*The Tatars*

*of*

*Crimea*

*Central Asia Book Series*

# The Tatars of Crimea

RETURN TO THE HOMELAND

*Studies and Documents*

*Second Edition, Revised and Expanded*

EDWARD A. ALLWORTH, EDITOR

*Duke University Press, Durham and London*

1998

© 1998 Duke University Press   All rights reserved

Printed in the United States of America on acid-free paper ∞

Typeset in Adobe Caslon by Keystone Typesetting, Inc.

Library of Congress Cataloging-in-Publication Data appear

on the last printed page of this book.

## Contents

Central Asia Book Series   vii

Preface   xi

1  Renewing Self-Awareness   EDWARD A. ALLWORTH   1

### I
### Forming a Modern Identity   27

2  A Model Leader for Asia, Ismail Gaspirali
ALAN W. FISHER   29

3  Ismail Bey Gasprinskii (Gaspirali): The Discourse of Modernism and the Russians   EDWARD J. LAZZERINI   48

4  Symbols: The National Anthem and Patriotic Songs by Three Poets   SEYIT AHMET KIRIMCA   71

5  Rituals: Artistic, Cultural, and Social Activity   RIZA GÜLÜM   84

6  Structures: The Importance of Family—a Personal Memoir
MÜBEYYIN BATU ALTAN   99

7  Documents about Forming a Modern Identity   110

### II
### The Ordeal of Forced Exile   153

8  The Elders of the New National Movement: Recollections
AYSHE SEYTMURATOVA   155

9  Mass Exile, Ethnocide, Group Derogation: Anomaly or Norm in Soviet Nationality Policies?   EDWARD A. ALLWORTH   180

10  Mustafa Jemiloglu, His Character and Convictions
LUDMILLA ALEXEYEVA   206

11  The Crimean Tatar Drive for Repatriation: Some Comparisons with Other Movements of Dissent in the Soviet Union
PETER REDDAWAY   226

12  Documents about the Ordeal of Forced Exile   237

## III
### Returning to Crimea 249

13 The Elusive Homeland EDWARD A. ALLWORTH 251

14 Politics in and around Crimea: A Difficult Homecoming ANDREW WILSON 281

15 Crimean Tatar Communities Abroad NERMIN EREN 323

16 Documents about Returning to Crimea 352

Bibliography of Recent Publications in English about Crimea 361

Notes on the Authors 371

Index 375

## *Central Asia Book Series*

Thinkers at least as ancient as Herodotus, Plato, and Plutarch have recorded biographies cited in swings in the Western debate about whether history does more to make the leader or the leader more to make history. Some Central Asian annalists no later than Narshakhi, Biruni, and 'Abd al-Razzaq referred to sacred traditions and persistently sought explanations for strong human character and leadership in the power of the deity and the influence of the changing juxtapositions of the planets in their courses.

In 1943, the American philosopher Sidney Hook formally contributed to another modern discussion when he first copyrighted his original volume analyzing leadership, entitled *The Hero in History: A Study in Limitation and Possibility* (New York: John Day, 1943). It came out at a moment of international turmoil, full of fearsome ideologies, loathing, and total war. That strife occurred as the Soviet system still lacked stability and as Europe and North America only haltingly emerged from a deep economic depression. Hook advanced several arguments meant to distinguish a leader's historical fame from his historical significance and the true leader from the merely opportune one. His full-fledged hero, or leader, had to perform in history as an "event-making man" or woman, not merely an "eventful man" or woman.

The real hero, by that definition, makes things happen. His or her "actions are the consequences of outstanding capacities of intelligence, will, and character rather than [simply] . . . accidents of position." The event maker creates crucial opportunities for actions that he or she makes occur through exceptional leadership ability.

Also in 1943, in a small Crimean village, the wife of Abdüljemil, Makhfure, warily celebrated the birth of her fourth child, a new son, Mustafa, in November, in a region under the frightening military occupation of Nazi invading forces. Within barely half a year, the Red Army retook Crimea, and violence again shook the peninsula. Punitive Soviet security troops soon roughly herded all Crimean Tatar "traitors" of the region, including Makhfure and her infants and youngsters, into boxcars and forcibly shipped the survivors of that ruthless mistreatment three thousand kilometers to the East (the father of the family, like many other Crimean Tatar men, then served in a Soviet army unit at the front).

Growing up in Central Asian exile under a strict police regimen, Mustafa quickly recognized his disconnection from a nurturing culture and relevant place. The strange absence of a significant community started him on a daring lifetime quest for his people's soul under a vindictive political system. By young adulthood in Tashkent, Uzbekistan, Mustafa had already educated himself about Crimean Tatar history and helped erase some of the deficiencies in the education of his compatriots. His actions from that time forward reveal the behavior of an event maker as he, initially in a deliberately undifferentiated group of activists, persistently fought his people's enemies and won the profound esteem of his elders and other exiles. He accomplished this through self-sacrifice and fortitude and by repeatedly outwitting the overpowering goliath through strategies implemented without resort to violence. A great part of that victory resulted from his extraordinary ability to communicate with Crimean Tatars and with the larger worlds of allies in the Soviet Union and with the foreign journalists, scholars, and politicians interested in events affecting the Soviet Union's vulnerability in nationality affairs.

*The Tatars of Crimea* devotes itself principally to seeking an understanding of what lies behind the resilience of that nationality and its effects. In that respect, probably no prominent figure in the Crimean Tatar group more effectively represents his community than the event-making leader, Mustafa Jemiloglu. As a result of his deeds, ideas, and strategies, he projects a large figure in several parts of this book.

In a focus on the Crimean Tatars, perspectives of scholarship owe their effectiveness or ineffectiveness to the extent of their mastery over the multiple frameworks within which inquirers work to pull out insights and understanding about the intellectual problems they hope to solve. Events flowing from the Soviet Empire's formal demise in late 1991 greatly influence later scholarship concerning people of that territory, for loss of the familiar enclosure left the configuration shapeless or, rather, with an unfamiliar shape still eluding exact identification. The subject of Crimea and its exiled Tatars had merited and received attention long before the parts of the Union of Soviet Socialist Republics disassembled, but, after the outline of that Union disappeared from the map, study of Crimean Tatars proved almost as intractable as before. The two editions of the present book mean to contribute to a better understanding of these problems while Crimean Tatars reenter the international arena. Geopolitics somewhat obscure that emergence, for indigenous sources report that they live in three sovereign countries instead of one, as before. Around 50 percent of ex-Soviet Crimean Tatars as of this writing remain inhabitants of Siberia and of Kyrgyzstan, Tajikistan, and Uzbekistan in Central Asia, and the other half now reside in Crimea, part of the independent Republic of Ukrayina.

The Central Asia Book Series publishes mainly original studies and documents like this one, travel accounts, documents, and reference works relating to twentieth-century affairs. It selects works based at least in part on the local languages of the area used in pursuit of original insights into the modern and postmodern developments, attitudes, and ideas motivating or typifying the people of Central Asia and related areas.

Edward A. Allworth, Editor of the Series
*Columbia University*

Andras J. E. Bodrogligeti, Advisory Editor
*University of California, Los Angeles*

Richard N. Frye, Advisory Editor
*Harvard University*

# *Preface*

Most aspects of life in the Crimean Tatar community have undergone tremendous change since *Tatars of the Crimea: Their Struggle for Survival* first appeared in 1988. A completely new opening chapter and the entire third section in this substantially revised edition of the book reflect that drastic turn of events. Three scholars have written four new chapters and translated documents specifically concerning the experience of the most recent period, especially the developments of the late 1980s and early 1990s. The book also provides an up-to-date bibliography on this subject. The flow of unofficial (samizdat) documentation from Crimean Tatar activists that played such a vital part in the earlier edition has ceased. Rather, the open press now appearing in Crimea, along with the frequent travels abroad of Tatar intellectuals and politicians, plus free public access to the region itself for outsiders, including some of these authors, to meetings, congresses, and people, in the peninsula, all these have provided a largely different basis for research. And uncensored book publishing in Crimean Tatar and in Russian suddenly offers useful additional sources for serious inquiry.

*The Tatars of Crimea: Return to the Homeland, Studies and Documents* reflects these changes without trying to become the purveyor of the latest news from Crimea. (That book title also embodies a shift in terminology away from the old Western usage that regularly placed the definite article *the* ahead of the place name or ethnonym *Crimea*, just as the names *Lebanon* and *Ukrayina* [Ukraine], like most independent countries and autonomous regions, now stand alone without the article that formerly introduced and, some felt, demeaned them.)

The general aims of the book remain the same: to discuss the main developments in Crimean Tatar life, culture, history, and, to some extent, politics in the twentieth century. Throughout, the authors intend to give specific meaning to the studies by analyzing the motivations underlying and the important consequences arising from those developments. First, the authors of part 1 demonstrate the impact of the cultural reforms, initiated late in the nineteenth century and continued into the next, pre-

Soviet era, for the modernization of the group's outlook and self-identity throughout the twentieth century, as evinced in its cultural expression. That established in the study, the chapters in part 2 proceed to the Crimean Tatar ordeal, mainly since 1944, when the Soviet regime forcibly removed the entire nationality from Crimea overnight and deported it to restricted zones in the Urals region and in Central Asia. Treatment of the consequences of that action focused the second part of the book on the efforts of Crimean Tatars to reconstitute their nationality after the shattering trauma.

The disassembly of the Soviet Union in late 1991, perhaps influenced to some extent by the Crimean Tatars' effective public demonstrations of the failure of Soviet nationality policies, accelerated Crimean Tatar efforts to reclaim the homeland. Part 3 considers the opportunities offered by the loss of that Soviet control, which simultaneously created many new problems for Crimean Tatars. The most pronounced of them arose from the fact that multiethnic Crimea no longer lived under Moscow's jurisdiction but relied on Kyiv (Kiev) and the economically distressed government of Ukrayina for support and protection from the violence and political excesses of the numerically predominant Russian military and civilian immigrants settled in Crimea since World War II. Part 3 looks primarily at issues raised by the slackening and cessation of Soviet control and refocuses attention on Crimea and some cultural, social, and political dilemmas engrossing the Crimean Tatar community in the Republic of Ukrayina.

By necessity, the second edition of *The Tatars of Crimea* has replaced to some degree, with newer material, many of the documents published in English for the first time in the 1988 edition. Readers may consult that edition for texts of Crimean Tatar proclamations, records, and statements especially reflecting affairs during the period 1966–87. Edward Allworth, Nermin Eren, Alan Fisher, Edward Lazzerini, Andrew Wilson, and Nancy Workman have translated a selection of original texts, placed at the ends of the three main sections of this inquiry, from documents written in the Crimean Tatar, Kazan Tatar, Turkish, Turkistanian, and Russian languages. Because these accounts relate closely to the studies making up the largest part of this volume, the translators provide no separate commentary about them. The authors contributing to this research come from the emigrant community of Crimean Tatars, from England, from North America, and from Turkiye. Crimean Tatar and Russian intellectuals in

Crimea invited to contribute to this edition could not spare the time and attention it demanded from their most pressing responsibilities there to submit finished chapters in time for this edition of *The Tatars of Crimea*. In the future, they will have a great deal to teach foreign scholars about the realities of Crimean and continued Central Asian life when they have the opportunity to communicate it to the world.

The editor especially thanks President of the Crimean Tatar Mejlis Mustafa Jemiloglu and Madam Safinar Jemiloglu for their kindness in having recent documents, photographs, and publications made available for this research. Some financial support for the preparation of the revised manuscript came from the Ismail Gaspirali Fund, Columbia University, for which the editor wishes to register his gratitude. Thanks for advice and/or assistance in the substantive as well as technical side of the effort also gladly go especially to Abdurrahim Demirayak, Nermin Eren, Ahmet Kanlidere, Seyit Ahmet Kirimca, Edward Kasinec, John R. Krueger, Martha Merrill, Alexander Motyl, Halim Saylik, Robert Scott, Peter Sinnott, Svat Soucek, Andrew Wilson, Fikret Yurter. Walter Barnard and Sarah Spurgin of the Columbia University Libraries repeatedly gave useful advice, as did Natalia Zitselsberger in the New York Public Library.

Transliteration from alphabets of the Union of Soviet Socialist Republics and successor republics follows an adaptation of the system published in the directory *Nationalities of the Soviet East: Publications and Writing Systems* (1971), by Edward Allworth. In the present book, references to certain consonants in the Romanized Turkish alphabet appear as digraphs as employed in English: Turkish ç = English *ch*; Turkish ş = English *sh*; Turkish ğ = English *gh*; Turkish c = English *j*; umlauts indicate Turkish vowels ö, ü, and velar ï. In the bibliography, notes, and text, this method of transliteration applies also to personal names written in Turkish, except for instances where the persons mentioned have established a certain spelling in English for their own names: for example, Kirimca rather than Kirimcha; Inalcik rather than Inaljik. With the demise of the Soviet Union, many proper names have reverted to traditional forms. President Jemiloglu had long been known in Russian-language sources as Mustafa Dzhemilev (its transliteration Anglicized to Jemilev). In his and many other instances, but not all, the Russian patronymics *-ev*, *-ov*, *-ova*, and *-ovna* have disappeared, in some cases replaced by Turkic patronymics *-oglu* and *-qizi*. In the emigrant journal *Emel* and some other publications from Turkiye, readers will see the form Mustafa Abdüljemil Kïrïmoghlu, showing his father's name as the second name and the substitution of Kïrïm as a last name in place of the shorter form, Mustafa Jemiloglu, adopted in this book from the Mejlis president's signature.

Crimean Tatars' own name for their homeland, *Qïrïm*, deserves the general acceptance owed to regional and country designations. The editor prefers to accept such self-names and forms, but the use of *Qïrïm* among nonspecialists and specialists has yet to find the immediate recognition that could overcome the confusion that might result from the adoption of *Qïrïm* in place of *Crimea* in English. Nevertheless, the repeated appearance of that self-name in this book in references and direct quotations, literary titles, and the like should help prepare the ground for a shift from the Russian-based form *Krym/Crimea* found in European languages to *Qïrïm*, the indigenous Crimean Tatar form and spelling of their name. Such naming receives significant attention in chapter 1 below.

Christopher Brest prepared the original cartography for the map covering the northern Black Sea littoral, which shows the distribution of the returning Crimean Tatar population of the former Soviet Union in Crimea near the end of the twentieth century. Abdurrahim Demirayak and Senol and Sinan Utku deserve sincere thanks for providing photographs and other graphic materials important for the design on the paperback cover of this book and for documentation of recent events in the studies.

E. A.   New York

*The Tatars*

*of*

*Crimea*

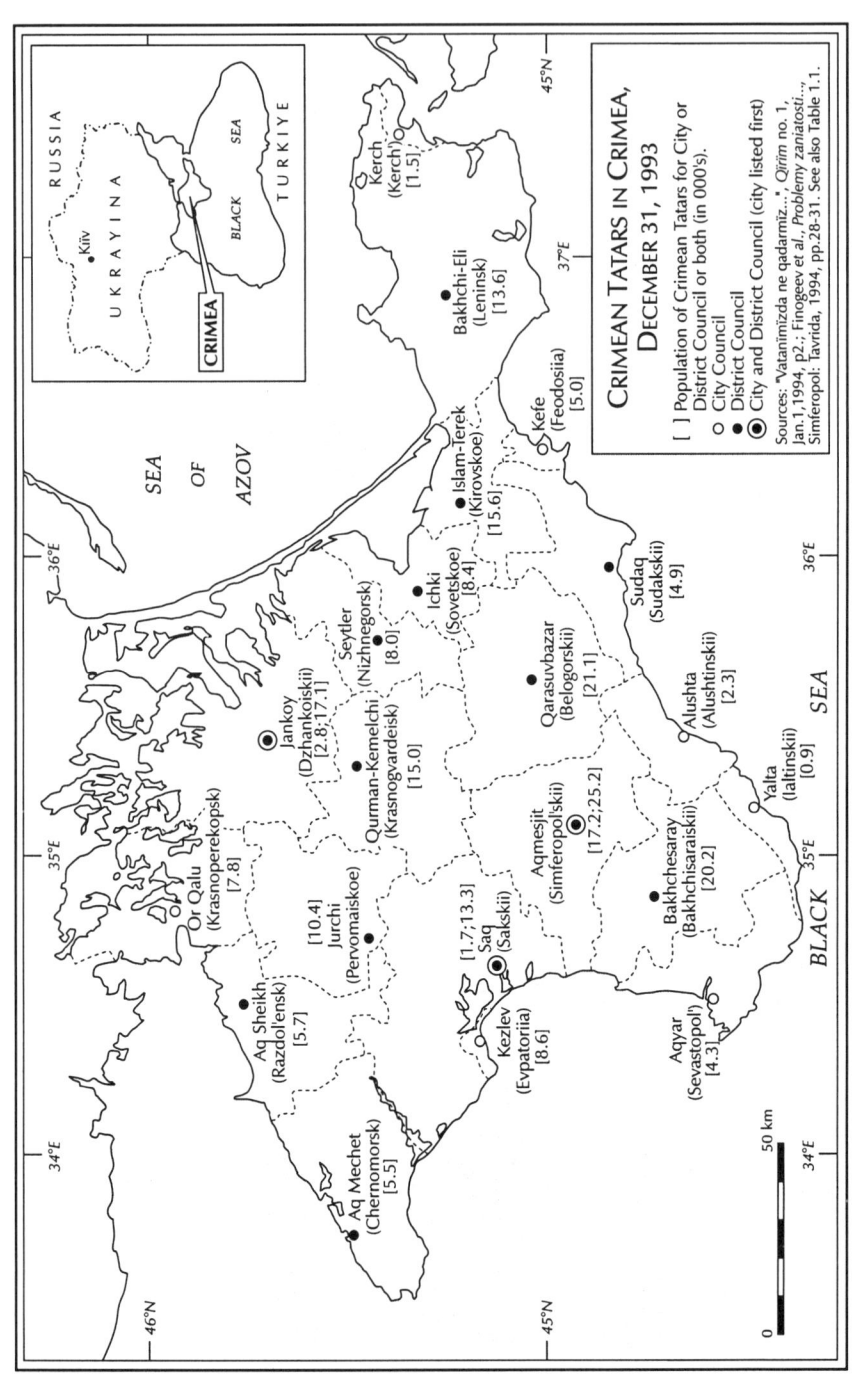

# 1

## *Renewing Self-Awareness*

EDWARD A. ALLWORTH

The ill treatment endured by Crimean Tatars during the last half century has tested them severely. When other nationalities might have faltered, these Tatars have persevered. Immersed in a hostile cultural, economic, and social environment created by a Russian oligarchy, they found great strength to carry them through the man-made threats to the survival of their community. What sorts of resources and support have proved indispensable in sustaining the group to this extraordinary degree?

Two reflections of this strength, in particular, attract immediate attention: steadiness in the face of each new danger and a fearless determination to defend themselves, spiritually and culturally, against formidable opponents.

### Expressions of Attitudes and Values

Those same traits reveal themselves person by person. The seemingly tenuous networks that tie individuals to a common cause may exist and reveal themselves most of all in the cultural values, moods, and attitudes expressed through words and other symbols. The literature, language, art, and related bearers and creators of signs serve more fundamentally than other factors to shape and support the outlook of Crimean Tatars in the postmodern season of the group's life. These mediums reach beyond bolstering courage and conviction. They convey a necessary appreciation of beauty, joy, and an affirmation of life that can give people the stimulus to act with imagination in hostile surroundings.

The way people express their feelings about their community and their place in this immediate post-Soviet period tells more about their group's viability under contemporary conditions than does news about their political life and institutions. A shattered community's many spokesmen and -women must participate in the process of reidentifying their group with its central nervous system, its significant core. Those talented enough to convey their feelings and ideas memorably in literature, music, and the arts probably exert the strongest influence in restoring and sustaining people's faith in the one community.

Crimean Tatars benefit in this respect from a small but active circle of writers, poets, composers, and other creative artists, men and women who have found that eloquence. Rather than conventionally idealize, they visualize their community and place in phrases and images that reaffirm them aesthetically in the minds and hearts of their audience. Where, under the circumstances, readers, listeners, and viewers might expect anger or hostility, more often than not the poets and artists speak softly, portray gently. A lyrical reengagement with suppressed feelings of longing seems all the more remarkable in view of the most recent history of the group. Decades of enduring an often harsh Central Asian exile have marked Crimean Tatars as surely as other previous, recent experiences. Nevertheless, the poetry and art publicly circulated usually accents a positive vision.

Although composing verse in Uzbekistan exile before the rise of glasnost as public policy in the Soviet Union after the mid-1980s, Eskender Fazïl guardedly conveyed his thoughts in notably terse lines that skirted strong feelings. Under the heavy censorship then especially limiting the literary efforts of Crimean Tatars in Central Asia, the young writer's collections of poetry—*The Violet* (*Melevshe*) had appeared in 1970 and *The Old Beechtree* (*Qart emen*) in 1976—enjoyed the select company of only twelve companion titles by various authors created and issued in the Crimean Tatar language.[1] But, because the Communist Party then continued to deny the crucial attributive *Crimean* to these Tatars, the colophon to *Gesture of Respect* (*Temenna*, 1982) specifies only that this poetry appears in "the Tatar language." The experienced writer Cherkez Ali, one of whose verses this chapter cites, below, functioned as editor of the booklet, and Aidar Osmanov, once editor of the Crimean Tatar literary journal *Yïldïz*, wrote brief comments for *Temenna*, giving the younger poet strong backing in those difficult times.

Yet in that booklet's opening poem, ostensibly intended for young readers and devoted "To Mothers of the World" ("Dyun'ya analarïna"), poet and teacher Eskender Fazïl examines the human condition in the Soviet Union and beyond. In this eighty-six-page booklet circulated in only two thousand copies for the hundreds of thousands of potential readers, he searches for an understanding of the origins of the cruel as well as the merciful individuals in his society and others and, by implication, the institutions among which he and his people live:

| | |
|---|---|
| White, | (Beyaz, |
| Yellow, | Sarï, |
| Black colored, | Qara renkli, |
| Tenderhearted mothers— | Merametli analar— |
| Tenderhearted, | Merametli, |
| Just | Adaletli |
| Bear children. | Doghuralar balalar. |
| | |
| Or hard-hearted, | Ya tash yurekli, |
| Black blooded | Qara qanlï |
| Who bore the merciless one? | Djellyatnï kim doghurghan? |
| The liar, | Yalandjini |
| The troublemaker | Fitnedjini |
| What sort of "mother" bore? | Angi "ana" doghurghan?[2]) |

The tone and rhetoric of literature, such as this poetry composed in the period of exile under severe restrictions, naturally remained more guarded, more circumspect, than most writings toward the end of and following the breakup of the Soviet Union.

In a later, lyrical turn, one of the personal voices heard frequently toward the end of the 1980s and 1990s sounds in the poetry of Lilia Budzhurova. She revels in beautiful perceptions of Crimea, usually tinged with a nuance of sadness. Budzhurova's short verse (in Russian) "What Is the Homeland's Scent?" (1989) exemplifies this sensual evocation:

Of what does the homeland smell?
Of a dry blade of grass,
Caught in a child's hair,
Of a pine branch, of bitter wormwood,
Or, of separation, buried in the heart?
Or, of lamb's wool, of aromatic coffee,
Tinkling as it pours into thin little cups,
Of mountain tea, of almonds, fragrant with mint,
Of today's reality, of yesterday's dream?
Or, of the searing cry of a lone seagull?

> Or, of the snowy peak of Chatïr-dagh?
> Of distant music from an ancient song?
> Oh no, my homeland smells of hope.³

Because this short lyric expressed such strong feeling about the Crimean homeland, Soviet censors in Central Asia would not accept it for publication. In her personal notes (see document 3, chapter 16), the poet mentions that such verses circulated in manuscript form. The first samizdat edition of it came out as a kind of underground pamphlet issued somewhere in the Baltics. This contrasts strikingly with the intellectuality of a later, topical poem dedicated to the delegates to the Second Qurultay, "We Returned Today" (June 1991), again in Russian:

> Our happiness comes from being together,
> In spite of the awful calamity [*bespredely*],
> We gathered in the old place, in order
> Once more to make our history.⁴

If literature and the representational arts supply much of the glue that holds in place the thinking and values of a nationality, the symbolism offered in the familiar, ever-present names of places and terrain features presents a second, potent source of identity for the group.

## The Resonance of Names

Self-names supply most important symbols signaling the collective identity that unifies a community of people. Reliable linkage between name and people, and often place, ordinarily forges strong bonds, securing group identity. The Crimean Tatar poet Rustem Ali speaks to this central theme for his people. In the expression of loyalty cited below, taken from the short poem "Crimea" ("Qïrïm," 1992), he affirms that, in spite of long-enforced separation, Crimean Tatars have neither neglected nor forsaken their true name or the memory of a place that nourishes them as a maternal presence with its verdancy symbolic of renewing life. This passionate expression concerning the name and the place often characterizes late twentieth-century Crimean Tatar written literature, some of it lyrical, much of it melancholy:

| Crimea, Crimea, Mother Crimea, | (Qïrïm, Qïrïm, Qïrïm Ana, |
| We did not forget our name. | Unutmadik adïmïznï. |
| We did not, Mother Crimea, | Dengishmedik, Qïrïm Ana, |
| Exchange our isle for another's. | Bashqasïna adamïznï.5) |

Crimean Tatars sometimes refer to Crimea as their "green island," or, as in this instance, merely as "our island," because it is connected to the mainland only by a very thin neck at the northern extreme of the peninsula. A prominent anti-Soviet Russian author, Vassily Aksyonov, has written a novel, *The Island Crimea* (1981), based partly on this premise.

When something interrupts or breaks that connection between group and name, both self-awareness and unity can suffer. The name adopted long ago by Crimean Tatars has experienced no simple or direct history. Invaders, conquerors, and internal opponents over several centuries leading up to the 1990s have repeatedly misunderstood, erased, or tried to change the self-name of Crimean Tatars.

Reviewing the nationality's stormy life, the matter of historical onomastic right becomes less than clear. Attempts to explain exactly how and when the present name originated and replaced the ancient *Chersonesus Taurica* (Tauric Chersonese) have yet to satisfy everyone. Reputable European historians in the nineteenth century surmised that *Crimea* derived from the name of the Cimmerian people driven from their habitat in the peninsula by Scythians as early as the eighth century B.C.,[6] but centuries had elapsed; moreover, the Cimmerian center lay in the eastern extreme of the peninsula, on the site of today's Kerch.

In the late nineteenth century, some scholars hypothesized from the peninsula's peculiar geography—the aforementioned narrowness of the northern isthmus making it almost an island—that Tatars and Turks at the end of the thirteenth century regarded the place as a highly defensible fortress and named it *Qrïm* (Russian *Krym*). Etymologists reasoned that the word *crimea* originally meant "stronghold" "because this word, by Forster's explanation, means *krepost'* [Russian for *fortress*], and can be connected with the Mongol word *kerm* [meaning] 'wall.'" A seventeenth-century Mongolian royal document shows the place name as *Qaram*, a form phonetically incompatible with *kerm/kerem* and therefore deriving from another original term.[7]

Russian lexicographers had developed a somewhat similar etymology for *Krym* more than a century earlier, shortly after the imperial acquisition of the peninsula, although the eighteenth-century version asserted that *Krym* meant "fortress" in Tatar.[8] Mongol hegemony over Crimea in the thirteenth century made that sort of etymology seem plausible. It did not explain whether the use of the term *Tatar* in this context referred to the Turkic language of Crimea's Tatars or to the Mongolian of Chinggis Khan and his commanders and descendants, whom Russians commonly called Tatars.

Much earlier, Qipchaq Turkic horsemen roaming the strip of territory just north of the Black Sea at the edge of the huge Desht-i Qipchaq had ridden down across the narrow isthmus to penetrate into the peninsula known as Tauric Chersonese in the ancient and early medieval world. Later, as the main force of troops under Chinggis Khan's commanders, those horsemen in 1223 did drive all the way to Sudaq, on the southeast coast of the peninsula, and withdrew in the same year.

Of the many cruelties connected with Crimea and its naming, an episode in the brutal rivalries among Mongol rulers seems to have prompted the earliest recorded use of the toponym *Crimea* for the peninsula. It appeared in the final part of a chronicle entitled *A Short History of Mankind* (*al-Mukhtasar fi akhbar al-bashar*) by the Arab writer and statesman Isma'il Ibn-'Ali Abu-l'Fida in the year H. 700/A.D. 1300–1301. He records details concerning the war between Mongol princes of the Golden Horde, Jöge and his opponent, Toqta. To gain favor with Toqta, a ruler of Trnovo in north-central Bulgaria betrayed Jöge, who had fled to him for refuge. He confined Jöge in his citadel, executed him, and "sent his head to Crimea, and the kingdom of Noqai passed to Toqta."[9]

Additional evidence indicates that the medieval town of Solkhat/Solhat received the name *Qrïm/Eski Qrïm* after the place already served as an administrative and cultural center of the peninsula for the Genoese, for Armenians, and, in the second half of the thirteenth century, for Qipchaq plainsmen. That renaming of Solkhat apparently occurred before the rise of the Muslim Giray dynasty to mastery over Crimea during the 1420s, when their center remained still outside Crimea, up the Itil (Volga) River at Berke's Saray, near the site of the modern Volgograd.[10]

A more lasting presence seemingly made itself known in the application of names to places. A learned etymology offered by a modern European scholar attributes the name of the town Eski Qrïm and that of the peninsula to the language of the Crimean Tatars and the Turks. He cites as the root for *Crimea* (*Qïrïm*) the term *qurum*, "defense," from *qurimaq*, "to defend, protect," which he says the Qalmyq language absorbed from Turkic as *kharm*. The postmodern Crimean Tatar lexicon conserves the meaning "defending" for *qoruma*, from the verb *qorumaq*, "to guard, defend."[11]

Thus, it appears that the early version of *Crimea* appeared first as a practical term for a defensive position at the neck of the peninsula, then as the toponym or a descriptive attribute for an administrative center (*Solkhat* becoming *Qurum* and its derivative, *Qrïm* and then *Eski Qrïm*, i.e., "Old Crimea"). Subsequently, that Qrïm nomenclature extended to the surrounding territory. Very likely, after the first decades of their establishment on the peninsula, Crimean Tatars themselves consistently referred to their land as *Crimea*. From this point, the term may have passed into usage as part of the distinctive name for Tatars who lived there and some decades later initiated their rule over the area in governments under the Giray dynasty. Its tenure as an official designation, with the area sometimes overseen by foreign powers such as the Ottoman Empire up to 1774, lasted until imperial Russian troops occupied Crimea and the governors changed its name.[12]

When administrators of the czarist Russian state annexed the peninsula that gave a home to Crimean Tatars in 1783, for a place name they returned to the classical toponym and immediately designated it the *Taurida* district (*Tavricheskaia oblast'*) of their realm. The fact that the Ottoman Turks had called that peninsula *Crimea* since they held sway over it beginning in the late fifteenth century may have motivated the Russian choice of a different (Greek) name. As late as 1914, Russia's rulers continued to use the name *Tavrida*, rather than *Crimea*, for that *oblast'*.[13]

Readers of the main writings of the great Crimean Tatar reformist Ismail Bey Gaspirali (to whose contributions chaps. 2 and 3 of this volume directly pertain) do not encounter in them calls for the ethnic self-determination of his people. Rather, Gaspirali writes constantly of the Muslims of Russia, including his own people, as part of that community. In matters of language, Gaspirali emphatically promotes the use of an ethnically neutral all-Turkic tongue and literary medium more or less based on Ottoman Turkish, again avoiding any partiality for the distinctive linguistic identity of Crimean Tatars. In his collection of articles *Russian Islam* (*Russkoe musul'manstvo*, 1881), he writes of "Tatar-Muslim traits" but, significantly, does not choose the form *Crimean Tatars*. Later, he specifically attacks the narrow kind of nationalism put forward by Russians and other Europeans. In an article entitled "Turkism" ("Turkchilik," 1907), he writes: "Let the cosmopolitans and others of the old persuasion speak of nationalism. This is their affair, but we have a different understanding."[14] Gaspirali defined his nation as the Muslim community of which he and the populations of coreligionists in the Russian Empire were a part.

He mentions Tatars of Kazan or Tatars of Crimea in such important tracts as his "Russian-Oriental Relations" (*Russkoe vostochnoe soglashenie*, 1896), but not "Crimean Tatars."[15] (A full English translation of this pamphlet is provided in chap. 7 of this volume.) In the modern cultural history of the Crimean Tatar nationality, Gaspirali has surely played a key part. His importance lies especially in the contributions he made to educational innovation and to a new, universalist perspective for his and other Muslim Turkic people and, in retrospect, in the tremendous amount he accomplished in renewing Crimean Tatar culture. In no sense a nationalist, only indirectly did he strengthen the singularity of his kinsmen's ethnic attachment through their reverence for his prominence and purity of motives for enlightenment of the Muslims in the Russian-wide empire. Not long after Gaspirali passed from the scene, in 1914, many other influential persons and events further clouded the definition of group identity and confused the naming of Crimea's Tatars and like groups.

When in 1921 Soviet authorities designated an administrative-territorial unit embodied in the peninsula as the Autonomous Crimean Socialist Soviet Republic (ACSSR), they merely emulated the earlier selection of place name by Crimean Tatars themselves. The Constituent Assembly (Qurultay) convened by Crimean Tatars in Bakhchesaray on 26 November 1917 proclaimed the establishment of a new, multiethnic, autonomous republic coextensive with the Crimean peninsula and named it the Crimean government (or administration) (*Qrïm Idaresi*, in Tatar) and the Crimean People's Republic (*Krymskaia Narodnaia Respublika*, in Russian). That logical selection of political name for their government and state probably stands as the first official use of *Crimea* for the purpose since the czarist Russian annexation of the region in 1783.

By 14 January 1918, heavily armed Russian naval forces had captured Aqmesjit (Simferopol'), then the capital of Crimea. They arrested defenders, including many Tatars, and dissolved the multiethnic Qurultay of

Paradoxically, a decade and a half later, in a speech delivered on 25 November 1936 to the Eighth All-Union Congress of Soviets, Joseph Stalin did imply, perhaps inadvertently, that the ACSSR took its name from the Crimean Tatars, although Soviet politicians normally rejected that notion vehemently. In that instance, Stalin meant to quash any dreams that Crimean Tatars might have cherished about elevating their namesake administrative-territorial unit to the level of union republic (or Soviet Socialist Republic, SSR). He meant to ensure that Russia's main semitropical playground and naval base on the Black Sea could harbor no technical ambitions to secede from the Soviet Union.

In its usual fashion, the dictator's rhetoric plodded on as follows in this regard:

What are the grounds for transferring Autonomous Republics to the category of Union Republics [the highest level in the territorial-administrative hierarchy]? . . . First, the republic concerned must be a border republic. . . . Secondly, the nationality which gives its name to a certain Soviet republic must constitute a more or less compact majority within that republic. Take the Crimean Autonomous Republic, for example, it is a border republic, but Crimean Tatars do not constitute the majority of that republic. . . . Thirdly, the republic must not have too small a population; it should have a population of, say, not less but more than a million, at least.[21]

The purported significance of these rankings lay in the practically meaningless prerogatives allowed a union republic: to call itself sovereign although it exercised no authority over its important domestic or foreign affairs; to have the right (but no plausible political means) to secede from the Soviet Union; to have its token foreign minister; to send larger delegations than could the ASSRs to Soviet Supreme Council sessions in Moscow; to have an anthem and banner that Moscow specified; and, after World War II, to send occasional representatives to sessions of the United Nations in New York and other international meetings.

In 1936, Communist Party of the Soviet Union (CPSU) Secretary Stalin would have known from statistics estimated for his information, and a few years later surely from data compiled in the then-unpublished 1939 Soviet census, that the population of Crimea (1.13 million) did, indeed, exceed the minimum required for union republic status. Of course, the 218,879 Crimean Tatars registered in that census made up only 19.4 percent of the peninsula's total. Stalin knew also that, years before the all-out deportation of 1944, the regime, on ideological pretexts fueled by Russian hostility to Tatars and other non-Slavs, had already diminished the Crimean Tatar proportion by shipping thousands from Crimea to exile in Siberia and elsewhere.[22] Nevertheless, that 1939 census showed some growth in Crimean Tatar numbers after 1926, but not in their proportion, which had fallen from the 25 percent (179,094 of a total population of 713,979) reported from the peninsula in 1926.[23]

Inconsistency did not deter the Communist chieftain from delivering such remarks in his speeches and writings. Evidence of this discrepancy between fact and political pronouncement lay in sources for all to see. The numbers of the Soviet Union's Turkmens (631,920 in 1926) and Tajiks (617,130 in 1926), each endowed with the rank of union republic (in 1925 and 1929, respectively), failed to pass the test. A decade later, around the time of his 1936 comments, the unpublished census data showed Stalin's aides that the population of neither group yet came close to reaching the requisite million within the boundaries of its namesake SSR (Turkmens, 741,488 in 1939; Tajiks, 883,966 in 1939). The aggregate of all nationalities residing in each of those SSRs—somewhat more than 1 million but fewer than 1.5 million—then matched the combined total in the Crimean ASSR fairly closely.[24]

In 1940, not long after Stalin's cynical statement about qualifications for union republics, he and his politburo elevated the Karelian ASSR to the status of union republic, calling it the Karelo-Finnish SSR. When this occurred, the area, bordering on Finland, according to 1939 data, housed but 469,000 people all told, 23.2 percent (109,000) of whom identified themselves as Karelian.[25]

After Soviet security forces deported Crimean Tatars from Crimea on 18 May 1944, the Soviet regime resorted to a comprehensive replacement of the anthroponymy and onomastics native to Crimea. By decree of the Supreme Council of the RSFSR, in December 1944, all main provinces and provincial centers received new, usually Russian, designations: Aq Mechet became Chernomorsk, Qarasuvbazar became Belogorskii, and so on. Also in 1944, the *Oblast'* Committee of the Crimean ASSR summarily ordered the replacement of all other traditional toponyms, including those of rivers, mountains, villages, and towns—commonly thought to have originated from Crimean Tatars but in reality coming, as well, from many earlier civilizations layering the peninsula. An eyewitness has reported that this order went to the executive secretary of the Russian-language newspaper *Krasnyi Krym*, who happened to serve as duty officer on the night the order came to its offices. He consulted two Russian books that lay on his desk, one a nineteenth-century treatise about horticulture, the other a recent treatment of how the Soviet military forces reconquered Crimea from the Nazi armies. These volumes account for the multiplicity of places and terrain features on the map of Crimea with names, often duplicated, such as *Abrikosovoe* (apricot), *Vinogradnoe* (vineyard), *Sadovoe* (orchard), or *Gvardeiskoe* (the guards) and the disappearance of nearly all the previous, universally used traditional names with their power to evoke a strong sense of personal identification for every normal inhabitant of the peninsula.[26] Distortion mangled the forms of a few place names that remained. On the map today, inhabitants find the Crimean Tatar names *Aqmesjit* (for *Simferopol'*) and *Aq Mechet*, a Russian version of the same toponym (for *Chernomorsk*). Crimean Tatar scholars have pointed out additional examples, including *Qïrq Or*, which Russian historians mistransliterated from *Qïrq Yer*, the authentic rendering from the Arabic script previously used by Crimean Tatars.[27]

Equally damaging to self-recognition and esteem within the Crimean Tatar nationality, the authorities decreed that Crimea's Tatars could no longer call themselves *Crimean*. In passports and other official documents, people now had to refer to themselves as "Tatars, formerly living in Crimea." Later on, when token amounts of publishing began appearing in their language, the name *Crimean Tatar* remained eerily unmentioned. During the absence of the deportees, Russian settlers disposed as they pleased of the property and real estate of the exiles. Not only did place names change; the new inhabitants of the region simply obliterated some of the former settlements, as they did the village of Chukurja, about four kilometers from Aqmesjit (Simferopol'). They dammed up the Salgir River in order to form an artificial lake just southeast of the city for recreational boating. That pond, now called Simferopol' Reservoir, submerged Chukurja village, among other places.[28]

Not until fifty years later, early in 1994, would an official action rectify the deprivation of their distinctive group name. The provincial government, the Republic of Crimea, authorized the restoration of *Crimean* to individuals and the group in the following resolution (full text):

Led by principles of humanism and social justice, with the aim of removing discrepancies in the interpretation of the name of the nationality "Crimean Tatars" and "Tatars," the Supreme Council of Crimea resolves 1. to restore the official name of the nationality, "Crimean Tatars"; 2. [to direct] the Ministry of Internal Affairs of Crimea to determine the procedure before 15 January 1994 and enter into the passports of citizens of Crimean Tatar nationality the appropriate changes. Chairman, Supreme Council of Crimea, N. Bagrov, 9 December 1993, Simferopol'.[29]

This belated action affirmed a return to the use of the distinction between Crimean and other Tatars that had already occurred in statistics compiled and published at the time of the Soviet population census in 1989 and in other treatment. Its major significance lay elsewhere, as a reflection of the strong sense of rightness characterizing the Crimean Tatar nationality in its reemergence from unwarranted censure by the corrupt Soviet regime. Although practice had already preceded the formality, the group's insistence on even such a tardy official correction and redress of this wrong perpetrated under that regime presaged much of its own dogged campaign and rationale that would appear in things to come.

With the official restoration of the nationality's self-name, a firm, legal, name linkage establishing a correspondence between the self-name of at least one nationality and the designation for the peninsula has, after fifty years, finally returned. Old Tavrida undeniably now carries the name *Crimea*, and so do the Crimean Tatars and no others. That holds great significance if group names evince connections to like-named places. When Crimean Tatars say that they have no place to live other than Crimea, it shows that they believe that they have the right to the land that gave them their distinctive name.

That victory over arbitrariness evinced the Crimean Tatar understanding that renaming disturbs the continuities needed to sustain a society's cultural identity. For persons with long years behind them, another change in authority can permit a reversal and welcome return to traditional names. That rehabilitation, presently overdue in Crimea, suggests the reversion to a previous, often Crimean Tatar form of countless street, village, town, and other place names from the Slavic coinages imposed during World War II. Such action would replace the several repetitions of Russian place names, such as *Lazarevka* and *Zavetnyi*, as well as names like *Schastlivyi* (Joyful) and *Izobil'noe* (Abundant) even more offensive to the sensibilities of Crimean Tatars. But an appeal based on an article published in the union-wide Moscow press in 1988 for just such renewal of the old names brought no response from the Soviet Cultural Foundation to which its authors had addressed it.[30] The map of Crimea continues to bear hundreds of Slavic place names devised in the mid-twentieth century. Table 1.1 supplies Crimean Tatar and Russian names for Crimea's main population centers and regions and gives the numbers and ethnic proportions of their inhabitants.

Despite the justice implicit in such corrective manipulations, had they occurred, few could grant those born between 1944 and 1991 any ready familiarity with an irretrievable emotional tie to the previous nomenclature. Notwithstanding the likelihood that younger people heard from family or read about the place names of the past, their immediate experience had detached those designations from daily life. To them, both the Russian substitutes and the erased and then reinstated traditional place names had to seem new, the pre-1944 designations necessarily lacking the resonance they instantly aroused in Tatar elders. An example of such potential difficulties in relating to the symbolism of a renamed place shows itself in the representation elected to the Third Qurultay of Crimean Tatars during late June–early July 1996. Of the 154 delegates, 115 persons in the cohort thirty to fifty years of age belong to the generations born in exile, most of whom returned to Crimea only in recent years. Twenty of the 154 delegates have yet to immigrate to Crimea from Tajikistan, Uzbekistan, and the Krasnodarskii Krai of the Russian Republic (twelve of those twenty were born before the 1944 deportation from Crimea).[31]

Until the establishment of the myriad associations between person, society, and place names needed to make Crimea's toponyms their own, the younger generations will remain alien to the restored names; that is, until those names enter the everyday vocabulary and thus into unself-conscious usage, the restored and substitute names will seem equally foreign to the younger speakers of the vernacular language.

## The Language Link

For almost fifty years, the Soviet government refused to permit a public educational program anywhere to teach in the Crimean Tatar language. For that reason, children of the group grew up speaking, reading, and writ-

Table 1.1  Crimean Tatars Registered in Crimea, 31 December 1993

| Distribution District Councils and City Councils: Tatar/Russian Name | Crimean Tatar Population (thousands) | Tatars as % of Total Population in the Area |
|---|---|---|
| Or Qalu/Krasnoperekopsk (city) | 7.8 | 7.4 |
| Aq Sheikh/Razdol'ensk | 5.7 | 15.6 |
| Aq Mechet/Chernomorsk | 5.5 | 15.2 |
| Kezlev/Evpatoriia (city) | 8.6 | 6.5 |
| Saq/Sakskii | 13.3 | 16.7 |
| Saq/Saki (city) | 1.7 | 4.2 |
| Aqmesjit/Simferopol'skii | 25.2 | 17.5 |
| Aqmesjit/Simferopol' (city) | 17.2 | 4.5 |
| Bakhchesaray/Bakhchisaraiskii | 20.2 | 19.9 |
| Aqyar/Sevastopol' (city) | 4.3 | 1.0 |
| Yalta/Ialtinskii (city) | .9 | .5 |
| Alushta/Alushtinskii (city) | 2.3 | 3.9 |
| Qarasuvbazar/Belogorskii | 21.1 | 28.4 |
| Sudaq/Sudakskii | 4.9 | 15.1 |
| Kefe/Feodosiia (city) | 5.0 | 4.0 |
| Bakhchi-Eli/Leninsk | 13.6 | 16.0 |
| Kerch/Kerch' (city) | 1.5 | .8 |
| Islam-Terek/Kirovskoe | 15.6 | 23.3 |
| Ichki/Sovetskoe | 8.4 | 19.6 |
| Seytler/Nizhnegorsk | 8.0 | 12.8 |
| Jankoy/Dzhankoiskii | 17.1 | 18.6 |
| Jankoy/Dzhankoi (city) | 2.8 | 5.0 |
| Qurman-Kemelchi/Krasnogvardeisk | 15.0 | 13.9 |
| Jurchi/Pervomaiskoe | 10.4 | 21.0 |
| Crimean Tatars in Crimea | 235.7 | 8.8 |
| Entire population in Crimea | 2,672.2 | |

*Sources:* "Vatanïmïzda ne qadarmïz ve onïng angi yerinde yashaymïz?" *Qïrïm*, no. 1 (1 January 1994): 2; B. L. Finogeev, E. M. Liumanov, and G. D. Bodner, *Problemy zaniatosti krymskotatarskogo naseleniia kryma (analiticheskii obzor)* (Simferopol: "Tavrida," 1994), 28–31, with data from the Komitet po Delam Deportirovannykh Narodov i Otdel Mezhnatsional'nykh Otnoshenii Soveta Ministrov Kryma; Enver Memetovich Abdullaev and Memet Umerovich Umerov, *Ruscha-qïrïmtatarja oquv lughatï: Russko-krymskotatarskii uchebnyi slovar'* (Aqmesjit: Qïrïm Oquv-Pedagogik Neshriyatï, 1994), 369–83. Finogeev et al. give data as of 1 January 1993, whereas "Vatanïmïzda . . ." provides data as of 31 December 1993. By year's end, figures for Crimean Tatar registrations rose in all places except Alushta.

Andrew Wilson (*The Crimean Tatars: A Situation Report on the Crimean Tatars* [London: International Alert, 1994], 38) reports that Crimean Tatars estimate that a further 50,000–60,000 of their countrymen had migrated back from exile without official registration, thus totaling, by September 1993, 250,000–260,000.

ing Kazak, Tajik, or Uzbek, for example, and Russian. A memorandum (*Otchet*) presented to the government of the Republic of Ukrayina by the Crimean Tatar Mejlis confirms the existence of that policy. No earlier than 1993 did the first school since the World War II–era deportations using the Crimean Tatar language for instruction come into being. The community established another in the following year. Both schools owed their start to private funding.[32] The younger Crimean Tatar emigrants earlier educated in Samarkand or Tashkent—the main places of urban residence for them in Uzbekistan during the postwar Soviet era—today speak and write excellent Uzbek and Russian.

Partly as a reaction to this situation, many Crimean Tatars preferred the use of Russian to a Central Asian tongue. Russian offered broader international communication than did a local medium and neutralized the assimilatory threat of the Central Asian languages. Observers have often noticed that Crimean Tatars born after 1942 seem most at home speaking and writing Russian, and some understandably lack a perfect control of their own language.

The president of the Mejlis, Mustafa Jemiloglu himself, has said that he delivered his report to the Second Qurultay in the Crimean Tatar tongue because he considered the meetings in 1991 a historic event, despite the knowledge that visitors to the Qurultay might not understand his language. He undertook this even though it required a few days of his busy time to translate the speech into what he called the Turkic (Crimean Tatar) language from the Russian in which he composed it. Many other speakers in those sessions simply delivered their messages in Russian,[33] possibly because they could not so fluently address the Qurultay correctly in their own language, or perhaps from a sense that many Crimean Tatars themselves felt more at home in Russian. In any case, urban Crimean Tatars lived at a crossroads important to the larger world and participated in a cosmopolitan traffic of ideas, languages, and people. Their preferences included mediums such as the bilingual press (fig. 1.1) that permitted them easy communication abroad and with the foreigners traveling and living in Crimea.

Denial of the right freely to publish, speak, and study their own language has taken its toll on Crimean Tatar youngsters, as well. A sympathetic Slavic resident of Crimea comes on a cluster of Crimean Tatar boys on a street corner chattering in Russian and asks them, "'Why don't you

Figure 1.1. Front page of Crimean Tatar/Russian bilingual newspaper *Qïrïm* (formerly *Dostluq*), no. 39 (25 September 1993).

speak Tatar with each other?' After an awkward silence, they reply, 'We're shy.' I understand the desire of the kids not to be singled out, not to be tactless with others, but also understandable to me is the tragedy of this situation, when you are reticent about speaking the native tongue."[34] That reticence reflects the feeling, pervasive among young and old, that, by blending into the social surroundings and speaking the prevailing language, they can cast off the stigma wrongly placed on them by the Soviet regime in 1944.

Deprivation of the use of their tongue in education and other intellectual discourse has produced yet another side effect. Crimean Tatars regard the native language as a treasure worth preserving for its own, symbolic sake, not only for normal communication. The poet Remzi Burnash captures something of that attitude in lines from his verse entitled "My Mother Tongue" ("Ana tilim"; trans. by Edward Allworth with S. Ahmet Kirimca):

| | |
|---|---|
| Each nation has its own tongue | (Er bir khalqnïn oz' tili bar |
| In which lovers confide, | Yaresinen sïrdashqan, |
| To it, that tongue is sweeter than honey, | Baldan tatlï o til' onga, |

| | |
|---|---|
| It will never be forgotten. | O bir vaqït unutïlmay. |
| My nation of kinsmen, too, | Menim tuvghan khalqïmnïn da |
| Has its own tongue that sings, | Oz' tili bar yïrlashqan, |
| Amid a thousand and one stars | Bin bir yïldïz arasïnda |
| This tongue, in my cradle, | Bu til' meni beshigimde |
| Raised me with its lullaby, | Ayneninen os'tyurgen, |
| It pulled forward from my youth | Yashlïghïmdan yetekley o |
| Holding me by the hand.... | Tutïp menim qolumdan....)[35] |

Portraying with words in some ways differs little from painting with oil and watercolors. Each medium in certain hands makes more palpable to observers scenes and moods imagined by creative artists. The Crimean Tatars' culture has generated artists who could remind them of the places and situations the exiles have longed to experience. On 18 September 1993, the Art Museum of Aqmesjit (Simferopol') opened a one-man show of works painted by Ramazan Useinov (born in 1949 in Samarkand). His became the sixth such exhibition hung for Crimean Tatar artists in Crimea. Viewers found works that symbolized his own spiritual return to Crimea, where he had evidently never previously lived. Some of the pieces bore titles especially significant to Crimean Tatars, such as *The Return*, *Ayu Dagh Mountain*, and *Bakhchesaray*. Critics sensed in his rather abstract, generally more universal visualizations, in particular among those completed in the 1990s, a more somber, melancholy mood than they had noticed in much of his earlier painting.[36] That shift may have reflected the change perceptible in some literature, as well, as creative artists descended from the optimism and high expectations of the late 1980s and very early 1990s to a cautionary realism (in poems cited above, Lilia Budzhurova refers to Crimea as a place redolent of hope but not devoid of the pangs of separation). Renditions by their creative intellectuals in the different fields of art, literature, and music, whether pessimistic or affirmative, contributed significantly to the regrowth of self-identity among Crimean Tatars.

Familiar words set to popular melodies carve another facet into the sensory configuration making up the group's self-awareness. In Central Asian exile along with his countrymen, the Crimean Tatar composer and folklorist Yahya Sherfedinov (born in 1894) came from a poor family of Kefe (Feodosiia). His talent earned him admission to the Petersburg School of the Arts. He finished teachers' seminary and taught in Kefe. He took his diploma from the Moscow conservatory in 1931. At his behest, during 1955–56, people in the Bekabad, Uzbekistan, zone of exile collected from their older countrymen and -women over seventy folk songs and melodies. When Uzbek Radio began broadcasting these in its Tatar programming, they were "the first melodies that reminded [Crimean Tatars] of the native land, which Sherfedinov's countrymen longed to hear." Every Crimean Tatar family attended live performances of these songs, dances, and other music presented throughout the zones of exile at concerts of the ensemble Qaytarma, reestablished in 1957 (see the discussion of the Qaytarma Ensemble in chap. 5 below). For Crimean Tatars, that troupe was "definitely a symbol of the ethnic group [*narod*]."[37]

## Yet Another Testing Time

The exiles needed such musical, moral support in order to overcome the ordeal they had to endure. A new shock came from discovering how vicious the hatred had grown, whether from fear or guilt, of Slavs toward Crimean Tatars during the last half of the 1980s and the early 1990s. It seemed to Tatars as if the arrival of something a step closer to parity among nationalities, in particular greater equality for Crimean Tatars, had aroused a kind of fury in the deposed dominant ethnic group. Before 1990, many acts of willful destruction struck Crimean Tatars. In August 1989 rose the first tent city of Crimea in the late Soviet era, erected on land occupied by Crimean Tatars in Sevastianovka village, Bakhchesaray *raion*. Such actions continued and soon provoked strong reprisals. Slavic vigilantes destroyed a similar self-constructed habitation in the village of Molodezhnoe, near Aqmesjit (Simferopol'), on 9 September 1989 (see fig. 1.2); they destroyed another near Nizhnie Oreshka, in Qarasuvbazar (Belogorsk) *raion* on 12 September 1989. Local thugs demolished an old Muslim mosque in the village of Azek (Plodovoe) in Bakhchesaray *raion* on 7 October 1989 and yet another group of temporary habitations on 14 December 1989 at the village of Degirmenka, near Alushta, with militiamen participating in the action.[38]

Russian militiamen and vigilantes continued the physical destruction and theft of Crimean Tatar housing, materials, and facilities in 1990 and 1991, on 16 August 1991 again razing to the ground the mosque rebuilt from

Figure 1.2. Crimean Tatars around the ruins of their new mosque at Molodezhnoe suburb, 2.25 kilometers north of Aqmesjit (Simferopol'), demolished in August 1991 by Slavic thugs. Photo courtesy of Mme Safinar Jemiloglu, wife of the president of the Crimean Tatar Mejlis.

the materials left after the first destruction of housing in Molodezhnoe on 9 September 1989.³⁹ Demolition of tents and other temporary structures made up only one of the miseries besetting the returnees. On announcing, "'In the name of Allah [*Bismillah*...]' at the very first moment when they set foot on [what they called] that 'sacred ground [*muqaddes topraq*],'" Crimean Tatars singled out as the most severe among "a thousand different hardships" they suffered on returning to Crimea the difficulty of getting land.⁴⁰ When some of them received assignment to more permanent accommodations, they found further problems. A collective letter from forty-six Crimean Tatar residents of a dormitory complained in detail about the sorry conditions under which fifty-six families, including those with little children, with ill or demented members, tried to live. With neither functioning bathing or indoor plumbing facilities nor kitchens or gas for heating and cooking, paying rent higher than their living allowances for more than two years for grossly overcrowded quarters, they found no response at all from the authorities in their district to reports they made about the delapidation.⁴¹ And so it goes.

But it mouths no empty cliché to observe in this case that hardship builds character. The harsh conditions and the hostility of Slavic settlers awaiting young Crimean Tatars emigrating from Central Asia to Crimea for the first time in their lives have tested and tempered them. In the early 1990s, a young couple, expecting a child, squatters on a plot near Aqmesjit (Simferopol'), consider "Crimea . . . a remote, provincial place, compared to Tashkent," where they came from. The return to Crimea means "exchanging relative prosperity [in Central Asia] for poverty," but, they say, "all of us are returning." Asked by an interviewer if they fear more persecution after the repeated imprisonment of their parents for flouting discriminatory regulations here, they laugh: "We have survived so much, we no longer fear anything." Outsiders confirm the rudimentary living conditions of many Tatars in Crimea.⁴²

In the final analysis, the resoluteness characteristic of the group—one expression of its optimism—grows out of the understanding that a mature sense of loss overcome but not forgotten sustains the group. Mejlis president Mustafa Jemiloglu has expressed that conviction in similar terms: "We can be optimistic in these difficult times, because we have survived much more dismal periods in the past; [and] . . . we do not forsee an easy future."⁴³ Related to that outlook arises the belief that the ashes of martyrs and other ancestors validate the group's linkage with Crimea. The cemetery of the khans in Bakhchesaray and the Qaraim graves in Mangup Qale, both in Crimea, had been plundered repeatedly by Russian and other treasure hunters long before Soviet authorities in the 1940s authorized and executed the destruction of local graveyards, removing all identifying signs and markers. In contrast, visits by Crimean Tatars to some well-kept graves of what are thought to have been three royal Crimean Tatars buried, apparently, in the eighteenth century in Chatalja, Turkiye, have confirmed for the living that "the sacredness of a grave has been considered indisputable among Muslims since ancient times."⁴⁴ From such attitudes have grown the strongly shared views about Crimea itself: "Our nationality has been returning one by one to our sacred [*asret*] Homeland [*Vatan*] for fifty years. Not a single thing can measure the holiness [*asretligi*] of the Homeland [*Vatan*] [to us]."⁴⁵ (For further discussion of this idea, see chap. 13.)

An important part of real group self-awareness comes from avoiding denial of the melancholy past as well as of the happy history of a nationality and its place. One reason for venerating ancestors arises exactly from a mature sense of loss leading to a more meaningful present life. Visits to the old cemeteries and grieving over the vandalizing of Crimea's mausoleums and Crimean Tatar cemeteries perform an important function as part of the process of absorbing both the regrettable and the salutory in truly strengthening a group's self-identity. Such things replace rather than merely propagandize a quasi-realistic past fabricated to fit an ideological treatment of times gone by like that in most Soviet versions of Crimean Tatar history.

In his day, Ismail Bey Gaspirali expressed the conviction that religious community, not language family, ethnic group, or political organization, constituted the main source of group strength for his people.[46] Late in the twentieth century, faith combines with the personal traits of Crimean Tatars—an acute traditional sense of moral and human rights, of ultimate honor and justice, combined with good name and redemption—to make a firm concept of self-worth and clear identity. This has developed because of and despite the vicissitudes involving traditional symbols, places, and an alien hegemony that have tormented and then strengthened them. They very paucity of visible signs of man-made Crimean Tatar physical identity in the landscape gives the scattered remnants of mosques, palaces, and relics of tombs all the more worth to them.[47] Overshadowing stone monuments, shared values and attitudes shape the imagined ties that endow a resolute community with mighty sinews of self-awareness leading to firm group identity.

## Notes

1. *Pechat' SSSR v 1976 godu: Statisticheskii sbornik* (Moscow: "Statistika," 1977), 21, tables 9, 43.
2. Eskender Fazïl, *Temenna: Shiirler* (Tashkent: Ghafur Ghulam adïna Edebiyat va San'at Neshriyatï, 1982), 6. (Unless otherwise noted, Edward Allworth made all translations.) Fazïl had published many poems in Central Asia before *Gesture of Respect* (*Temenna*), a copy of which he kindly inscribed to the author of this chapter.
3. Lilia Budzhurova, "Kak pakhnet rodina?" *Nekuplennyi bilet. Sbornik stikhov* (Baltic Region [city not named]: Krymizdat, 1990), 32.

4. L. Budzhurova, "My segodnia vernulis'," *Avdet*, nos. 15/16 (11 July 1991): 8.

5. Rustem Ali, "Qïrïm," *Dostluq*, no. 15 (1992): 3 (translated by Edward Allworth, with Ahmet Kirimca).

6. J. B. Bury, *A History of Greece to the Death of Alexander the Great* (London: Macmillan, 1900), 111.

7. Communication from John R. Krueger, 11 June 1996.

8. N.G., "Krymskii poluostrov," in *Entsiklopedicheskii slovar'* (St. Petersburg: F. A. Brokgauz/I. A. Efron, 1895), 16A:872; *Novyi i polnyi geograficheskii slovar' Rossiiskago Gosudarstva ili leksikon opisuiushchii azbuchnym poriadkom geograficheski, topograficheski, idrograficheski, fizicheski, istoricheski, politicheski, khronologicheski, genealogicheski i geraldicheski, namiestnichestva, oblasti i uiezdy; goroda, krieposti, reduty, fortposty, ostrogi . . . obshirnoi Imperii Rossiiskoi v nynieshnem eia sostoianii, v tsarstvovanie Imperatritsy Ekateriny Velikiia . . .* (Moscow: V Universitetskoi Tipografii, u N. Novikova, 1789), pt. 5, p. 205.

9. [Abu'l-Fida,] *The Memoirs of a Syrian Prince, Abu'l-Fida', Sultan of Hamah (672–732/1273–1331)*, trans. P. M. Holt, Freiburger Islamstudien, vol. 9 (Wiesbaden: Franz Steiner, 1983), 8–9, 36, 39.

10. Stanley Lane-Poole, *The Mohammadan Dynasties: Chronological and Genealogical Tables with Historical Introductions* (Westminster: Archibald Constable, 1894), 235–37; Valerii Vozgrin, *Istoricheskie sud'by krymskikh Tatar* (Moscow: "Mysl'," 1992), 20, 127, 130; Begäli Qasimaw, *Ismailbek Gäspräli (Tänishtirish Yolidägi bir Täjribä)* (Tashkent: Ghäfur Ghulam namidägi Näshriyat-Mätbää Birläshmäsi, 1992), 21.

11. Maks Fasmer, *Etimologicheskii slovar' russkogo iazyka* (Moscow: Progress, 1967), 2:389; E. Abdullaev and M. Umerov, *Ruscha-Qirimtatardja oquv lughati* (Aq Mesdjit: Qirim Oquv-Pedagogik Neshriyati, 1994), 120–21. Abdullaev and Umerov give *kerman* as the Crimean Tatar equivalent of *fortress* (p. 152).

12. Clifford Edmund Bosworth, *The Islamic Dynasties: A Chronological and Genealogical Handbook* (Edinburgh: Edinburgh University Press, 1967), 154, 157–59.

13. Erik Amburger, "Russisches Reich: Verwaltungsgrenzen von 1914: Europäischer Teil," separate folding sketch map included with *Geschichte der Behördenorganisation Russlands von Peter dem Grossen bis 1917* (Leiden: E. J. Brill, 1966); see also p. 373.

14. Begäli Qasimaw, *Ismailbek Gäspräli (Tänishtirish yolidägi bir täjribä)* (Tashkent: Ghafur Ghulam namidägi Näshriyat-Mätbää Birläshmäsi, 1992), 32; Ismail Bey, "Turkchilik," *Tärjuman*, no. 36 (1907), cited in Qasimaw, *Ismailbek Gäspräli*, 31–32.

15. Ismail Bei Gasprinskii, *Rossiia i Vostok: Russkoe Musul'manstvo: Mysli, zametki i nabliudeniia Musulmanina; Russko-Vostochnoe Soglashenie: Mysli, zametki i pozhelaniia* (Oxford, 1985; reprint, Kazan': Fond Zhien, Tatarskoe Knizhnoe Izdatel'stvo, 1993).

16. Vozgrin, *Istoricheskie*, 394, 398, 400.

17. Ibid., 402–3.

18. Ibid., 386, 390–91.

19. "4 goda natsional'noi politiki Sov. vlasti," *Zhizn' natsional'nostei*, no. 24 (122) (5 November 1921): 1; M. O. Reikhel, *Sovetskii federalizm* (Moscow and Leningrad: Gosudarstvennoe Izdatel'stvo, 1930), 216, citing the act of the VTsIK "Ob avtonomnoi Krymskoi SSR," *Sobranie Uzakoneniia RSFSR*, 18 October 1921, art. 69-546.

20. Walter Russell Batsell gives a translation of the constitution in his *Soviet Rule in Russia* (New York: Macmillan, 1929), sec. 36.

21. Joseph Stalin, "The National Question and the Soviet Constitution," in *Marxism and the National Question* (New York: International, 1942), 220–21.

22. *Vsesoiuznaia perepis' naseleniia 1939 goda: Osnovnye itogi* (Moscow: "Nauka," 1992), table 16, "Natsional'nyi sostav naseleniia po respublikam, kraiam i oblastiam," p. 67. Except for some summary figures, detailed data from the Soviet census conducted in 1939 remained unpublished until after the collapse of the Soviet Union.

23. *Vsesoiuznaia perepis' naseleniia 17 dekabria 1926 g: Kratkie svodki*, issue IV, "Narodnost' i rodnoi iazyk naseleniia SSSR" (Moscow: Izdanie TsSU SSSR, 1928), table III, p. 71.

24. *Vsesoiuznaia perepis' naseleniia 1939 goda*, 72–75; *Vsesoiuznaia perepis' naseleniia 17 dekabria 1926 g.*, table III, p. 130.

25. *Vsesoiuznaia perepis' naseleniia 1939 goda*, 66.

26. Vasilii Subbotin, "Bor'ba s istoriei: Rasskaz-vospominanie," *Literaturnaia gazeta*, 30 January 1991, reprinted in Alieva, comp., *Tak eto bylo*, 3:68–69; *Atlas turista Krym* (Simferopol': Kimmeriia, n.d.), large (scale 1:200,000) four-sheet map of Crimea in color printed in Russian, with great detail.

27. Server Ebubekir, "Problemy toponimiki i istoriia Kryma," *Kasevet: Istoriko-etnograficheskii zhurnal* 24, no. 1 (1995): 3.

28. Cengiz Daghji, *O topraklar bizimdi: Roman* (Istanbul: Varlik Yayinevi, 1972), 5.

29. "Postanovlenie Verkhovnogo Soveta Respubliki Krym o nazvanii natsional'nosti 'krymskie tatary,'" *Avdet*, no. 25 (90) (16 December 1993): 1.

30. N. Ivina, "Zachem nam otrechen'e?" *Literaturnaia gazeta*, 6 April 1988, cited by Emil Amit in Alieva, comp., *Tak eto bylo*, 3:111.

31. Kurtegen Asanov and Zaira Kakura, "Kto predstavliaet krymskotatarskii narod?" *Avdet*, no. 12 (151) (24 June 1996): 3.

32. "Parallel'nyi otchet Medzhlisa krymskotatarskogo naroda ob osushchestvlenii mezhdunarodnogo Pakta ob ekonomicheskikh, sotsial'nykh i kul'turnykh pravakh v Ukraine (k tret'emu periodicheskomu dokladu, predstavlennomu Ukrainoi v sootvetstvii so stat'iami 16 i 17 pakta ot 19 sentiabria 1994 goda)" (pp. 10–11 of a typescript prepared by Nadir Bekirov, member of the Mejlis).

33. "Kurultay v litsakh," *Avdet*, nos. 15/16 (26/27) (11 July 1991): 8.

34. Iu. I. Zaporozhchenko, "Zakon o iazyka—eto politika," *Avdet*, no. 20 (85) (7 October 1993): 4.

35. Remzi Burnash, "Ana tilim," in *Qïrïmtatar edebiyatï: 7-indji sïnïf ichyun derslik-khrestomatiia*, comp. Alie V. Veliulaeva and Lenie A. Alieva (Aqmesjit: Qïrïm Devlet Oquv-Pedagogik Neshriyatï, 1993), 165.

36. G. Kurtaliev, "Vozvrashchenie v dukhe abstraktsionizma," *Avdet*, no. 19 (84) (23 September 1993): 4.

37. G. Kurtalieva, "Ostanovite Belialova!" *Avdet*, no. 13 (78) (8 July 1993): 2.

38. M. N. Guboglo and S. M. Chervonnaia, eds., *Krymskotatarskoe natsional'noe dvizhenie*, vol. 2, *Dokumenty: Materialy: Khronika* (Moscow: Rossiiskaia Akademiia Nauk Tsentr po Izucheniiu Mezhnatsional'nykh Otnoshenii, Institut Etnologii i Antropologii im. N. N. Miklukho-Maklaia, 1992), 310.

39. Ibid., 23 May–27 August 1991, pp. 321–25.

40. "Topraqnï ich bir maniasïz almalïmïz," *Dostluq*, 1 August 1992, 2.

41. "Obshchezhitie, gde nema, v-obshchem, zhitiia . . . ," *Qïrïm*, no. 25 (24 June 1995): 1.

42. Urszula Doroszewska, "Crimea: Whose Country?" *Uncaptive Minds* 5, no. 3 (21) (Fall 1992): 44; James Rupert, "Coming Home to Poverty; Tatars' Return Roils Crimea's Politics," *Washington Post*, 5 January 1996.

43. Urszula Doroszewska, "Interview with Mustafah Dzhemilev," *Uncaptive Minds* 5, no. 3 (21) (Fall 1992): 58.

44. G. Kurtalieva, "Chuzhie sredi svoikh," *Avdet*, no. 2 (93) (27 January 1994): 4.

45. Sabe Useinova, "Qash yaqadjaq alïp koz'siz qalmayïq," *Yangï dyuniya*, no. 27 (30 June 1995): 4.

46. Ismail Bey Gasprinskii, "Russkoe Musul'manstvo: Mysli, zametiki i nabliudeniia," in *Rossiia i Vostok*, 38–39.

47. S. M. Chervonnaia, *Iskusstvo tatarskogo Kryma* (Moscow: Rossiiskaia Akademiia Khudozhestv, Nauchno-Issledovatel'skii Institut Teorii i Istorii Izobrazitel'nykh Iskusstv, Medzhlis Krymskotatarskogo Naroda, 1995), 297–301; see also the pictorial appendix, plates 1–13.

# I

Forming a Modern Identity

# 2

## *A Model Leader for Asia, Ismail Gaspirali*

ALAN W. FISHER

Crimean Tatars have been blessed with a number of outstanding leaders over the past hundred years who are in large part responsible for the remarkable ability that Tatars have shown to survive, even thrive, as a vital nationality within the Russian Empire and the Soviet Union. Most recently, Mustafa Jemiloglu has provided direction and leadership to the small Crimean Tatar nationality in the Soviet Union, especially those residing in the Tashkent region. The tasks for Jemiloglu are extremely difficult ones, as over the past two decades Crimean Tatars have faced challenges to their identity much more severe than their ancestors experienced under czarist rule: official refusal to consider them a legitimate nationality, refusal to permit their return to their territorial homeland, and refusal to give them the even limited encouragement granted to other, more acceptable ethnic and national groups. Yet Jemiloglu's example, hard work, perhaps stubbornness, have permitted Crimean Tatars in the Soviet Union to be among the most energetic national groups in the realms of literature, journalism, and political activities.

About one hundred years before Jemiloglu, the most important Crimean Tatar leader was Ismail Bey Gaspirali. The challenges facing Crimean Tatars in his day were quite different from those that confront Jemiloglu. Then it was a matter of survival, in the cultural sense, in the face of clear Russian political, economic, and educational superiority. Understandably, Gaspirali's responses to the different challenges were of a different order than those used, or appropriate, today; Gaspirali's emphasis lay on educational and spiritual renewal, not politics. Indeed, he found nothing wrong with the idea of close cooperation with the Russian political and cultural authorities, for he could not conceive of a set of circumstances in which Crimean Tatars would be without a homeland. But, without his efforts and accomplishments, it seems unlikely that Crimean Tatars would have survived long enough to produce the political and national movement that inspires them today.

When Ismail Bey Gaspirali (Gasprinskii)[1] died on 11 September 1914 in Bakhchesaray after a long illness, most of the important Turkic newspapers and journals in the Russian and Ottoman Empires published obituaries that reflected an outpouring of emotion and grief about what they generally agreed was a major loss to Turkic society.[2] In *Iqbal*, an Azeri journal in Baku, Saifi Ibrahimov wrote:

Who was Ismail Bey? We don't yet have an answer to this question. In Russia, in Turkiye, in Egypt, in Arabia, in India, in Afghanistan, in Iran, in Turan, everywhere his name was known and beloved. Ismail Bey was everything, everyone, our all, the entire nation. Ismail Bey was the genius and the conscience of our modern language, our heart, our literature, our writers, our readers, our press, our *maktabs* and *medreses*, our pupils and students, the entire being of all of us.[3]

Yusuf Akchuraoghlu wrote in *Türk Yurdu* in Istanbul:

Ismail Bey was a good teacher, a skillful journalist, a distinguished editor, a social and political intellectual, and an active member of our national societies and institutions. But all of these attributes do not add up to or even describe Ismail Bey. In the Turkic and Islamic world of the past half century, it is possible to number twenty or thirty persons whom I knew who possessed qualities worthy of eulogy. But Ismail Bey was unique—*tek adam*—who belongs among a handful of persons in the Islamic and Turkic world over the last several centuries to be singled out for especial praise.[4]

A year later, Osman Akchokrakli wrote a long essay in Ismail Bey's own *Terjüman* in which he concluded:

In 1903 Ismail Bey wrote in this journal: "We are making progress. But our national education remains yet to be born." What is *Terjüman*? It is our national treasury. Yes, *Terjüman* is our national literature, our national education, the treasury of our modern national history. Do we have a national public library? Do we have a national public museum? Do we have a national public academy? What we have is twenty-three volumes of *Terjüman*. This is our great national treasury.[5]

Dozens of such statements appeared through the Turkic press in 1914 and the following months,[6] as in *Vakit* (Orenburg) by Fatih Kerimov, "Great National Grief"; in *Yoldïz* (Kazan) by Abdullah Battal-Taymas, "Difficult Event"; in *Koyash* (Kazan) by Fatih Emirhan, "Small Memory of a Great Nationalist." Finally, in a very important article published in

Figure 2.1. Ismail Bey Gaspirali and his new-method schooling pressed under the Russian bear and reactionary Muslim *ulema*. From the satirical Azeri journal *Mulla Nasreddin*, no. 17 (1908).

*Jumhüriyet* in Istanbul, fourteen years later, Fuad Köprülü wrote about Gaspirali and his journal *Terjüman*: "*Terjüman* had an important effect not only on the Crimea, but in Kazan, the Caucasus, Turkistan, Chinese Turkistan, Siberia, Romania, Bulgaria, everywhere in the Ottoman Empire, in short, in the entire Turkic world. It produced great hope, laid foundations for the accomplishment of that hope, of a national renewal for the Turks, especially for the Russian Turks. Its editor's name, Ismail Bey, is known everywhere" (fig. 2.1).[7]

These were evidence of Ismail Bey's immediate legacy throughout the Turkish and Turkic world. In order to determine what might remain today, more than eighty years later, of a direct and identifiable legacy from Ismail Bey in the Turkic world, it is necessary to examine studies produced in the Soviet Union and Turkiye relating to the history of Ismail Bey's period and to the history of Islamic education and renewal in and outside Russia and studies of the Turkic and Tatar political and nationalist movements written in Turkiye, the West, and the Soviet Union.

It is surprising that works by the leading Soviet Turkologists do not for the most part even mention Gaspirali. In his important study of the turn-of-the-century period (first published in 1966), Muhammad Gainullin, perhaps the leading Soviet Tatar historian of Tatar literature and journalism, completely ignored not only Gaspirali but *Terjüman* and almost any author who had published in it. Because Crimean Tatars were officially rehabilitated by the Soviet government no earlier than 1967, presumably his book about Tatar literature in the nineteenth century, published in 1975, would have rectified the earlier omission. It also seemed likely that Gainullin's revised edition of his first book, expanded and considerably changed, published in 1983, would have had something to say about Ismail Bey and *Terjüman*. But in all his works there is total silence on the subject.[8] Ismail Bey is not credited with contributions to Turkic, Tatar, or Islamic educational reform in such works as those by M. Z. Tutaev, V. M. Gorokhov, or R. I. Nafigov, which deal specifically with the Jadidism initiated by Gaspirali.[9]

But it is not only Soviet works on the subject that downplay or avoid mention of Ismail Bey. Many of the most important works on modern Turkish history, literature, and journalism produced in Turkiye and the West ignore Gaspirali and his contributions.[10] Indeed, besides the Crimean Tatar authors and historians themselves, in their Istanbul journal *Emel*, in *Dergi* published for several years in Germany, and in *Türk Kültürü*, which devotes a good deal of attention to Turks outside Turkiye, almost nothing about Ismail Bey and his influence appeared in Turkiye either[11] before 1991.

In works by Western scholars interested in Soviet nationality affairs and history, more has appeared about Ismail Bey.[12] Almost all such studies focus on the existence and importance of Ismail Bey's journal *Terjüman* and especially on the meaning of the motto that appeared on the masthead of the journal's later issues: "Dilde, fikirde, ishte, birlik" (Unity in language, thought, and action). Most have placed the importance of his work within the broader topic of pan-Turkism.

None of the early obituaries, or even essays discussing Gaspirali that appeared in the 1920s, such as that by Fuad Köprülü, mention this motto, and they certainly do not claim that Ismail Bey's chief importance lay in the political movement relating to pan-Turkism, Turkic nationalism, or Turkic unity. Rather, they all focus on language, literature, and especially renewal through education.

Finally, two very important studies by Western scholars focusing almost exclusively on Ismail Bey Gaspirali must be mentioned and credited with drawing our attention back to the really important elements of his work and life. These are the dissertation by Gustav Burbiel on the language developed by Ismail Bey and used in *Terjüman* and the dissertation by Edward Lazzerini on Gaspirali's ideas. No modern evaluation of Ismail Bey's contributions may ignore the information and ideas presented by these two scholars.[13]

The first task in identifying the true legacy of Ismail Bey is to determine what he considered most important and to establish his intellectual contributions. It is possible to divide his concerns into four main categories, which, although separate, are obviously interrelated: the general question of Islamic renewal and relations between the Islamic and various Western worlds; language and its role in Islamic renewal; women's rights and emancipation as an essential ingredient for renewal; and, finally, for Ismail Bey the panacea for the first three, education in a form new to the Islamic world. It is also very important to place Ismail Bey's ideas in their own context, both in the Islamic communities of the Russian Empire in which he lived and operated and in the larger Islamic world of his time. Finally, with the above at least outlined and identified, it is possible to note Ismail Bey's immediate impact at home and abroad and to make some suggestions about his possible long-term legacy.

First, Ismail Bey believed that the rapidly changing political and cultural relation between Muslims and Western states and peoples made necessary an immediate and rapid Islamic renewal. He summarized his views on the problem succinctly in a long article in *Terjüman* in 1907, which was translated and partially published in the London *Times* by Arminius Vámbéry:

> In paying due attention to the relations of the Muslim world, we shall be grieved to notice that, wherever and under whatever rule they be, they always remain behind their neighbors. In Algiers the Muslims are superseded by the Jews, in Crete by the Greeks, in Bulgaria by the Bulgarians, and in Russia by everybody. . . . We must investigate into the causes of this deplorable state, for admitting, for example, that

the Algerian Jews surpass the Algerian Arab, it is astonishing and quite inexplicable that the poor and devout Buddhist should get ahead of the once energetic Muslim.[14]

Gaspirali's views here were aimed at encouraging the organization of a pan-Islamic congress to meet in Cairo to discuss the broad issues of Islamic revival.

Again, Gaspirali wrote that "it is an indisputable fact that contemporary Muslims are the most backward peoples." "They have been left behind in virtually every area of life by Armenians, Greeks, Bulgarians, Jews, and Hindus. . . . We have remained behind them and now regard them with amazement."[15] What was even worse was the fact that a number of areas of the Muslim world that had only recently been independent were losing their sovereignty in the face of European expansion and imperialism. What were the causes of this misfortune? What remedy was available to stop the decline and recover the losses? He noted more than once that he did not accept the widespread belief in the West of his time that Christianity and Judaism had innate strengths that no other religion or religious tradition could match. Islam once had itself dominated both Jews and Christians in politics, economics, and even culture. Rather, Gaspirali placed much of the blame on Islamic religious leaders who had "stifled progressive ideas, placed thought in a vice, and closed the doors to scientific research."[16] It was not Islam as a religion or as a culture that was at fault, but its leading practitioners.

Ismail Bey's attitudes toward the West were only partly produced from his firsthand experience. He had lived for a few months in Paris early in his career and apparently could read French. But his views, for the most part, about Western-Islamic relations were the result of his experiences in Russia, his study of Russian culture and institutions, and his good knowledge of the Russian language.

Ismail Bey wrote in the editorial in the first issue of *Terjüman* in 1883:

Exactly 100 years ago, on 8 April 1783, the small [Crimean] khanate, worn out by disorder and bloodshed, was made a part of the greatest empire in the world and received peace under the patronage of a mighty power and the protection of just laws. Celebrating this day together with all the other peoples of the Russian Empire, the Crimean Muslims cannot fail to recall all of those good deeds by which they have already profited for 100 years.[17]

While one might note that Gaspirali needed the approval of the Russian government's censorship committee before the journal could be issued and that such an editorial might well be aimed at gaining such approval, Ismail Bey was not hostile to the idea of Russian political domination of the Turkic communities in the empire and did truly believe that the Turks there had a great deal to gain from a close association with the Russians.

Gaspirali had written a small book in 1881, in Russian, entitled *Russian Islam: Thoughts, Notes and Observations of a Muslim* (*Russkoe musul'manstvo: Mysli, zamietki i nabliudeniia musul'manina*) in which he called for the total and immediate renewal of Russian Islam. This could be done, indeed, had to be done, in concert with the Russian government. He believed that Russia "would be one of the greatest Muslim states in the world," that Russia was the heir to the former Tatar possessions, and that sooner or later Russians and Tatars would enjoy the same rights. He was convinced that the Russian government would itself in the end come to its senses and abandon its policies that had been often admittedly hostile to Muslims and other minorities. "I believe that the Russian Muslims shall be more civilized than any other Muslim nation. We are a steady nation, give us the possibility to learn. You, great brothers, give us knowledge.... The Russians and Muslims shall come to an understanding in this way."[18]

Some years later, in 1896, Gaspirali wrote an essay in which he elaborated on these ideas. This essay was written long enough after 1883 to emphasize the point that he was writing at least in part from belief and not merely as an effort to please the censor. His essay, *Russian-Oriental Relations* (*Russkoe-vostochnoe soglashenie*) (translated in full in chap. 7 of this volume), emphasized not only agreement between and understanding of one another by Russians and Muslims but an actual drawing closer together—*sblizhenie*. "Muslims and Russians can plow, sow, raise cattle, trade, and make their livings together or side by side.... We think that sooner or later Russia's borders will include within them all of the Tatar peoples.... If Russia could have good relations with Turkey and Persia, she would become kindred to the entire Muslim East, and would certainly stand at the head of Muslim nations and their civilizations, which England is attempting so persistently to do." Gaspirali was not in favor of or did he believe probable the disappearance of Muslim or Turkic identity among the more numerous and more advanced Russians. "The key to the future of both the Islamic community and the Russian Empire was the active cooperation of an enlightened Russian government with an awakened Muslim people."[19]

In his views toward Russia, with his relatively positive attitude toward Russian-Muslim cooperation, Gaspirali resembled a contemporary in Central Asia, Ahmad Mahdum Donish, a scholar, a poet, and for a while the court astrologer in Bukhara. Donish looked to Russia, however, not so much as a model to be imitated as a useful source of knowledge and of tools to rebuild and renew Bukharan society, to save it from total extinction at the hands of the West (Russia). Donish apparently believed that there was room for cooperation between Bukharan Muslims and Russians, even when the relationship was so unequal in power.[20]

There were many Muslims of the late nineteenth and early twentieth centuries who were highly critical of their own society and who looked at the West with some envy or at least respect. In this regard, Ismail Bey was not different or unique, even within the Russian context. One can compare him, for example, with Ziya Gökalp, who is in fact often mentioned when discussions of Gaspirali are conducted. Gökalp was more circumspect, however, in calling for close cooperation with the West. Of course he lived in a state where he could write about such matters with more freedom than could Gaspirali. Yet in 1911 Gökalp sneered at those in the Ottoman Empire and outside who seemed to accept European civilization unquestioningly, "like someone who buys ready-made suits. . . . We Muslims cannot imitate fixed models of civilization. We need clothes made to measure principles of life which fit our figure. We have to create a new civilization from our own spirit."[21]

Gökalp and Gaspirali were both accepting, perhaps without doing so knowingly or clearly, the idea of the possibility of progress and basic change, and a change with positive value. Even in the Europe of Gaspirali's time this was a relatively new idea, and the Muslim world should not be overly criticized for being slow to accept it. The discovery that institutions were capable both of novelty, which was not mentioned or even hinted at in the Bible, and of development, by which one kind of institution would grow out of another, was an idea that was not centuries old in the West. Indeed, one of the most important Western theoreticians of the idea of progress of this sort was Lewis Henry Morgan, who died only in 1881.

The Islamic world, in Russia and outside, was in desperate condition in the minds of many reformers. Without some major change it might collapse entirely. Gaspirali saw no real danger in cooperation and growing closeness between Muslims and Russians or other Westerners. He apparently did not believe that Islam itself would have a difficult time surviving such proximity. And his prescriptions were quite different from those offered today by many within the Islamic world, who raise the same questions about danger and survival but who call for rejection of cultural relations with the West and call for a return to pure and early Islam.[22]

What were Gaspirali's specific prescriptions for survival? First of all, Ismail Bey focused on language, particularly in its written form: "Everyone knows what happens to a person without a language; there is no need to explain. If it is bad for a man, it is the same for a nation."[23] "It must not be forgotten that the language of a people is no less important an element in daily life than is religion."[24] Ismail Bey was convinced that at least the Turkic Muslims of the Russian Empire must have a common literary language—the critical mass for a viable culture and society was larger than any single part of that Turkic world. Such a common language would associate Russian Turkic Muslims with Turks outside Russia—in the Ottoman Empire, in Persia, and so forth. Such contact, communication, and resulting cooperation would greatly benefit the renewal of their society.

Ismail Bey was convinced that the language he used in *Terjüman* was just such a language, that in its simplified form it would be understood by Turkic readers anywhere and would facilitate the drawing together of Turks throughout the world. The language of *Terjüman* was, for all practical purposes, however, only a simplified form of Ottoman Turkish used in Istanbul at the time. It was criticized by a number of Gaspirali's contemporaries as not being understood easily by Turks in Central Asia, even in the Volga region. What is important to note here is that Gaspirali was interested in such a common literary language in order to facilitate renewal, not for any political purposes. He did often write of a Turkic nation (*kaum*), but where is the evidence that he dreamed of using this as a base for facilitating or creating a unified greater Turkic independent state or political entity?[25]

We remember that throughout the nineteenth century intellectuals in the Ottoman Empire grappled with the language question too. Ibrahim Shinasi, a young Ottoman intellectual and poet, had several decades before Ismail Bey published a journal, *Terjüman-i Ahval*, the name of which served as a partial model for Gaspirali's own journal. He had emphasized as Ismail Bey would later the simplification of the written language to facilitate wider readership.[26] Ziya Pasha, too, had written an article, "Poetry and Prose," in 1868 criticizing the Ottoman language as a useless literary medium for the vast majority of Turkish readers. This is ironic when one takes into account the fact that Gaspirali modeled his journalistic language on Ottoman.[27]

Some years later, Shemseddin Sami also focused attention on the necessity of creating a common literary language for Turks from Bukhara and Kashgar to the Balkans: "The first symbol of a nation and a race, its foundation, and its common property, shared equally by all its members is the language in which it speaks.... Each people and nation must therefore first of all bring order into its language."[28] Ziya Gökalp looked on language as the foundation stone of nationality and regarded independence in the sphere of language as a necessary condition for political independence.[29]

Gaspirali's contemporaries in the Russian Empire, Muslim and Turkic, often agreed with his emphasis on language and increased literacy. But the movements toward national development among many of the Turkic people and other non-Russians in the late nineteenth and early twentieth centuries proved to be divisive forces too strong to permit the adoption of a "neutral" common language among the Russian Turks. The Kazan Tatar intellectual Nashirvan Yanishev, who usually supported the idea of Islamic solidarity and cooperation, did not believe that Gaspirali's focus on a common literary language was useful or possible. He wrote that "no one, with the exception of the Azeris, can understand the language of *Terjüman*; the farther north you go, the fewer the people who read *Terjüman*."[30]

Policies pursued in the late nineteenth century by the Russian government helped encourage the separate development of minority languages. N. A. Il'minskii had argued that the ultimate goal of assimilating these nationalities into the mainstream of Russian culture was best and most quickly achieved by creating Russian schools for the nationalities, using the children's own language at the early stages of education to introduce them to the rudiments of Russian culture, but their language transcribed in Cyrillic characters. Ultimately, Russian itself would be used at the upper school levels. (These views bear some resemblance to current policies in the United States on bilingual education.) These Russo-Tatar schools would compete with purely Muslim schools; Gaspirali himself both attended and taught in such a school.[31]

Against this negativism, Gaspirali, in some exasperation, wrote in 1912 that "the desire of each Turkic people to create its own language is in agreement with democratic principles, but it is harmful for the future."[32] To the end of his life, Gaspirali held firmly to the idea he had expressed in *Terjüman* in 1906, that "without a national language there can be no progress, because a national language, a common literary language, is the means and source most fundamental and necessary for the advancement of education, literature, religion, and national hopes."[33] The statement has a great deal of meaning today, and his focus was not off the mark, for his judgment of language's importance was sound.

A second interest of Gaspirali's, which proved important for the national development of Russia's Turks, and particularly for the Volga and Crimean Tatar communities in the future, was that of women's rights and emancipation. In the legal sphere, he wrote little about women, although emphasizing the equality of women with men in matters of marriage, divorce, and inheritance.

Knowing how sensitive an issue this was among most Muslims in Russia and outside, Gaspirali made greater efforts to stress his Islamic orthodoxy. "I beg the reader to understand that I am not suggesting that the Sheriat be changed; this is impermissible."[34] Instead, he pointed out that the Qur'ân demanded the equitable treatment of women. What masqueraded as Islamic law and custom relating to women was nothing more than "some Asiatic concept." Beyond the legal questions, Gaspirali raised the issue in terms that sound strikingly modern. He pointed out to his readership that, since more than half the Muslim and Turkic population was female, for the Muslims to deny women the right and possibility to contribute to national development was to deny themselves half their human resources.

Ismail Bey firmly believed and often stated that without female participation it would be difficult, if not impossible, for Islamic society to raise its level of existence to that of the West. There was an intimate connection between the assurance of a vigorous and enlightened national life and the raising of the conditions of women's lives. All this had to begin with education, as with virtually everything else Gaspirali called for. "Whoever loves his own people and wishes it a great future, must concern himself with the enlightenment and education of women, restore freedom and independence to them, and give wide scope to the development of their minds and capabilities."[35]

Ziya Gökalp, too, had raised the women's issue in Turkey itself. He called for women's participation in social life, especially in the economic sphere, and free and unhindered entrance into the professions. Gökalp called for the equalization of educational opportunities for men and women, just as schools for women were so important to Gaspirali.[36] Whether Gaspirali's and Gökalp's hopes have been realized is a matter for debate. But it seems clear that women play a more important, at least public and visible, role in Turkic-Tatar life than in most other areas of the Islamic world.

While Gaspirali's slogan "Dilde, fikirde, ishte, birlik" is more widely used in scholarly discussions of his legacy, the term *usul-i jadid* (new method) more accurately reflects his importance. *Usul-i jadid* referred originally to the new method of instruction of language—phonetic transcription, simplified grammar, and simplified vocabulary. It soon came to mean the style of instruction in all subjects used in the *maktabs*, with an expanded curriculum as well as a new method of teaching. This curriculum at the *maktab* level (which was the level of greatest importance to Gaspirali) was to include the traditional Muslim elements—Qur'ân, calligraphy, Islamic traditions, but also a genuine ability to read in Arabic. But beyond these subjects Ismail Bey believed that a student should study the grammar and literature of his native language, the history of Islam and Islamic societies as well as of other religions and other societies, geography, arithmetic, and at least enough science to make an impact on the student's own lifestyle. He was convinced that no genuine renewal of Turkic-Tatar Islamic society was conceivable without educational renewal. His society needed "an army of learned men" and an "enlightened public."[37]

An American's dissertation shows that the *usul-i jadid* required reform in the actual physical environment for education, relating to size of classes, a regularization of beginning and ending school years, regularized school days, and a set curriculum of courses and levels. The school itself must be designed as a school, and the teachers must be prepared specifically in the subjects that they would teach.[38] Gaspirali was convinced that a sound and full *maktab* education was a prerequisite for a meaningful *medrese* experience. Admission to the higher level would require solid grounding in the *maktab* "basics."

To the south, the Ottomans, too, produced educational reformers who recognized the inadequacy of their traditional system. They had made great strides in identifying educational problems and had introduced a number of innovations that would be important later on as influences on Gaspirali, who spent some time in Istanbul. The idea of *maarif*, the process of becoming acquainted with things not known, was a direct challenge to the *ilm* of the *ulema*. The introduction of *fan* and the establishment of commissions and of ministries of education all reflected deep concern and innovative responses.[39]

There were important obstacles to overcome, however. In the decree of Mahmud II that supposedly made primary education compulsory, it was said:

While, according to Muslims, learning the requisites of religion comes first and above everything else and while these requisites take precedence over all worldly considerations, the majority of people lately avoid sending their children to school. This condition is the cause not only of widespread illiteracy but also of ignorance of religion, and hence, has been a primary cause of our misfortune. As it is necessary to deliver the Muslims from these worldly and other-worldly misfortunes, and as it is a religious obligation for the entire *ummah* of Muhammed to learn the affairs of religion and the faith of God, no man henceforth shall prevent his children from attending school until they have reached the age of adulthood.[40]

Again, in 1845, in addressing the Supreme Council, discussing the foundation of a Council of Education, Sultan Abdul Mejid defined the aims of education thus: "To disseminate religious knowledge and useful sciences, which are necessities for religion and the world, so as to abolish the ignorance of the people. It is a necessity for every human being to learn first his own religion and that education which will enable him to be independent of the help of others, and then and only then to acquire useful sciences and arts."[41]

At least in the Ottoman Empire, however, the government endorsed the goals and methods of educational reform. In Russia, Gaspirali faced opposition from the existing Muslim educational profession, the teachers in traditional *maktabs* and *medreses*, as well as the government. Russian officials too feared the outcome of successful Muslim educational reform, and, as already noted above, N. A. Il'minskii particularly opposed these reforms. He wrote, "A Muslim fanatically hostile to the infidels was less dangerous for the Russian state than a Muslim educated in the European style, with a degree from a Russian or Western university."[42] K. P. von Kaufman, governor general of Turkistan after the Russian conquest, believed that "the best way to undermine the influence of Muslim education was to create Russian schools to which Central Asian children would be admitted." This had the double advantage of drawing them away from Muslim schools, either traditional or of a new sort, and of bringing Muslim and Russian children together. He believed that the latter would assimilate the former when placed side by side.[43]

Russians established schools to compete with the very popular Jadid schools of Gaspirali. These Russian-native (*russko-tuzemnaia*) schools were for Muslims only, however, to acquaint the children with Russian culture through the medium of their own language and with elements of the Russian language. The first was opened in 1884 under the headmastership of a Russian orientalist, V. P. Nalivkin. In 1911, there were almost ninety of them in Turkistan, and, by 1913, there were more than 150 in the Kazak plains. This was an important recognition of the enormous success of Gaspirali's new-method schools.[44]

There is considerable disagreement about the number of *usul-i jadid* schools established by the time of the Russian Revolution in March 1917. But it seems clear that the number exceeded five thousand.[45] Gaspirali traveled widely in the Muslim areas of the empire doing his best to persuade the local dignitaries of the importance of these new-method schools. He was more successful in some regions than in others. In Kazan *guberniia*, where interest in educational reform and social renewal predated Ismail Bey's career, his new method corresponded exactly with the needs of the powerful Tatar bourgeoisie, and in the city of Kazan alone by 1916 there were more than a dozen Jadid *maktabs*. The presence of ten Jadid *medreses* in Kazan *guberniia* must have reflected some years of reformist primary education. One set of statistics published in the 1920s in Kazan argued for the proposition that these reformed schools were at least as successful as their Russian counterparts, producing a claimed Tatar literacy rate on the eve of the March 1917 revolution of 20 percent, compared to 18 percent for the Russians and between 5 and 9 percent for the other non-Russian minorities in the *guberniia*, the Chuvash, Mordovians, Votiaks, and Cheremisses.[46]

Gaspirali visited Central Asia, and under his influence Jadid schools were opened in Andijan in 1897, in Samarkand and Tokmak in 1898. These early Central Asian schools were exclusively for the local Tatar population. It was only in 1901 that the first Uzbek Jadid *maktab* was opened in Tashkent. The first Jadid school in Samarkand began operation in 1903.[47]

Ismail Bey had less success in Bukhara and Khiva, whose political leadership wavered on the issue and then succumbed to pressure from the local clergy to prevent such schools' establishment. Gaspirali made a trip to Calcutta, where he claimed to have succeeded in creating a Jadid school, using Urdu. An examination of educational literature published in India and Pakistan fails, however, to verify any lasting result in that region; the main evidence of his achievements there appears in his own essays in *Türk Yurdu* in 1912, "Hind Yolundan" and "Hind'den Dönerken."[48]

Strong enough backing for Gaspirali's educational ideas emerged throughout the Russian Islamic political movements so that the Third Muslim Congress in August 1906 at Nizhni Novgorod adopted three resolutions, one of which was to press for school reform in Islamic areas and to conduct education in the *maktabs* in the mother tongue of the pupils and with classes in *medreses* in the language espoused by Gaspirali. In May 1917, the Pan-Russian Muslim Congress held in Moscow adopted a resolution offered by Zeki Kadyrov on school reform that conformed in all important ways to the ideas of Gaspirali.[49]

A number of important Central Asian, Tatar, Azeri, and Turkish intellectuals credited Gaspirali with providing models and leadership that influenced them heavily. Modernists like Yusuf Akchuraoghlu, Akhundzada, Huseyinzade, Ahmed Maksudi, and Fatih Kerimi on the one hand, and editors of journals and newspapers such as *Vaqt*, *Yulduz*, and *Ay Qap*, all recognized the path breaking of Ismail Bey and *Terjüman*.[50] The great surprise, then, in looking at Gaspirali more than eighty years after his death was to discover that his accomplishments were given so little credit either in the Soviet Union or in the larger Turkic world in general.

Ismail Bey's language reform and any idea he may have had for a cultural (or even political) unity of the Turkic Muslim world would not overcome the desires of each Turkic group, the Azeri, Tatar, Uzbek, Kazak, and Turkish peoples, to focus on local and parochial political goals. But Gaspirali's evaluation of the weaknesses of Islamic society, his directions in educational reform, and his journalistic achievements produced immediate, dramatic, and long-lasting results. What a pity that *Terjüman*, viewed by many who wrote the obituaries appended in this volume (see chap. 7, document 3), has not been republished and has not been seriously studied by scholars who would have much to learn from it. If it served in 1914 as the "treasury" of Tatar culture, it is a treasury that remains to be discovered and mined today.

## Notes

1. Ismail Bey's name appears in scholarship and on his own published work as either *Gasprinskii* or *Gaspirali* (the Russianized or local Crimean Tatar form). I have preferred to use *Gaspirali* in this chapter.
2. For some of these obituaries and statements about Ismail Bey, reflecting a wide range of opinion, see chap. 7 in this volume.
3. Saifi Ibrahimov, "Büyük ve Tarihi Millî Matem," *Terjüman*, 1 October 1914, taken from *Iqbal*.
4. Yusef Akchuraoghlu, *Türk Yurdu*, no. 12 (1911).
5. Osman Akchokrakli, "Millî hazinemiz," *Terjüman*, no. 202 (1915).
6. See, e.g., Fatih Kerimov, "Great National Grief," *Vakit* (Orenburg), 1914; Abdullah Battal-Taymas, "Difficult Event," *Yoldïz* (Kazan), 1914; and Fatih Emirhan, "Small Memory of a Great Nationalist," *Koyash* (Kazan), 1914.
7. Fuad Köprülü, "Ismail Bey Gasprinski," *Jumhüriyet* (Istanbul), 7 March 1928.
8. Mukhamed Gainullin, *Tatarskaia literatura i publitsistika nachala XX veka*, rev. ed. (Kazan: Tatknigoizdat, 1983), and *Tatarskaia literatura XIX veka* (Kazan: Tatknigoizdat, 1975).
9. M. Z. Tutaev, *Oktiabr' i prosveshchenie* (Kazan: Tatknigoizdat, 1970); V. M. Gorokhov and V. P. Rozhdestvenskii, *Razvitie narodnogo obrazovaniia v Tatarskoi ASSR* (Kazan: Tatknigoizdat, 1958); R. I. Nafigov, *Formirovanie i razvitie peredovoi tatarskoi obshchestvenno-politicheskoi mysli* (Kazan: Tatknigoizdat, 1964).
10. N. Berkes, *The Development of Secularism in Turkey* (Montreal: McGill University Press, 1964); I. Bashgöz and Howard Wilson, *Educational Problems in Turkey, 1920–1940* (Bloomington: Indiana University Press, 1968). Other studies of Turkic educational reform that ignore Gaspirali while discussing the Jadid movement include T. P. Dadashev, *Prosveshchenie v Turtsii v noveishee vremia* (Moscow: Izdatel'stvo "Nauka," 1972); A. D. Zheltiakov and Iu. A. Petrosian, *Istoriia prosveshcheniia v Turtsii (konets XVIII–nachalo XX v.)* (Moscow, 1965); Mustafa Asiler, *Türk eghitiminin ana davalari* (Istanbul, 1960); Nafi Atif, *Türkiye pedagoji tarihi* (Istanbul, 1929); Osman Ergin, *Türkiye maarif tarihi*, 5 vols. (Istanbul: Osmanbey Matbaasi, 1943–45); Nuri Kadamanoghlu, *Türkiye'de eghitim* (Ankara, 1963).
11. The main exception is a biography of Gaspirali by Kirimli Jafar Seydahmet, *Gaspirali Ismail Bey* (Istanbul: Matbaajilik ve Neshriyat Türk Anonim Shirketi, 1934); see also Zeki Velidi Togan, "Ismail Gaspirali," in *Encyclopaedia of Islam*, 2d ed. (Leiden: E. J. Brill, 1965), 2:979–81.
12. Serge Zenkovsky, *Pan-Turkism and Islam in Russia* (Cambridge, Mass.: Harvard University Press, 1960), 30–37, 81–82, 107–8; Charles W. Hostler, *Turkism and the Soviets* (London: Praeger, 1957), 123–30; Geoffrey Wheeler, *The Modern History of Soviet Central Asia* (New York: Praeger, 1964), 194–207; Alexander

Bennigsen and Chantal Lemercier-Quelquejay, *Islam in the Soviet Union* (New York: Praeger, 1967), 38–39, 47, 78, 128.

13. Gustav Burbiel, "Die Sprache Ismail Bey Gaspyralys" (Ph.D. diss., Hamburg University, 1953); Edward Lazzerini, "Ismail Bey Gaspirali and Muslim Modernism in Russia, 1878–1914" (Ph.D. diss., University of Washington, 1973). See also Bertold Spuler, "Djadid," in *Encyclopaedia of Islam* 2:366.

14. Lazzerini, "Ismail Bey Gaspirali," 109–10, citing and translating Arminius Vámbéry, "A Mahomedan Congress in Cairo," *The Times*, 22 October 1907, 15.

15. Ibid., 153, citing and translating from *Terjüman*, no. 45 (26 November 1895); and A.L.C., "Le Congrès musulman universal," *Revue du monde musulman* 3, nos. 11–12 (November–December 1907): 499.

16. Ibid., citing and translating from "Ulema-yi asiriyun," *Terjüman*, no. 40 (17 February 1913).

17. Ibid., citing and translating from *Terjüman*, no. 1 (10 April 1883).

18. Bennigsen and Lemercier-Quelquejay, *Islam*, 41; Zenkovsky, *Pan-Turkism and Islam*, 33–34.

19. Lazzerini, "Ismail Bey Gaspirali," 14.

20. Seymour Becker, *Russia's Protectorates in Central Asia: Bukhara and Khiva, 1865–1924* (Cambridge, Mass.: Harvard University Press, 1968), 202.

21. Uriel Heyd, *Foundations of Turkish Nationalism* (London: Luzac, 1950), 78.

22. Khurshid Ahmad, "The Nature of the Islamic Resurgence," in *Voices of Resurgent Islam*, ed. John L. Esposito (New York: Oxford University Press, 1983), 218–29, esp. 220.

23. Lazzerini, "Ismail Bey Gaspirali," 225, citing and translating "Jan yani dil meselesi," *Terjüman* (22 January 1908).

24. Ibid., 207, citing and translating "Vopros o iazyke," *Terjüman*, 4 November 1905.

25. Tadeusz Swietochowski, *Russian Azerbaijan, 1905–1920: The Shaping of National Identity in a Muslim Community* (Cambridge: Cambridge University Press, 1985), 31–32; he argues that in Azerbaijan an average reader could understand the language of *Terjüman*, which influenced the "Ottomanization" of the Azeri press.

26. David Kushner, *The Rise of Turkish Nationalism, 1876–1908* (London: Frank Case, 1977), 57–58.

27. Ibid., 58.

28. Ibid., 62.

29. Andreas M. Kazamias, *Education and the Quest for Modernity in Turkey* (London: Allen & Unwin, 1966), 108–10.

30. Zenkovsky, *Pan-Turkism and Islam*, 114–15, citing *Yulduz*, no. 786 (1912).

31. Alexander Bennigsen, "The Muslims of European Russia," in *Russia and Asia: Essays on the Influence of Russia on the Asian Peoples*, ed. Wayne Vucinich (Stanford,

Calif.: Hoover Institution Press, 1972), 152; Zenkovsky, *Pan-Turkism and Islam*, 28–29; Wheeler, *Modern History*, 199.

32. Zenkovsky, *Pan-Turkism and Islam*, 115, citing Gaspirali's statement in *Türk Yurdu*, 16 May 1912.

33. Lazzerini, "Ismail Bey Gasprinskii," 225, citing and translating "Kerain-i kerame hutab," *Terjüman*, 25 September 1906.

34. Ibid., 247–48, citing and translating "Gdie koren' zla?" *Terjüman*, 15 September 1903.

35. Ibid., 23–27, citing and translating *Molla Nasreddin*, no. 3 (1913), which is also cited in M. Kasumov, *Boevoi revoliutsionno-demokraticheskii zhurnal "Molla Nasreddin"* (Baku, 1960), 32; Thomas Kuttner, "Russian *Jadidism* and the Islamic World: Ismail Gasprinskii in Cairo, 1908," *Cahiers du monde russe et soviétique*, nos. 3–4 (1975): 390.

36. Sechil Akgun, "Women's Emancipation in Turkey," *Bulletin of the Turkish Studies Association* (March 1986), 1–11, about a positive effect of American missionary schools on the growth of women's education; Heyd, *Foundations*, 94; Berkes, *Development of Secularism*, 390.

37. Lazzerini, "Ismail Bey Gaspirali," 172; Bennigsen and Lemercier-Quelquejay, *Islam*, 39; Wheeler, *Modern History*, 202–3.

38. Lazzerini, "Ismail Bey Gaspirali," 184–95; see also Kuttner, "Russian *Jadidism*," 389.

39. Berkes, *Development of Secularism*, 99–100.

40. Ibid., 101.

41. Ibid., 173.

42. Bennigsen, "The Muslims," 152; V. M. Gorokhov, *Reaktsionnaia shkol'naia politika tsarizma v otnoshenii tatar Povolzh'ia* (Kazan, 1941), 201–5.

43. Wheeler, *Modern History*, 201.

44. Ibid., 201–3.

45. Bennigsen and Lemercier-Quelquejay, *Islam*, 39; Lazzerini, "Ismail Bey Gaspirali," 195–99.

46. Kushner, *Rise of Turkish Nationalism*, 12–14; Tamurbek Davletshin, *Sovetskii Tatarstan: Teoriia i praktika Leninskoi natsional'noi politiki* (London, 1974), 47–48; Tutaev, *Oktiabr' i prosveshchenie*, 13–14, gives no mention of Gaspirali in discussing new-method schools; Alexandre Bennigsen and Chantal Lemercier-Quelquejay, *Les mouvements nationaux chez les Musulmans de Russie: Le "Sultan Galievisme" au Tatarstan* (Paris: Mouton, 1960), 39–40, 59–60; Hélène Carrère d'Encausse, *Réforme et révolution chez les musulmans de l'empire russe: Bukhara, 1867–1924* (Paris: Armand Colin, 1966), 137–42.

47. Becker, *Russia's Protectorates*, 203–5; Hélène Carrère d'Encausse, "The Stirring of National Feeling," in *Central Asia: A Century of Russian Rule*, ed. Edward Allworth (New York: Columbia University Press, 1967), 177–78, 194–95, 200.

48. Paul Dumont, "La Revue *Türk Yurdu* et les Musulmans de l'Empire Russe, 1911–1914," *Cahiers du monde russe et soviétique*, nos. 3–4 (1974): 321.

49. Swietochowski, *Russian Azerbaijan*, 48–49; Bennigsen and Lemercier-Quelquejay, *Islam*, 78–79.

50. Manuel Sarkisyanz, "Russian Conquest in Central Asia: Transformation and Acculturation," in *Russia and Asia*, ed. Vucinich, 255; François Georgeon, *Aux origines du nationalisme turc (Yusuf Akchura, 1876–1935)* (Paris: Editions Institut d'Etudes Anatoliennes, 1980), 18–21, 45, 54.

# 3

# *Ismail Bey Gasprinskii (Gaspirali): The Discourse of Modernism and the Russians*

EDWARD J. LAZZERINI

## Language, Thought, and Action

> What modernism then represents is a passage from a discursive
> exchange within the world to the expression of knowledge as
> a reasoning practice upon the world.[1]

In the early summer of 1867 a young Crimean Tatar and a schoolmate embarked on one of those youthful escapades immortalized by Mark Twain: they ran away from home. Having endured an academic year at a military institute in Moscow, the teenagers journeyed by rail to the southern port city of Odessa to secure steamship passage to Istanbul. Once ensconced along the Bosporus, they expected to join the Ottoman army—at that moment embroiled in action on Cyprus—in a gesture that defied the anti-Turkish sentiment fashionable in certain Moscow circles. Odessa authorities thwarted the adventure when the youths failed to produce the required exit visas.

Anecdotes attract hyperbole, and this one, briefly related and drawn from the life of Ismail Bey Gaspirali (1851–1914), is probably no exception. Born in a Crimean village near Bakhchesaray (former seat of the ruling khans), Gaspirali would mature into the most celebrated advocate of Turko-Muslim modernism in the Russian Empire. While supporters cite this episode to prove that an anti-Russian and pan-Turkic orientation emerged early in his intellectual development, it may better serve to introduce a general inquiry into Gaspirali's thinking on Russian society and authority. Any such effort must be framed by a consideration of certain general caveats: the complex and polysemous character of his discourse; the dynamics of power and culture among imperial Russia, the various domestic and foreign Islamic societies, and the West; the necessity for

Islamic cultures to embrace modernism and, to that end, assistance from Russia; and the enormous ambiguity that the empire presented, in the perception of an ethnic non-Russian, as a metaphor for the West—already possessing certain signs of modernity—and yet something other, not definitively Western or Asiatic, modern or traditional. Gaspirali, the Turko-Islamic modernist movement, and the Russian state came to form a trio whose strains were always intricate and unpredictable, sometimes harmonious, but often cacophonous. Analysis of this relation goes well beyond biography and intellectual history to facilitate our grasp of several larger phenomena: (1) the relations of internal colonialism in the Russian Empire; (2) the Islamic cultural renaissance there during the nineteenth century and the early twentieth century and Gaspirali's pivotal contribution to it; and (3) the place of that renaissance in the general Islamic and global network of colonialism, dependency, modernization, and reaction that has distinguished international affairs for the past hundred years.

In this century, Continental literary theorists, philosophers, and historians have forced a fuller appreciation of the varied cultural and systematic claims that social context—time and place—makes on everyone. Linking the work of Marx, Nietzsche, and Freud for their critical posture and for their articulation of "the possibilities and the rules for the formation of other texts," they have opened up imaginative lines of inquiry, even as our intellectual mainstream has gradually "domesticated" these essentially radical methods.[2] All have riveted their attention on language in its relation to thought and action, on language and discourse caught "within a network of contextual relations, within a definable if exceedingly complex environment, from which . . . [it is] inseparable."[3] Forever changing, discourse reflects yet shapes being to create a system of meaning in every time and place. Language, then, is hardly neutral, never aimless; moreover, it bears multiple levels of meaning, including that which all authors seek to mask or helplessly repress. ("Even in the absence of substantial social pressure, men lie quite readily about their most intimate beliefs.")[4]

The first value, then, of much recent critical thought is its unremitting reference to the discursive process, to the hidden in language as much as the explicit, the unexpected as much as the intentional. A second value derives from emphasis on a particular time and place: the modern age in the context some conveniently label *Western culture.* Here the focus is much less on the material aspects of modernization than on the collective mental reorganization that accompanied that process. Attention to the discourse of modernism—the language of the modern age—indissolubly linked to this reorganization, has engendered new and different ways to probe and comprehend the era.[5] Both concerns enhance the analysis contained in this chapter.

As one of the Russian Empire's preeminent nineteenth-century social activists and a leader of the Islamic renaissance in the period 1860–1930, Ismail Bey Gaspirali deserves the scholarly attention that other luminaries within the international Islamic community (such as Muhammad Abduh, Jamal ad-Din al-Afghani, and Sir Sayyid Ahmad Khan) have long attracted. His distinctions were many, his labors indefatigable, and his vision expansive; moreover, as Alan Fisher shows extensively in chapter 2 in this volume, his influence ran deep even outside his homeland. Underlying his life's work was a determination to challenge the Turco-Muslim peoples—beginning with his own Crimean Tatars—to engage in community self-examination. The challenge was a broad one, demanding that Muslims understand and respect their history, frankly assess their contemporary attainments and capabilities, recognize and accept the possibilities and benefits of social progress, and join together in a united campaign to forge a future consonant with both the spirit of Islamic teachings and the many realities of modern life.[6]

Success in this great, revolutionary enterprise, Gaspirali reasoned, depended primarily on essential change in the character and content of organized education. His lifelong advocacy of basic literacy through innovative pedagogical techniques (commonly designated *usul-i jadid*, "new method"), his insistence on practical training in conjunction with moral schooling, his promotion of secular knowledge as well as religious wisdom, and his concern for the education of women all attest to his abiding belief in mankind's perfectibility and the privileged status of human reason.

Despite his frequent reference to Islamic tradition, much of what Gaspirali argued rested solidly on the accumulation of Western wisdom since the Renaissance. Through education, travel, and social contacts, he personally assimilated the mentality of modernism and its discourse, seeking to extend it to his people and their presumed brethren inhabiting that vast territory from Istanbul to Kashgar. Intellectually, the modern age entails a fundamental epistemological break with the past. It refuses to take the future for granted, to assume that things to come are predictable. Rather, as a contemporary German historian contends, to the modern mentality the future is something that "must be prepared for" because it is "in the bounds of calculable experience."⁷ Thus, rational prognosis, at the heart of Gaspirali's own epistemology, promises some control over the outcome of history. Hence, the often excessive confidence in the human potential for individual and collective reform. No stranger to such optimism, Ismail Bey urged his Turkic-Muslim listeners to transcend their current limitations, embrace a novel future, and reshape their lives by treating knowledge in the modern way: "as a reasoning practice upon the world."

Among the many aspects of Gaspirali's enterprise that threatened to exhaust his optimism and derail his efforts, none proved as troublesome as the ultimate fact of his marginality. On the personal level, the consequences were minor. Moving with relative ease back and forth between Western and Islamic cultures, he does not appear to have suffered unduly from his incomplete assimilation by either. He was educated in Russian schools, lived for a few years in Moscow as a teenager, resided in Paris in the mid-1870s, traveled extensively within the Russian Empire, and had frequent contacts with Russian public officials. Conversely, he visited Muslim India, Egypt, the Ottoman Empire (sojourning in Istanbul for one and a half years), and Bukhara, while calling his home Bakhchesaray, still the most Muslim of Crimean cities in the early twentieth century.

Intellectually, however, his effort to force the discovery and valorization of a marginal ideology produced enduring problems that always, it seemed, occupied his attention. His audience was understandably complex and "read" him in endless ways. Ethnically alone it included diverse Russians, domestic and foreign Muslims, and Europeans of various nationalities, each bringing his or her own peculiar cultural experiences to bear. But even these distinctions are insufficient to capture the range of opinion that Gaspirali attracted. He had his supporters, and their numbers grew over the decades; yet so did his detractors, who, if not legion, were frequently more influential.

Among the latter could be found Orthodox missionaries, ardent Russian nationalists, and at least some bureaucrats. The last condemned his entire enterprise as politically threatening, likely to destabilize the borderlands, exacerbate certain international tensions, and destroy the territorial integrity of the empire. Whereas Gaspirali believed that the voice of the people could speak creatively if brought within the realm of rational discourse, such Russian opponents as Nikolai Ivanovich Il'minskii, Nikolai Petrovich Ostroumov, Vladimir Petrovich Nalivkin, Aleksandr Efimovich Alektorov, M. A. Miropiev, and indirectly the more well-known and influential

Konstantin Petrovich Pobedonostsev recoiled from the unpredictability of such a measure.[8] They rightly deemed rational discourse as access to power—a privilege the few dared not share with the many.

Fear of the multitudes unrestrained was compounded by the otherness of the Muslim as one of the legally designated *inorodtsy*, or ethnoreligious aliens inhabiting an empire officially defined as Russian and Orthodox Christian. For those like Gaspirali, who expected the popularization of modernism to wash away the accumulated layers of myth, superstition, and prejudice that stayed progress within the Islamic world, his Russian antagonists evinced only derision and cynicism. He was charged with being cunning (*khitryi*) for printing his newspaper *Terjüman/Perevodchik* (Interpreter) in both Tatar and Russian since, as Il'minskii insisted, the use of Russian would "inspire confidence and even interest" and would fill "Russian eyes" with a false sense of Muslim "rationalism and liberalism."[9]

"Cunning" was a characteristic that Russian polemicists had for centuries attributed to all Orientals, particularly to Tatars, with whom they had had the longest continuous contact. Il'minskii, for one, applied this cultural axiom in 1890 when, in reference to Gaspirali, he wrote that "the Tatars are devious [*khitryi*]; they do not give their secrets to everyone."[10] One scholar recently observed how the same adjective was apparently first applied to the "many unfamiliar new skills and techniques which foreigners [Europeans] brought with them [to Muscovy] in the sixteenth and seventeenth centuries."[11] The paradoxical synthesis of Oriental and European *khitrost'*, represented in Gaspirali, made him doubly suspect. Not surprisingly, all manner of intentions were ascribed to his effort to "spread the European Enlightenment among the Muslim subjects" of the empire and to unite them culturally regardless of linguistic or customary distinctions. So too did some misapprehend, deliberately or not, such of his statements as "Russia is becoming more and more a Muslim land, and everyone is predicting that in the future she will stand as one of the greatest Muslim countries."[12] That Gaspirali intended something other than his antagonists claimed is apparent from the following statement: "In the future, I hope the near future, Russia will become one of the significant Muslim states without detracting from her role as a great Christian power."[13] Nevertheless, by reading negative meaning into Gaspirali's utterances, his detractors sought to deflect their positive significance and reduce his impact.

Gaspirali's critics also included many Muslims, led by traditionalist mullahs—the so-called *qadimists* (from *usul-i qadim*, the "old method")—who apprehended in his progressivism and Western experience an assault on sacred teachings, on their exclusive right to interpret those teachings, and on the centrality of religious dogma in the civic and private lives of the faithful. Whereas Russian opponents invariably focused their ire on the politically disruptive implications of Gaspirali's views, Muslims tended to represent those views as sacrilege. Like other religions, Islam has not been immune to reformist movements during its long history, and such as have emerged have always been associated with renewal (*tejdid*) and draped in a mantle of moral righteousness rather than ecumenism or liberalization. For the *müjeddid* (renewer) and his followers seeking to regenerate the Islamic way, reform (*islah*) has meant reaffirmation of Qur'ânic uniqueness and authenticity, a literalist interpretation of scriptural teaching and its strict application to human needs, without recourse to borrowing from non-Islamic traditions. Reformers, then, have been "radical" in their designs to rearrange social forces, but their movements were always firmly within an Islamic framework.[14]

From Gaspirali Muslim traditionalists heard a message neither of renewal, although he frequently used the word, nor of return to a pristine, original Islam. Although he argued that the proper application of Islamic teaching had once provided the dynamism that underwrote the great achievements of historic Islam and claimed that those glorious times were repeatable, his opponents discerned in his innovation (*bid'at*) only heresy, the inevitable result of his dabbling in Western learning. One of the most vocal of *qadimists*, Ishmuhammed ibn Dinmuhammed, accused the modernists (Jadidists) of "spreading among Muslims books from abroad, especially by French atheists," and seeking to replace the "old Muslim ways with European ones."[15] He was essentially correct, of course, but his conspiratorial interpretation of these activities sought to deny them any legitimacy. In an appeal to Muslims to face the lethal challenge of modernism, another *qadimist*, Il'iajeddin Muhitdinov, wrote: "In the world three things exist to which one cannot give rein—an enemy, fire, and sickness—and against which one needs immediately to take up a weapon, water, and medicine . . . ; the enemy is the new customs (of which the chief is instruction by the new method), the fire is the study of [these new customs], and the sickness—the results of that study."[16] More dogmatic was Ishmi Ishan's blunt assertion that "whoever believes in God and Muhammed must be an enemy of the modernists. For them the *Shar'ia* demands the death penalty."[17]

Not surprisingly, both Russian and Muslim critics of the modernist program gradually proved willing to make common cause against Gaspirali and other advocates, feeding mutual suspicions with rumor and innuendo, while taking advantage of circumstances to thwart, for example, the spread of new-method schools after 1905–6. In the semantic universe of both camps, Gaspirali posed a contradiction, challenging the hegemony of assumptions and attitudes, of complex knowledge/power relations that determined public policy and that he viewed as obstacles to "social progress." The authority his opponents claimed was ultimately questioned and placed on the defensive by Gaspirali's appeal for Islamic modernism. Because they were so ideological themselves, the Il'minskiis and Dinmuhammeds easily recognized the enemy for what he was: a heterodox harboring a latently subversive ideology. Russia's imperial power and traditional Islam's cultural hegemony were, in their respective eyes, at serious risk. Quoting Matthew 13:25, Il'minskii could have spoken for his Islamic counterparts as well when he wrote: "But while men slept, his enemy came and sowed tares among the wheat, and went his way."[18]

Yet, as important as winning over his Muslim critics was for Gaspirali, his relationship to the Russians proved more crucial. Colonial reality incited Gaspirali to pay extraordinary attention to the attitudes of the empire's primary ethnic component and its spokesmen. How to minimize Russian resistance to his project was a question too significant to underestimate. That Gaspirali did not is attested by the volume and span of his writings devoted to the theme. His goals required not merely Russian neutrality but official acceptance in order to move as broadly and rapidly as possible along a front of change. Even more, he sought Russian commitment and support, believing that whatever destiny awaited the Muslims would be determined to a large extent by Russian assistance, by the guidance of "our elder brothers," as he frequently called them before the turn of the twentieth century. Attracting them to his cause was to be his great task.

## Message to Russia

*Light, give us light, elder brother, otherwise we shall suffocate, rot, and contaminate the country. We Muslims are still children.*
—ISMAIL BEY GASPIRALI

In the documents section of part 1 of this volume, readers will find in translation a pamphlet Gaspirali penned in 1896, addressed primarily to the Russians. This was not the first time that he had written to that audience; in fact, fifteen years earlier, at the beginning of his career as a publicist, he turned to it with words of praise, friendship, empathy, and hope. Then, in a series of articles subsequently reissued separately under the title *Russian Islam* (*Russkoe musul'manstvo*), he endeavored to dissipate the fictive imaginings that he feared filled the Russian mind about his coreligionists so that the two groups could achieve the *sblizhenie* (rapprochement) from which both would benefit. He knew from personal experience, although he hated admitting as much publicly, what prejudices shaped the attitudes of Muslim and Russian toward one another, and the longer he labored, the more his worst fears were realized.

To his Russian critics Gaspirali was "that" *inorodets*, educated in Russian schools, conversant with the Russian language, privileged by the imperial context, yet setting out to apply his blessings inappropriately in pursuit of a cause ultimately detrimental to the empire and its presumed interests. Because he strove, as one critic charged, "to use all the advantages of Russian culture to defend [his] nationality," he could not be trusted; despite his partial assimilation, some believed, he continually evinced an anti-Russian bias, as if to prove the implicit message of the anecdote opening this chapter.[19] Unlike Ibrahim Altinsarin, for example, a Kazak protégé of Il'minskii's and a "good" native, Gaspirali transgressed the rules of proper behavior by acting autonomously and presuming an interpretive privilege to which he had no right. As a Russianized Muslim, he was a partial insider who, it was feared, knew how to turn the dominant discourse against itself. Foreign yet familiar, distant yet near, self yet other, to certain Russians Gaspirali presented a threat all the more terrible for its ambiguity. He could move with ease across the cultural boundary separating two worlds, scattering within the heart of the dominant culture invisible seeds of subversion that would sprout poisonous shoots. The specter he evoked was too awful to contemplate.

Such strident views and negative stereotypes may have been atypical of most educated Russians, yet more subtle prejudices did act to obstruct Gaspirali's plans. In response, he consciously adopted the shrewd and effective tactic of appearing perfectly orthodox, of working within parameters set by authority, while proferring moderate criticism of the status quo and suggesting its reform. Unquestionably sincere in his quest for a Russian-Muslim rapprochement—he neither "ran away" nor encouraged others to do so, despite ample opportunity to emigrate—yet he was just as certainly clever, if not cunning, in his use of this ideal to assuage Russian fears and make possible the realization of his many other goals. From early in his career he articulated a rhetoric of reason designed as much to mollify as to persuade. A perusal of his texts treating the Russians' relationship to native Muslims and those inhabiting other lands will highlight his approach and expectations.

However paradoxical its use might seem in view of subsequent Soviet policy, the term *rapprochement* for Gaspirali symbolized the fusion of creative energies likely to issue from close Russian-Muslim contacts. Its achievement—a cooperative, mutually encouraging, and egalitarian society—would provide substance to the otherwise romantic notion of a Russo-Islamic world sitting astride the Eurasian continent and separating the West from the greater Orient. In place of enmity between Russian and Islamic peoples would come respect, forging an unassailable compact able to defy external threats and overcome ill-considered prejudice; instead of discord would come harmony, opening up greater opportunities for pursuing joint interests bound to serve the modernist cause of progress, power, and prosperity. For all its utopian charm, the promise of these two peoples working hand in hand was cradled in a web of argument redolent with the calm reason and logic the modern West apotheosized. Three prominent strands provided this web its shape. The first, although least significant, set the potential relationship in historical and cultural perspective; the second lent the strength of geopolitical arguments; while the third sounded a Kiplingesque note proclaiming a "white man's burden" for the Russians.

Relations between Russians and Muslims, Gaspirali often reminded his readers, had had a long history. By the late nineteenth century, czarist troops and administrators were just completing several hundred years of gradual, piecemeal absorption of neighboring Muslim people—the cumulative effect of "moments of historical necessity," so he described it.[20] Natural borders to define the ultimate extent of the empire seemed finally attained. Gaspirali viewed Russian territorial expansion with equanimity; as a fact of history, the reality of power could hardly be denied. Still, he spoke frequently and glowingly of the benefits that attended absorption into the Russian Empire, whether in the deeper past or in the more immediate present. Writing during the one hundredth anniversary of the conquest of his native Crimea, he contended that the local population could not fail to "recall all of the good deeds from which it has profited for a century."[21] In anticipation of similar long-term consequences for the Turkmens, he applauded the seizure of their oasis settlement at Merv in 1884, an event that all but capped the conquest of Central Asia.[22] As a general position, Gaspirali consistently and without reservation defended Russian military actions and successes, and not only against the smaller and less powerful societies of Central Asia. More prominent neighbors like Afghanistan, Persia, and even the Ottoman Empire had, in his view, little about which to complain. They were less the victims of unjustified Russian advances than misguided provocateurs who obstinately "failed to look upon Russia as a good neighbor."[23]

But history revealed other pertinent lessons for Gaspirali to sustain his insistence on the logic of *sblizhenie*. First, in the style of a sixteenth-century Muscovite propagandist determined to enhance the authority and status of his political patron, he proposed that Russia was the legitimate successor of the Golden Horde that once ruled both the Russian lands and much of Central Asia. There followed Russia's historical obligation to restore territorial unity to a world once whole. And not by chance did he designate the Russian emperor the "white czar," in subtle reference to the Russian lands' geographic position at the western (hence "white") end of the Tatar/Mongol domain. Moreover, the Tatar yoke, however burdensome for Russia, had the unintended effect of fostering unity among the principalities and the emergence of a single national and political territory.[24] Thus, the Turkic-Muslim people, Gaspirali argued, deserved compensation, not in "old Asiatic coin, but in the new European variety; that is, by spreading among us European science and knowledge generally."[25]

Second, ordinary Russians and ordinary Muslims had for centuries coexisted in harmony, he contended, engaging in the same economic activities, working the same land, living in adjacent settlements under the same law—"in Crimea, Tatar and Russian villages differ in only one respect: the former have mosques, the latter churches."[26] The humaneness of the Russian explained the ease with which Muslims had always fit into and been accepted by Russian society; it further explained the more benign manner with which Russia traditionally (at least since Catherine II) approached imperial administration. Compared to the English, French, or

Dutch, in whose presence the "sons of Asia . . . [feel] an artificiality, an offensive condescension," the Russian possessed a warmth and conviviality that charms as well as an "elemental affinity" that elicits trust:

> Neither in Marseilles nor in Paris do you find a colony of Algerian Arabs; nor is there an Indian quarter in London; nor should one look for a single . . . Malay Muslim in the Hague. Yet thousands of Muslims inhabit Moscow and St. Petersburg, where they have their own streets, mosques, and so forth. While the greater part of them are Tatars, you will also find in all the large cities of central Russia, let alone in frontier areas, Persian merchants and Turkish bakers.
>
> What leads them to and keeps them in Russia other than elemental affinity? Why is the man of the Orient not drawn to trade or earn his living in the West? Could it be more difficult to get from Algeria to Marseilles than from Kazan' to St. Petersburg or Arkhangel'sk?[27]

What had been casual companionship and good neighborliness historically, what Gaspirali discerned as "nothing more than the consequence of a *barely perceptible quality of the Russian national character*," could—indeed must—serve in the future as the natural base for "a closer kinship, as that between children of the great family of people inhabiting Russia."[28]

If history and culture had forged a natural bond between Russian and Muslim, contemporary geopolitical factors made conscious enhancement of that bond imperative. "Were we to cast our eyes over a map of the Eastern Hemisphere, we would see that [several] Muslim countries and Russia share a long common border." This Russo-Islamic world formed for Gaspirali—who loved to encourage his readers to peruse maps—the nexus of Eurasia, a "crossroads of all commercial, cultural, political, and military routes and relations."[29] It was thus exposed to external pressure from both Europe and the Far East, which it separated and which had designs on it, wished it ill, and would overwhelm it unless Russian and Muslim recognized the common danger and responded jointly. England and Japan, island powers at opposite ends of Eurasia and the special focus of Gaspirali's suspicion, posed the greatest threats (fig. 3.1). The former had a long tradition of international competition that more and more brought it face to face with Russia; furthermore, as an imperial nation with global interests, it was actively involved in the affairs of various Islamic populations, exercising its extraordinary power to influence attitudes toward Russia, subvert Russo-Islamic ties, and sap Russian strength by fo-

Figure 3.1. European politicians in the East. Ismail Bey Gaspirali excludes Russia from the British-French-German colonialist club oppressing the "gnats" of their Islamic countries. From the satirical Azeri journal *Mulla Nasreddin*, no. 26 (15 July 1907): 2.

menting trouble with its neighbors. For the moment, no more formidable foe challenged the Russian Empire.

Lurking beyond the eastern horizon, however, gathering its strength in consequence of a decisive commitment in 1870 to modernization, lay a nation about to take its place among the major powers. Japan, the "yellow peril" in Gaspirali's sadly ironic phrase, would reveal just how much progress it had made when it easily defeated first China in 1894–95 and then Russia itself a decade later. These successes did not surprise Gaspirali, who as early as the 1880s recognized the implications for the Russo-Islamic world of a Japan transformed, powerful, and aggressive.[30] He was drawn to that nation with mixed feelings, on the one hand fearful of its newfound might, yet on the other awed by the accomplishments that conscious, determined effort had achieved in so short a time. Japanese success proved one of his major contentions: that modern life and capabilities were not secrets reserved for Europe and its offshoots but were available to all societies willing to face the challenge of change and willing to sacrifice worthless tradition for progress. Would that his own brethren, frequently depicted as slumbering by their own satirical press after 1906, might waken to test the winds of change and head off in the same direction.

One can sense throughout his writings Gaspirali's urgency concerning the fate of Muslim peoples in a world dominated by power of a kind qualitatively different from any previously known. Membership in the "club of modernism" was now a precondition of survival, and time was vital. A context wherein one's nation was economically backward, educationally unsophisticated, technologically naive, and even uncomprehending of its plight required help from "friends."

Who, then, were the friends of the Islamic people? On the basis of historical and cultural relations, and considering the state of world politics, Gaspirali believed them to be the Russians. To this theme he added an appeal to ethnic sensibility. If couched in moral terms, his quite blunt advocacy of a civilizing mission for Russia in the Islamic territories within and outside the empire also stroked—and not incidentally—Russian pride. The possibility for such a role was created at the beginning of the eighteenth century by the reforms of Peter the Great, which for Gaspirali launched the empire into the modern age. Now, with well over a century of experience and development, Russia could provide leadership and guidance to those, like the Muslims, clinging to the past. In 1881, he lamented the failure of central Russian authority to take up the task of leading "the Muslims to progress and civilization." The government, he charged, was focusing too narrowly on administrative concerns so that "Russian power among the Muslims has not gone beyond the demands of the state treasury and the maintenance of social order and tranquility. . . . Is there nothing more to . . . the great civilizing mission of Russia in the East? . . . Do administrative changes really constitute all that that mission entails?"[31] Throughout the remainder of his life he criticized lost opportunities as well as shortsighted and inconsistent policies that limited the positive influence that Russia could have had on his brethren. Inevitably, he complained, both suffered immeasurably.

Mutual understanding, encouraged by Russian assistance and openness to Muslim secular needs, was the key, in Gaspirali's judgment, to improving relations and awakening in Russian society a sense of the enormous value to be derived from fulfilling its responsibility: "Give them the possibility to acquire knowledge, improve their access to new ideas and principles; then you will see how quickly the Muslims come alive and lose their apathy."[32] Active, loyal, productive subjects were Gaspirali's promise in return for enlightened, generous, and liberal Russian attitudes toward Muslims. Why not? "*Except for religion, everything else* draws [the two] together and binds them fast." What was good for Russians, he was convinced, was good for Muslims; moreover, what benefited the latter unquestionably redounded to the empire's favor, even as the whole is blessed by the strength of its parts. "Russia," he emphatically declared, "has nothing to lose and everything to gain from the good opinion of Muslims."[33] What needed cultivation on both sides was belief that, for all their cultural differences, the empire's peoples had common interests and aspirations that far outweighed all other considerations. Thus, Gaspirali bristled at charges by certain Russians that Tatars were guilty of separatist intentions because they strove to become modern and yet retain a separate cultural identity.[34] For him, this was the height of misapprehension, an unfortunate attitude that served at best a negative social purpose. Hence the meaning of a remark he made in response to complaints about the publication of the *Interpreter* in Turkic as well as Russian: "There are only Russian newspapers," he wrote, being published in the empire; the single difference is that they "appear in various languages."[35]

While acknowledging the legitimacy and appropriateness of Russia's civilizing mission, Gaspirali was careful to distinguish it from imperial policy commonly identified with Russification. The latter he defined as total assimilation of all groups by the Russians for the sake of ethnic homogeneity and a presumed augmentation of control over the empire's entire population. Such a policy would serve the interests of bureaucrats and administrators concerned above all with power, but it bore within itself "the character of constraint, of limitation on the rights of a given nationality" in relation to another. As such, Gaspirali admonished, administrative Russification lacked justification (except for authority and "hotheaded patriots"), was historically counterproductive, and would be in the long run ineffective and harmful. Better to unify people and groups "on the basis of equality, freedom, science, and education," to Russify them "morally" by valorizing ethnoreligious differences and allowing cultural autonomy, and thus build bridges leading to *sblizhenie*.[36]

Such bridging became Gaspirali's life's work, forming the underlying theme of his discourse and explaining the very existence of his extraordinary newspaper, *Interpreter*. From its founding in 1883 until his death in 1914, this publishing venture represented two cultures—Russian and Islamic—in language, content, and intention, yet they were cultures not meant to remain separated or hidden from one another. Rather, they were to be "interpreted" (hence the newspaper's title), translated into each other's idiom, opened up to comprehension and respect, and linked. *Interpreter* served from its inception as a vehicle for the kind of noble and practical civilizing mission that Gaspirali allotted to Russia and consistently advocated. It needed to, because he would face from many Muslims incessant resistance to his unyielding demand that they (even if spiritual leaders) learn the Russian language as well as their own, be willing to enroll their children in state-sponsored schools when necessary, and read the secular literature available from not only Russian but other European sources. Without Russian help, "the social and intellectual isolation of the Muslims, their profound ignorance in all areas, their deathlike sluggishness, gradual impoverishment, . . . and disastrous emigrations" would continue unrelieved.[37] Russians had to realize, however, that assistance must be rooted in common sense, careful study of Muslim society, and a desire to ensure truth and justice (*pravda* and *spravedlivost'*).[38]

Failure to do so would prohibit *sblizhenie* and ensure power as the untempered factor in Russo-Islamic relations, free to institute discriminatory measures that, in an age of intensifying nationalist sentiment, would likely be blatantly and crudely Russifying. Preventing the Muslims from remaining or becoming firmly "the other" in too many Russian minds, from being condemned by and excluded from the dominant culture unless they accepted it all (including, above all, religion), from being victimized by a game that assigned truth, rationality, and social value arbitrarily to those inside the dominant culture, all were goals implicit in Gaspirali's program, however differently expressed.

They were there in the ink he used to write, polemicize, and propagandize. So too were other ideas, sentiments, and concerns unarticulated or only unintentionally revealed, resonances of the unconscious among what is permitted expression. Some of these deserve consumption, in the manner of Borges's curious and imaginary monkey, who absorbs what is left by the writer he dialogues with: "This animal, common in the north, is four or five inches long; its eyes are scarlet and its fur is jet black, silky and soft as a pillow. It is marked by a curious instinct, the taste for India ink. When a person sits down to write, the monkey squats cross-legged nearby with one forepaw folded over the other, waiting until the task is over. Then it drinks what is left of the ink, and afterward sits back on its haunches quiet and satisfied."[39] Like the simian, with attention, patience, and a reading of Gaspirali's texts as more than mere tokens of a mode of discourse, students can learn more than he intended and complete their own dialogue.

## Ignoring Power

> The economic and industrial might of the Russian people
> is incomparably less dangerous than is the West's.
> —ISMAIL BEY GASPIRALI

In *Russian-Oriental Relations* (*Russko-vostochnoe soglashenie*) (see the full translation of this essay at the end of part 1), buried among numerous statements formed and arranged to sustain an extended argument proclaiming that Muslims were better off living within the Russian Empire than elsewhere, is the epigraph that introduces the final section of this chapter. In its original context, the sentence is easily passed over for its seeming insignificance within that forest of Russophilic and overwhelmingly positive reasons for *sblizhenie* that have already been examined at length. Because its argument is so different from the constant and soothing message with which Gaspirali endeavored to entice his Russian audience, and because he did not pursue its sense at all either in this particular essay or in his larger corpus of writing, the reader is subtly encouraged to dismiss the statement as inconsequential. To follow first impulses, however, might close off a promising line of interpretation. On closer examination, Gaspirali's seemingly offhand comment provides a fascinating illustration of the complexity of human thought that often eludes both its creator and its observers, each intent on making ideas fit a pattern with as few contradictions as possible. In this case, the idea leashed within the statement is threatening to Gaspirali's carefully orchestrated appeal for Russian support because it suggests at least two issues best ignored: the negative side of Russian colonialism and the potential for disharmony in future Russo-Islamic relations.

Regarding the first issue, the reality of Russian power surely weighed heavily on Gaspirali's mind as he pondered the best ways to overcome Islamic feebleness, whether economic, technical, educational, or political. Yet, although he never admitted as much in any source available, objection to Russian domination could not have been a guiding sentiment in him—contrary to the implications of the anecdote that opens this chapter—because as a responsible person he did not believe that a reasonable alternative existed. Once he accepted that assumption, his public thought and private decisions were psychologically shaped and policed to match perceived reality. Despite the myriad and complex developments occurring across the empire in the twilight of the old order, Gaspirali remained consistent even as he responded with a degree of flexibility and adjustment. We have seen that he did at times fawn over the Russians and exaggerate their benevolence and good nature, controlled and tempered his criticisms of their imperial policies, drew analogies with French and British measures in order to criticize colonialism safely, and exhibited a pronounced sensitivity to that which was reasonably possible under current circumstances. Caution, common sense, pragmatism, and patience so characterized his mode of thinking that they produced echoes again and again in both public and private statements. Three brief examples from among many will serve as illustrations: the first, when he wrote in *Interpreter* that "every reform, every innovation, achieves its goals when it is timely and receptible";[40] the second, found in a 1911 letter to Yusuf Akchura, declaring, "You know that I am not a coward, but I have said that a mountain cannot be crossed by those who set out barefooted and without fully provisioned saddlebags";[41] and the third, central to an autobiographical short story, whose hero (author) proclaims: "Between principle and action there is something very important and strong: life. It has its own demands, its own laws, which are often in opposition to the inclinations of our hearts."[42]

This answer to the proverbial Russian question, *Chto delat'?* (What is to be done?), permeated his being, guiding and defining him despite objections from the many Muslims who often charged him with treachery or weakness. In an 1888 interview, Gaspirali acknowledged that some "accuse me of betraying my people, almost of betraying Islam. There are those who say that I am more of a Russian than is a Muscovite."[43] The evidence suggests that he worried little over such opinions. More challenging was the attitude of those like the Bashkir nationalist who recorded in his memoirs: "I remember saying . . . that Ismail Bey had been too servile. . . .

It was dangerous for us to encourage the Russians to approach us in the guise of a big brother, . . . make love to us in order to betray us. It was better for the future of the colonial people to refrain from close mingling, as the English did."[44]

Of course, his success in publishing as extensively as he did with little difficulty from the authorities for over thirty years owes much to this approach. So too does his refusal to become even moderately political until very late in his life. The evidence of Gaspirali's aversion to politics, at least until 1908, is substantial and ranges from his refusal to include radical opinion in his newspaper to his critiques of socialist thought, his reluctance to see Muslims ally themselves in 1906 with the Constitutional Democratic Party, and his rejection of political issues from the agenda of the Third All-Russian Muslim Congress meeting that same year in Nizhniy Novgorod. Even after 1908 his political activity was decidedly mainstream, on the conservative side, and always legal.[45] Finally, coming back to the quotation at the beginning of this section, it suggests why dealing with the Russians may have been "less dangerous" than dealing with other great powers.

Yet the Russians were dangerous and oppressive, the least of several evils at best. And this brings us to the second issue to which Gaspirali's statement draws attention: if it is safe to deal with the Russians now because they are themselves relatively weak, not really modern (or Western), will the situation remain the same in a generation or two after further development of their own? Will the Russians, an "other" as well from the European perspective, really welcome a revitalized, vigorous, prosperous, and, above all, competitive Muslim minority without evincing signs of jealousy and anxiety? If the Muslims are now like "children" in their inability to contribute to the unfolding of modern life and, like children can for now be manipulated and controlled, what will happen when they grow up and become autonomous, willful, articulate, and self-directed (and terribly modern and Western)? Would relations between Russia and Islam evolve as Gaspirali insisted, or would Muslims want, as some of his most ardent critics argued and coreligionists proved, political independence as well? And then, what fate awaited the territorial integrity of the empire, and what, conversely, of the Turkic identity that Gaspirali continually espoused as a cultural goal? Would not the one be undermined while the other was increasingly promoted beneath a blatantly political flag?

These are questions to be posed on the basis of hindsight and a certain reading of Gaspirali's substantial body of extant writings. They are, however, also questions that Gaspirali doubtlessly entertained in some form, worried over, but ultimately kept from influencing his work to any significant degree. "Some thoughts are forbidden to us," he wrote during the upheavals of 1905–6. "Let us leave these to the generations that will come later."[46] Leaving them, however, proved impossible, given the colonial nature of the domestic Russo-Islamic relationship, the character of the czarist political order, and the growing impact of nationalist ideology worldwide. Whatever his intentions, Gaspirali's modernist program was inherently subversive and dangerously volatile as it worked its way through society, transforming and generating much more than planned for. It refused to recapitulate in practice the key metaphors of the time, even as Gaspirali continually restated them: for example, that czarist policies toward czarist nationalities were good government; that modernism was an apolitical and nonthreatening tendency; or that Russia was Western culture. Aspirations notwithstanding, his program could never be assimilated into the status quo.

"I have never doubted the truth of signs," says a character in Umberto Eco's novel *The Name of the Rose*; "they are the only things man has with which to orient himself in the world."[47] Appreciating the increasingly shared positive meaning attached to economic growth, mass education, beneficent government, and social justice, Gaspirali sought not to preserve but to transform a society. Recognizing the signs—*symbols* might be a better term—through which such public concerns are mediated, he relied on their understood truths as much as possible to deflect opposition, whether Russian or Muslim, and advance his cause. Familiar signs were thus useful to reorient whoever would listen, disarm their opposition, or calm their anxieties; to threaten effectively the traditional sense of order without violating conceptual categories or raising issues coded as taboo.[48] The most significant constellation of signs of the times—modernization—was irresistible to both Russian and Muslim. The trump in Gaspirali's hand, it allowed him to mediate not only between Russian power and Islamic needs but also between—although not in the limiting binary sense—modernist and traditionalist, progressive and reactionary tendencies possessed by both ethnoreligious contexts.

Gaspirali was no charlatan, trickster, or unprincipled manipulator, although manipulate metaphors he did. He was a heterodox who, despite personal distaste for the phenomenon, contributed to the most fundamental kind of revolution imaginable: one that ignites "fire in the minds of men." His texts are radical in ways he never intended or wanted to contemplate. They form the interstice separating orthodoxy and subversion, participating in both simultaneously, as those of all modernists have done. They are instigators, breaking some boundaries while proclaiming their preservation, promising a vastly different future without any cost save for expenditures of physical and mental energy and the exercise of reasoned choice. His texts are wishful above all, romantically faithful to the blessings of modernization and the syncretic possibilities of culture. Rich and meaningful in their ambivalence, they raised a great stir and bore their author's influence beyond his most ambitious expectations.

With passing time, state power would predictably intrude on and bludgeon the possibilities that Gaspirali sought to actualize. Complex power relations were the one phenomenon that he sought to render insignificant, not as would a deliberate and open subversive (by confronting it with ridicule), but by pretending it was of little consequence. Intentionally ignoring power gave Gaspirali's program much of its idealism, appeal, and lasting impact. On the other hand, doing so left it abjectly vulnerable to those Russians and Muslims for whom the exercise of power was the central fact of life.

## Notes

*Gaspirali* is one Turkic variant of Ismail Bey's adopted family name. Like others, it derives from a small village (Gaspra) located in the foothills facing the southern shore of Crimea. It entered usage only at some point following the Russian conquest of the region in 1783 and then in imitation of Russian practice. Ismail Bey himself always employed a Russified variant—*Gasprinskii*—in his public discourse, as did many other Muslims inhabiting the empire. It may have been his private preference. In any event, the Russian variant takes on added significance, perhaps, in view of the arguments herein regarding Gaspirali's attitudes toward the empire's dominant ethnic group.

1. Timothy J. Reiss, *The Discourse of Modernism* (Ithaca, N.Y.: Cornell University Press, 1982), 30.
2. Michel Foucault, "What Is an Author?" in *The Foucault Reader*, ed. Paul Rabinow (New York: Pantheon, 1984), 14.
3. Reiss, *Discourse*, 10.

4. Stephen Greenblatt, "Invisible Bullets: Renaissance Authority and Its Subversion," in *Glyph 8* (Baltimore: Johns Hopkins University Press, 1981), 43.

5. For a thoughtful discussion of what can and needs to be done in intellectual history, see Dominick LaCapra, "Rethinking Intellectual History and Reading Texts," in *Modern European Intellectual History*, ed. D. LaCapra and S. L. Kaplan (Ithaca, N.Y.: Cornell University Press, 1983), 47–85.

6. These general observations about Gaspirali's views are more fully discussed in my "Ismail Bey Gasprinskii and Muslim Modernism in Russia, 1878–1914" (Ph.D. diss., University of Washington, 1973). Azade-Ayse Rorlich ("'The Temptation of the West': Two Tatar Travellers' Encounter with Europe at the End of the Nineteenth Century," *Central Asian Survey* 4, no. 3 [1985]: 39–58) has written one of the few other studies of the reaction to modern and Western culture by specific Russian Muslims.

7. Reinhard Koselleck, "Modernity and the Planes of Historicity," in *Futures Past: On the Semantics of Historical Time*, trans. Keith Tribe (Cambridge, Mass.: MIT Press, 1985), 13.

8. Typical Russian expressions of harshly critical attitudes toward Gaspirali can be found in N. I. Il'minskii, *Pis'ma N. I. Il'minskago k ober-prokuroru Sviateishago Sinoda Konstantinu Petrovichu Pobedonostsevu* (Kazan': Izd. "Pravoslavnyi Sobesiednik," 1895), esp. 61–66, and "Izvlecheniia iz pisem N. I. Il'minskago k N. P. Ostroumovu," *Pravoslavnyi Sobesiednik*, pt. 2 (July–August 1900): esp. 43–45, 50–51, and 58–61 (4th pagination); N. P. Ostroumov, *Chto takoe Koran? Po povodu statei G. Gasprinskago, Devlet Kil'deeva i Mirzu Alima* (Tashkent, 1883); and M. A. Miropiev, *O polozhenii russkikh inorodtsev* (St. Petersburg: Sinodal'naia Tipografiia, 1901), esp. chap. 1, as well as his "Kakiia nachala dolzhny byt' polozheny v osnovu obrazovaniia russkikh inorodtsev-musul'man," *Rus'* 4, no. 17 (1 September 1884): 24–41.

9. Il'minskii, *Pis'ma N. I. Il'minskago k ober-prokuroru*, 63–64.

10. Il'minskii, "Izvlecheniia iz pisem' N. I. Il'minskago," 59.

11. James H. Billington, *The Icon and the Axe* (New York: Knopf, 1967), 121–22.

12. A. E. Alektorov, "Islamizm i kirgizy," *Moskovskiia viedomosti*, no. 301 (1897), summarized in A. E. Alektorov, ed., *Ukazatel' knig, zhurnal'nykh i gazetnykh statei i zamietok o Kirgizakh* (Kazan': Tip. universiteta, 1900), 90.

13. Ismail Bey Gaspirali, *Russkoe musul'manstvo: Mysli, zamietki i nabliudeniia musul'manina* (Bakhchesaray: Tip. Spiro, 1881), 4.

14. These comments on Islamic reformist movements rely heavily on John O. Voll, "Renewal and Reform in Islamic History: *Tajdid* and *Islah*," in *Voices of Resurgent Islam*, ed. J. L. Esposito (New York: Oxford University Press, 1983), 32–47.

15. Ishmuhammed ibn Dinmuhammed, *Vypiska iz knigi "Isharet-el-meram," prinadlezhashchei imamu Khatybu i mudarrisu der. Tuntar, Urbarskoi volosti, Malmyzh-*

*skago uezda, Dinmukhametova*, trans. G. Akhmarov (Kazan': Lito-Tip. I. I. Kharitonova, [1910?]), 1.

16. Il'iajeddin Muhitdinov, *Povolzh'e*, vyp. 1 (1903): 20. The quotation dates from 1899.

17. Ishmi Ishan, *Mir Islama* 12 (1913): 870.

18. Il'minskii, "Izvlecheniia iz pisem' N. I. Il'minskago," 52, from a letter dated 3 February 1888. Documentary evidence of the complicity between *qadimists* and the czarist bureaucracy was published in A. Arsharuni and Kh. Gabidullin, *Ocherki panislamizma i pantiurkizma v Rossii* (Moscow: Izd. Bezbozhnik, 1931), 123–29. In his "Introduction: Secular Criticism," in *The World, the Text, and the Critic* (Cambridge, Mass.: Harvard University Press, 1983), 1–30, Edward Said offers a cogent statement, applicable to the concerns of this chapter, about the hegemonic tendencies in every culture.

19. N. P. Ostroumov, as quoted in K. E. Bendrikov, *Ocherki po istorii obrazovaniia v Turkestane (1865–1924 gody)* (Moscow: Akademiia Pedagogicheskikh Nauk RSFSR, 1960), 255.

20. Gaspirali, *Russkoe musul'manstvo*, 3.

21. I. Gaspirali, "Stolietie," *Terjüman/Perevodchik*, no. 1 (10 April 1883): 1. Hereafter, citations to his newspaper will bear the abbreviation *T/P*.

22. I. Gaspirali, untitled article, *T/P*, no. 19 (21 May 1884): 43–44.

23. I. Gaspirali, "Rossiia i Vostok," *T/P*, no. 8, suppl. (10 June 1883), and *Russkoe-vostochnoe soglashenie: Mysli, zametki i pozhelaniia Ismaila Gasprinskago* (Bakhchesaray: Tipo-litografiia gazety "Perevodchik," 1896).

24. I. Gaspirali, *Russkoe musul'manstvo*, 4. The reference to "white czar" is found in *Russko-vostochnoe soglashenie*, 15.

25. I. Gaspirali, *Russkoe musul'manstvo*, 12.

26. Ibid., 25.

27. I. Gaspirali, *Russko-vostochnoe soglashenie*, 6. For other uncomplimentary critiques by Gaspirali of Western European imperial policies, see untitled article, *T/P*, no. 2 (13 January 1895): 3, untitled article, *T/P*, no. 19 (14 May 1895): 45, "Angliia i Vostok," *T/P*, no. 28 (30 July 1895): 81, and "Anglichanin i russkii," *T/P*, no. 48 (17 December 1895): 161. In a remarkable essay that appeared in 1884–85 (*Avrupa Medeniyetine bir Nazar Muvazene* [Constantinople: Matba'a Ebu'l-Ziya, 1884–85]), Gaspirali placed serious restrictions on the value of Western culture for non-Western peoples.

28. Gaspirali, *Russkoe musul'manstvo*, 5, 10.

29. Gaspirali, *Russko-vostochnoe soglashenie*, 1.

30. Besides his comment concerning Japan in *Russko-vostochnoe soglashenie*, see the following Gaspirali articles: untitled article, *T/P*, no. 37 (16 October 1894): 73,

"Mongolism," *T/P*, no. 16 (23 April 1895): 33, and "Zheltyi vopros," *T/P*, no. 6 (20 January 1904): 13, where he employed the phrase "yellow menace."

31. Gaspirali, *Russkoe musul'manstvo*, 9, 5.

32. Ibid., 30.

33. Gaspirali, *Russko-vostochnoe soglashenie*, 19.

34. This issue was a source of polemical jousting between Gaspirali and writers for such periodicals as *Okraina, Vostochnoe obozrenie, Moskovskiia viedomosti, Novoe vremia, Russkaia zhizn'*, and *Novoe obozrienie*.

35. I. Gaspirali, untitled article, *T/P*, no. 13 (18 April 1893): 25, and "Po nevolie," *T/P*, no. 6 (22 February 1891): 11.

36. Gaspirali, *Russkoe musul'manstvo*, 16–17, 31. For a revealing interpretation of Russian imperial policy during the crucial reign of Alexander III (1881–94) by a liberal-minded bureaucrat, N. Kh. Bunge, see George E. Snow, "The Years 1881–1894 in Russia: A Memorandum Found in the Papers of N. Kh. Bunge: A Translation and Commentary," *Transactions of the American Philosophical Society* 71, pt. 6 (1981): 22–46.

37. Ibid., 7.

38. Ibid., 18–19.

39. Jorge Luis Borges, "The Monkey of the Inkpot," in *The Book of Imaginary Beings*, trans. N. di Giovanni (New York: Dutton, 1969), 160.

40. I. Gaspirali, "Oblegchennaia azbuka," *T/P*, no. 39 (6 October 1903): 169.

41. Cited in Kirimli Jafer Seydahmet, *Gaspirali Ismail Bey* (Istanbul: Matbaajilik ve Neshriyat Türk Anonim Shirketi, 1934), 54.

42. I. Gaspirali, "Gün Dogdu, yani Yeni Zaman ve Yeni Kishiler," *T/P*, no. 92 (7 November 1905): 184.

43. S. Filippov, *Po Krymu: Otrazheniia* (Moscow: Tip. A. Levenson, 1889), 76.

44. Ahmed Zeki Velidi Togan, *Bugünkü Türkili (Türkistan) ve yakin tarihi* (Istanbul: Göven Basimevi, 1942–47), 556.

45. A contrary view, seriously weakened by its almost total reliance on Gaspirali's three-issue newspaper *Al-Nahda*, published in Cairo in 1908, is offered by Thomas Kuttner, "Russian *Jadidism* and the Islamic World: Ismail Gasprinskii in Cairo—1908," *Cahiers du Monde russe et soviétique* 16, nos. 3–4 (July–December 1975): 383–424.

46. Quoted in A. Deliorman, "Ismail Gaspirali ve Terjüman Gazetesi," *Türk Kültürü* 6, no. 69 (1968): 655.

47. Umberto Eco, *The Name of the Rose*, trans. William Weaver (New York: Harcourt Brace Jovanovich, 1983), 492.

48. Mary Douglas, *Purity and Danger: An Analysis of the Concepts of Pollution and Taboo* (London: Routledge & Kegan Paul, 1966), 35.

# 4

## Symbols: The National Anthem and Patriotic Songs by Three Poets

SEYIT AHMET KIRIMCA

By 1914, the state of affairs in Crimea had divested Crimean Tatars of their own imperial past and most national monuments. The only institution with which the people could now identify was the newspaper published by Ismail Bey Gaspirali, *Terjüman* (Turkish *Tercuman*). From this situation arose the next generation of educators and leaders for the nationality. Outstanding among those was Numan Chelebi Jihan (1885–1918), first president of the Crimean national government, who had been educated in one of the new-method schools established by Gaspirali before his death in 1914. Jihan also studied in Istanbul, becoming the first elected mufti (religious authority) of Crimea since Russia annexed Crimea formally in 1783. He wrote the song that rose to the status of a national anthem. Another cultural leader, Shevki Bektore (1881–1961), became the teacher who in 1924 created the first Arabic-script alphabet modified specifically for Crimean Tatars. His song "My Tatarness" gained wide popularity and a permanent place in the repertory of Crimean Tatar patriotic music.[1] A third intellectual leader, Bekir Sitki Chobanzade (1893–1938), studied in Crimea, then in Istanbul on a stipend offered by the Students' Benevolent Association established by Ismail Bey Gaspirali. As a poet, he added verses to Bektore's original version of "My Tatarness," making the song even more popular than before. As professor of Oriental languages, Chobanzade later (1928) also participated in romanizing Bektore's Crimean Tatar alphabet. Common to the ideas of these three was an attempt to modernize the educational system of Crimea. By using the vernacular language, these men helped form the Crimean Tatar national identity. The very same thought—preserving the nationality by saving its literary language—would recur much later during the Central Asian phase of Crimean Tatar history.

On 26 November 1917, after Friday prayers and Muslim rituals, to the tune of the "Marseillaise," with the sky-blue field and golden scales of the Qurultay flag and a revolutionary banner flying, Crimean national government president Jihan opened the national parliament (Qurultay). As the parliament began its work on that day, its members sang "I Pledge" by popular demand as a kind of oath of office. Standing in Bakhchesaray's old Palace of the Khan in the Babi Divan salon, he spoke about the symbolism of the event, the place, and the new institution. Among other things, President Jihan said: "My dear parliamentarians, today we are reactivating our political history. It had ceased for the last century and a half. Today the Crimean parliament has convened in the Council of State to resuscitate the Tatar national will that was destroyed by the government of Russia."[2]

Thus, Crimean Tatars found a new leader and fresh symbols to accompany remaining traditional signs of group identity. The thesis in this chapter is that under adverse conditions a nationality may yet look to its culture and art to provide the significant symbolism so necessary for group survival. One such enduring symbol came from the pen of Numan Chelebi Jihan. Written about 1910, during his student days in Istanbul, the poem "I Pledge" ("And ätkämän") turned into a patriotic national hymn for his people. The song became known mainly by word of mouth, for it appeared in print rarely, once around 1917 in a handwritten collection (an early kind of samizdat) issued by a mullah from Kezler, Omer Hajji Hasan Efendi. It came out again in 1918 in Istanbul.[3]

The anthem of a nationality usually projects images of past struggles and present heroism. It challenges the people's enemies, who may deprive them of hard-won liberty. It assures its singers that they will be free forever because of the rightness of their cause. An anthem may also serve as the foundation of a nationality or a cause worth defending. However, "I Pledge," the Crimean Tatar anthem, deals with the actual conditions under which Crimean Tatars live. It also applies to the condition of Crimean Tatars in Central Asian exile since 1944. The song does not suggest any bravado. It observes and records the daily anxiety and pain suffered by people and speaks about personal resolve to lessen the suffering of terrible experiences shared by kinsmen. It calls for self-reliance and sacrifice.

The second stanza of "I Pledge" begins: "I Pledge to bring light to this darkened home. / Why should two brothers not see one another?"[4] These lines refer to the divisiveness and darkness in Crimean Tatar life brought by Russian police terror in Crimea. And they hint at the banishment that patriots underwent when the authorities arrested them. That state terror caused people to fear one another and suspect family members of betrayal to the police. The poet reassures his countrymen when he calls for Crimean Tatars to trust each other and bring unity to the nationality. Russian politicians saw danger in the words of "I Pledge." Scores of people went to jail and were exiled as a consequence of singing the anthem in public or private. Political police charged a Crimean Tatar man named Nuri, from Bakhchesaray, with fomenting the establishment of the Crimean national Qurultay. Nuri's defense, drunkenness, did not save him from Siberian exile in 1927.[5] Similarly, the police arrested the composer responsible for the score to which the poem was set, Hasan Refatov, son of the accomplished musician Takatuka Mahmut Efendi from Bakhchesaray. Hasan Refatov, interned as a nationalist along with many others, died in 1932.[6] As a song, "I Pledge" evidently could be played and sung, so long as its performance did not lead to political demonstrations. Another version of it came out in a collection entitled *Songs of Crimea* (*Pesni Kryma*) compiled by A. K. Konchevskii, with a foreword contributed by Minister of Soviet Education A. V. Lunacharskii, in Moscow in 1924 as a matter of ethnographic and evidently educational interest.[7] This early adoption of a national anthem by the Crimean Tatar public illustrates the rapid development of a sense of nationality consciousness and unity among them. By comparison, Central Asian Turkic and Iranian nationalities such as Uzbeks and Tajiks wrote and adopted their first official Soviet-era anthems in 1947 and 1945, and the Soviet Union did not adopt its latest anthem until 1944.[8]

As it had in the time of the Crimean khans, poetry continued to enjoy great popularity. Poets, called by the people *keday* and *akey*, traveled and sang their verses. They would stay in the special guest houses built in each village and opened to visitors free of charge. According to the childhood recollections of Ajemin Jagarli, now deceased, families used to listen to visiting *kedays* from early in the evening until the morning hours. Crimean Tatars of the older generation remember that itinerant *kedays* often employed patriotic themes in their songs. One senior emigrant from Crimea recalled a *keday*'s singing: "My mother, the daughter of Crimea, is a young lioness. She embroidered the sky-blue flag. She is the Tatar star" ("Benim anam Kirimlidir, aslan Tatarin kizi. Kök bayraghi o ishledi, o dur Tatar yildizi"). These *kedays* also played an important role in spreading the songs "My Tatarness" and "I Pledge" throughout Crimea.[9]

The current popular poems that helped form Crimean Tatar identity fit into that cultural niche of the nationality. The first line in the third stanza of "I Pledge" changed through usage to its present form as early as 1917. Originally, it read: "I pledge, give my word to die for knowledge [*bilmäk ichun*]." Popularly, this has become "I pledge, give my word to die for the nation [*millät ichun*]."[10] These alterations seemed to mean that people had begun working for cohesion and intended to reclaim the symbols of past independence to rebuild the Crimean Tatar nationality. Part of the same idea lay behind the action taken by Chelebi Jihan on 21 October 1917 to establish the Palace of the Crimean Khans (Khansaray) as a national museum.[11] Finally, the very last line of the anthem reads: "Still one day the gravediggers will come to bury me." Ironically, the poet did not enjoy the remote, quiet interment he hoped for in "I Pledge." On 23 February 1918, when he was only thirty-three, Slavic sailors murdered him and threw his body into the Black Sea; it was never recovered.

The three stanzas of Chelebi Jihan's "I Pledge," translated from the 1918 edition, follow:

> I pledge to heal the wounds of Tatars,
> Why should my unfortunate brothers rot away;
> If I don't sing, don't grieve for them, if I live,
> Let the dark streams of blood in my heart go dry!

> I pledge to bring light to that darkened country
> How may two brothers not see one another?
> When I see this, if I don't get distressed, hurt, seared,
> Let the tears that flow from my eyes become a river, a sea of blood!

> I pledge, give my word to die for knowledge
> Knowing, seeing, to wipe away the teardrops of my nation
> If I live a thousand unknowing, unseeing years, if I become
>     a gathering's chief
> Still one day the gravediggers will come to bury me!

Transliterated from the Crimean Tatar of 1918, these stanzas read:

> And etkämän tatarlarin yarasini sarmagha,
> Nasil bolsun bu zavalli qardashlarim churusun;
> Onlar ichun okunmäsäm, qayghumasam, yashasam.
> Yuräkimdä qara qanlar qaynamasin, qurusun!

And etkämän shu qaranghi yurtqa shavlä särpmägä
Nasil bolsun iki qardash bir birini kormasin.
Buni korub buusatmasam, mughaymasam, janmasam,
Kozlarimdän aqan yashlar, därya dängiz qan bolsun!

And etkämän, soz bärkämän bilmäk ichun olmaga
Bilub korub millätimin koz yashini silmägä
bilmiy, kormiy bin yashasam qurultayli khan bolsam
Yänä bir kun mäzarchilar kelir beni kommägä!¹²

A Turkified version of this anthem has become widely known and sung in the emigration. The leading Crimean Tatar journal published outside the former Soviet Union, *Emel*, has published the words to the song at various times under the title "Ant etkemen."¹³

## Chelebi Jihan

Chelebi Jihan was born in 1885 in the village of Sonak, in the Congar region of Crimea, the son of Ibrahim and Jihanshah Chelebi. His education started in Sonak's new-method school, which the Russian authorities soon closed. He then studied under Mustafa Efendi, a doctor of Muslim theology. Chelebi Jihan continued his studies briefly at Akchora Seminary near Jankoy, then in the Rustiye Medrese of Aqmesjit. His father had graduated from the teachers' college. The family owned large parcels of land in Sonak. When he sided with the village poor against the Russian government officials, they contrived to force him into bankruptcy.¹⁴ His uncles from Kitay village financed his further education in Zinjirli Medrese. The seminary, which functioned in the village of the future Salajik, near Bakhchesaray, had been founded by Mengli Giray Khan in 1500. This institution became the center of intellectual activity in Crimea. In 1907, Chelebi Jihan briefly enrolled in the Vefa preparatory school, in Istanbul. The next year he enrolled in Medrest-ul Kuzat law school. The uncles financed his education, beginning with Zinjirli Medrese through law school.¹⁵

In 1908–9, Chelebi Jihan became a founding member and was elected chairman of the Association of Crimean Students (Qïrïm Talebe Jemiyeti), within which he formed a second group called Motherland (Vatan), which focused on the political future of Crimea. Along with Habibullah

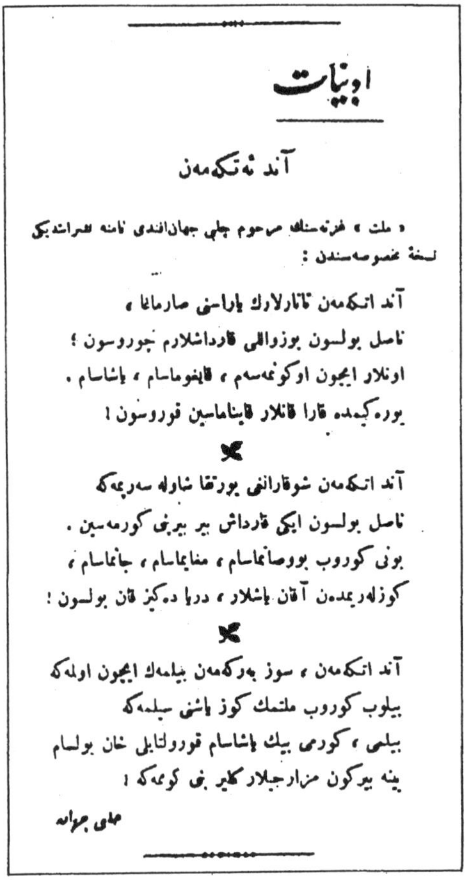

ادبيات

آند ئەتكەمەن

« ملت » غزته‌سنك مرحوم چلبي جهان افندی نامنه نشراتدیکی
نسخهٔ مخصوصه‌سندن :

آند اتکەمەن تاتارلارك یاراسنی صارمانا ،
ناصل بولسون بوزواللی قارداشلارم چوروسون ؛
اونلار ایچون اوکونمەسەم ، قایغوماسام ، یاشاسام .
یوره‌کیمده قارا قانلار قاینامامسین قوروسون !

آند اتکەمەن شوقارانغی یورتقا شاوله سەرپەکه
ناصل بولسون ایکی قارداش بیر بیرینی کورمەسین .
بونی کوروب بووصانماسام ، مناغماسام ، جانماسام ،
کوزلەریمدەن آقان یاشلار ، دریا دەکیز قان بولسون !

آند اتکەمەن ، سوز بەرکەمەن بیلمەك ایچون اولەکه
بیلوب کوروب ملتمك کوز یاشنی سیلمەکه
بیلمی ، کورمی بیك یاشاسام قورولتایلی خان بولسام
ینه بیرکون مزارجیلار کلیر بنی کومەکه !

چلبی جهان

Figure 4.1. Early edition of the Crimean Tatar Anthem "I Pledge" ("And ätkänmän"), signed by (Numan) Chelebi Jihan. From the original version in the newspaper *Millät*, reprinted in the journal *Qrim*, no. 8 (1918): 147.

Temirjan and others he established the Young Tatar Writers' Group (Yash Tatar Yazijilari Jiyini). It published brochures written by Chelebi Jihan: "I Pledge," "Swallows' Prayer" ("Kirilgajlar duasi"), and many others. He wrote these short stories and poems in the Crimean Tatar literary language, following his motto: "People must be addressed in their own tongue." On graduating from the school of law in Istanbul, he returned to Crimea, married, and then enrolled in the Psychoneurology Institute in St. Petersburg.

After 25 March 1917, when he was elected chief mufti of Crimea, he became instrumental in founding the Dar-ul Malumat, a school for women, and Dar-ul Muallimin, a teacher's institute for men, both in Aqmesjit. In establishing these schools, he followed his principles concerning national unity. When he opened the new national museum on 21 September 1917,

Chelebi Jihan said: "Nations require four foundations to advance their civilizations. They are literature, science, business, and diplomacy. We have been denied these for the last 150 years."[16] He wrote other memorable poems during his compulsory military service in World War I and when he was later imprisoned for nationalism, but his song "I Pledge" lived on to sustain Crimean Tatars through very difficult years.

People sang the verses of a second poem, "My Tatarness" ("Tatarligim"), along with "I Pledge" (see fig. 4.1). Because singing "I Pledge" became a political gesture or symbol and therefore a political risk, Crimean Tatar exiles in Central Asia or elsewhere in later years adopted "My Tatarness" as an unofficial anthem. A Crimean Tatar emigrant of the late 1970s from the Tashkent region has confirmed that status for "My Tatarness." Neither of these songs appeared in a large collection of Crimean Tatar songs issued a decade ago in Central Asia. They spread among people by word of mouth only and even then very cautiously, between the most trusted friends.[17] Both these songs encapsulate the Crimean Tatar experience in history since the Russian annexation of 1783 and the forced exile of 18 May 1944. They were current for Crimean Tatars in the Soviet Union as well as those who lived in the emigration. Such songs may endure more readily under circumstances of exile than in a nationality residing within its homeland.

"My Tatarness" is well known in two versions, the first the original, full poem, the second a version created by people who merged this poem by Shevki Bektore with one by Bekir Sitki Chobanzade. Here is the current wording of "My Tatarness":

> Since my childhood I loved my Tatarness and my birthplace.
> I cried, suffered, and felt for them many a time.
>
> Wherever I went, I traced many. I saw the scattered Tatars.
> They haven't a single flowering rose to smell.
>
> They became true wanderers in their own homes and gardens.
> But to whom can you really tell them, these secrets?
>
> They have been thrown to the mountains, stony places and battles
>     by a strong wind.
> This imperfect world has become a grave for Tatarness, for the Tatar.
>
> I paused and poured tear drops on top of every grave.
> For every one of them I made a headstone from my songs.

> Palms raised, I prayed to God from my heart.
> Let Him give a long, happy life to Tatarness, to the Tatar.

The following verse, by Chobanzade, customarily comes in place of the final two given above:

> To those who ask if there are Tatars, I am a Tatar.
> I am the young Tatar who knows his ancestry.
> To those degenerates who don't know their ancestors,
> I will shout: You aren't needed [in this struggle]![18]

## Shevki Bektore

Shevki Bektore came from the village of Kavlaklar, in Dobruja, Romania. During his childhood, his family emigrated to Turkiye, where he took his primary and higher education. As World War I began, Bektore was working in Crimea as a private schoolteacher. The Russian government interned most Turkish citizens at Tambov, but Bektore eluded this measure and fled via Azerbaijan to Turkiye. After the war, he went back to Crimea as one of fifty teachers. Beginning in March 1918, he worked in Crimean education in different institutions. In 1922, he wrote a Crimean Tatar–language grammar book, and, in 1924, he drafted an important symbol, the first specifically Crimean Tatar alphabet based on Arabic script (fig. 4.2.).[19]

Beginning in 1926, Bektore worked in Turkmenistan, and, in late 1933, the authorities had him arrested for nationalism and sentenced to labor camps in Zarafshan and then Zengiata, in Uzbekistan.[20] The police released him only in 1945 in a general amnesty but restricted him to the Yangiyul area. Thus, Shevki Bektore paradoxically lived in one of the regions of exile to which the Soviet government and Communist Party sent the 1944 generation of displaced Crimean Tatar persons. In a sense, he and his song "My Tatarness" welcomed the new wave of exiles from Crimea to Central Asia. As late as 1956, he emigrated from the Soviet Union on a Russian passport, published his memoirs, *Red Flows the Volga* (*Volga kizil akarken*), in the 1960s, and died in Istanbul in 1961 (see also chap. 15).

His song and the anthem "I Pledge" possess great importance as symbols of identity and cohesion from Crimean Tatars in the diaspora. In the absence of a true capital city, of a national museum, of a national seal and

Figure 4.2. *The Crimean Tatar ABCs* (*Tatar alifbesi*), an elementary school textbook in the modified Arabic script prepared by Shevki Bektore. Front cover from the edition of the Qrim Hukumat Nashriyati, 1925.

flag, and of other conventional marks of nationality, these songs have for a time become the only palpable symbols remaining for Crimean Tatars to rally around. "My Tatarness" comments on shared national and personal experiences from birth to death. It seems unique to Crimean Tatars and in that way echoes the emotional history of the Crimean Tatar nationality. The line "Wherever I went, I traced many. I saw the scattered Tatars" points to the dispersal of Crimean Tatars from Romania, Bulgaria, and Turkiye to the distant places in the Russian Empire. The line about lacking a flowering rose to smell refers to the lack of happy, prospering families in exile. And the allusion to wandering in their own homes and gardens indicates the predicament of Crimean Tatars who have been deprived of a suitable place in their own homeland. Speaking about building headstones, the poet refers to the organized destruction of Crimean Tatar cemeteries in Crimea as well as to the many people who perished during banishment and had to be left unburied beside the railroad.[21] The poem's despair was augmented with a feeling of determination by another intellectual who contributed to this symbolic work and to many other aspects of Crimean Tatar culture.

## Bekir Sitki Chobanzade

Chobanzade (1893–1938) wrote the later, last stanza of "My Tatarness," translated above. He concentrated on an image of the struggle necessary for the group identity required for the survival of the nationality. Senior Crimean Tatar emigrants remember in their very young childhood reciting "My Tatarness." And, as they recall, while singing that last stanza, "they proudly beat their breast and announced themselves to be the young, educated Crimean Tatar in that poem."[22] Bekir Sitki Chobanzade was born in Argin Koy near Kefe, son of Abdul Vahap, a shepherd (*choban*). When the boy reached the age of seven or eight years, he used to help his father pasture the sheep at the Karabay plateau summer camping area. His education started in his village grammar school. At thirteen, in 1905, he enrolled in the Qarasuvbazar Turkish Rustiye *medrese* and graduated with honors in 1909.[23] A poor but bright student, his further education, in Istanbul, gained financial support from the Hayriye Jemiyeti of Qarasuvbazar. Such associations, first established there by Ismail Bey Gaspirali, helped needy students. After graduating from the lycée with honors in 1915, he returned to Crimea and then went to study Russian in Odessa. Three years after enrolling in the University of Budapest he graduated, again with honors, with a degree in Oriental languages and philology.

Back in Crimea in 1920, Chobanzade taught in the Aqmesjit pedagogical institute while he worked as department head in the Crimean central educational department. In 1922, he became a professor of Oriental languages in the University of Aqmesjit, where he taught Turkish. Actively publishing scholarly articles, he became noticed and in 1924 received an appointment as professor of philology in the University of Baku, Azerbaijan. He collected his poetry, written starting in 1914 in the northern (Qipchaq) branch of the Crimean Tatar language, and in 1927 published it in a small book entitled *The Whirlwind* (*Boran*). Following his principle of writing his verse in the language people understood, he composed poems such as "Mother Tongue" ("Tuvgan til"): "I found you in Crimea and in

Kazan / I found you as my heart soared and overflowed / . . . / Mother tongue! Nothing else comes into my mind, / The enemies do not know my great secret."[24] He also played an instrumental role in converting the alphabet from Arabic to Roman in 1924. In 1936, along with others in the Turkological Section of the Pedagogical Institute of Crimea, he was exiled to Siberia, where he died in the winter of 1938 on the banks of a northern river at Troitsko-Pechorsk somewhat west of the Ural range of hills. In his short life as a learned man, he authored around ninety scholarly articles about Uzbek language and literature, Chaghatay poets, and other subjects. As one of his poems declared: "I was born in a house. / I will build a *medrese* for young students. / Let the books be open for rich and poor!"[25]

Unified in spirit, these three poets of Crimea made contributions in many other vital spheres of life. After the Crimean national government had been quashed in 1918 by Soviet armed forces, the example and actions of these men and many others firmed and developed modern Crimean Tatar national ideals. They directly and indirectly contributed much to the cultural renaissance that took place in the Crimean Autonomous Soviet Socialist Republic organized by the Soviet government from 18 September 1921 until at least 1928. In that period of flowering Tatarness, many schools, libraries, theaters, and museums opened and advanced the culture still more. A few of the educated persons from this creative period somehow survived the later Communist Party purges, World War II, and the mass deportation of 18 May 1944 to rekindle Crimean Tatar cultural life in Central Asia as well as outside the Soviet Union. In Central Asia, the publication of a newspaper, the *Banner of Lenin* (*Lenin bayraghi*), in Tashkent, helped revive Crimean Tatar literary life and language and thus enabled Crimean Tatars to find one another again. That newspaper played a role similar in some ways to *Terjüman* at the turn of the twentieth century. It, too, brought Crimean Tatars together and visibly as well as spiritually symbolized their Tatarness. Once again, the nationality desperately needed at least a minimally unifying institution. The anthem and patriotic songs of the three poets provided it. Popular sayings sustained the group seeking renewal. One proverb predicted revival in these lines: "A surviving orphan will grow up lamenting, but one day will drink water from a golden cup."[26] Now the newspaper, its language, and the special Crimean Tatar (Cyrillic) alphabet used in it added more recognizable signs of identity to complement the inner strength and self-awareness conveyed in "I Pledge" and "My Tatarness." These were not enough, but they provided a symbolic beginning.[27]

## Notes

1. Sh. Bäktorä, *Tatar älifbäsi* (n.p.: Qrim Hukumät Näshriyati, 1924).
2. Müstejib Ülküsal, *Kirim Türk-Tatarlari* (Dünü, Bugünü, Yarini) (Istanbul: Baha Matbaasi, 1980), 176–77.
3. Shevki Bektöre, "Antli shehit," *Kirim yayinlari*, no. 1 (1961): 26.
4. Chäläbi Jihan, "And ätkämän," *Qrim mäjmu'asi*, no. 8 (1918): 147. Thanks to Hakan Kirimli for supplying this very early printed version of the poem.
5. Conversation of the author (New York, October 1986) with Süleyman Sarana, who emigrated from Crimea to Turkiye in 1935.
6. Riza Gülüm, "Kirim Tatarlarinin Milli Oyunlari, Sharki ve Muzik," *Kirim bülten*, no. 114 (December 1977).
7. M. Goldstein, "Sovyet haraketine ugrayan Krim Türk Halki ve onun Milli Kültürü," *Dergi*, no. 59 (1970): 27.
8. "Gimn," in *Ozbek sawet entsiklapediyäsi* (Tashkent: Ozbekistan SSR Fänlär Akädemiyäsi, 1972), 13:345.
9. Halim Saylik, New York, 1986. Conversation with the late Ajemin Jagarli related by Halime Öztunç, grandmother of Halim Saylik. Quotation from Hatice Öztunj of Ayranci, Konya, Turkiye, ninety-nine-year-old matriarch whose family emigrated from Crimea to Turkiye in 1933.
10. "Ant etkemen," *Emel*, no. 146 (January–February 1985): 20.
11. Ülküsal, *Kirim Türk-Tatarlari*, 170, 172.
12. Chäläbi Jihan, "And ätkämän," *Qrim mäjmu'asi*, no. 8 (1918): 147 (translation by Seyit Ahmet Kirimca with Edward Allworth).
13. "Doghumunun 100, shahadetinin 67. Yildiriminde—antli kurban Chelebi Jihandan: 'Ant etkemen,'" *Emel*, no. 146 (January–February 1985): 20.
14. Bektöre, "Antli shehit," 20.
15. M. Serdar, "Chelebi Jihan," *Kirim yayinlari*, no. 1 (1961): 2.
16. Ibid., 7; Ülküsal, *Kirim Türk-Tatarlari*, 120.
17. Conversation between the author and Ayshe Seytmuratova, New York, October 1986; Yahya Sherfedinov, "Kirim Tatarlarinin türkü ve danslari," in *Yangiray qaytarma* (Tashkent: Gafur Gulam adina Edebiyat ve Sanaat Neshriyeti, 1978), trans. Abay, cited in *Emel*, no. 147 (March–April 1985): 3.
18. Bektöre, "Antli shehit," 24 (translated by Seyit Ahmet Kirimca with Edward Allworth).

19. Shevki Bektöre, collection of his songs, *Kirim bülten*, no. 85 (December 1972): 1–11, and "Antli shehit," 23–24; Saadet Bektöre, *Volga kizil akarken* (Istanbul: Nur Yayinlari, 1960), 26; Shävki Bäktorä, *Tatar älifbäsi* (n.p.: Qrim Hukumät Näshriyati, 1925).

20. Saadet Bektöre, *Volga kizil akarken*, 27–28, 55–57, 148.

21. Alan W. Fisher, *Crimean Tatars* (Stanford, Calif.: Hoover Institution Press, 1978), 95.

22. Conversations between the author, Yunus Ezgin, and Mehmet Muhittin Sevdiyar, New York, October 1986.

23. Ülküsal, *Kirim Türk-Tatarlari*, 267.

24. Ibid., 151, 268; Bekir Sitki Chobanzade, "Tuvgan til" (reprinted along with a modern Turkish version entitled "Ana dil"), *Emel*, no. 115 (November–December 1979): 27–28.

25. Fisher, *Crimean Tatars*, 145–46; Ülküsal, *Kirim Türk-Tatarlari*, 268; Emel, "Bekir Sitki Chobanzade," *Emel*, no. 46 (May–June 1968): 17, 23.

26. Boztorgay Ahmet-Nagi Ali, *Folklor toplami* (Bucharest: Kriterion, 1980), 303.

27. Edige Kirimal, "Kirim türkleri," *Dergi*, no. 59 (Munich 1970): 9, 15.

# 5

## Rituals: Artistic, Cultural, and Social Activity

### RIZA GÜLÜM

In addition to its subject matter or content, group expression through art, culture, and social organization supplies probably the most important means by which a nationality provides itself continuity and focuses its collective identity at the same time. These creative resources give a nationality the opportunity to articulate—through gesture, word, representational medium, or ritual—assertions of its self-awareness as well as its unconscious belonging to its own group. When most other channels of such declaration become closed off through deprivation or strict censorship, when political possibilities remain out of reach, some aspects of cultural or artistic life usually seem to offer outlets for the necessary enunciation of a nationality's sense of self-worth and identity. Moreover, in this instance, the Crimean Tatar community in the former Soviet Union spun off beyond its core many small satellite bodies often rotating outside the boundaries of the country. Artistic and cultural expression among Crimean Tatars inside the Soviet state functioned as crucial supporting factors in the maintenance of the nationality. In a significant respect, similar activity proceeding in the non-Soviet diaspora served a comparable purpose. The outside activities complemented and in a necessary manner, for the group, reflected Crimean Tatar particularity back to the main group (see chap. 15).

The activities of the home group of Crimean Tatars, closely controlled by Crimea's political authorities, extended a rich heritage that reaches back even before the turn of the twentieth century. These restricted expressions of artistic, cultural, and social life had fundamental meaning for the nationality and its corporate identity. They continue to play that role under trying conditions back in Crimea.

### Songs, Music, and Folk Literature

Crimean Tatars love and create songs and music, folk songs, and other folklore. They have done so since very old times. Holidays, feasts, and public celebrations were full of Crimean Tatar songs and music to provide people with a good time. In the midst of this joyfulness, these expressions relate to their work as well as to play. Crimean Tatar hospitality meant the preparation of special food, showing great courtesy and serious respect for guests attending celebrations. A Crimean Tatar reveres the guest because people regard him as Allah's visitor, and they respect every command of Allah. The land of Crimea itself provides one of the reasons for these traditions. People sang specific, very popular folk songs (*manes* and *chins*) in the particular regions where they lived. They performed *manes* in the main towns in the mountainous parts of Crimea, but people sang *chins* everywhere on the peninsula. The farmers of the agricultural areas of Crimea originated the *chins*. The singing of *manes* by younger boys and girls survived until the present time. And many famous performers among mature singers—Jangazi Sherafettin, Ismail Saled, Uzun Mahmut, and others—have earned renown for their renditions of *manes* and *chins*.[1]

Some of these old folk songs survived, others came into popularity later, but performers render them even now in the Central Asian area of Crimean Tatar exile. One of these older songs from Jangazi Sherafettin laments the difficult times of czarist Russian domination: "During the cruel czarist times / We would want to die. / Our lives disgusted us. / Nothing to wear, barefooted, / We would stroll along the roads." The style of this early bard reveals itself in another *chin*: "Here I come; may greetings be upon you; hello, brave sirs, who will notice paupers like us? / Greetings, welcome, someone kicked by a mare, / You are a brainless grain scatterer. / I heard of a carriage of gold with a silver pole, / Greetings, welcome Seyd Ali the drunk. On fields, shocks of grain, in a garden, large haystacks look nice. / One trouser leg up, the other not down."[2]

Another well-known man of letters, Osman Akchokrakli, has served Crimean Tatar folklore very well in citing memoirs about Crimean Tatars by Jan Muhammad. Here is a poem taken from the book *Journeys over Poland* (*Polonya üzerine seferleri*) (1648–49) by Islam Giray Khan II and Bohdan Hmelnitskii:

> Shoe the pintos, oil the bows,
> Burnish the saddle wood, fry the meat.
> Take down the sword and sharpen it,
> If your sword is white, your eye won't dim.
> If you hang two leg cuffs and one rope on the pommel of your saddle,
> Put a red leather charm on my horse's head.[3]

Jan Muhammed's beautiful poem combines art with forceful lyrics. An examination of a book about the *manes* and *chins* reveals not only that more than a thousand have been collected but that these very folk poems are still being sung in Crimea and Uzbekistan by Crimean Tatars.[4] The compiler's opinion is that there are still many people who write down *manes* and *chins*. Folklorists Semadin Bekirov and Abdurrahman Bari contributed much information about them. Also, Sabriye Selametova memorized her mother's *chins* and thus enriched the history of this national literary form. Many others have also collected specimens of them, and Crimean Tatar scholars, such as Eshref Shamizade and Kerim Jamanakli, have studied them. The following is an example of the four-line *mane*:

> The bottom of a river is reedy,
> When a rose blooms, it is summer.
> I can't call you a rose,
> A rose's life is short.
>
> Derya tübü saz olur,
> Gül achilsa yaz olur.
> Men sana gül deyalmam,
> Gülnin omürü az olur.

Next is an example of the two-line *chin*:

> What is a *chin*, if you know how to put it together,
> If you make me mad, I'll sew a shepherd's jacket out of *chin*.
>
> Chin degenin nedir o kelishtirsen,
> Chindan chekman tikermen, erishtirsen.[5]

Folk poetry appealed greatly to people partly because it offered vigorous verbal performance of lively, entertaining material. For similar reasons, theatrical presentations attracted attentive audiences, although the modern form came rather late to Crimea.

## Theater and Drama

Dramatists Yusuf Bolat (died 1986) and Abdullah Balin relate a great deal about Ümer Ipchi's biography, about the theater, and about literary activities. Ümer Ipchi's era saw the beginning of the modern Crimean Tatar theater, an institution that served the nationality in very important ways.[6] A single ordinary person does not make history. Societies and renowned leaders make things happen. Ümer Ipchi (1897–1944) is one of the individuals who took a great role in starting Crimean Tatar theater. He not only wrote plays but served as a master director. He was one of those who first organized the theater. When it turned professional and received state support in 1923, he became the first administrator. The foundation of this theater emerged long before 1917, but at that time actors were amateurs. The founders of organized theater, Ipchi, Jelal Muinov, and Ayshe Tayganskaia, faced considerable difficulty, for Crimea lacked experienced directors and dramatists. When the state took over the Aqmesjit (Simferopol') drama group and changed it into the Crimean Tatar State Drama Theater (CTSDT), it attracted a number of strong performers and theater people, including Hayri Emir Zade, Halil Gurjü, and Ava Kilicheva from other Crimean towns. In addition, Ipchi brought in a famous actor, Jelal Baykin, and his wife, Sara, from Kazan Tatarstan to perform and Sulva Valiyev to direct productions in the Crimean theater.[7]

Ümer Ipchi also went to Moscow, Ufa, and Kazan to study theatrical activities there and to meet some actors and managers. He obtained a few plays from them. During 1923–24, the subjects of his plays were mainly historical or legendary. But, in 1924, he started working on other subjects and putting on plays from neighboring countries. In this he found success. He always focused on the latest social problems in the dozen or more plays he wrote. In 1925, his drama *The Prostitute* (*Fahishe*) was staged. Before long, a number of Russian dramas had been translated into Crimean Tatar and put on in Crimea. Likewise, works written by Kazan Tatars and Azerbaijanians were presented.[8]

Ipchi also worked for the newspapers *Qirim muhtar Jumhuriyeti*, *Yeni Dünya*, *Yash kuvvet*, and *Qizil Qirim*, for which he wrote poetry and other works. One of his new plays, *Alim the Crimean Brave* (1926), became so well received after it was produced in Crimea as *Alim Aydamak* that the actress Ava Kilicheva translated it into Russian. In that version, the Kievan cinema director, Tasin, read it and made the play into a film with actors from the CTSDT. It enjoyed great success. As a result, Ipchi lost actors to other Soviet theaters, but he found a new, talented leading lady in Lütfiye Chalbash. She worked in an Aqmesjit pastry and preserve factory but simultaneously acted in the amateur drama group of her factory. Within a year after Ipchi recruited her for his CTSDT, she performed extremely well. Among other roles, she played the character Catherine II in Ipchi's historical drama *Shahin Giray*. Later, she too left this theater and emigrated to Turkiye. In part to provide new talent for Crimean theaters, in 1926–27 the Crimean Ministry of Education ordered the CTSDT to organize a drama school. This institution opened in 1928. The ministry required every town in Crimea to send boys and girls to this school. Ümer Ipchi personally selected the talented young people from each town and invited them to the CTSDT in September 1928 to take examinations. Some thirty-five to forty competed, and judges selected twelve of them to study in classrooms all morning and in the drama studio afternoons. Osman Akchokrakli, Asan Refatov, Abdullah Laif Zade, and other senior teachers taught at the school and served as administrators. Ümer Ipchi continued to give his all to the theater and the school and persisted in writing plays and translating others from foreign languages.[9]

The twenty-one actors and actresses appointed to the staff of the theater included Gani Murad, Ismail Abduraimov, Alime Muqaddesova, and Ali Temindar. After accepting these talented young performers in 1929, Ipchi resigned as director and principal of the school and concentrated on his own writing, occasionally directing a performance. He staged his last play, *The Enemy* (*Düshman*), himself in 1932 and resigned from the theater officially.[10]

Yusuf Bolat came after Ümer Ipchi, and his plays merit mention. He staged the works of Russia's or Western Europe's well-known playwrights so that Crimean Tatar audiences could see the famous plays. Through him, Crimean Tatars came to know works by Shakespeare, Gogol, Carlo Gozzi, Gorky, and many others. Dozens of great dramas and comedies, including *Hamlet*, *Othello*, *Princess Turandot*, and *Marriage*, were staged in Crimean Tatar translations.[11]

## Folklore in Exile

Not until 1957 did the authorities permit the deportees in Central Asia to organize a Crimean Tatar folk dance group to replace the one destroyed during the mass exile thirteen years earlier. On this occasion, they specified

Figure 5.1. Advertisement for a Crimean Tatar exile performance in Central Asia of the musical drama *The Girl Arzi* (*Arzi qiz*), book by Yusuf Bolat, music composed in 1937 by Ilyas Bakhshish and Yahya Sherfedinov. From a later edition (Eskishehir, Turkiye: Eskishehir Kïrïm Folklor Derneghi Yayïnlarï, 1991), 28.

that the group could perform folk dances and songs, modern songs, large musical compositions, plays, sketches, and concerts. At first it was impossible to realize all these aims, but eventually everything in that agreement became a reality. Managers of the troupe accepted many new, young performers, and the ensemble became stronger than before. By 1959, the Qaytarma group's president and general manager, Ilyas Bakhshish, a well-known composer, felt the troupe to be strong enough to stage a performance. He decided to put on the musical drama *Arzi qiz* by Yusuf Bolat, the Crimean Tatar playwright (see fig. 5.1). The troupe made an accomplished presentation. A second attempt in this sphere, offering the comedy *Mother-in-Law* (*Kaynana*) by Azerbaijanian playwright Mejit Shmahal, achieved even greater success. The prominent Crimean Tatar actor Gani Murat, who directed the performance, said about the theater and the Qaytarma group: "At last, in 1960–61 they made me programmer and general manager of the Qaytarma National Dance Troupe. For two years and three months I added one-act plays, fifteen-minute comedies, and short sketches to the first part of scheduled concerts. I also staged *The Reluctant Bride* (*Zoraki gelin*) by the famous dramatist Yusuf Bolat. I translated two of Ilya Finkin's plays from Russian to Crimean Tatar and put them on stage: *A Remedy for a Liar* (*Yalanjiya bir ilach*) and *I Want to Marry* (*Evlenmek istiyorum*)."[12] Thus, on a new basis, the Qaytarma ensemble of Crimean Tatars in Central Asia had to carry on the tradition of the theater school that branched off from the CTSDT in 1933. Among the graduates of that school who later became important actors and actresses was Ayshe Ditanova. Persons like her played significant roles not just on stage, for in the 1920s and early 1930s women seldom participated in the theater.

## A Celebrated Singer, Poet, and Actress

Sabriye Erejepova devoted her life to Crimean Tatar songs, music, and theater. Known as a sweet-voiced singer and actress, she lived in exile for thirty-three years and died on 18 September 1977.[13] Of all Crimean Tatars, she sang the most songs and produced the most recordings. She had a great share in the making of Crimean Tatar popular music. She also sang in other languages. Her own compositions were based on folk art. She tried to bring back the old songs for her people.

She was born in 1912 in the city of Bakhchesaray into the family of a teacher. As a child she attended the Uner Terbiye School, and Hanbekova served as her first music and folk song teacher. On graduation, the Crimean Central Radio, newly organized, accepted her as a singer. From then on she devoted her life to music. Some of her songs that became famous on recordings were "Mother-in-Law" ("Kaynana"), "I Fear Three Things in This World" ("Bu dunyada uch nesneden korkarim"), and "A Lamb Came Down from the Mountain" ("Daghdan endi bir kuzu").[14] She composed many songs, recorded many, and kept more than four hundred in her repertory. She also worked under the Crimean Central Radio music department of Aqmesjit (Simferopol') and its director and composer, Yahya Sherfedinov. Russia and surrounding countries heard her voice.[15] In 1973, Sherfedinov recalled:

It was in the last days of autumn 1932. At that time I was working in the Aqmesjit Crimean Central Radio administration as music department director. One day a fair-skinned young girl of medium height came in. She was Sabriye Erejepova....

We needed folk singers. She heard about this from the pianist Hanbekova and applied for the position. . . . After hearing her beautiful voice in the practice room, I recommended her for the job. . . . She became known during the first year she started. . . . At my suggestion she attended the music school and was very satisfied with it. . . . She added Russian traditional songs to her repertory. A reason for her creative success is that she was very reliable and never gave up on anything before she reached her goal. All these wonderful characteristics made her the beloved and famous singer among Crimean Tatars. When Uzbekistan was celebrating its fortieth anniversary as a Soviet Socialist Republic in 1964, she was chosen as the most popular singer in Uzbekistan.[16]

The composer Ilyas Bakhshish says that, from her earliest informal renditions of songs like "I Had To" ("Mejbur oldum"), audiences listened attentively and admiringly, standing and applauding before she could finish. Her songs gave pleasure and joy to Crimean Tatar and other listeners. Bakhshish collected several hundred of them in a volume published the year of her death in Central Asia.[17] Sabriya Hanim, as Crimean Tatars called her, said this about how she approached these national songs: "First, it is very important to respect the original song. To understand the real meaning of the song, one has to examine her people or the people the song belongs to, and this requires very hard work. I would always want the audience to feel what I feel and try to make them understand the meaning and beauty of the song."[18] Bakhshish commented that, when the singer was still very young, she challenged him to compose music for her song "Love to the Village" ("Köye sevgi"). He managed it successfully, and she later recorded it in Moscow in 1967.[19]

Ilyas Bakhshish (see fig. 5.2), popular Crimean Tatar composer, was born in Aqmesjit on 23 March 1913, too young to participate in the historic changes between 1914 and 1921, but late enough to take part in many subsequent events that affected the life of the nationality profoundly. After elementary school in his hometown, he received music lessons from Fazil Chergiyev, who introduced him to the world of music. At a music school in the same city he studied under a student of Rimsky-Korsakov's, Ivan Chernov. From Chernov, who understood and loved Crimean Tatar music, he learned a great deal about notation, orchestration, and instrumentation.[20] As a young composer he wrote his first music, "Working youth" ("Chalishan gench"), and other works before 1937. In that year he and Yahya Sherfedinov wrote the music for Yusuf Bolat's play *Arzi qiz*, for

Figure 5.2. Ilyas Bakhshish, composer of music for *Arzi qiz* and other stage works. From *Qïrïm* no. 1 (1 January 1994): 3.

Nasrettin Hoja's musical comedy *The Golden Cradle* (*Altin beshik*), and for many others. At the time Bakhshish served as conductor and music director for CTSDT.[21] At the end of World War II he was among the Crimean Tatars exiled from Crimea to Uzbekistan. During his exile years in the town of Farghana he worked in the Russian City Drama Theater and contributed music to the Russian plays *Chimes of the Kremlin* (*Kremil kurantlari*) and *Maria Stuart*. Before the war he composed seven pieces for symphony orchestra and wrote many others for chorus and solo voices. He became the first Crimean Tatar composer to write a suite for ballet. He notated almost a hundred Crimean Tatar folk songs.[22]

A skillful organizer, not only did Ilyas Bakhshish function as the creative director of the Crimean Tatar National Dance and Song Troupe in 1940, but in 1957, in exile, he also supervised the development of the Uzbekistan National Opera and Theater. He also organized folk dance, song, and music groups. Until returning from exile, he worked as the principal of a music school in the Chilanzar quarter of Tashkent, where he served over twenty years.[23]

## Dance

The institutions in the arts trained a number of choreographers who could introduce Crimean Tatar folklore and theater to the general public. Heading the list of such masters of dance were Hayri Emir Zade, Hüseyin Bakkal, Seitov Bilal, and others who worked as ballet and folk dance teachers. Almost all the national dances of Crimea were created by Hüseyin Bakkal. He not only invented and staged dances but schooled the best dancers. When he directed, acted, danced, and choreographed at the CTSDT, he also provided choreography for the Aqmesjit workers' cooperative's folk dance group.[24] Simultaneously, he taught at the young artists' school of the CTSDT. Bakkal had a very rich style of his own, a style he never changed. The many dances he created and staged include *Cotton Dance* (*Pamuk oyunu*) and *Party Games* (*Jiyin oyunlari*).[25] The talented Hüseyin Bakkal participated in world and national folk dance festivals in Berlin, Munich, Leipzig, and Dresden. In 1936, Soviet authorities imprisoned him as a "nationalist." When World War II began, he escaped from prison and returned to Crimea, where he was welcomed warmly. There he supervised a production of *The Golden Cradle* (*Altin beshik*), dramatized by Ibrahim Bakhshish and composed by Ilyas Bakhshish and his assistant composer, Abdullah Kavri. Among its elegant scenes were comedian Bilal Parik's "Tim Tim" dance and quick dances by beautiful young girls. This musical remained on stage for many months.[26] *Bakhchesaray Fountain* (*Bakhchesaray cheshmesi*) and other works also reached the stage between 1941 and 1943.

These works of art, plays, rich music, and beautiful costumes composed part of Crimean Tatar history. Hüseyin Bakkal said: "To make a historical play you first have to examine the country's history deeply. You have to know where an incident took place, the dances, costumes, music, and the setting at that time, or else the play will not succeed." Hüseyin Bakkal dedicated fifty years of his life to Crimean and other Turkic Muslim dances of the Soviet Union. He died in exile at the age of seventy-three, but he left behind his daughter, Remziye Bakkal, who also loved folk dances and possessed great talent for teaching and creating new dances.

Remziye Bakkal gained fame in Tajikistan as an actress and choreographer and won the Tajikistan Soviet Socialist Republic (SSR) state prize. Zülfira Asanova studied under Remziye Bakkal.[27] She became famous when still very small. By the age of ten she had won all the awards in the youth and student festivals in Moscow and international competitions. After Zülfira Asanova graduated from school she entered the Leninabad Musical Drama Theater named for A. S. Pushkin, where Remziye Bakkal also worked for twenty years. Asanova worked there long afterward. She danced Tajik, Uzbek, Crimean Tatar, and other Asian dances with great artistic mastery.²⁸ The famed poem by Aleksandr S. Pushkin "Bakhchesaray Fountain," based on a Crimean Tatar legend, was staged in the Leninabad Theater. Zülfira Asanova played the role of Zarema with great aplomb and success. She continued, when she had already become renowned, to follow her teacher's finger movements with great admiration. Asanova faithfully performed the dance "Tim Tim" that Remziye Bakkal had made famous.

Another accomplished student of Remziye Bakkal's was her own granddaughter, Elzara Asanova. She became the leading lady of the Opera and Ballet Theater in Dushanbe and a popular actress throughout Tajikistan. She tirelessly worked and raised young students, including Zebo Aminzade and Malika Qalandarova. They too gained wide recognition. Remziye Bakkal functioned as a leading choreographer of the Leninabad Theater for a long time. Her dances made up the heart of the concert celebrating the sixtieth anniversary of the November 1917 revolution. In 1980, her dance entitled *Friendship* (*Dostluq*) earned a great response in opening ceremonies for the Moscow Olympic Games. She also served as an authority on the dance ensemble Qaytarma. She complemented their routines with new steps and added six more female dancers. She also traveled to Tashkent and staged several pieces for the Qaytarma ensemble. Remziye Bakkal helped ensure the future of Crimean Tatar dance by guiding her two daughters and her son into art and music. Gülnara became an orchestra conductor for Leninabad's S. Hafiz School of Music, and Dilara worked as a music teacher in the same school.²⁹

The Bakkal generation caused Crimean Tatar national art to become widely known. Leaders of the arts following Remziye Bakkal helped propagate these dances. Through their efforts Crimean Tatar folk dances continue to live on. Many ties linked Hüseyin Bakkal's granddaughter, Elzara Asanova, to the world of the arts. Her own grandmother, Zöre Bakkal, had played piano in the CTSDT. Elzara Asanova's mother, Pakize Bakkal (Asanova), held the position of principal in the music division of the Tajikistan SSR Puppet Theater. Elzara Asanova's father, Rifat Asanov, danced and sang in the Qaytarma troupe for many years.³⁰ She once said, "When I was four or five years old, my grandfather, Hüseyin Bakkal, taught me several dances.... When I was six or seven, he used to take me by the hand to the Children's Leninabad City Concerts to participate in the festival dances. When I did well, he used to be as happy as a child. He would say that he saw his younger days revived in me."³¹ Elzara Asanova studied under her grandfather and later in the Tashkent school for choreography in the division for national dances. In 1965, she graduated from the school with honors, and the Academic Opera and Ballet Theater of Tajikistan admitted her at once. The young performer danced in a play, *Son of the Homeland* (*Vatan oglu*), by T. Osipov, in *Gypsy Girl* (*Jingene qizi*), and in *Layla and Mejnun*, a ballet by Balasanyan. She soon became a solo dancer and won a large following, dancing in the Ten-Day Festival of Tajikistan's Art and Culture in Moscow in 1967. The following year she toured with the Tajikistan Academic Opera and Ballet Theater throughout the larger cities of the Soviet Union as well as in Afghanistan. In 1976, she won the State Prize of the Soviet Union and that same year the award for leading actress in the Tajikistan SSR. In the 1970s, she also performed in Eastern Europe and Iran. She played leading roles in a number of films, such as *Shepherd Boy* (*Choban oglan*).³² The career of Elzara Asanova has demonstrated that women can make great contributions to the public life of the Crimean Tatar community through their art.

Men also communicated the national aesthetic through creative performance and composition. Modern Crimean Tatar arts began to develop actively late in the second decade of the twentieth century. Performers adorned holidays and weddings with folk dances and music. Earlier, the fathers and grandfathers had celebrated good harvests and other occasions, and these traditions still continue. Crimean Tatar folk dances express a distinct color, artistic form, appearance, life, and meaning. Among the more prominent masters, the late Hayri Emir Zade (Karaosman) created the shepherd dance and handkerchief dance and gave them artistic identity. In these dances, heroes portrayed people's hostility toward external enemies.³³ The shepherd dance is thought to portray the Crimean Tatars' situation within the Russian Empire.

After studying about a year in Petersburg, Hayri Emir Zade went to Odessa's Trade School. After graduating from it in 1913, he started to work in Ukrayina, where he taught the Turkic language. In addition, in 1914 he worked as a driver in order to send his sisters through school. One sister became a dentist, and the other graduated from Moscow University. During vacations, Hayri Emir Zade returned to visit Crimea, where he would embellish his performance of the shepherd dance and participate with the Qaytarma ensemble of Crimea. His successes in these folk dances later on brought him into the newly founded official CTSDT. In it, he first performed *Tahir and Zuhra*, *Leyla and Mejnun*, and additional plays.

Hayri Emir Zade was brave, handsome, a gentleman. By his acting in dances and plays he won people's affection and respect. In imitating a shepherd who had lost his flock of sheep he was so effective on stage that the audience, responding to the presentation, also acted as if they participated on stage themselves.[34] People used to describe Hayri Emir Zade as a strange, special actor; while on stage half of his face laughed while the other half cried. He served as a member of the CTSDT, and as a film actor he worked in Mosfil'm, Ukrainfilm, and Azerbayjan studios many times in leading roles. His first role came in a film called *Halim*, depicting the daily life of Crimean Tatars. He left Crimean Tatar theater after 1926 and worked in Ukrainfilm studios. In that connection, Ümer Ipchi always blamed himself for encouraging Emir Zade to take roles that brought the actor great popularity outside Crimea and ultimately drew him away from home.

Hayri Emir Zade came into the world in 1898 at a village named Dereköy, near Yalta. His father owned the village store. His two sisters, Ayshe and Maryam, and he were orphaned in 1913.[35] In 1922–23, both sisters married Crimean Tatars and moved to Central Asia, settling in Samarkand. By then, Hayri himself had mastered the famed Crimean Tatar shepherd dance. Later on, he staged this dance all over Crimea and gained fame from it. Without doubt he gave his people recognition with this dance and in addition drew the approval of government officials. His closest friend and an elder of the community, Jelil Uygun, observed: "We studied together in Dereköy public school and in Aqmesjit, Crimea's capital city, for three years. On graduating, he left for Petersburg, where he wanted to become a painter. There, he met and found friends among Crimean Tatar students and learned the shepherd dance from a young man named Mustafa, of the Argin family."[36] As has been noticed, performances of this work aroused people's feelings of nationality because it conveyed a story of bravery and heroism.

Increasingly in 1927–28, Crimean Tatar nationalists came under great pressure. Veli Ibrahimov, president of the Crimean Autonomous Soviet Socialist Republic, was hanged, and Soviet authorities deported members of the Association for National Salvation. Hayri Emir Zade had many close friends among the deported nationalists. He too was forced to leave

Crimea. He relocated in Baku, Azerbaijan. While there, he acted the leading role in the film *26 Baku Commissars*. He died in 1959 without ever being able to return to his homeland. Nevertheless, he and all the other prominent performers and creative artists of those formative years provided an irreplaceable cultural legacy for the Crimean Tatar nationality. That endowment has become ever more important to succeeding generations now living inside and outside Crimea. Their experience and the instruction that successors have received from them have shown that the most lasting inheritance that one age may pass on to another probably remains the intangible sense of identity that comes from the subtle nuances conveyed in artistic expression of the values and will of a nationality's inner life. This group identity can be carried by everyone, rich and poor, powerful and weak, in the community. Outsiders to the group can scarcely ever reproduce it, distort it, or efface it entirely.

## Notes

1. Riza Gülüm, "Kirimtatarlarinin milli oyunlari, sharki ve muzikleri," *Kirim*, no. 114 (November 1977): 13; Riza Fazil, *Maneler ve chinlar: Halk agizinin yaratijilighinin lirika haznesi* (Tashkent: Gafur Gulyam adina Edebiyat ve Sanat Neshriyati, 1975), 10.
2. "Edebiyat haznemiz, Kedaylar," *Kirim*, no. 133 (April–November 1982): 11, 13.
3. Riza Gülüm, "Buyük Alim, Osman Akchokrakli," *Kirim*, no. 138 (October 1983): 15.
4. Fazil, *Maneler ve chinlar*, 8.
5. A. Osmanov, "Maneler," *Lenin bayraghi*, 15 July 1986, 3; Isa Ablakimov, "Chinlar," Shevket Dushayev, "Eski devir hakkinda Chinlar," and Seitnafe Murtazayev, "Beyitler," all in *Lenin bayraghi*, 29 November 1975, 3; A. Mejitov, "Osmanov Chinlari," O. Abselamov, "Choban Chinlari," and A. Kravchenko, "Kartanamnin Chinlari," all in *Lenin bayraghi*, 15 July 1986, 3.
6. Yusuf Bolat, "Umer Ipchi, hikaye ustasi: Edebiyat konsultatsiya yerine," *Lenin bayraghi*, March 1977, 3.
7. Gani Murad, "Umer Ipchi, teatr erbabi: Aktornin hatira defterinden," *Lenin bayraghi*, 27 March 1975, 3.
8. "Kirim Devlet Tatar Tiyatrosu," *Azat Kirim*, no. 11 (February–March–April 1972): 3; Riza Gülüm, "Krim Devlet Tatar Tiyatrosu," *Azat Kirim*, no. 13 (September–October–November 1972): 4; Murad, "Umer Ipchi, teatr erbabi," 3.

9. Mustejib Ülküsal, *Kirim Turk-Tatarlari* (Istanbul: Baha Matbaasi, 1980), 235, 303; Murad, "Umer Ipchi, teatr erbabi," 3.
10. A. Dermenchi, A. Balich, D. Bekirov, and Ilyas Tarhan, *Edebiyat khrestomatiyasi* (Tashkent: Oqituwchi Näshriyati, 1971), 213; Gülüm, "Kirimtatarlarinin milli oyunlari, sharki ve muzikleri," 15; Murad, "Umer Ipchi, teatr erbabi," 3.
11. Murad, "Umer Ipchi, teatr erbabi," 3.
12. Ibid., 3.
13. "Bizim edebiyat: Sabiriye Erejepova," *Kirim*, no. 114 (November 1977): 20–21.
14. "Halkimiznin sevimli yirjisi," *Lenin bayraghi*, 24 April 1973.
15. "Bizim edebiyat: Sabiriye Erejepova," 21.
16. Yahya Sherfedinov, "Onu ilk ben dinledim," *Lenin bayraghi*, 24 April 1973, 3.
17. Ilyas Bakhshish, "Khalq sharqilari onun omürü," *Lenin bayraghi*, 24 April 1973, 3.
18. Ülküsal, *Kirim Türk-Tatarlari*, 272–73.
19. S. Abkelamova, "Sanada kechken omür," *Lenin bayraghi*, 29 March 1986, 3.
20. S. Abkelamova, "Kompozitor hakkinda besh interviyu," *Lenin bayraghi*, 26 March 1983, 3.
21. "Altin beshik tiyatro," *Azat Kirim*, no. 55 (9 July 1943): 4.
22. Abkelamova, "Kompozitor," 3; Gülüm, "Kirimtatarlarinin milli oyunlari, sharki ve muzikleri," 15.
23. Ilyas Bakhshish and Edem Nalbantin, comps., *Sabahnin seher vaktinda* (Tashkent: Gafur Gulam adina Edebiyat ve Sanaat Neshriyati, 1977). This collection gives 367 songs and popular ballads.
24. Gülüm, "Kirimtatarlarinin milli oyunlari, sharki ve muzikleri," 15.
25. Enver Arifov, "Halk oyunlarinin ustasi," *Lenin bayraghi*, 5 October 1977, 4.
26. Riza Gülüm, "Meshhur korograf, Hüseyin Bakkal," *Kirim*, no. 127 (March–April 1981): 2.
27. Sh. Ramazanov, "Remziye Bakkal ve onum talebeleri," *Lenin bayraghi*, 9 April 1983, 4.
28. A. Kozli, "Unvan hayirli olsun Zülfira," *Lenin bayraghi*, February 1975, 4.
29. Ramazanov, "Remziye Bakkal," 4.
30. Ablamit Umerov, "Elzaranin yenishleri," *Lenin bayraghi*, 1 January 1979, 4.
31. A. Veliyev, "Elzara oynaganda," *Lenin bayraghi*, 10 January 1985, 4.
32. Umerov, "Elzaranin yenishleri," 4.
33. Enver Arifov, "Khalq oyunlarinin ustasi," *Lenin bayraghi*, 5 October 1977, 4.
34. Murad, "Umer Ipchi, teatr erbabi," 3.
35. Haydar Sarachoghlu, "Hatiralarimdan bir parcha," *Kirim*, no. 133 (April–November 1982): 18–19.
36. Jelil Uygun, "Kirim Türklerinin halk artisti, Hayri Emir Zade: Unutulmaz portreler," *Kirim*, no. 12 (June 1961): 191–93.

# 6

## *Structures:*

## *The Importance of Family—A Personal Memoir*

MÜBEYYIN BATU ALTAN

Without their autonomous republic, and without their homeland, the Crimean Tatar people would have been deprived of a cultural environment in which they could enjoy, as nearly all other ethnic groups in the Soviet Union did enjoy, the cultural heritage of their nationality. What happened to Crimean Tatars in this respect was tersely expressed in 1966 in one of many appeals by their representatives to the Communist Party of the Soviet Union: "Everything was done in order (1) to destroy the statehood of Crimean Tatars; (2) to obliterate the culture, art, and literature of Crimean Tatars; (3) to destroy the history of these people; (4) to finish their language; (5) to terminate their customs; (6) to do everything possible to make every Crimean Tatar feel ashamed to call himself a Crimean Tatar; (7) to prove to every representative of this nation that neither he nor his children, nor his descendants still unborn has any future."[1] Notwithstanding the enormous pressure from the political authorities of the Soviet Union to keep this nationality totally disorganized, Crimean Tatars most actively and determinedly stood up against the Soviet government. They demanded that officials restore their nationality and human rights as well as their autonomous republic status.

Where did Crimean Tatars get this stubborn will to survive? What makes this small ethnic group not only live on but also continue to fight for its rights against foreign politicians? One of the foremost reasons for that firm will to prevail appears to lie in the might of the Crimean Tatar family. It is a source of strength and faith. A conversation demonstrating some of this power took place in 1969 between Dina Kaminskaia, a leading attorney defending Soviet dissidents Mustafa Jemiloglu and Ilya Gabay, and a Crimean Tatar pupil: "'What do you want to be when you grow up,' I asked the ten-year-old. 'I'll be a teacher in a Tatar school,' he said. 'When I'm grown up, we'll be living at home.'"[2] That ten-year-old could not have

Figure 6.1. Crimean Tatar family in a newly self-built house in Crimea. Photo courtesy of Mme Safinar Jemiloglu, wife of Mustafa Jemiloglu, president, Crimean Tatar Mejlis.

gotten this idea of becoming a Crimean Tatar schoolteacher from his own instructors. Nor could he have learned it from his schoolmates, and he obviously could not find it in his Soviet textbooks. The source of the idea had to be his family.

The Soviet system publicly denied thousands of Crimean Tatar youngsters a knowledge of their nationality's history, language, and culture, yet privately these children became quite aware of their nationality identity. In the absence of structured institutions to inculcate their group history, civilization, and tongue, it became an obligation of the family to fulfill this duty. Crimean Tatars born since the early 1940s grew up listening to stories about their families and their ancestral homeland. They heard this from parents and grandparents, uncles, aunts, and other close relatives. More than in most modern nationalities, either the immediate or the extended family exclusively molded the future generation of Crimean Tatars.

The family gave them understanding of and hope for the future, a sense of direction and goals, and a sense of identity. It has provided the backbone for the Crimean Tatar nationality's durability. The group also realizes that the family was and still is its last stronghold against complete Russification. Crimean Tatars therefore pay special attention to the family. Knowing its importance, they were and are ready to preserve it at whatever cost, even at great personal sacrifice.

After the promulgation of a decree on 5 September 1967 that exonerated Crimean Tatars of Stalin's wartime libel, hundreds of families attempted to return to the Crimea. Some of these families managed to settle there legally, and others are still trying hard to live on the Crimean peninsula (see fig. 6.1). The Crimean Tatar families who returned to Crimea were once again subjected to humiliation and mistreatment by the authorities. Thugs attacked women and children and evicted them from their ancestral lands, but it did not stop people from returning. They continue to endure great hardship in order to be closer to their families, relatives, and friends. The following extract from a letter relates an appeal written by one of those who returned to Crimea:

I, Emine Sherfe Ametova, was born in 1936. I was five years old when the war broke out. My father and brother were called up for military service and were killed in action [against the Germans] in 1943. My mother, my two brothers, and I were deported to Central Asia like all Crimean Tatars. Now, I have my own family—three children and my old mother, age 81. . . . My oldest brother, Jemil Shalverov, moved legally to Crimea. . . . Left alone with my family, I decided to move nearer to my brother, and in July 1977 I went to Crimea.[3]

Documents show that hundreds of Tatar families then lived in Crimea, but that was still a tiny fraction of the nationality. In two Crimean *raions*, Islam-Terek and Qarasuvbazar (Kirov and Belogorsk), alone in the early 1980s lived 721 families, including 3,050 people.[4] From these figures it is evident that family size in Crimea today averages between four and five members. The data do not specify how many of these 721 families have some kinship to one another. But, if the letters cited in this article give an indication, it would not be surprising to find that a substantial percentage of those families are in fact related. When the opportunity arises to study the location of Crimean Tatar families closely, the findings reveal a pattern of kinship wherever they have settled.

After the mass deportation of the spring of 1944, Crimean Tatars had to settle in various parts of Central Asia, mainly in Uzbekistan. Even in that extreme case, related families somehow contrived to congregate in the same cities and towns or in areas close by. I was able to collect some original correspondence exchanged between Crimean Tatars in the Soviet Union and their relatives in the United States. In most of these letters, the writers specifically mentioned that the majority of the related families settled in close proximity to each other and often in the same town. One of the letters makes that point clear: "All of us are in the same village except uncle Ali's two sons and uncle Osman's children. The rest of us are all in the same area" ("bizler hepimiz bir koydeyik, yaliniz Ali emjemin eki oglu ve Osman emjemin balalari bizden ayri. Kalganimiz hepimiz bir yer-deyik").[5] I have read numerous letters like this from different families that strongly emphasize the same thing, that most relatives do live in the same area. This is true whether the settlement region is Uzbekistan, Ukrayina, the North Caucasus, or elsewhere in the former Soviet Union.

Furthermore, there are refugees who have left the former Soviet Union who have maintained continuous contact with their families who remained behind. A small group of Crimean Tatars that was able to leave Crimea just before the mass deportation to Central Asia resettled in the United Nations refugee camps in West Germany, where they lived until 1950. Their desperate search for families and kin gives another instance of how important the family became for Crimean Tatars. I grew up in those refugee camps listening to stories about my relatives and my elders' homeland just like Crimean Tatar youngsters in the Soviet Union did. I also grew up longing for the rest of my family and for Crimea. Administrators in Germany gave my family a chance to immigrate to the United States directly from the refugee camps in Germany. Economically, it offered a good opportunity for the family, but we had to consider everyone in it, including my paternal grandmother, two uncles, and two aunts. My grandmother, now the family leader, decided that it served the interests of the entire family best to resettle in Turkiye. There, she determined, it would be much easier to continue our lives as Crimean Tatars and Muslims. Once that decision was made, there was no more discussion, and the entire family resettled in Turkiye, as our elder wished. Yet another sign is that refugees in Turkiye received land and financial aid from the Turkish government for resettlement. My oldest uncle, whom it assigned to a faraway province, declined government assistance rather than separate from the remainder of the family. He and his family came to live with us. This meant that ten people lived in a small, one-bedroom apartment. We were uncomfortable, but extremely happy, for the family links had not been broken.

In 1957, a family friend got a letter from his brother in Uzbekistan. This became one of the first communications the refugees had received from families they had left behind. The news spread very fast, and shortly the entire refugee community began to gather at our friend's house to get news from their families in Central Asia. From these channels my family found out where our relatives lived and who had survived the deportation. Suddenly hope renewed for reunification. The mere idea of this made our life happier. It showed that, although thousands of miles separated us, the emotional ties remained.

Not until 1981 did we meet one of our cousins from the Soviet Union, who came to visit us for the first time in thirty-eight years. We spent a month together talking about our families. We never felt like strangers in spite of such an extended separation. We felt as if we had grown up together. In a way, we had. Our cousin grew up listening to stories about us, and we matured to adulthood in the West hearing anecdotes about her and her parents, brothers, and sisters. I have personally witnessed reunions of numbers of families who also experienced and expressed the same feelings of family unity, regardless of time and distance between members. I know of a father's anguished search for his family, a wife and two young daughters left behind. One of those daughters, only four years old when he left, arrived in New York thirty-seven years later. I saw this heartfelt reunion and listened to the recounting of their continuous search for each other. I also observed the reunion of two distant cousins reunited by sheer luck. Their only clue to each other's whereabouts lay in an old address that the cousin from the Soviet Union had been carrying around for forty years. When the cousin from the Soviet Union came to visit her son, she decided to make one more attempt to locate her relatives and finally found the long-lost cousins.

In all these reunions that I personally witnessed, people expressed the same strong theme over and over: "I can't believe we have been away so long. It seems as if we have never been separated." The short summary of a letter I received from a Crimean Tatar conveys the same spirit. It also shows that Crimean Tatars were held in exile longer than most other ethnic groups in the Soviet Union, and for that reason family members around the world felt compelled to continue the endless search for kinsmen:

We are an old family of Aqmesjit. . . . I was born in Cairo. . . . I am tremendously interested . . . in everything that concerns my Crimean country, my Crimean countrymen, my Tatar brothers and brothers in Islam. I am deeply proud of our history. . . . I was quite young when my father died. I only knew when he died that I had one uncle living in Istanbul and one aunt, a doctor living in Iran. . . . When I started to grow older I began feeling my own deep roots. . . . During that time . . . I had the opportunity of meeting Professor Yusuf Velisah Ural-giray, who had been one of my father's friends. I also started to search for my uncle's Istanbul address, but did not succeed [in finding it] in Cairo. I tried again in Italy and finally succeeded. So, I went to Turkiye and for the first time met my uncle and learned about another uncle and relatives.[6]

The Soviet authorities attempted to isolate the subject of Crimean Tatars from academic researchers and others. Those ideologists deliberately omitted the name *Crimean Tatar* from the list of Soviet nationalities. But they failed to neutralize the cohesiveness of the Crimean Tatar community. That is because the Crimean Tatar family showed its strength in responding to the threat against the entire ethnic group. As a whole, Crimean Tatars have managed to sustain the nationality's unity tenaciously because of the great attachment to the family and relatives. This has enabled us not only to survive but to form one of the most effective human and nationality rights movements. A French scholar has noted that in it "a new generation has grown up and stands in the forefront of the struggle for return to Crimea."[7]

An important part of that strength derives from the tight family attachment that encourages younger Crimean Tatars to marry within the Crimean Tatar community. They were known as one of the most endogamous people in the Soviet Union. According to unofficial statistics, the rate of endogamy is 90–91 percent, which means that only 9 or 10 percent of Crimean Tatars marry outside the group. Such a rate compares favorably with the percentage for nationalities of Central Asia.[8] That is remarkable, considering their dispersion among other Turkic, nominally Muslim nationalities as well as among segments of Russian and other Slavic ethnic groups. So long as Crimean Tatars can sustain their tight family unity as well as they have so far, the Crimean Tatar nationality will survive. That solidarity produces strong personalities. One who is now the heart and soul of the Crimean Tatar nationality's drive for recognition and repatriation, Mustafa Jemiloglu, was sent an invitation to come to the United

States to visit some relatives (although his immediate family then lived in Central Asia). In one of his letters he responded to that offer: "Your invitation has not yet arrived. Even when I receive it, it is doubtful that they will allow me to go and visit you. If they do permit me to go, after what they have done to our old man [General Petr Grigorenko], it may be quite dangerous to accept your invitation. I have no desire to leave this country permanently. After all, I have my people, my parents, relatives and friends here."[9]

From this, Jemiloglu makes clear that he, who spent much of his most productive life in Soviet prisons, would rather sacrifice his personal freedom than leave his family, relatives, and friends permanently behind. That communication perfectly conveys the sense of belonging that characterizes the Crimean Tatar family and, by extension, the nationality itself. In all this, a revival of a special kind of clan life appears to emerge as a response to the group's need and determination. A new and closer kinship returns to the center of group existence under such circumstances. Not only does it sustain the group; all testify that it seems to bring joy and satisfaction to its members.

Finally, I wish to attach to this memoir a few translations I made of selected letters from Mustafa Jemiloglu and other Crimean Tatars in the Soviet Union that expressed these attitudes and values concerning family more fully and personally.

## Personal Letters

*Mustafa Jemiloglu to his cousin Fikret Yurter,*
*New York, 13 March 1978 (translated from the Crimean Tatar language)*

*Greetings, dear Fikret Aga:* We received your letter dated 18 February [1978] on 6 March. Asan [M.J.'s brother] had begun to write to you, but he had to go away on a work-related assignment. I was going to write to you after our telephone conversation; then I said to myself "what is the sense of writing a letter right after a telephone conversation"; I did not like to supply the archives of "the organization" with more written documents. Nevertheless, I decided to write one more time.

We received your package; many thanks, it was a great help to us.

How is your health and job? How are my sister-in-law Hatije, the children, and your father-in-law? Please extend my greetings and sincere wishes to all of them and to my compatriots there. My parents in all their letters send special greetings to you. Their health nowadays is fair.

A short while ago our famous poet, Eshref Shemizade, passed away in Moscow. In his will, he wished to be buried in his homeland, Crimea. There were some friends from here who attended his funeral. After they returned here they told me that they had seen my parents and informed me about my parents' health.

I had close contact with Eshref Shemizade. When I received a telegram from his son, Vildan, about his father's death, I wrote to the local militia for permission to attend this funeral. I was turned down. Then, I asked them for permission to visit my parents. They did not give me permission for that, either. On my application they wrote [in Russian]: "Under conditions of open administrative surveillance, leaving the limits of the city of Tashkent prior to the completion of the specified period is not permitted. 20 March 1978. [signature]." They are telling me now that they will send me to a factory in Tashkent, where they will give me a job and a place to stay in a dormitory. If I don't agree to their offer, I am told that they have the right to keep me in prison. My health is not good. I cannot do the work they offered me because I suffer from a severe stomach ulcer. And that is my situation now. They may keep me in prison. I will not be able to see my father, my sisters Dilara and Gilizar in Crimea, and many of my friends. . . .

One of these days I shall send you some Crimean Tatar recordings, and after I send you the recordings I'll write to you again. If you get a chance, send me some Turkish recordings.

If you write to our relatives in Turkey, send them my greetings. It is my childhood dream to visit Turkey someday because for me it is a continuation of our homeland.   *Mustafa*

*Mustafa Jemiloglu to his niece Ayser Yurter,*
*New York, 29 November 1980 (in English)*

*Dear Ayser:* I was very happy to receive your photo enclosed in your father's letter. You have become a very nice and charming girl I see. Although it is rather late already, however, I congratulate you on your birthday—it became known to me only during our conversation with your father by phone some days ago. I wish you, dear Ayser, strong health and great happiness in your life.

I am sending you our photo too. Next to me on this photo you see my wife (and your aunt) Safinar. She sends to you her greetings and best wishes as well. Your father asked me by phone about her age and birthplace, but because of nasty audibility I could not answer him. Please, tell him these "personal particulars": She was born on 23 June 1948 in town Yangiyul (Uzbekistan), her parents were born in Bakhchesaray, by speciality she is a teacher of German in elementary schools. Her son (and now my son as well, because his own father died three years ago from cancer) Eldar Ebubekirov was born on 31 May 1972 (?) in Yangiyul, where he lives now with his grandparents.

How about your correspondence with Safiye? She is very ill now and was placed in the hospital a few days ago. By the way, she wanted very much to have some fairy tales or another book for children in Turkish, but I could not get any. If it is possible, please, send her some books, she would be very glad.

I do not know whether you can write and read in our native language enough well, so I decided to write you in English, although, as you see, my English is very far from to be perfect. But, of course, we would be happy to receive letters from you in our own language.

Best regards to your parents and to your brother Abdulla from me and aunt Safinar.

We congratulate your family on the coming New Year.

*Your uncle, Mustafa 'Abdaljamil* [*surname written in Arabic script*]
*P.S. I'll answer your father's letter* [*one of*] *these days.*

*Mustafa Jemiloglu to Fikret Yurter,*
*New York, 24 October 1981* (*translated from the Crimean Tatar language*)

*Esteemed Fikret Aga:* We have received your congratulatory telegram on [the birth of] our child; thanks very much. But, there has been no letter from you for a long time. Are your health and work all right? How are your garden plantings? The last time I wrote was to little Ayser on 18 March. News that it was received, that is, "notification" [*uvedomleniia*] came back, but no reply arrived.

Our health and situation, thank Allah, are not so bad. Our son is already seventy-one days old. I am sending you his pictures; they were taken when he was twenty-six and fifty days old. His health is all right, but of course there are some days when he does not feel so good. I work as before in the oxygen plant. Safinar is at home with our son day after day. We constantly get letters from our relatives and friends. Our parents send you their warm greetings. In the middle of September they went to Uzbekistan. They will stay there for a month or two. Reshat [Jemilev] aga sends his greetings to you in all his letters, but I have not heard from him for quite a while. From what I heard, he is in the same situation that I was in the summer of [19]75.

Say hello to all our relatives, countrymen, the elders [the Grigorenkos], and to friends from us. We await your letter. Keep well.

*Mustafa 'Abduljemil [surname written in Arabic script]*

*A Crimean Tatar in the Soviet Union to relatives in the West, 19 July 1966 (translated from the Crimean Tatar language)*

*Greetings my dear relatives, brother-in-law, sister, and grandchildren.* Warm and longing greetings first of all from me and my family, from my father and mother, from your mother and brother and his family, to all of you and to Ismail Aga.

Dear relatives, I have received your last letter. I also received the family picture that you sent. It made me extremely happy, may Allah make you happy as well. I went to your mother right away, read the letter, and showed her the picture and told her: "I am not going to give you this picture, this one I'll keep for myself, no hard feelings, please." She agreed, and I kept the picture. I had given her all the other pictures you have sent us previously. I asked your mother, "You, too, should have your picture taken so we could send them your picture." She agreed to have her picture taken.

If you ask any news from us, we are all well nowdays. We have our own homes with spacious gardens. Our lives and health are very good. My father's family consisted of three boys and two girls. The oldest, uncle Ali, died in 1934. His two sons and one daughter are alive. Next was our uncle Osman, who died in 1947. His one son and three daughters are alive. Then comes my father, Ibrahim, whose four daughters and one son (myself, Muhammad) are all alive. My father (eighty-three years old) and mother (sixty-eight years old) are still alive and well. My sister S . . . has three sons and two daughters. . . . Your mother is the youngest of the family. We are all in touch with each other. We all live in the same village. Only Uncle Ali's two sons and Uncle Osman's children live away from us. The rest of us are all in the same area.

In conclusion I wish you all great health and success in your work and am waiting impatiently for your letter. I hope you can read my writing. Please forgive me for writing this way. [*Signature withheld*]

## Notes

1. "Documents of the Crimean Tatar Movement (1966–1973)," *Chronicle of Current Events*, nos. 28–31 (1975): 141–42.
2. Dina Kaminskaia, *Final Judgment—My Life as a Soviet Attorney* (New York: Simon & Schuster, 1982), 331.
3. Emine Sherfe Ametova, samizdat documents received by the Crimea Foundation (New York, 1979).
4. *Materialy samizdata*, RFE-RL, vypusk no. 18/84, 8 June 1984, *Arkhiv samizdata* no. 5224, 1:3, trans. Central Asia Center, Columbia University, 1986. See chap. 16 below.
5. Rashit Memedov, private correspondence in the archives of the *Crimean Review*, Boston, 1986.
6. A. Yakup, private correspondence in the archives of the *Crimean Review*, Boston, 1986.
7. Hélène Carrère d'Encausse, *Decline of an Empire: The Soviet Socialist Republics in Revolt*, trans. Martin Sokolinsky and Henry A. LaFarge (New York: Newsweek Books, 1979), 198.
8. Wesley Andrew Fisher, *The Soviet Marriage Market: Mate-Selection in Russia and the USSR* (New York: Praeger, 1980), 228, 230, 236, 244.
9. Mustafa Jemiloglu, private correspondence dated 13 March 1978, in the archives of the Crimea Foundation, New York.

# 7

## *Documents about Forming a Modern Identity*

Document 1

Ismail Gasprinskii, *Russko-vostochnoe soglashenie: Mysli, zametki i pozhelaniia* (Russian-Oriental Relations: Thoughts, Notes, and Desires) (Bakhchesaray: Tipo-Litografiia Gazety "Perevodchika," 1896). Translated from the Russian by Edward J. Lazzerini.

*Preface*

In 1881 I published a pamphlet entitled *Russian Islam* in which I discussed measures for the education of Russia's Muslims and their most intimate possible rapprochement [*sblizhenie*] with the Russians. Among other remarks I stated that "the Russian takes up easily and gets along splendidly with other nationalities, charming them by the simplicity, responsiveness, and humanity natural to the Russian character. This explains why the Muslims do not feel as strangers in Russia and do not shun personal contact and rapprochement with the Russian people."

These words were written neither lightly nor for effect. Having grown up in Russia, and having lived in the West and the Orient from 1871 to 1875, I have shaped the aforementioned view from personal observations and impressions. Since that time fifteen years have passed, yet my opinion has grown all the firmer despite certain voices—emanating from people with narrow or partisan views on Russian-Muslim relations and on Islam in general—that one comes across in the press. As in everything, however, life compensates for reservations and rejects errors no matter where committed.

In that same pamphlet I urged the small number of educated Russian Muslims to work to enlighten the Muslim masses by expanding the curriculum of the religious schools, publishing in the vernacular [*rodnoi iazyk*], and popularizing Russian schools and the sciences.

While exhorting others I could not sit with my own arms folded. In 1883, on a weekly basis, I began publishing a [bilingual] Russo-Tatar newspaper, *Interpreter* [*Perevodchik/Terjüman*]. Although my publication was earmarked for the Muslims of Russia and was adapted to their comprehension and thinking, its dissemination abroad in other Muslim lands led me to study both the economic and political situations there as well as the peculiarities of their relations with Russia.

At this point I propose to discuss briefly my views on these relations. I recognize, of course, that I could easily err while treating complex international questions, that I am a dilettante in matters political, and that I am little more than a publicist for whom the view from beautiful Bakhchesaray may distort reality. Nevertheless, I shall write what I think with conviction but without any pretension.

By offering my opinions I hope only to have them discussed and weighed by my Russian and Oriental readers.[1]

I

Were we to cast our eyes over a map of the Eastern Hemisphere, we would see that [several] Muslim countries and Russia share a long common border and certain seas like the Caspian and the Black. The Russo-Muslim world—if such an expression may be permitted me—stretches, in the one direction, from the Arctic Ocean to the depths of equatorial Africa and, in the other direction, from the Baltic and Adriatic to the great China wall and the Indian Ocean. To the east of Russia and the Muslim lands throng some five to six hundred million people within the Mongol-pagan world, and to the west seethes and churns a vigorous Europe with two hundred and fifty million inhabitants. Thus situated between the Europeans and Mongols, the Russo-Muslim world finds itself in the center of the hemisphere, at the crossroads of all commercial, cultural, political, and military routes and relations.

Both these neighboring worlds—the European and the Mongol—are overpopulated, and their excess forces them to seek the less crowded territory that is settled precisely by the Russians and Muslims. Thanks to the advantage of maritime transportation, the Japanese and Chinese have already flooded the Pacific Ocean and Southeast Asia with their surplus population. The United States struggles against this influx with restrictive measures. As soon as steam-driven transportation reduces overland distances within the Chinese Empire, we can expect that Chinese emigration and then political views will turn of necessity westward, threatening the Russo-Muslim world. That China was defeated not long ago by little

Japan ought not reassure us; rather, the rapid development of Japanese military power shows that the same could be repeated with China. Thirty years ago no one could have imagined Japan as presently constituted. And it, like China, was considered as closed off as a sepulcher and distinguished by deathlike immobility, amusing customs, and a ridiculous army.

From the west, Europe applies pressure to the Russo-Muslim world. For now the pressure points are few—German colonies dispersed throughout the Russian south and extending already into the territory of Turkiye, including Palestine—but they hint at a not-very-distant future when such movement by necessity will be directed at "land more or less spacious." The political aspirations of the West seem perfectly clear. The scorn for a savage and schismatic Muscovy prior to Peter I as well as the struggle with Russia during the last two centuries are nothing other than the consequence of Europe's inevitable expansion eastward. This tendency, sometimes conscious, sometimes instinctive, explains European politics beginning with Charles XII's conflict with Peter the Great and ending with the recent disorders in Armenia so exaggerated by the English. Are not the occupation of Polish territory by the Germans, the seizure of Algeria and Tunis by the French, Bosnia and Herzegovina by the Austrians, Cyprus and Egypt by the English, and the shores of Abyssinia by the Italians tangible evidence of this movement? And this is not all. Having encircled the East, Europe, represented by the English, has already contested Russian interests in South Asia, in Afghanistan, and on the Pamir plateau.

Acting in this manner vis-à-vis both Russia and the Muslims, Europeans, in each instance, extract profit and advance. Thus, they supported and then pressured Turkiye during the reign of Catherine the Great. They wanted to divide Turkiye up with Russia in the days of Napoleon 1, and worked together with her for the liberation of Greece, but then protested the Treaty of Unkiar-Skelessi between Russia and Turkiye. Subsequently they incited the Porte to war and together besieged Sevastopol'. Finally, after venomously applauding the recent war of liberation, they met in Berlin and turned upside down the results of that difficult and costly conflict. Having ceded to Russia one fortress and one port—Kars and Batum—they took for themselves nearly a third of the territory remaining to Turkiye.

If we examine with what callousness Europe oppresses the entire Orient economically and with what brutality it acts in every situation over a pence, a centime, or a pfennig, then it becomes obvious that the East can expect nothing good from the West.

In my opinion, neither Western Europe nor the Mongol-pagan East can or will entertain positive sentiments toward the peoples who inhabit the central regions of the Eastern Hemisphere. Advancing one *arshin* or a hundredth of a mile, both must by necessity expand ethnographically, economically, and politically to the central, less populated Muslim and Russian lands.

II

If the future of the Mongol-pagan world appears obscure and uncertain, the tasks and aspirations of a vital, civilized West are delineated. To sow distrust and enmity toward Russia among Muslims, to present Russia as a destructive and implacable enemy of Islam and Western culture—these are the frank calculations of the Europeans. Adroitly and systematically (here I beg the forgiveness of Russian and Oriental diplomats) they exploit misunderstandings in the relations between Muslims and Russians, misunderstandings fatal [to both] but remarkably beneficial to the Europeans. To plunder economically the entire Orient, while maintaining the appearance of friendship, and to weaken Russia by periodic wars with Muslims equipped and armed by Western friends—such is the policy that the West never sheds, for even those small nations liberated by Russia and related to her, with the exception of the glorious Montenegro, turn their hands to the West, even though the powerful and fraternal help of Russia might be indispensable. This observation, to be sure, does not concern the simple folk, the masses, who, we know, never play a leading role [in public affairs].

Muslims who receive an education in the West or who hear lectures by professors invited from there or who study the science in translation from Western books and newspapers gain, of course, an extremely vague and incorrect idea about Russia and the Russian people. Arabs, Turks, Persians, let alone Indian Muslims, knowing Russia from English, German, and French sources, and not having a single independent work on their great northern neighbor, always yield easily to their Western friends and see the world willingly through the latter's spectacles. From readers of *Interpreter* in Egypt, Turkiye, and Persia we frequently receive questions about how long *medreses* [Muslim religious schools] have been opened in

Russia, how long Muslims have been permitted in civil service and in the universities, when is the call to prayer from the minarets allowed, and so forth. Obviously, these gentlemen are surprised that Muslims live in Russia as they do in any Muslim country. Unfortunately, [one must admit,] for us in Russia the study of and acquaintance with the Orient has not achieved its proper development either. In spite of the fact that more than twelve million Muslims inhabit the territory of Russia, there are few among us who are familiar with the teachings of the Qur'ân and with the way of life and situation of the Muslim people. It is impossible to speak of "study and knowledge" when the Qur'ân is viewed as a pernicious book in which, nevertheless, some two hundred million people believe to the point of abnegation; it is impossible to call "understanding" the opinion that Muslims are incorrigible fanatics and the enemies of all knowledge and civilization [*obshchezhitie*].

To our extreme regret literary work and pamphleteering about the Orient fails to dispel such absurd ideas. We have only the instinct and happy turn of the Russian character to thank for the amicable and trusting relations that continued to be strengthened and improved. It would be desirable if Russians and Muslims came to know one another better and directly, without either preconceived [ideas] or prejudice. Thus, they might see that, *except for religion, everything else* draws them together and binds them fast. Religion, the domain of God, should not impede the good in secular life and activity; and it does not, for the Qur'ân has not been an obstacle to an alliance between the Turks, the English, and the French, and the Gospels have not prevented Emperor Nicholas [I] Pavlovich from concluding a treaty of friendship with Turkiye. In private life and actions we quite often see excellent relations between Christians and Muslims. These need to be developed, expanded, and consolidated while by no means infringing the religious sentiments so dear to each of us.

For Muslim peoples, Russian culture is closer to their own than is the West's. The economic and industrial might of the Russian people is incomparably less dangerous than is the West's. Together or side by side the Muslim and the Russian can still plow, sow, raise their livestock, earn their living, and engage in commerce. Their skills are not essentially different, but next to the European the Muslim is impoverished and becomes a farm laborer. And so it is. But in Russia, with the exception of the nomadic Kirgiz, Muslims do not fall into poverty; on the contrary, they enrich themselves. Undoubtedly, in the future the Kirgiz [Kazaks] will build their lives on more civilized bases.

The cultural, that is, elemental, affinity existing between the Oriental and the Russian peoples manifests itself by the fact that nowhere do the sons of the East live more easily than in Russia. Neither in Marseilles nor in Paris do you find a colony of Algerian Arabs, nor is there an Indian quarter in London, nor should one look for a single Achits or Malay Muslim in the Hague. Yet thousands of Muslims inhabit Moscow and St. Petersburg, where they have their own streets, mosques, and so forth. While the greater part of them are Tatars, you will also find in all the large cities of central Russia, let alone in frontier areas, Persian merchants and Turkish bakers.

What leads them to and keeps them in Russia other than elemental affinity? Why is the man of the Orient not drawn to trade or to earn his living in the West? Could it be more difficult to get from Algeria to Marseilles than from Kazan to St. Petersburg or Arkhangel'sk?

One prominent Turkish writer—whose name I do not have the right to reveal—said to me: "The Ottomans must and will defend their independence to the very last, sacrificing to that end what is humanly possible; but, if the fatal hour must strike, then I would rather our people pass under the authority of Russia than of any other power. The reason is not Russophilism—I am an Ottoman and nothing more; rather, to live with the Russians would be better and easier. They are closer to us in spirit and culture than are the peoples of the West."

We have much to gain from good relations with the Orient and from the latter's goodwill toward Russia. Taking advantage of the geographic proximity of Russia to the East, we must develop the most brisk and wide-ranging commerce. The Orient needs the finished products of Russian industry, while Russia requires the raw materials of the hot, southern lands. Why, then, do Russia and the East not work out mutually advantageous commercial ties as an example to other countries? To be sure, Europe will not appreciate this; nevertheless, we must strive for its achievement so as to prove the value of establishing such relations.

III

It is advantageous and satisfying to the West if in Russia and the Orient people find historical, geographic, and theological reasons for mutual enmity and distrust. But would it not be better, in that same history and geography, to search for arguments and a raison d'être favoring reciprocity and agreement? I think that it would be better, although the West would fulminate endlessly about it to the Russians and the Muslims.

As early as the beginning of my publishing career, in an article entitled "Russia and the Orient," which appeared in *Interpreter* (no. 8, [1883]), I wrote: "Russia was forced into war with Muslims in part for reasons of its own development and in part so as to ameliorate the condition of eastern Christians. These wars did not have as their goal the destruction or weakening of Muslim countries; rather, such were the consequences of wars for which the Turks themselves must share the blame by failing to acknowledge Russia as a good neighbor and by listening only to their Western friends. The latter always cleverly took advantage of hostility between Turkiye and Russia in order to exploit the former while sapping the strength of the latter as much as possible. We think that it would be reasonable and beneficial to forget the past for the sake of the sincere rapprochement of Turks and Russians. Since Europe will not want or permit this to happen, all the more reason to press for its benefits and utility. Europe is the common enemy of Turkiye and Russia." Today this viewpoint is all the more valid and significant.

By proposing little by little, yet systematically, the idea of rapprochement between Russia and the East, by transmitting without bias information about Russia, by entering freely into polemics with Russian publications whenever necessary, and by throwing light on the calm and peaceful life of Muslims in Russia, I have achieved a success that I dared not hope for. Not only the simple folk, for whom I have written and continue to write, but also educated ulema, great khans, and enlightened pashas have begun to read *Interpreter*. We cannot explain the success of *Interpreter*[2] other than by the emergence of interest in Russian affairs by Orientals, something that [foreign] Muslim newspapers evidence by continually reprinting verbatim all the information on Russia to be found in *Interpreter*.[3]

Presently, the Muslim East comprises Afghanistan, Persia, Egypt, and Morocco. Leading the way is Turkiye with its sultan, also recognized as caliph, that is, the religious head of all Islam, the vicar of the Prophet. All these Muslim states are considered independent, yet to a significant degree they are deprived of their independence and exist thanks to the political competition of the great powers and their support for "equilibrium" in

Europe and, now, in Asia. But what is it about these Muslim countries that disturbs Russia, and what is it about Russia that disturbs them? It is said that Russia needs the Straits in order to have free access to the Mediterranean and defend its southern border. The Straits are in Turkish hands. An outlet to the Mediterranean, Persian Gulf, or Indian Ocean is needed for the vast expanses of Asiatic Russia. Persia, however, separates us from the Gulf, while Persia and Afghanistan do so from the second. Owing to this, it is claimed, Russia must break up and destroy these states so as to take their place. It is said, moreover, that Russia has the highest moral duty to demolish and carry off the Crescent everywhere and replace it with the Cross.

I do not give much credence to these opinions, for the following reasons. Imagine that it is the Serbs and Bulgars who are masters of Kazan' and Crimea, and not the Tatars; and that they alarm Russia with continual raids and block her roads to the east and south. And imagine that it is the Greeks and not the Turks who control the Straits, watched over by the Europeans. In these circumstances would Russia deny its natural and pragmatic push toward open space and the ocean? She would take possession of Kazan' and Crimea just as she had done from the Tatars, and she would be just as interested in the question of the Straits [which serve as] a gateway to and from Russia. In general I do not find sufficient reason for considering the actions of states or popular movements in the abstract, without taking account of actual causes. Many say and write that the Arabs engaged in conquest for the sake of Islam and the Qur'ân. I cannot accept that because I understand well how the Arabs, united by their new religion, rushed to conquer the rich, profitable lands of Syria, Iraq, and Egypt, having left behind the barren, deserted lands of Arabia, where the faith was not yet consolidated. While preparing the conquest of Constantinople, Mehmed II hardly thought about converting St. Sophia into a cathedral mosque; rather, his granting of concessions to the defeated Christians shows him to have been an astute politician and not a warrior of God. Moreover, an earlier warrior, Caliph Omar, on seizing Jerusalem, made clear that he had not come to take possession of houses of worship or see their destruction.

All the more reason that I cannot admit that the Russians have played the role of crusaders in the twentieth [*sic*] century.

It would be much better to examine the question from its practical, positive side alone. All the more so because, if Russians and Muslims are occupied with abstractions, then others, probably, will grasp reality, and that would not be desirable.

The significance for Russia of the Straits and a southern outlet to the ocean is patent. The natural (and, consequently, legitimate) push to the open seas of the most extensive continental country is determined by its economic and political life and development and therefore ought not to be considered by Muslims as [reflecting] a "thirst for conquest" or, even more, as "hostility toward Islam." For the statesmen of the East to admit the natural necessity of a powerful neighboring people, while preserving their own situation, would be proof of the greatest political sagacity. On the other hand, we dare to believe that it would be equally important for Russia to find the means for an understanding with its eastern neighbors so that it can peacefully and without sacrifice achieve what is necessary to ensure the defense of its southern borders and the development of its commerce.

The entire series of military clashes between Russia and the East during the last two centuries, having had enormous consequences for the emancipation of Eastern Christians and the amelioration of their lives, has not brought us closer to a resolution of the [fundamental] question of Russia's proper well-being and needs—the question of the Straits. Europe has and will have no objections to measures leading to the creation of Christian principalities in the Balkan Peninsula, but with the indispensable condition that Russia be confined to the Black Sea and that Europe could elbow its way through the Straits as needed. After the unsuccessful [Crimean] War, the Treaty of Paris deprived us of [access to] the Straits; after the successful [Russo-Turkish] War, the Berlin Congress affirmed this loss even more. There is no reason to expect that in the future Europe will not maintain this situation with all its power, seeing that to do so is to its advantage.

IV

Many will recall, I think, the agitation that seized Europe as a result of rumors that circulated at the beginning of this year concerning the conclusion of a Russo-Turkish alliance. Why did these rumors so alarm the European press? Why did they force the diplomats to prick up their ears so that in Constantinople and in St. Petersburg [the authorities] found it necessary to refute them? It goes without saying that Europe was not troubled by the expectation of a Russo-Turkish invasion but understood that an alliance between the white czar and the Islamic caliph would completely jumble the cards with which Europeans are accustomed to playing. That such an alarm could be raised in Europe, each time a rumor circulates about a Russo-Turkish rapprochement or alliance, is testimony to the major significance [such a rapprochement] could have. Yet its significance would be even greater if the question were placed in a broader context and not limited to Turkiye, if it entailed—think of it!—the rapprochement and solidarity of the entire Orient with Russia.

Imagine that Russia has entered into sincere, amicable relations with Turkiye and Persia. This friendship would affect rather perceptibly relations with Egypt and the Arab world, on the one hand, and with Afghanistan and the Indo-Muslim world, on the other.

Under the enormous authority of the caliph, the entire Muslim community would turn its trust and sympathy to Russia. At the Straits, which lead to southern Russia, would stand not simply the Turks but friends of Russia with whose [Russian] aid the Straits could be so reinforced that they would actually become impassible to enemies that border them. At the Persian Gulf, on the left flank of Asiatic England, would stand Persia and perhaps Afghanistan, who would be sympathetic to Russia. Securing Russia's southern border in Europe and Asia by means of solid relations with neighboring Muslim states would provide extraordinary freedom to Russian might in the West and the Far East.

Such relations are more easily achieved than by the conquest of these countries. As for Russian outposts in the Mediterranean and anywhere in the vicinity of the Indian Ocean, they could be acquired or obtained from Turkiye and Persia. In its agreement with Turkiye, England has received for its fleet [access] not only to a port but to an entire island, Cyprus. Why could not a similar accord be worked out betwen Russia, Turkiye, and Persia once they establish mutually advantageous conditions and desire to enter such an agreement?

The Russo-Eastern accord has a purely defensive character, without menace to whoever might not be involved. It could be strengthened by the fullest commercial relations based on the concession of special privileges for the products of the contracting countries.

For Turkiye and Persia an accord with Russia would mean that they might better defend themselves against European exploitation and might not be dependent on the whim of every power or the caprice of the theory of equilibrium. Relying on this accord, they might more boldly and more composedly envision the future and more tranquilly busy themselves with a domestic renaissance, adopting forms *not from the West but from Russia*, a country closer to them in terms of civilization and mode of national life.

I will not expatiate on the mutual benefits of a Russo-Oriental rapprochement; they are self-evident. Moreover, the principalities of the Balkan peninsula would find themselves in more comfortable circumstances.

As for how such a rapprochement could be realized, it is necessary to note that every accord implies obvious responsibilities whose acceptance, in any event, binds the negotiating parties. This, of course, is inevitable. It is up to the statesmen to determine whether the expected advantages balance the obligations acquired. Russia must be convinced that she has in the Muslims faithful and reliable allies, and the Muslims must be assured that Russia and her people do not have any need or desire to encroach on their political order or religious beliefs. For this to occur, the accord must be founded on clear and precise stipulations. The contracting parties must grant one another every term and advantage possible. While negotiating, [the two parties] ought not to dupe one another but ought to find a solid basis for an honest accord and a guarantee of mutual interests and the peaceful development of peoples. It is incumbent on statesmen to elaborate the most appropriate conditions for such an accord.

Having risked discussing this subject, I make only one claim: that such an accord would be beneficial to both the Russians and the Muslims.

v

Against a Russo-Oriental rapprochement various domestic and foreign policy objections could be raised. Above all, we suppose the following: while guaranteeing the security of the Muslim lands, such an accord would tie Russia's hands and alter her historic mission. I do not think [this would happen]. Among the great powers Russia is not a stranger to such guarantees; and by giving them freely she, of course, will ensure corresponding advantage for herself.

To me, as a Muslim, it is improper to speak of Russia's mission in the religious sense, but I can say that her rapprochement with the East will facilitate her civilizing mission in the wider sense.

In Istanbul and Teheran one can hear people talking and whispering, suggesting that an intimate accord with Russia would deprive these states of their independence, that the Turkish sultan and Persian shah would find themselves in a position comparable to that of the khans of Bukhara and Khiva. This is not true at all. On the contrary, the accord would strengthen the position of these governments and countries, by delivering them from the, at times, intolerable influence of one or the other great power. What kind of independence in the international arena does Turkiye presently exercise when she could not, in 1885, save her own Rumeli governor-general from a small band of Bulgarians, let alone respond effectively to the seizure of Tunis, Egypt, and other [countries]? Rather than diminishing the power of the sultan and shah, an accord with Russia would assure them both great [political] stability and considerable spiritual and material power.

Europe will, to be sure, struggle against such an accord with every truth and untruth. She will pull out all the stops in St. Petersburg, Istanbul, and Teheran, bristling and threatening war, but this accord could nevertheless be effected through the goodwill of the leaders of Russia and the East.

Allying itself to Turkiye and Persia, Russia would draw close to the entire Islamic East and, thanks to the especially pleasant quality of the Russian national character, would actually provide leadership for the Muslim people and their civilization, something that England so stubbornly pursues.

Good relations between the white czar and the Muslim caliph would give to the thoughts and sympathies of seventy million Islamic faithful in India a completely different orientation, and the English would find it difficult to spread tales about the [alleged] mission of the "Cossack" to destroy Islam, as if it were defended by England and its free institutions.

In Russia we are poorly acquainted with the system by which England treats the Muslim peoples. This system is well considered, yet British conceit and aloofness undermine it. If the British were as easy to get on with and were as simple of character as the Russians, the East would adore them in spite of their money grubbing and cupidity. In any event, until now the English have marched along with the East as friend to caliph and Muslim. They have persuaded the East that they are protecting Moscow from the feeble impulses of France and Spain, that they continually defend the caliph and Persia against Russia, that they have temporarily occupied

Egypt in order to save it from the grasp of France, and that in India they are not lords but allies of the local princes and people. To convince the Muslims further, they obtained from the sherif of Mecca [the declaration] that "India is an Islamic country" and that Muslims ought to reconcile themselves to British rule. English policy can be summed up as, Give us commercial advantages, and we will defend you and provide you with the fruits of civilization, while encroaching on neither your politics nor your religion. Even recent attacks on the sultan and the notorious "Armenian Affair" are explained in no other manner than by the wish to strengthen Turkiye, having compelled the latter to take up reforms and grant free institutions to its people. By playing with the facts or putting them in a false light, the English will convince the Muslims of Russian enmity to them and their world. Nevertheless, the Armenian events and the "protection" of Egypt that has already lasted too long have raised the curtain from the English game, and the East has begun to look more critically at the whole history of English friendship.

How far the reaction of the Oriental public against their longtime friends has progressed is manifest in Muslim newspapers: those that hew the English line find themselves without many readers, while those of nationalist character are filled with anti-English articles.

The newspapers *Vatan* (Bosnia), *Gayret* (Bulgaria), and *Kipr* (Cyprus), as well as part of the Arab and Indian press, have begun to speak out, in seeming concert, against England. And I will not even discuss the bitter truths that were revealed at a meeting of Muslims this very year in London itself, nor will I cite the complaints of Indian newspapers about English invective against the sultan-caliph. I will limit myself only to noting the speech given by the Indian scholar Muhammed Abdulgani Efendi on 2 (14) February of this year in Newcastle, at a gathering of the local geographic society. Having apprised the audience of the global distribution and significance of the two hundred million Muslims inhabiting the planet, the aforementioned Muslim scholar completed his speech with the following relevant words:

One-fourth of the entire Muslim population in the world finds itself under English governance. This imposes on those Muslims well-known obligations of a civil and political character. But we should not forget that deeper and more subtle ties bind this population to the caliph as Islam's religious leader. It is true that this fact does not hinder Muslims in fulfillment of their civil duties to Great Britain, but it would be tactless to subject to some great test the feelings that Muslims have toward the state and those they have toward their religion and caliph. We must not forget that, wherever Muslims are maltreated, they and their brethren throughout the world will be displeased because all Muslims belong to a single religious community.

It is well known that Russia can count on a number of supporters from among the so-called Old Turks and the Persian nobility. But the Young Turks, partisans of a constitutional order, understand the value of good relations with Russia. In their own publication *Meshveret* (Deliberation), which appears in Paris, they acknowledge that Turkiye can have an agreement with Russia, but not now when Turkiye is weak. The latter must strengthen itself first; otherwise an entente with Russia would place Turkiye in the position of a vassal. In its French supplement, this newspaper wrote: "We do not profess any animosity toward Russia. While she has her historic mission we have concern for our independence and dignity. Are there no means to reconcile what appear to be two irreconcilable points of view? We believe there are."

However and whenever the existing cycle of political dependency or semidependency ends for Muslim monarchs and princes, the two-hundred-million-strong mass of Muslims, solid and united by the Qur'ân, will be there. This mass, which attributes the highest significance to faith, and which attaches no importance to differences of birth, language, or country for men who follow the Qur'ân, cannot be underestimated on any account.

One should not be nonchalant about the goodwill and sympathy, the hostility and distrust, of this massive part of humanity toward the states and peoples who have been called by history to have the closest ties with them—whether as neighbors, allies, or rulers.

They understand this perfectly well in London. So too does that [English] subsidized part of the Arab/Indian press that continually pushes on the Muslim masses the idea of solidarity between English and Muslim interests. In the words of these organs, only Russia is a threat, not only to Muslim rulers, but to the very way of life and religion of Muslims. England, they say, because of its interests (witness the frankness!) is called to protect the rulers and people of Islam; and, for Muslims under such protection and governance, England guarantees a free life, religious toleration, and [economic] development.

It seems to me that it would be of some use for the Muslim world to know the truth about Russia since it holds a very distorted view of that country at present. Muslims should be persuaded that Russia does not harbor any hostile sentiments toward Islam or the people who profess it. Muslims who inhabit or visit Russia can confirm this by their personal examples and words.

Russia has nothing to lose and everything to gain from the good opinion of Muslims.

Completing my remarks, there remains for me to add only that, by submitting to the influence of England and Germany, Turkiye would acquire sufficient guarantee for a proper existence for the caliphate and [Ottoman] dynasty, but an existence that would be limited to external pomp. Turkiye would also acquire guarantees regarding religious affairs. We know that the Emperor Wilhelm has personally visited the sultan in order to draw him into the Triple Alliance; but the sultan preferred the strictest "neutrality" and made his point so tactfully that he preserved the best relations with Germany. Evidently, the sultan sought more than the Western alliance could grant him.

We want our Oriental readers to know that while suggesting a Russo-Oriental entente we do not mean to impose our views. Let the Muslim states exist and develop outside such an entente. But, if at some point they feel it necessary to pursue this or that political combination, we suggest that they remember mighty Russia and the wonderful Russian people. Russia can live and flourish on her own, without any alliances or agreements, but Muslim states do not have that luxury. We cannot lose sight of this fact.

It is also important not to forget that the traditional friend of the East—the *Ingelez-efendi*—has established himself at the Suez Canal and at the Straits of Bab el Mandeb. He has transformed an Arab sea into an English lake; that is, he has appropriated for himself the keys to Mecca and Medina, without having compensated the amicable but needy caliph with a single commercial or tariff concession. What kind of "friendship and community of interests" is this, gentlemen?

I have said my piece. Now I will readily listen.   *Bakhchesaray (March 1896)*

## Document 2

Mähmud Khojä [Behbudiy], "Isma'il bey häzrätläri ilä sohbät" (Conversation with the Esteemed Ismail Bey [Gaspirali]), *Ayinä*, no. 49 (27 September 1914): 1162–64. Translated from the Turki—and Farsi—language eulogy by Edward Allworth with Obeidullah Noorata. Mähmud Khojä was the leading Turkistanian Jadid (Reformist).

It was at prayer time before sunset [about 3 P.M.] on the twentieth of June [1914]. A respected medrese instructor from Marghilan and I walked on a shaded path of Gulkhane Park in Istanbul. In front of us a Tatar in a Tatar-style karakol lamb's-wool hat went along slowly with a fez-wearing Turk. We quickly walked past. The two of them seemed familiar to me. Putting my hands to my breast I gave a sign of greeting and passed by. It came to me that this Tatar looked like Ismail Bey [Gaspirali]. Perhaps it was someone who resembled him. As for the fez-wearing Turk, he was the esteemed editor Hamdullah Subhi Bey. We scarcely went on even ten steps when I heard a friendly voice say from behind me, "Oh, Khojä." My heart thumped, and, no doubt remaining about the aforesaid individual's being the esteemed Ismail Bey, we turned back and clasped hands. It seems Hamdullah Subhi Bey had clarified the question of who we were. During the encounter the esteemed one said: "Why are you becoming old-looking so fast?" He meant, Why is your mustache turning white so quickly? Without thinking, I asked: "Sir, why are you getting so thin?" The esteemed Master responded: "What can one do, it's this way for all of us." I declared that in the morning I would set out for Syria and Egypt. "If that is so, let us have a talk," the esteemed one remarked. I said thank you. His honor took leave of Mr. Hamdullah Subhi Bey. I, too, parted from the honorable *medrese* instructor. Going out of the park and getting into a carriage, we came to the place where the esteemed Master stayed [Shahin Pasha Oteli]. The honorable one ordered some food, but he had no appetite.

The esteemed one's voice was weak, and every three or four minutes he coughed lightly and expelled phlegm. In the hotel room the esteemed one spoke to me about Russia, about Turkistan, about the world of Islam in general, and about what was happening. Speaking about the progress Muslims are making from one day to another, the honorable one was content. The honorable one said further: "Mahmud Khojä, now let me see what you have to say." I talked about Samarkand, Bukhara, Tashkent, Khiva, and Farghana, summing up about each one of them. "Thank Allah, it seems the Turkistanian brothers are starting to enroll their children in the government's primary schools. Today you have two newspapers and one journal. In your schools, too, there is progress; but, of course, for others who are capable there is no progress. Enroll your children a bit more in the government's primary schools, indeed, and don't flee from the culture of the Russian. . . . Oh, I don't know; what will become of that Bukhara?" the esteemed one remarked. I said, "My dear Sir, one cannot hope for anything from Bukhara until our government, that is, Russia, trains Bukhara." So, the esteemed Master said, "Yes, in the end it will have to come about that way"; again the dialogue went in another direction. Several times I requested his permission to leave. "Perhaps your honor wishes to rest." The esteemed Master said, "Khojä, sir, if you are here, my comfort is the more. And, if you depart, I shall set to writing a letter." The esteemed Master, having gone to Petrograd in February, when he came with Muhammad Fatih Afandi and others to inoculate the Muslim faction [of the state duma deputation] caught cold accidentally. Since then, as a consequence of his feeling unwell, he had not been able to attend the assembly and consultations taking place in Petrograd, and because of this his honor felt extreme regret. And, if the climate of Istanbul were suitable, the esteemed one intended to stay for some period. If Allah would take care of the winter ahead of us, the esteemed one, spending it in Cairo, Egypt, in that case, too, intended to work out some matters. Having invited me to Bakhchesaray on [my] return and driving around together by automobile, the esteemed one promised to show me Crimea. I, too, gave a promise to come into Bakhchesaray on returning. But this inauspicious conflict [World War I] prevented it. The respected Master had become emaciated; his honor constantly engaged himself with coughing and phlegm. Every time I wished for permission [to retire], the esteemed one gave no answer. Asking leave to send for a bed, stretching out [on it], the esteemed one talked for hours. When I looked [at a watch] one time it seemed the time had passed midevening by an hour [it was about 10 P.M.]. That is, it seemed we conversed a full seven hours. Hardly granting permission [even yet for me to leave], accompanying [me] to the head of the stairs, the esteemed one over and over made me promise to come into Bakhchesaray on returning [from my journey]. Seven years earlier, the esteemed Master came to Samarkand as the guest of the renowned [teacher] Shakuri and ourselves. Compared with that time, the esteemed one just now seemed to be extremely thin. I had never dreamed of seeing the esteemed Master and conversing [with him] in Istanbul. By the grace of Allah, finding such a bounteous gift from the unique seven hours of conversations of the esteemed Master, I remained content, so that [merely] by telling [about it] I cannot repay the debt [I owe for this]. And the delight of that conversation will absolutely never leave me. If only I had not departed for Damascus on the morrow, I would have conversed with the esteemed Master a bit longer. Oh! Now we let that perfect Master slip from [our] hands. And he flew to the world of spirits. Perhaps in dreams and visions we shall converse with the spirit of that possessor of laudable quality. [Farsi:] That past pleasure, which will not again recur, yesterday got away from [my] hand but will never leave my memory.   *Mähmud Khojä*

## Document 3

"Ismail Bey Gasprinski, 1851–1914," *Shura*, nos. 21 (1 November 1914), 22 (15 November 1914), 23 (1 December 1914), 24 (15 December 1914): 641–44, 673–75, 705–8, 737–41. Translated by Alan W. Fisher.

This very long obituary for Ismail Bey appeared in four issues of the Tatar-language journal *Shura*, published in Orenburg in November and December 1914. Published bimonthly from January 1908 to January 1918, *Shura* was one of the most important literary and political Tatar journals in the last years of the Russian Empire. Its editor was Rizaeddin kadi Fahreddin, a reform-minded religious official. As readers can easily see in the obituary that follows, "*Shura* was certainly, of all Muslim journals, the most deeply influenced by Russian culture."[4] I wish to thank Edward Allworth for both informing me of this obituary's existence and providing me with a photocopy of it.

### *1 November 1914: Ismail Bey Gaspirali, 1851–1914*

Ismail Bey was someone who was respected in the world for his preoccupation with the affairs of humanity; he was a man of ours who was revered for his writings about and on behalf of our nation; our man and our leader, Ismail Bey Gaspirali, is now at rest and has departed for another abode. It was the product of Ismail Bey's pen that gave us the route to follow for the future; he provided for us the necessary lessons to learn in order to reach the future. With the death of Ismail Bey, Russian Muslims have lost a person with "a thousand" faces, a person who himself was our educational center and institution. We are now separated from the person who was most clearly the servant of knowledge for and among our people.

He was born in a very traditional village, moved to the city, and spent his life there. He had a sharp intellect, great ability, natural aptitude, courage, and firmness, was a hard worker, and, because of all these, contributed as much as any one man can to the well-being of Russia's Muslims. He showed them, through his own example, what their potential for renewal is. He was the cause of a revolution among Russia's Muslims that was all encompassing: in science, in literature, in their society as well as in their economy. Until today there has been no Muslim in Russia who has contributed as much as Ismail Bey.

His entire adult life Ismail Bey devoted to serving his nation, his people, his society [*millet ki, khalq be jemaat ki*]. He helped all the rest of us develop our material and intellectual welfare and potential. He was a servant to all of us without parallel.

The lives of our people have greatly benefited from all the years, months, days, and even hours of Ismail Bey's own life. It is unfortunate indeed that someone who is of such great service to his people and all humanity is so short lived. Yet his good works and services remain behind as his legacy. Too often the long lived of us contribute far less to society than does someone who has a relatively short life. Let us be grateful, however, for his short life, for it was so important to the very fiber of our existence.

Although Ismail Bey's life was not long, it was filled with "a thousand" blessings and good deeds for the rest of us. Everyone who knew him, and knew of him, recognized that everything he did was for the benefit of knowledge and the people. Let us all rejoice in Ismail Bey's life, not be too sad about his death!

All the important people as well as the ordinary people have a great debt to Ismail Bey. He was indeed one of God's greatest gifts to mankind. Let us raise our thanks to God Almighty for this gift. Ismail Bey would have wished that we remember him most for what he did to improve the intellectual and spiritual life of our people. While there were and are many who remain pessimistic about the future of Islam and humanity in general, Ismail Bey showed us how to attain a good future.

Our nation [*millet*] will benefit forever from what Ismail Bey accomplished. He led the way in showing how to raise and educate the next generation of young people who will be the ones to serve our nation in the future.

Ismail Bey's contributions have become the guide [*rehber*] for the difficult-to-find route out of our difficult present, the warnings against mistaken policies, and the plans for our nation's future. For these reasons, it is important that his biography be written and that it be studied by all the students in our schools. However, until now, this has not been written. This must be written so that we can fully appreciate what Ismail Bey did and so that we will be able to benefit from his accomplishments.

Because of Ismail Bey's death, we have lost a man who was of use to our people in a thousand ways. He was a man who worked hard, remained firm in his convictions, and now he is gone. Today we feel deep grief and believe we have experienced a great calamity. But God knows best, and let us take up the paths that Ismail Bey has built, to complete the tasks that he has begun. This is the best way for us now to serve our nation.

Although some elements of Ismail Bey's biography have appeared in our newspapers and journals over the past several years, no serious attempt has yet been made to provide a complete story of his life. At *Shura* we have decided to begin that task by providing here an outline of his biography. We hope that in the future a much more serious and complete effort will be made. We have benefited in our project from the information printed in *Terjüman* by Hasan Sabri Efendi, who was one of Ismail Bey's closest friends and associates.

*Biography.* The founder of the newspaper *Terjüman*, Ismail Bey Gaspirali, was born on 8 March 1851 (1267) in a village called Uchuköy, which was a two-hour journey from Bakhchesaray. His mother came from a Crimean noble family and was named Fatma Hanim. His father, Mustafa Aga, came from a noble family of the second rank. Mustafa Aga had been born in the village Gaspra, which was on the Crimean Black Sea coast. Ismail Bey took the name Gaspirali from this origin. (Information on this fact was published in *Terjüman*, no. 19 [1884].) There is some evidence that Ismail Bey's ancestors originally came from the Khazar Turkish branch, but the information is unclear. Some time ago, in *Terjüman*, in an article entitled "Gun Dogdu," a story was presented about Ismail Bey's possible ancestors. A certain Daniyal Beg came to Crimea from the Circassian region and was considered by some a Circassian, by others a Turk. Ismail Bey believed that this Daniyal Beg was one of his early ancestors. We are not taking a position on this question, which does not seem very important anyway.

Ismail Bey's father and mother lived in Aqyar (Sevastopol) during the 1855 war and at its end moved to Bakhchesaray. At this point Ismail Bey was four years old. When Ismail Bey was ten years old, he found a girlfriend named Habibe, who lived in Bakhchesaray. After attending a military training school in Moscow, Ismail Bey went to Istanbul and then to Paris. After his stay abroad, he returned to Russia and to his own homeland. In 1874 (1291), Ismail Bey became a teacher in Yalta, where he taught Muslim adults the Russian language. Two years later he came to Bakhchesaray and gave Russian lessons at the Zinjirli *medrese*.

In 1879 (1296), he was elected mayor [*golova*]. In this position he served four years. After that period he began what would become his life's work. He would also make a number of journeys in the coming years: in 1885 to Baku, in 1893 again to Baku and then on to Bukhara, in 1907 and 1908 to Egypt, and finally in 1911 to India.

About his second journey to Baku, Ismail Bey wrote a short account in *Terjüman*, a portion of which we include here:

In 1893, I found myself for a second time in Baku. On my first trip I traveled with Sefer Ali Bey Velibeyov. I passed through the Caucasus on the way to Baku, that first time. We were particularly interested in learning about trade and commerce as it was conducted by Muslims living there. Sefer Ali Bey was a merchant and was himself interested in making some investments in the Caucasus and in Baku. We met with a number of the rich merchants and industrialists. Sefer Ali Bey purchased one large establishment and decided to begin the publication associated with it of a newspaper. Those with whom he dealt could not understand the sense of starting a newspaper, which could certainly not be profitable. And few were willing to consider a newspaper that would be modeled on *Terjüman* and that would not be essentially Muslim in nature. They were not particularly interested in new forms of newspapers, of education, of literature. They said: "For us it is enough to trust in God." Happily Sefer Ali Bey persisted in his plan, and the newspaper was eventually started.

We also noted then that many of the educated elements of that society spoke Farsi, and the local ordinary population found it very difficult to speak with them.

Now, on my second journey, I am happy to report that Turkic is being used by all, the newspaper is thriving, and the people of the area are entering a new future.

*His Family.* Ismail Bey married in 1879 (H. 1293), but, after a number of years, he divorced that woman. In 1882 (1299), Ismail Bey married Zahire Hanim, the daughter of Isfendiyar Akchurin from Siberia. These two lived together for twenty years. (A biography of this lady appears in the book *Meshhur Hatunlar.*) Although after Zahire Hanim's death Ismail Bey married one of her sisters, it was Zahire Hanim who was his prime companion throughout his active life.

Ismail Bey had three sons, Rahmet Bey, Mansur Bey, and Haydar Bey, and three daughters, Hatije Hanim, Shafiqa Hanim, and Nigyar Hanim. He had one living sister, Zeyneb.

*His Education.* Ismail Bey studied first with Haji Ismail. At that teacher's death, Ismail Bey entered the gymnasium at Aqmesjit and, after two years' study there, entered the Veronezh military academy. From there he advanced to the Moscow higher military school. It is interesting to note that Ismail Bey, who spent more than thirty-five years serving the interests of Russian Muslims and Turkish nationalists, had his first educational experiences in Russian schools. Yet his nationalist activity ultimately cut him off from the Russian families he grew to know and love, the Russian writers, and the Russian professors.

On this touchy question, Yusuf Bey Akchurin once wrote:

People often think that their nation, their ideas and culture, are unique to them. They think it wrong to mingle with other cultures. Muslims today are among the worst in this regard. We forget that, long ago, Muslims were open to other cultures and ideas. Al Ghazali was one such philosopher who was open to such foreign ideas. Ismail Bey received his very first education within Islamic tradition. But soon he branched out. Among his best friends were the Katkov family. Ismail Bey cannot be said to have suffered from these associations. He may well have benefited.

Ismail Bey found the strength to remain firm against those who were uneasy about change, against those "masters" of the past who waivered on the question of renewal. He understood better than they that true service to our religion required an acceptance of renewal. He often wrote in *Terjüman* that the old stone "walls" were crumbling and that they needed to be rebuilt with new materials. He learned from Katkov that Russia and Russians also needed renewal, that their own "walls" were in a state of deterioration. He knew that it was not necessary to pursue renewal in exactly the same way that Katkov and Russians were doing it but that one did not need to fear what they were saying solely because they were Russians. Indeed, he learned a great deal from the newspapers that such Russians were publishing, especially the *Moscow Gazette* [*Moskovskiia Viedemosti*]. Journalism needed men who were knowledgeable about the world. Ismail Bey was a man whose strength and desire combined to produce for us a useful and modern journalism that could address the needs of our people. He believed that Katkov was just such a man for the Russians too. When Katkov died, Ismail Bey showed sincere grief and in *Terjüman* offered sympathy for his family. He wrote that Katkov had provided great service to the Russian people through journalism, that he had worked hard at that task for thirty years, that Russians would recognize the true value of his service. And he concluded that he hoped, after he had completed thirty years of service, that our people would consider him [Ismail Bey] in the same light.

During his time in the Moscow military academy, Ismail Bey began to develop a great affection for his own Turkic-Tatar nation. After those years, although he traveled as far as Paris and Istanbul, he thought about the problems of our schools and our books. He decided on these trips that he would focus much of his life on improving the intellectual life of our schools and books and would emphasize renewal of the teaching and journalistic professions.

*15 November 1914*

Ismail Bey published a book, in Russian, entitled *Russian Muslims*. With this work, Ismail Bey initiated a debate on some very important questions. He wrote, "Our ignorance is the main reason for our backward condition. We have no access at all to what has been discovered and to what is going on in Europe. We must be able to read in order to overcome our isolation; we must learn European ideas from European sources. We must introduce into our primary and secondary schools subjects that will permit our pupils to have such access." Ismail Bey found the means necessary to introduce these ideas among the Turkic-Tatar people. He understood that this means was primarily the responsibility of the publishing industry.

Because of this, he published on 8 May 1881 a volume entitled *First-Born* [*Tonguch*], which was soon followed by a second, *Daybreak* [*Shefak*]. Together, these two works have been considered to be the famous "Ismail Publications." In the years since, Ismail Bey explained that it was the reception that these two works found that persuaded him to venture the publication of his famous newspaper *Terjüman*. Although Ismail Bey was not able to gain assistance from any quarter at first, and despite the fact that such a venture was considered to be extremely bold at the time, Ismail Bey persisted and produced the first issues of *Terjüman* on his own. Ismail Bey had to travel to St. Petersburg in order to receive permission to begin publication and had to incur considerable personal expense in time and money. But, on 10 April 1883 (1300), the first issue appeared. Ismail Bey continued to face one obstacle after another, but the issues of *Terjüman* continued to appear. In 1882, he also published a *Turki Yearbook* [*Salname-i Turki*] and a beautiful almanac. In the introduction to the former, Ismail Bey wrote: "We have put together a *Turki Yearbook* and an almanac for the benefit of all Muslims in Russia, both for the first time. We are conducting an experiment to see if what is regularly done in Russian, Ottoman, and French languages, which provide statistical and geographic information for those peoples, can also serve a useful purpose for Russian Muslims."

Throughout his life, Ismail Bey published innumerable books, brochures, essays, treatises, and collections, all with the purpose of serving Russia's Muslims. But the most beautiful and most useful of all the things that he published was *Terjüman*. This newspaper allowed Russia's Muslims to awaken, to come out of seclusion, to enter the world. It permitted Russia's Muslims to cease being so far behind the rest of the civilized world and provided the needed remedy for many of our ills.

Ismail Bey once wrote about the costs and rewards connected with *Terjüman* in this way:

Today *Terjüman* enters its third year. Let us inform our readers what we see as the use and purpose of *Terjüman*, that it has aimed at improving the health and happiness of our homeland [*vatan*], of the Turks as well as other Muslims who live in Russia. We have aimed at providing the essentials for the education of our nation, of the Turks and all Muslims in Russia. When the first issue of *Terjüman* was printed, we produced only 320 copies, and we perhaps thought that we would find it difficult to have a readership warranting that many. In December 1883, however, we needed to print 406 copies. For 1884 we had to increase our operating budget, and by December we had 1,000 subscribers. Let us describe briefly who these 1,000 subscribers were. 300 were in Crimea; 300 were in Astrakhan, Samara, Orenburg, Ufa, Kazan, and Perm; 150 lived in Dagistan; 50 were Siberian Muslims; 200 were in Central Asia and Turkistan. 150 appeared to be from the upper and wealthy classes; 300 were ordinary working people; 500 were urban merchants, teachers, artisans. Our readership comes from all over the Russian Muslim world and includes all sorts of people. (*Terjüman* 1885)

In an editorial appearing in *Terjüman* in 1903, in the twentieth anniversary issue, Ismail Bey wrote the following, referring to ideas he had presented in the very first issue in 1883:

The first service that *Terjüman* will provide is news that will be useful for our society's livelihood and information about Russian society that can be useful and important for our own society. The road ahead of us is long and difficult. We thus ask God's help and guidance, both of which we will need in abundance. But it will be our readers who will decide if our aims have been achieved, if we have proved useful to the needs of our society. In twenty years we have produced several hundred issues of *Terjüman*, and of these we believe more than a million Muslims in Russia and Muslims living within the Ottoman state have read our issues. What has been our effect, our impact? We have received much information that is very gratifying. Letters from our readers indicate a wide degree of support. And even more important are the tangible results of our efforts. Schools for Muslims in Russia are changing, are improving, and we believe some of the credit for this development belongs with what has been published in *Terjüman*. Foundations for more than one thousand primary schools have been laid, and, in many of them, our "phonetic method" of instruction is employed. Our young writers and scholars have produced in these twenty years as many as three hundred scientific and literary treatises. In eight of our cities, societies have been established to work for the social and cultural benefit of our people. The spiritual and intellectual health of our world of Islam is greatly improved. We hope that God is pleased with what has been achieved. But much still remains to be accomplished. We hope very much that a Muslim university may be established and several hundred more social and cultural societies may be founded. With God's help *Terjüman* will continue with its efforts to accomplish these goals.

In another issue of *Terjüman*, Ismail Bey wrote the following on the matter of renewal and reform within Islam:

Thirteen years ago there were innumerable forms of revolutionary and reform movements afoot in Russian Islam, many of them in opposition to one another. In essence, these movements raised five or six types of question: (1) Muslims who are subjects of the Russian government have to decide whether they are loyal to the czar or to some Muslim government or are loyal to their own homeland [*vatan*]. (2) What sort of education is proper and necessary for Muslims? Should it include the study of modern science? If so, is it necessary to learn Russian? Should there be Muslim schools that teach modern subjects? (3) What are the best means for training Muslims to live in the modern world of trade and industry? Should our schools branch out of our old traditional modes and offer new methods of instruction? Is this sort of education dangerous to the preservation of our culture? (4) Is it necessary that Muslims in Russia be trained in modern methods of agriculture? Is it possible to survive and thrive economically without acquiring new scientific agricultural knowledge? (5) If we establish our own national schools, to permit our youths to acquire an education without going to the Russian schools, should our own schools be modeled on the Russian ones? Should they offer the same subjects and teach our youths the Russian language? (6) What should be the role of our newspapers and journals in all this? Should they instruct, prod, incite, encourage? Should they take positions on these various issues? (*Terjüman*, 1895)

Toward the beginning of 1896, Ismail Bey published an evaluation of the various reform movements involving Russian Muslims:

It is interesting to compare the situation of Russia's Muslims at the beginning of 1896 with the situation in 1880. Today there are a great many Russian Muslims, who could not read or write before, who not only read but contribute to *Terjüman*. Over these fifteen years, in Russia and especially in the city of Kazan, many books have been written and published by Muslims. Although some of them still remain textbooks written in Arabic, our "literature" has really been born, and much is written in Turkic. Before, there was not much beyond the almanacs of Abdulkayyim al Nasri Efendi and the treatises of Radlov. Today, we have almanacs, geographies, and histories. And we can sense the beginning of the writing and publishing of poetry, dictionaries, fiction as well as nonfiction in Turkic. We no longer have to depend on learning Russian and using Russian books on these subjects. We see the birth of a "new literature" [*edebiyat-i jadid*]. But, in this new literature, how much is there of genuine new ideas? We have a great many schools. But are there genuine scholars, researchers, inquirers among their teachers? There is not nearly enough of "new method" or "new idea" in our schools in the cities and provinces where Muslims live. In fact, it is not in our secondary schools that our Muslim youths are really learning about the modern world in which they live; it is in the factories where they work that they come into contact with modernity. The real question that all of us should now be considering is this: How will our Muslim youths value their culture and traditions when they appear to be so out of touch with the modern world? If they learn one thing in school and another in the factory, what are they to make of it? The future, the independence, the sovereignty, the survival of our nation is at stake. It is absolutely essential that we produce new ideas in our schools that are in accord with the new world into which our youths enter. Fifteen years ago, it might not have seemed possible to achieve. Today, however, there is great hope. (*Terjüman*, 1895)

After founding *Terjüman* Ismail Bey made a journey along the Volga and then into the districts east of Itil. In Ufa he met with Selim Geri Mirza. He then traveled through the Caucasus. He learned of the current conditions of the Turkic and Tatar peoples living in these areas. He came to the conclusion that they were living in a deplorable situation, in a society that was gravely ill. Then, many years later, when he traveled to Egypt to attend the general Islamic congress, he learned that the Turkic world was not unique in this regard, that the entire Islamic world was gravely ill. He wrote there an essay that was published in Arabic and addressed these issues. He called for a plan for all Muslims to follow, to use new methods in education as the remedy for its grave illness.

The major obstacle that Ismail Bey faced in the Turkic world in Russia, and in Egypt, was the concern that many Muslims, even educated and intelligent ones, raised about the compatibility of new educational methods with Islamic tradition, with Islam itself. But Ismail Bey was willing to go to Egypt, even as far as India, in order to carry his message and concerns.

A great many people who wished to continue to rely on Islamic traditions as they understood them and who resisted considering many of the new ideas and new methods proposed by Ismail Bey put obstacles in the way of Ismail Bey at every chance they found. Books, pamphlets, essays, introductions to other books, all were used to oppose the new methods. But Ismail Bey countered every obstacle, responded to all criticisms, with his own books, pamphlets, introductions, and essays. It is our opinion that, in the contest, Ismail Bey won, and he achieved "checkmate" [*mut*] against his opponents.

He made a journey to Bukhara to confront some of the most influential of his opponents. There were many there, in the schools both secondary and primary, who argued that his ideas and methods were contrary to Islamic culture and law. He understood that even in the *medreses* of Bukhara the knowledge of the modern world had to be introduced.

Ismail Bey's road was long and difficult, but the correct one to follow. He was a modern man [*jadid bir adam*] who served truth and reality. He strove to free us from ignorance, from ideas that were both meaningless and useless. Muslim students, he argued, who attended *medreses* that remained deaf to modern ideas were a national waste. He was willing to devote all his time and energy at home and to make long and difficult journeys for no personal gain or profit, but on behalf of the possible gain and profit of all of us. The Islamic world has been restricted by the tight bonds of an outmoded past, of outmoded methods. He argued that Muslims should find themselves obligated to break these bonds, to free their imagination, to advance. Everywhere else, it was in the last century [nineteenth] that "modern civilization" was born. The Western peoples began to place knowledge and science at the forefront, to give them highest priorities. They were able to discover a great deal about nature and with these discoveries were able to greatly improve the life of their peoples. There have been "a thousand" real benefits to humanity from these discoveries. Merchants, factory owners and workers, artisans, all have found new skills, talents, abilities, as results of these discoveries. "A thousand" great works have resulted.

Russian Muslims have tended to experience the reverse of all that we wrote above. We have not had access to the discoveries, to the science and knowledge that the Western peoples have produced. And we have not been able to add our own contributions to those discoveries. The debate has centered on two issues coming from this state of affairs: Is it right that we do not contribute, and is it wrong to learn how to contribute?

Ismail Bey, and we, believe[d] that the Islamic world and the Muslims in Russia have the responsibility to join the people who are producing these discoveries. The Turkic language is an excellent means to achieve these goals; those who are determined to depend on Arabic and Persian as the official languages of our past will remain in the past. This was why Ismail Bey worked so hard to gain acceptance of a common Turkic language, "Turki."

In general, all Muslims and the Turkic people have the innate capacity to become leaders in the production of new knowledge. This action is not "against God." Rather, almighty God demands no less from human beings. We have a great inheritance from our ancestors, Turkic and Muslim. Our ancestors from centuries ago were leaders in the production of new discoveries and knowledge. They developed great talents and achieved great works.

The *Muqadamat* of Hariri is a good example of what we are arguing here. He wrote in Arabic, it is true. But he gained his knowledge, acquired ideas, from all over. His contributions were important for his age. What Ismail Bey has worked for in our own age is similar.

*1 December 1914*

According to Tabiri, Bedi Hamdani once wrote a poem that consisted of one possible act or accomplishment after another, intended for memorization and recitation as instructions for a future leader. But, according to Tabiri, this poem could be memorized and utilized only by one person in a given age or era, its effects meant for the one rare individual who is meant to dominate a particular time. Parts can be memorized by anyone, but the whole poem only by the one unique person. We know from other sources of such a poem, by Hariri, in the *maqam* form, written in Nishapur. This latter poem contained a story about talent and ability, and indicated that a man who has such rare talent and ability can fulfill his destiny only when his talent is used on behalf of religion and humanity.

1. Our own age has had such an individual who could have fulfilled Hamdani's precepts, a man who possessed such rare talents and abilities, who could have memorized the entire poem, and who used these talents and abilities on behalf of this nation. This was Ismail Bey Gaspirali. There is no doubt that Ismail Bey fulfilled what Hariri and Hamdani called for. Ismail Bey is an example of the sort of servant of religion and humanity that the great poets described.

2. Ismail Mirza himself wrote an article in *Terjüman* about the responsibilities that leaders have toward their people and all humanity. We summarize here the main points that Ismail Bey raised in that article: "Every form of useful activity for mankind and for society must be in tune with the ideal. Without forethought and planning the desired results cannot be achieved, whatever the activity. It must be carefully planned out and be in accord with the ideal."

3. Ismail Bey saw that it was necessary for all the Turkic peoples and groups to use a common "Turki" language in order for them to advance, to coordinate their activities in line with what he believed to be the ideal.

4. He pressed for reform of the religious *medreses*. This could be accomplished only through a comprehensive plan that instituted a common teaching curriculum using a common new teaching method beginning with the primary schools. About these matters, he wrote a great deal in *Terjüman*. One of his most important articles on this subject appeared in our newspaper in Ufa a few years ago, which we summarize here:

Our native language can best be preserved by instructing the children in our primary schools using the "phonetic method" of instruction. Without such instruction, the next generations of our Turkic youth will not speak the same language, will not be able to understand each other, cannot conduct their activities in accord with the common ideal. In places like Penza and Tambov, it will be Russian and not Turkic that provides the means to achieve any ideal. Clearly we need to focus on the language question if we wish to preserve our future.

Ismail Bey believed that the phonetic method of teaching literacy combined with the new method of general instruction was absolutely necessary. About this subject, we summarize some ideas that appeared in *Terjüman* a number of years ago:

The foundations of the oral method were established in Bakhchesaray in 1883 when the first new-method school was founded there. For the first five or six years, most of the people found it difficult to accept the innovations. But finally some began to notice that pupils were learning to read and write well after only two years of instruction in this school. They began to see the value of the new method. Now there are eight new-method schools in Bakhchesaray. It is possible to establish as many as one hundred of them in our *guberniia* alone. (*Terjüman*, no. 50 [1895])

5. A great deal on the reform of spiritual conditions has been published in *Terjüman*. Ismail Bey's ideas on this question were most clearly expressed in issue number 60 (1898) of *Terjüman* and may be summarized as follows:

We have for too long existed in a situation where we refuse to consider what may actually help us recover from our present condition. We exist as if we remain stretched out in bed, without arising. Everyone should strive for a set of ideas and ideals that can permit them to achieve the greatest possible accomplishments.

Everyone up to now has been satisfied to focus on one or two traditional sets of ideas. We need to have access to a thousand sets of such ideas, to be able to choose that or those that can be most useful for our future. To add new ideas and ideals is not to reject what is good and useful in our national or religious heritage. Those of us who wish really to be able to serve our people must be willing to recognize what is good and useful in other sets of ideas and ideals. Our local leaders, political as well as educational, may well continue to serve Islam by accepting the future. Our *ulema* do not need to focus only on the past. But those who believe that it is right and proper to place all trust and hope in God can nevertheless begin to serve also the needs and aspirations of our nation. The civilized nations are not necessarily Godless in their civilizing activity. But the challenge is great. It will not be easy to persuade our *muftis* and other *ulema* that Islam is not against change.

6. We summarize here some of Ismail Bey's ideas on the education of women as they appeared in dozens of articles in *Terjüman*:

Muslims have tended to diverge in recent periods from some of the precepts of Islamic law. They have sometimes done it without knowing that they were violating some of the earliest precepts. One of the examples of this sort of error relates to the education and upbringing of women. Some have argued that, by educating women, one is not keeping God's will, that one is in fact preventing such women from fulfilling their rightful responsibilities, that is, being married and raising children. This is absolutely an ignorant position to take. It is, in fact, itself a violation of God's will. Our young girls who pass through primary schools, and in many cases who enter gymnasiums, are *more able* to fulfill God's will than those who do not. Muslims in Kazan and in Ufa have begun to educate their daughters, and a number of them have learned to read and write. Some Muslims have cited religious reasons for opposing this development in Crimea, but many Crimean Muslims have seen the utility in female education and have supported it. These Crimean daughters are beginning to know the requisites of living in the modern world. The condition of these Crimean daughters should give useful instruction to Muslims living in the Caucasus and in Turkistan, where such developments are rare. There are too many people in the Caucasus and in Turkistan who say that what daughters need is instruction in how to fulfill God's will and nothing more. What they do not understand is the fact that God wills both men and women to develop their minds, to be educated, to learn science and other forms of knowledge. The daughters of all the Muslims in Russia must be introduced to education, just as it is important for their sons.

We must not be afraid of the people, male or female. We must not permit ignorance to flourish. We must not allow our daughters to become like Chinese girls and women. In China women are not permitted to become fully human. They exist only to serve men. This is a major difference between Islam and Chinese society and traditions. Unfortunately, many of us Turks have remained far too long under the influence of Chinese culture. One of the great blessings of the Turks' becoming Muslim many centuries ago was their liberation from Chinese culture and traditions. We were pagans then and ignorant. Islam afforded us the opportunity to become civilized, and the opportunity was available to both men and women.

There are those among our Muslim men who fear that education for our women will open them to the possibility of preferring foreign men and their ideas. What they forget is the fact that Chinese culture and traditions are foreign, to us, and to Islam. The foundations of civilization are built only through education. Perhaps Chinese women will some day arise and be freed from their subjection. It is about time that we encourage our own daughters to arise!

7. On the opening of social welfare societies and through them the renewal of society, there have been a great many articles in *Terjüman*, and we encourage our readers to consult them.

8. In order to establish firm foundations for our national literature, it is necessary that we develop a pure, clear, and understandable "Turki" language. We have discussed this subject, and Ismail Bey's intense participation in its success, above. Here we will mention some of the problems, and successes, in this development and draw from examples of the use of "Turki" by modern writers. Of all the hopes entertained by Ismail Bey during his life, this one may well be the most difficult to achieve. It is very difficult to change one's language consciously. It is much easier to learn a foreign language than to reform in a considerable way one's own. But the initial steps in the reform of our literature and its expression have been achieved already.

In an article appearing in *Terjüman* in 1888, Ismail Bey noted that the most active of our writers and literary figures used a language that was for the most part not understandable by most Turkic readers in Russia. He wrote that for literary style and even language these writers owed their major debt to the past "greats" within our literary history. He hoped that in the future outstanding writers would emerge who could write in a language that the ordinary literate Turk could understand. We are happy to note that, at the present time, many of our best writers have paid heed to Ismail Bey's call. Among our most active writers and literary figures today who would fit Ismail Bey's description are the following:

(1) Mirza Fath Ali Ahundov (Tiflis). He has published in the "Turki" language a number of plays. (2) Hasan Bey Melikov (Baku). He founded one of the most important "Turki" newspapers among Russian Muslims. (3) Said Ansi Zade (Tiflis). He publishes a Turkic newspaper named *Ziya-i Kafkasiya* and is the author of many short stories. (4) Jelal Efendi Ansi Zade (Tiflis). The brother of Said Ansi Zade, he is a writer and publishes the newspaper *Keshkul*. He wrote the wonderful treatise "A Short Guide to Knowledge." (5) Abdulselam Ahundzade (Shusha). He is the author of the highly respected book *The Conditions Necessary for Knowledge*. (6) Amiz Efendi Mekarav (Kuban district). He serves as a local *kadi* and is the author of the book *A Catechism*. (7) Ataallah Yabazidov. A writer in both Turkic and Russian of treatises on science. He is a lawyer in Petrograd. (8) Abdulkayyum Nasirov (Kazan). He writes almanacs in "Turki" and has authored five or ten treatises. (9) Shihab al din Merjani. A professor in the city of Kazan. He has written a number of important essays in "Turki" as well as in Arabic. (10) Husseyin Efendi Gaibov (Tiflis). He is a poet and has put together a number of books on the question of our national identity. He is also the *mufti* of Tiflis. (11) Muluka Bumajukov (Siberia). A poet who has published a great deal of poetry in "Turki." (12) Altinsarin (Orenburg). A Kazak poet. (13) Musi Akchibitov (Penza). A novelist of the first rank, author of the novel *Husam Mela*. (14) Zahir Bekiyev (Kazan). An author of novels in Tatar. (15) Abdulselam Kazyhanov (Kazan). He wrote and published a geography in "Turki."

Other writers who have appeared in the years since 1888 and who are contributing greatly to our national literature include Selizazim Shirvani, Habtalla Ayshan, Abulmunih Haji, Chukr Mehmed Ali Ishasi, and a "thousand" beautiful poets. However, it is important to place at the forefront of all the names mentioned above that of Ismail Bey.

Thirty years ago Ismail Bey explained to us what was necessary for us to really serve our people through writing. It involved making clear and available to our readers the most important ideas of our time. Ismail Bey was the best at doing this. One of his slogans might well have been "what is best for mankind is what is most useful for mankind." This slogan informed everything that he did.

At the opening of the General Islamic Congress that was held in Egypt a few years ago, Ismail Bey discussed these important questions openly and bluntly. He prepared a speech to present before more than three hundred guests and participants at the hotel Continental in the middle of October 1907. We summarize here the main issues that he raised, which we believe clearly focus Ismail Bey's aims at that time:

Although Muslims throughout the world are today plagued by a condition of backwardness, there are important new ideas that are appearing throughout the Muslim world that need to be discussed and absorbed. Many newspapers and journals have been founded on every side in the Muslim world, most of which are providing genuine service to the various Muslim nationalities. Humanity in general will only benefit from these developments. But they do not hide the fact that, generally throughout the Muslim world, poverty and ignorance seem to be the permanent state of affairs. In the Muslim world, *medreses* continue for the most part to be institutions of the past and continue to play the part of obstacle to progress and renewal. Muslims appear to be under the domination of traders and commercial interests. They appear unable to take charge of these affairs on their own. Despite the fact that there are supposed to be more than three hundred million Muslims throughout the world, trade and industry are not important among them. We have no successful commercial companies, no successful banking establishments, no leaders in international trade and commerce. We have inherited from our ancestors fertile lands and rich forests and great commercial traditions. But we cannot discover how to make use of them, to profit from them. We are dependent on others, from non-Muslim lands and traditions, to exploit our own riches. They are in Europe and America. Why do we have no successful merchants and traders within our Muslim lands? Surely, in Iran and Turkey, in Egypt and North Africa, in India, there is sufficient talent. It is my belief that, if the present situation continues for long, not only the traditions and values of the Muslims but their very existence is in question. It is ignorance that is primarily to blame. Greeks, Bulgarians, Jews, Hindus, all have in less than half a century made such strides in progress that they have left us far behind. It is nothing inherent in Islam that can explain this state of affairs. It is nothing inherent in Arab or Turkic culture that is to blame. Let us remember that Turks developed the highest culture and science in Samarkand, great works of civilization. This alone is proof of the fact that Turks, and Arabs, and all Muslims, are capable of these achievements today. Peoples who come from the same stock as Turks—Finns and Hungarians—are far ahead of us in science and knowledge. Are Muslims, who today appear to be without knowledge, without talents, slaves of outmoded ideas and systems, to remain in this condition indefinitely? Islam is a religion that should be able to offer us a solution to the current state of affairs. Islam is a religion that fosters science, knowledge, education, progress. Islam is not a religion opposed to any of the above. Why does it seem to be so today? I do not have all the answers to this question, the most important one we face today, perhaps the most important one we have ever faced. It will take serious, honest, bold, and blunt discussion.

After he delivered his speech, a great deal of discussion and argument took place. But the essence of the debate centered around the question of whether Islam could (should) be reformed or changed, whether Islam was doomed to fail or destined to succeed and survive. Ismail Bey was roundly applauded for raising the question in such a clear fashion.

One of Ismail Bey's greatest hopes was, in fact, that Islam would succeed and survive, that it would play what he believed to be its rightful role in the development of world civilization. But to do so it was necessary that Muslim teachers, particularly those who were involved in religious and legal education, be reformed and renewed. For this purpose, new and reformed teachers' schools would have to be founded.

It seems to us that in recent years this particular question has also been of utmost importance to the Turkic Muslim world. And it was in his last several years, when he was already becoming ill, that Ismail Bey began to focus more of his attention on the religious and spiritual education of Turkic Muslims. He was responsible for founding a special school in Bakhchesaray that would concentrate its efforts on such renewal of religious and spiritual education; it utilized the "mother" Turkic tongue and has set the foundations for continued renewal in Turkic Islam.

### 15 December 1914: Ismail Bey's Journey to India

In order to publicize his "phonetic method" of teaching literacy, Ismail Bey journeyed to India. He was prepared to use whatever energy was necessary and to undergo considerable personal sacrifice in order to persuade others of the benefits of this teaching method. In fact, however, he was not the first "Ismail" to make such a journey to India.

In the year 1751, another Ismail, a Bukharan by birth, and a follower of Said Biste, left Orenburg for a similar trip to India. It was one hundred sixty years later that the second Ismail, this time from Bakhchesaray, also journeyed to India.

Although the first Ismail went in an official governmental capacity, had with him a great deal of gold and silver, and was accompanied by many assistants and other officials, he had a great deal of difficulty reaching India and had almost no success when he arrived The second Ismail made the trip accompanied only by forty verses [*beyt*] and a ten-piece alphabet together with some additional school [*maktab*] materials. But this Ismail was able to meet with many of the great and important members of the Indian Muslim community. His major worry was that these important people would listen politely, would not appreciate the possibilities of this new teaching method, might not be truly interested in raising the literacy of the mass of Indian Muslims, and would put the new alphabet and method into a "museum" when he left.

Ismail Bey began his visit with a few days examining the Muslim schools in Bombay. The schools of the Indian Muslims, like those for Muslims elsewhere in the world, were in a decrepit state. The leaders of some of these schools were beginning to believe that the problem was with the use of Arabic letters and were beginning to consider the introduction of another, "more appropriate" alphabet. At least Ismail Bey recognized that some of these leaders saw the need for educational reform. After attending a meeting of the Enjumen-i Islam society in Bombay, Ismail Bey discussed his new method with school officials and, to the astonishment of society members and teachers, offered to demonstrate to them that he could teach illiterates to read in only forty days.

Some of these officials took up Ismail Bey's offer, and on 2 March 1910, with all the appropriate Muslim blessings made, the first "phonetic-method" school was established in India. The Enjumen-i Islam society agreed to provide two months' funding, to allow Ismail Bey to demonstrate the effectiveness of his method.

At the end of the forty-day period a number of the previously illiterate students were able to read some simple lines, and the firm foundations for a new era in Indian Muslim education were laid. Indian Islam had in glorious centuries past produced some of the leaders of Muslim intellectual and political life: emperors like Akbar Shah; philosophers like Mirzad-al Haruni, Muhiballah al Bukhari, and Mahmud al Chunkuri; poets like Feyzi and Azat; canonical jurists like Hamdani; statesmen like Ahmed ibn Abdulrahman; mystics such as Ahmed al Sahrendi and Abdul ar-Rashid al-Chunkuri; masters like Riziya, Sekinder Bey, and Shahjihan

Bey; writers like Abdullah and Sadik Hasan Han; rich merchants like Rahmetallah and Ahmed Han. It is indeed fitting that the first "phonetic-method" school was founded among the great Indian Muslims, and we can take great pride in the fact that it was a Russian Muslim who initiated this reform.

Ismail Bey said the following about his journey to India, as reported in *Ikdam*:

I went to India to conduct some research on a project on which I have been working for three years, to examine Indian Muslim schools, to see how my teaching method might fit in their existing schools, and finally to determine if it were possible to persuade the local Muslim school officials to adopt my "phonetic method." While I was walking around Bombay, I saw signs and papers written in two scripts, one of which resembled English and the other Hebrew. There was no place where the signs were written with the Arabic alphabet. Thus Muslims could not possibly be able to read the signs without having learned a new language. And the alphabets used, strange to the Muslims, did not permit them to even "sound out" the signs. Thus, the pressures among the Indian Muslim community were rising to adopt the Latin alphabet for their own language. In the province of Bombay there are twenty million people. Should they actually adopt the Latin alphabet it will be difficult to prevent it from being adopted elsewhere in the Muslim world.

Men whose occupations are involved with knowledge and science usually need a great deal of testing, trying, and evidence before they will give up one set of ideas for new ones, one established method for another. And it was not clear at first to such people that the new methods were in fact superior to the older ones. But Ismail Bey was extremely persistent, was willing and able to devote a long time to persuading such leaders to cease defending the old and to consider a new road or path. Of course, one of Ismail Bey's important discoveries was that any particular orthography can be closely linked to questions of national identity. Throughout a career of more than thirty years, Ismail Bey worked to protect the old orthography and the use of Arabic letters. He continued to be able to provide answers to questions raised by the opponents, within the nationalist movement, of the old alphabet and spelling. He firmly believed that it was possible to combine the old orthography with a new "phonetic method" of teaching reading. He kept this effort up until the end of his life.

Beginning with the appearance of *Terjüman*, Russian Muslims got in the habit of using the term *Tatar*, despite the fact that it was not entirely appropriate for all Russian Muslims. But after 1906 they began more often to use the term *Turk* as less specific and more accurate. The change was one that Ismail Bey fostered.

On learning of Ismail Bey's death, there appeared in the newspapers and journals of Turkey, Egypt, and Syria a great many outpourings of sorrow and grief. We provide below a sampling of statements and testimony from journalists who were influenced by the ideas and actions of Ismail Bey, some of which appeared in print in recent years.

1. Ahmet Midhat Efendi. This person, who was a follower of Ismail Bey, delivered a speech about Ismail Bey at an Islamic Congress held in Istanbul on 19 April 1909, in which he said:

Gentlemen! This evening Ismail Bey honored us by appearing before our gathering and presenting us with some thought-provoking ideas. He instructed us "not to pay attention overly to how one pronounces words, but to pay attention closely to the heart of the word itself." We should all ponder this carefully. In truth, it was absolute truth that Ismail Bey spoke. None of us can have any doubt that this view is certainly true.

Ismail Bey Gaspirali is a man with a mission, with a certainty of purpose. This man was responsible for introducing in Russia twenty-eight years ago the newspaper *Terjüman*. This man began to publish *Terjüman* at a time when the Russian Muslims had little or no access to news in their own language. He also understood that, in order to be able to make advances in knowledge and education, a sound system of primary schooling was necessary. Finally, he believed that, for the fulfillment of a sound national identity, Russia's Muslims needed a common language. Toward all these goals this man devoted his life. Ismail Bey might well have come to the conclusion that these goals bore too high a price. A great many people doubted the benefits of renewal and unity. But the warrior Ismail Bey was victorious in these struggles and was able to overcome all sorts of slander and false accusations that his detractors produced.

2. Jevdet Bey. This person, who was the leading journalist and one-time editor of the newspaper *Iqdam*, wrote a long article about Ismail Bey, a portion of which we publish here:

Ismail Bey is a man whose name one day will be a national monument. He comes from the true Turkic stock (of the Russian/northern-Turkic group). We have a number of illusions about ourselves [we Turks], and he realized what they were. In order to begin to address these illusions, he founded a school with perfection in mind. We seldom find among ourselves successful businessmen. We still live in a world of illusions and specters. This man had an idea that may well cure our deafness and insensitivity. There are many people who are fatalists, who are resigned to accept whatever God has planned for their future. He decided to challenge such people. Thirty years ago there was absolutely no one in our publishing world who would not have considered his ideas bitter tasting. We had no one who was willing to apply great efforts to solve our difficulties. We had no problem in creating obstacles for people such as Ismail Bey.

I know the goodness of this man; I have seen his works. Nothing has been published yet in modern Islamic languages that matches the works he has published to awaken Muslims to achieve modern sciences and knowledge. It is the custom among the people to place high value on inherited habits and ideas. According to this custom, Muslims tend to consider their own traditional ideas superior to all else. Otherwise intelligent people tend to call those who produce new ideas nonbelievers. But there is a big difference between new ideas and un-Islamic ones, just as one should distinguish between bigots and zealots. Even the ancients who provided commentary on Islamic law and traditions argued that one should be guided by more than what ideas one inherited from the past. There is no doubt that there are some people who now think otherwise, but most of our leaders still believe that there should be no teaching outside of what the Qur'ân offers. Ismail Bey has presented to us a way to overcome our blindness to the present and future. He has asked our people to awaken.

3. Huseyin Hüsnü. He is a sheikh of the Rufaiyah dervish order and has written a long article on Ismail Bey in the journal *The Nile* [*al-Nil*]:

In an article published in Bakhchesaray in the newspaper *Hizmet* recently, the founder and chief journalist of the newspaper *Terjüman*, the zealous, eminent, and famous Ismail Bey Gaspirali, is reported to have died and to have come face to face with his ultimate destiny.

We are deeply saddened because Ismail Bey and his associates have been true servants of our millions of religious brothers in Russia. We all place our trust in true servants of God such as Ismail Bey. The death of one who is also a true servant of our great nation [*millet*] brings us a great sense of loss. We are very grateful to Ismail Bey for having done what he did for our religion and for our people.

We take great pleasure in the fact that Ismail Bey was able to struggle so effectively against the lies and misunderstandings that have plagued us Muslims. The entire Muslim world is grateful for Ismail Bey's praiseworthy service.

Ismail Bey possessed a taste free from defect. He loved simplicity and for this reason wore simple clothes and ate and drank simply. His writing reflected this simplicity. He now is simply separated from us and is at rest. He eats his simple food there, drinks his coffee there, and remains at rest there.

He used to accept guests with hospitality at his home. He would arise early, at six or seven, would drink black coffee, and after that would begin to write. After the mail arrived, he would read his letters and daily papers. He took notes from his daily reading and marked up the papers with a colored pen. He did much of his work while stretched out on his bed [*kerevet*]. He wrote very quickly and was writing up to the time of his death.

He smoked tobacco. Around ten in the morning he would leave his room and walk to the editorial office of *Terjüman*. In his last days, he still visited his office, talked with the newspaper's staff, but would soon return to his home and stretch out on his bed. We know that now, after his death, he will still "be present" in the offices of *Terjüman*.

Both his room and his office were cheerful, nicely colored, with flowers. He liked beautiful music. He used to say, "The world is colorful and beautiful; so too should our press be colorful and beautiful."

For Ismail Bey the greatest pain and worst punishment would have been to have no work to do, to be idle. Thus he never spent a day without some productive work to be accomplished. He was constantly busy with writing or reading or speaking or thinking.

No matter how great the difficulty, Ismail Bey's spirit was never daunted, and he never lost hope. However frail he might have appeared, he had great boldness and firmness inside. He gave spirit to those without spirit, hope to those without hope. No one could ever say that he ever was without goal or aim. He had a sensitive and compassionate heart. He constantly preached moderation in the midst of deep crisis. He gave consolation to those experiencing sorrow, even to those who went morally astray.

In the city, no matter how rich and powerful his friends or acquaintances, no matter how important the society he kept, Ismail Bey never distinguished himself from the poor, weak, and hungry. He really preferred the simple customs and traditions of his people. While being in great demand in "high society" in the cities, Ismail Bey preferred to have a simple life, to wander about the bazaar with ordinary people, to go into small coffeehouses and drink coffee, to gossip with the people.

Ismail Bey did not much like food prepared in the European fashion. In culinary taste he was still an old-timer. He was not in favor of replacing the old traditional customs and values with European ones [i.e., Russian] and felt pained to see many of the young Muslims adopting European taste in food and dress and abandoning what he believed to be good in the old ways.

Ismail Bey placed high value on the arts. He did like some European music but preferred the Turkic national music as it was known and performed in typical Eastern villages.

Ismail Bey argued that even in traditional and isolated villages in Crimea, such as Aksar Temir Dulusu and Temirlenk Marashi, "one day there will be primary and higher schools that will produce physicians, philologists, poets, and painters. Let there be music conservatories and medical schools open to all Muslim children."

From the first weeks of 1914, Ismail Bey began to complain that he felt weak and ill. In February he went to Petrograd but soon found it necessary to return to Bakhchesaray and then to spend a couple of weeks at the shore taking in the Crimean sea air. By the beginning of summer, however, it was clear that he was very ill.

Throughout June, Ismail Bey was given a combination of the best waters and minerals, and it was hoped that these in combination with the wonderful Crimean air would restore him to health. Yusuf Beg Akchurin returned to be with him in Crimea. His condition continued to deteriorate.

Yet he was still able to get around. He had a photograph taken of himself with the staff of *Terjüman* and again with the members of his family. Experiencing a great deal of pain, on 27 June he went to a hospital in Aqmesjit, spent three days there, and even was able to do some writing while in bed. The doctors reported that the final stages of his illness were about to begin. But his condition stabilized, and he remained unchanged by the end of August. Every day he spent one or two hours reading the daily newspapers. He spoke on political questions. But on 8 September he lost his ability to stand up, and it became clear that he was beginning to make his final journey.

Ismail Bey called his family together on 9 September. They prepared a special bulgar pilaf for him, and, in order to show them that he was still competent and able, he read to them his last will and testament:

Since the end is growing near, I think it important to have my personal and financial matters in hand. Therefore, I have prepared and now read to you my testament and last wishes:

1. My grave: dig it on the east side of the *türbe* of Mengli Giray Khan beside the Zinjirli Medrese.

2. Please spend no more than forty rubles on my burial and funeral and related expenses. I want 200 rubles spent for the benefit of a *maktab* and mosque.

3. I do not want *Terjüman* to be divided up. I hope that *Terjüman* will continue to prosper and that the various members of my family will continue to profit from it.

4. After me, I hope that the editorship of *Terjüman* will be taken on by Hasan Sabri Ayvazov and that all members of my family will support him.

5. Whatever income derives from *Terjüman*, let it be divided equally among my children and sons-in-law.

6. Please give a fifty-ruble gift to the orphan I have befriended named Zeyneb.

Around noon on 10 September the "Yasin-i Sherif" [sura 36 of the Qur'ân] was read, and, afterward, Ismail Bey gathered together enough strength to say:

God is great! I have lived more than sixty-three years. I have devoted more than thirty-five of them to Muslim movements and Islamic renewal. I hope my efforts have provided long-lasting benefit to my nation and that my work has helped everyone else's work too. I have one more hope. But I do not now know whether this hope will be granted. It is that God will be pleased with what I have done and that God will approve of what all of you do after me.

This day passed. Everyone remained in his house, fearing the worst. The next day, 11 September, he remained in bed, although early in the morning he was strong enough to give some important advice to his close friends and family. But, at around eight in the morning, Ismail Bey died. Those around him wept bitterly.

On 12 September the Friday prayers were said. The funeral service was organized by the administration of *Terjüman*, and his casket was carried by six men, and he was buried, as he had wished, alongside the Mengli Giray Khan *türbe*.

News of his final illness and death, published in *Terjüman* and then immediately in the rest of the Muslim press, produced deep grief and mourning among the Turkic and other Muslims of Russia. But most expressed the hope that it would be his life and achievements, not his death, that would inspire what Muslims would do in the future, their hopes and service.

Ismail Bey was our master teacher. We should not weep but now should take great pride in what he accomplished. Among Russian Muslims, Ismail Bey was one of our greatest. While we, at *Shura*, have received statements of consolation from a great many people, the following list gives some indication of the great variety and breadth: from the village of Chakmak, the imam and *mudarris* Mehmed Shakir Ahmed Veli Oglu Feyzi; from Tashkent, Muhsin Efendi Shiir Mehmed oglu Hanifa Asimet; in Kerki, Abd al Habir Abdallah; in Samarkand, Sidiqi; in Irkutsk, Habibullah Garbidov; in Kazan, Jelal; and so forth. Clearly, Ismail Bey meant a great deal to everyone. We will miss him! But we will carry on.

# Notes

1. The present pamphlet is being translated into Oriental languages.
2. *Perevodchik* is distributed among foreign Muslims more than among those living in Russia.
3. For example, *Iqdam, Sabah, Gayret, Vatan, Diqqat, Hidmet, Agenk, Zaman, Kipr, Nil, Ahter,* and *Naasuri.*
4. Alexandre Bennigsen and Chantal Lemercier-Quelquejay, *La presse et le mouvement nationale chez les Musulmans de Russie avante 1920* (Paris: Mouton, 1964), 77.

# II

The Ordeal of Forced Exile

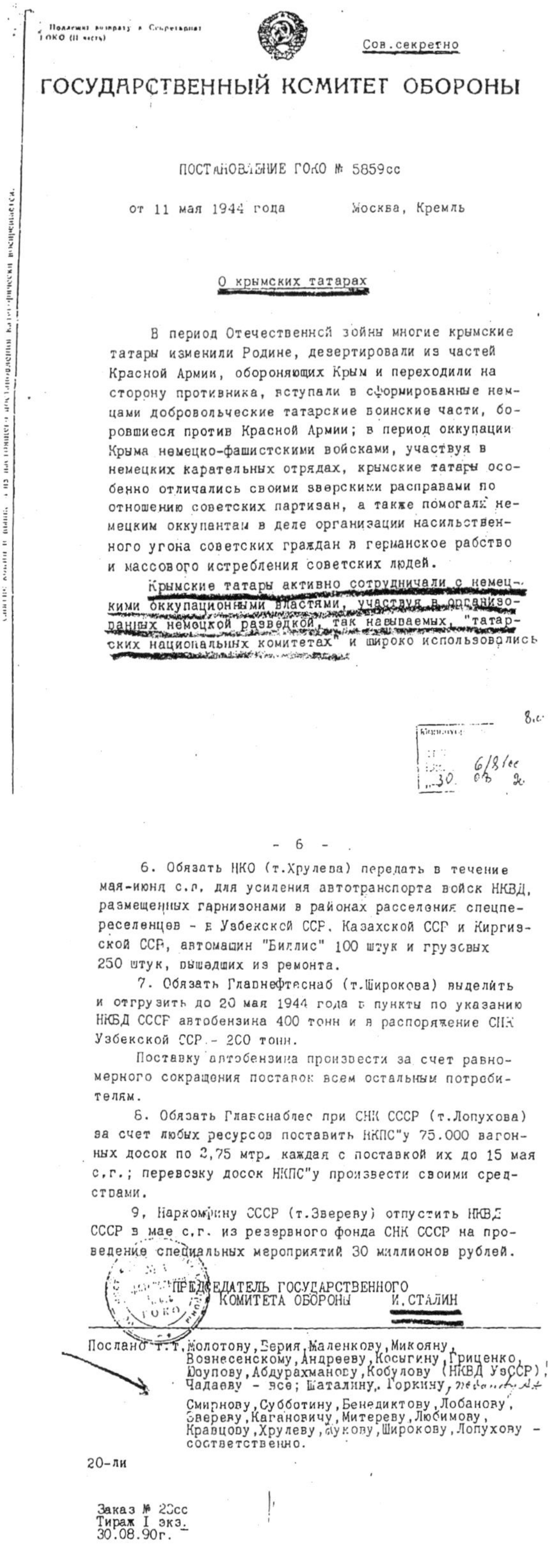

Подлежит возврату в Секретариат
ГОКО (II часть)

Сов.секретно

# ГОСУДАРСТВЕННЫЙ КОМИТЕТ ОБОРОНЫ

ПОСТАНОВЛЕНИЕ ГОКО № 5859сс

от 11 мая 1944 года    Москва, Кремль

О крымских татарах

В период Отечественной войны многие крымские татары изменили Родине, дезертировали из частей Красной Армии, обороняющих Крым и переходили на сторону противника, вступали в сформированные немцами добровольческие татарские воинские части, боровшиеся против Красной Армии; в период оккупации Крыма немецко-фашистскими войсками, участвуя в немецких карательных отрядах, крымские татары особенно отличались своими зверскими расправами по отношению советских партизан, а также помогали немецким оккупантам в деле организации насильственного угона советских граждан в германское рабство и массового истребления советских людей.

Крымские татары активно сотрудничали с немецкими оккупационными властями, участвуя в организованных немецкой разведкой, так называемых, "татарских национальных комитетах" и широко использовались

- 6 -

6. Обязать НКО (т.Хрулева) передать в течение мая-июня с.г. для усиления автотранспорта войск НКВД, размещенных гарнизонами в районах расселения спецпереселенцев - в Узбекской ССР, Казахской ССР и Киргизской ССР, автомашин "Виллис" 100 штук и грузовых 250 штук, вышедших из ремонта.

7. Обязать Главнефтеснаб (т.Широкова) выделить и отгрузить до 20 мая 1944 года в пункты по указанию НКВД СССР автобензина 400 тонн и в распоряжение СНК Узбекской ССР - 200 тонн.

Поставку автобензина произвести за счет равномерного сокращения поставок всем остальным потребителям.

8. Обязать Главснаблес при СНК СССР (т.Лопухова) за счет любых ресурсов поставить НКПС"у 75.000 вагонных досок по 2,75 мтр. каждая с поставкой их до 15 мая с.г.; перевозку досок НКПС"у произвести своими средствами.

9. Наркомфину СССР (т.Звереву) отпустить НКВД СССР в мае с.г. из резервного фонда СНК СССР на проведение специальных мероприятий 30 миллионов рублей.

ПРЕДСЕДАТЕЛЬ ГОСУДАРСТВЕННОГО
КОМИТЕТА ОБОРОНЫ    И.СТАЛИН

Послано: т.т. Молотову, Берия, Маленкову, Микояну, Вознесенскому, Андрееву, Косыгину, Гриценко, Доупову, Абдурахманову, Кобулову (НКВД УзССР), Чадаеву - все; Шаталину, Горкину,
Смирнову, Субботину, Бенедиктову, Лобанову, Звереву, Кагановичу, Митереву, Любимову, Кравцову, Хрулеву, Чукову, Широкову, Лопухову - соответственно.

20-ли

Заказ № 20сс
Тираж I экз.
30.08.90г.

Figure 8.1. First and final pages of the top secret document from the Soviet State Defense Committee (GOKO), signed by I. (Iosif) Stalin, the Soviet dictator, 11 May 1944, ordering the deportation of the entire Crimean Tatar nationality from Crimea. (A partial translation appears in chap. 13, page 271). From a copy made 30 August 1990 furnished by the Crimean Tatar Mejlis.

# 8

## *The Elders of the New National Movement: Recollections*

AYSHE SEYTMURATOVA

During the night of 17–18 May 1944, Soviet soldiers and agents of the NKVD (now the KGB) with automatic weapons in their hands forced their way into the homes of Crimean Tatars.

Peacefully sleeping children, women, and old men, whose fathers, husbands, and sons spilled their blood on the front during World War II in defense of the Soviet state, as well as intelligence officers and partisans, were yanked from their beds, and in the name of the Soviet state it was declared that, "for treason against the motherland, you are being exiled in perpetuity . . . to roll call in fifteen to twenty minutes."

Is it possible for one woman to wake, dress, and put shoes on a sleeping seven-year-old child in fifteen to twenty minutes, not to mention doing other things? This is what my mother had to do. Her oldest son was seventeen, and the youngest was two. I was seven.

They packed us barefoot and cold, dressed only in pajamas, into railcars and sent us off to Central Asia, along with the entire Crimean Tatar people. We Crimean Tatars call these Soviet railcars "crematoria on wheels." (For a reproduction of the document ordering the deportations, see fig. 8.1.)

So we were transported for weeks without proper food or medical attention. There was not even any fresh air, for the doors and windows were bolted shut. For days on end, corpses lay alongside the living.

And only out in the sands of Kazakhstan did the transport guards open the doors, so as to toss out the corpses alongside the railway. They did not give us time to bury the dead. Many people went insane.

It is grievous for me to write about this terrible tragedy. I am not only a witness to this tragedy, but a victim of it.

We, the Crimean Tatar children of the 1940s, grew up under the conditions of cruel state-sponsored terror on reservations—that has naturally left a deep imprint on our hearts.

I am not indifferent to the fate of my people. Along with my people, I have endured all the horrors of deportation: the hunger, the cold, the sickness, the insult, the injury, and the supervision of the special settlements. With my own eyes I have seen genocide, the destruction of the Crimean Tatar people.

And, as a Crimean Tatar woman, I have experienced discrimination.

I was born in Crimea in the village of Ajierin, not far from the city of Kerch.

My parents were peasant *kolkhoz* workers. There were seven children in my family: five boys and two girls. In autumn of 1941 my father was mobilized for and sent to the front.

He perished in the war against the fascists while defending the Soviet state. And we, his seven children and wife, were exiled in 1944 as traitors to the motherland from Crimea, along with the entire Crimean Tatar people.

A part of our people was deported to the Urals and part to Central Asia. Our family ended up in Uzbekistan, in the Samarkand district of the Khatyrchinskii region, at the mine "Lyangar."

At that Lyangar mine some sort of ore was extracted that was valuable to the military industry. I cannot recall the name of the ore. Among the people it is called *chirit*.

For the entire Crimean Tatar people a special regime was established—no Crimean Tatar had the right to travel farther than five kilometers from the settlement.

Other deported people lived at the Lyangar mine as well: the Koreans (deported from the Far East in the 1930s) and Volga Germans (deported in 1941).

The common national tragedy brought us, Crimean Tatars, closer to these peoples.

Uzbeks also lived at the mine settlement.

The living conditions were terrible at first. We lived in earthen huts or in barns with the cattle.

Later, barracks were built, where each family was allotted one room (no matter the size of the family).

We seven children and my mother lived in one small room.

Deportation, sickness, hunger, and cold did not allow me or my peers of school age to begin our studies in the years 1944–45.

Only in 1946 did I cross the threshold of a school. At that time there was not even a mention of schools or instruction in the Crimean Tatar language.

All children of deported peoples were coerced into attending Russian schools. I too studied in a Russian school. Although the school was called Russian, there were in fact only a few Russian students there. Basically, they were children of Crimean Tatars, Germans, Koreans, and people of other nationalities.

The teaching staff of our school was also international. I do not remember the names of my first teachers. But I do remember well that a Korean man taught my fifth-grade class mathematics; his name was Kim.

We the children of the 1940s did not have a childhood. My younger brother, sister, and I did not have a single toy. Of course, there were toys in the stores, but my mother often did not even have money for bread, let alone toys.

We lived at the Lyangar mine from 1944 to 1954. After Stalin's death in 1953 we moved closer to Samarkand, to the settlement of the Superfosfat factory, where we lived right up until our emigration to the West in 1978. My relatives to this very day live at that settlement. At the very same Superfosfat settlement I graduated from the tenth grade.

Since I was a child, I have been fond of sports: riding horses, playing basketball and volleyball, riding bicycles, doing gymnastics and light athletics. In addition, I like to read very much. I took out books not only from the elementary school library but also from the settlement's library and from the regional library in Samarkand, named for A. S. Pushkin.

To the best of my abilities I assembled a personal library.

It was my responsibility to keep the house in order and to do the wash. I cherished every minute and did not waste my free time. At school I made friends not only with Crimean Tatars but also with Russians, Koreans, and Uzbeks.

In 1958, I entered the Samarkand State University named for Alisher Navoy in the graduate department of history.

At school I hated history and the history teachers. And here is why. The elementary school teachers constantly slandered our people and history, calling us traitors and barbarians.

And only after the Twentieth Congress of the Communist Party of the Soviet Union (CPSU) in 1956, where the unjustified deportation of smaller ethnic groups during the war was loudly discussed, did the schoolteachers stop baiting us, Crimean Tatar children.

The fact that I decided to study history was made possible by the Twentieth Congress.

I wanted to learn why we were sent away and why, if we were not guilty, we were not returned home to Crimea. Other questions arose: for example, why we had no schools in our native language.

I began to seek answers to these and other questions in the graduate department of history at Samarkand University. At the same time I also studied at the two-year evening university of Marxism-Leninism at Samarkand University.

In 1963, I graduated from the department of history. As a student I had been a member of an academic society at the university. I often gave lectures at academic conferences.

I was fortunate enough to study under such historians as Professor I. I. Umnyakov and the reader D. N. Lev.

They were not only fine historians but fine people as well. They understood me and the tragedy of my people. These and other people protected me from taking a careless step.

In childhood, to uphold the honor of the people, it was sometimes necessary to use fists.

But, when we had grown up, to uphold our people's honor we used the pen.

After graduating from the university I worked as a teacher of history in a school and at the university in Samarkand. I dedicated all my free time to collecting documents and material on Crimea and Crimean Tatars.

I was especially interested in the battle of Crimean Tatars against fascism. For we, Crimean Tatars, were accused of treason against the motherland, and we needed facts, not only to rectify the slander of the Soviet government, but also to demonstrate to the peoples of the Soviet Union the hostility of the authorities toward a relatively small group of people.

So as to realize my dream of becoming a historian, I left for Moscow in October 1964 to take the postgraduate entrance exams for the Institute of History at the Akademiia Nauk (AN) USSR. Despite the fact that I passed all my exams, I was accepted, not in the Institute of History of the AN USSR, but in the Institute of History of the AN Uzbek Soviet Socialist Republic (UZSSR) in Tashkent. But alas! The director of the Institute of History of the AN UZSSR, Akhurova, plainly explained to me: "We train our own national cadres [Uzbeks]."

"And where do I belong," I asked her. "In Moscow I am a foreigner, and in Uzbekistan I am a foreigner. Tell me, where do I belong?" In a word, I was not accepted in Tashkent.

It was then that I deeply, deeply understood that we were like homeless people. And no one wanted to let us into his home.

I took several professors into confidence at Samarkand University, including Professor I. I. Umnyakov (now deceased).

Of course, I spoke with each of them separately. They all deeply sympathized with me and understood that "salt had been poured on my wounds." I studied for five years under these professors, and they knew me very well and understood better than I the injustice of the Crimean Tatar people's exile.

I am grateful to my teachers and professors at Samarkand University who taught me how to live and struggle. Each one of them advised me to unearth the history of my people and to acquaint Crimean Tatar youths with it.

In 1964, I was admitted to the history department of the university as an assistant. Without going into details, I'll say the following about how the initiators of the national movement of Crimean Tatars found out about me. Once a boy I knew rushed up to us and handed me a note that said that his father wanted to see me very much. The note also said: "I must speak with you right away." When I arrived at Ahmed aga's (aga: "uncle," conveys respect) house, I saw three men, totally unknown to me.

Ahmed aga introduced me to the men and briefly stated who they were and why they had come. All of them had been partisans and intelligence officers in Crimea during World War II.

I told them briefly that I wanted to become a historian and that I had been collecting documents and material about Crimean Tatars' participation in the war. The conversation went on late into the night. A week later we met again, but this time there were ten people. I had come up with a plan for work among Crimean Tatars.

I was asked to read my plan for work aloud. When I had finished, one of the *Aksakals* (elders) stood up, walked over to me, and kissed me on the forehead. Then he took the papers out of my hands and said: "Hold in your head everything that you wrote here and burn the papers. For such papers, I spent seventeen years in prison."

Everyone agreed with him, and the papers were destroyed then and there.

In the plan were the following:

1. Gather books on the history, archaeology, and ethnography of Crimean Tatars.
2. Gather Crimean Tatar folktales, legends, adages, sayings, and songs.

3. Gather national costumes and household articles.
4. Have young people in an amateur historical society.
5. Start a group called "Collectors of National Folklore" and a group for the study of Arabic script (since Arabic script had been our national form of writing). In 1926–27, our national writing—in Arabic script—was replaced by the Roman alphabet, and, in 1936, the Roman was replaced by the Russian alphabet.
6. Gather materials concerning deaths among the people in 1944.
7. Investigate the historical and artistic literature about Crimea and Crimean Tatars.
8. Establish a national museum and a national library.

All this work was aimed at enlightening people. As you can see, there was nothing against the state in the plan. But later I realized that our *Aksakal* was right. For, in searching my home, the KGB men took away not only papers that were written on but blank sheets as well. They introduced as evidence even things that were copied from Soviet books.

But, in 1964, I still thought that the authorities would not return to the Stalinist days.

In the autumn of 1965, I once again left for Moscow and met with the same results.

Director of the Institute of History Shtrakhov crudely explained to me, "No matter how well you do on your exams, we will not accept you."

When I asked why, Shtrakhov said nothing. I had to answer the question myself: "I understand why you don't want to admit me to the school of history; it's because I'm a Crimean Tatar, and you are the foremost falsifier of the history of Crimea and Crimean Tatars. But rest assured that from today on my people and I will struggle to return to the homeland in Crimea and to reestablish our own state. And the time will come when the Institute of History will train cadres for my republic."

The next day, after my talk with Shtrakhov, I went to the reception room of the Central Committee of the CPSU on Nogin Square.

I had with me many letters addressed to the Central Committee from Crimean Tatars living in the city of Samarkand. I gave them to the letter department of the Central Committee. In the reception room were about forty Crimean Tatars who had arrived from various regions of Uzbekistan.

I did not know any of them, and they did not know me. At about three or four o'clock the director of the reception room, Stroganov, invited all the Crimean Tatar representatives into his office for a talk. I entered the office as well.

Apparently his task was to "persuade" the Crimean Tatars to leave Moscow. Stroganov began to accuse us of interfering with official work; he said that it was not at all necessary to come to Moscow in such large numbers. In conclusion he said, "All your letters are collected in a bag and burned." This declaration by Stroganov greatly upset the representatives of the people.

The Crimean Tatars then declared to Stroganov, "As long as our national question remains unresolved, we will write and send our representatives to Moscow. We demand that our people's stigma as 'traitors to the motherland' be removed and that we be returned to Crimea."

In answer to Stroganov's question, "Who is insulting you by calling you 'traitors'—name names," I said:

> We are insulted by the Soviet government itself, and the "name" of that citizen is the disposition of the State Committee for Defense, from 18 May 1944. The second "name" is the law of the Presidium of the Supreme Soviet of the Soviet Union from 1946 [on the elimination of the Crimean Autonomous Soviet Socialist Republic (ASSR)]. And the third "name" is the edict of the Presidium of the Supreme Soviet of the Soviet Union from 1956 [on the prohibition of Crimean Tatars from returning to their homeland in Crimea].

I then ended my short speech with the words, "We are offended by Soviet laws from 1944, 1946, and 1956. And we Crimean Tatars don't have the legal right to take anyone to court. As long as these laws are not changed, we can be called 'traitors' by any citizen at all."

So you can see from comrade Stroganov that it is like the old saying, "A fish rots head first" (corruption starts at the top).

Just then Stroganov wrote down my name and realized that I worked at Samarkand University; he advised me not to get involved in this matter (the national movement).

When I got back to the hotel in the evening, a telegram was already lying on my table: "Return to the university immediately."

From that day on I was under pressure from the KGB. I began to be summoned to various offices: the dean's, the rector's, Party offices (although I was not a member of the CPSU), union offices, etc.

In the course of all the talks I upheld the right of my people to their homeland, Crimea.

And, when they understood that further conversations with me would be futile, they asked me to withdraw from the university "of my own accord." That I did.

I felt free, as if released from fetters, and I became actively involved in the national movement in Samarkand. I went from house to house having talks with Crimean Tatars about the right to the homeland.

In Crimean Tatar homes I held meetings of Crimean Tatars, and I invited representatives of Party and union organizations; I also invited representatives of the police and the KGB. We Crimean Tatars considered our struggle legal, and we did not hide from the government our desire to return to the homeland.

At these meetings I explained the right of our people to live among themselves in the homeland; I explained the constitutional right of every people to have schools in their native language and their own press (magazines, newspapers, books) as well as the right to a national culture.

I also read documents on the people, personal letters of Crimean Tatars to the Central Committee, Supreme Soviet of the Soviet Union, and the Council of Ministers of the Soviet Union, and also communiqués from representatives of Crimean Tatars in Moscow.

I collected signatures on people's documents, addresses, declarations, and inquiries; I collected money to fund the national movement. I helped write letters and declarations to partially literate Tatars. I took part in the composition of many universal people's documents.

I gave special attention to young people and women.

We Crimean Tatar women conducted several republican conferences: the first took place in the city of Bekabad in 1966; the second in Samarkand in 1968; and the third in Tashkent in 1970.

Yes, I was the author of many women's and young people's addresses to the Central Committee and to the Soviet government.

Moreover, I gathered documents and material on the intelligence officers, partisans, and participants in World War II. Thus, for example, I managed to seek out the commander, radio operator, and communications specialist of the intelligence group "Lyaki," which had been active in Crimea from November 1943 to April 1944. The commander of that group was Amet Kadyrov, and in 1974, after thirty years, he was decorated by the government for his heroism.

I gathered material on Crimean Tatar heroes of the Soviet Union.

I gave these materials to Crimean Tatar schoolchildren, who in their classes hung up clippings about Crimean Tatar heroes, partisans, and intelligence officers.

Thus, not only Crimean Tatar children were made aware of the heroism of Crimean Tatars during World War II, but also the children of other nationalities.

In Samarkand we formed youth groups that taught Crimean Tatar songs and dances and gathered folk sayings, adages, folktales, and legends.

In 1966, the Twenty-third Congress of the CPSU was to take place, so of course our initiative groups and activists in the national movement submitted a collection of documents on the destruction of the Crimean Tatar people in 1944–45, on the participants in the war, and on the barbarism of the German fascists in Crimea.

We had a meeting and familiarized Crimean Tatars with the address to the congress of the CPSU. On this address were more than 130,000 signatures of Crimean Tatars living in Central Asia.

In the summer of 1966, the Crimean Tatar inhabitants of Samarkand sent me to Moscow again as their representative.

In Moscow we visited the editorial staffs of the newspapers *Pionerskaia Pravda*, *Uchitel'skaia Pravda*, *Komsomol'skaia Pravda*, and others.

We demanded that the slander of the Crimean Tatar people on the pages of these papers be halted and that more be written about the heroes, partisans, intelligence officers, and model workers in industry from among Tatars.

In the summer of 1966, the authorities stepped up the persecutions of the Crimean Tatar representatives in Moscow. Corporal punishment in the reception room of the Central Committee of the CPSU in June 1966 was described by me in issues 24 and 25 of *Information*.[1]

Apparently, my activities in Moscow and Samarkand came to the attention of the penal authorities (the KGB in particular). In September 1966, I went to Moscow for the third time to take my entrance exams for the Institute of History of the AN USSR. But alas! I was not even allowed to take the exam. On 1 October, I returned to Samarkand, and, on 14 October I was arrested by the KGB and taken back to Moscow.

The KGB USSR kept me in solitary confinement in Lefortovo prison.

Before me, two other Crimean Tatar representatives had been arrested: Server Shamratov, a second-year student in the graduate school of Tashkent University, and Timur Dagji, a journalist and employee of the radio and television stations in the UZSSR. We were charged according to article 74 of the Ugolovnyi Kodeks (UK) RSFSR: "Incitement of ethnic discord."

But the absurdity of the charges against us was obvious. In our documents there was not a single word against any people; on the contrary, we called on the peoples of the Soviet Union to help us return to our homeland in Crimea.[2]

Our affair went secretly by the number 319, and the trial was secret and closed. Our courtroom, however, was full of high officials. Here I will not touch on the material of the investigation and the trial.

Rather, I will say that we were released from the courtroom and put on up to three years' probation. Our trial took place from 19 to 20 May 1967.

On 15 July, I again flew to Moscow as a representative of Crimean Tatars. This time more than four hundred people gathered. Among the representatives were pregnant women, schoolchildren, war veterans, and Communists.

And, on 21 July, the leaders of the Soviet state were compelled to receive twenty of us in the Kremlin.

I too was among those twenty. I kept a full shorthand account of the reception in the Kremlin in issue 50 of *Information*.[3]

At that time we were received by Yurii V. Andropov, the chairman of the KGB USSR; Rudenko, the public prosecutor of the Soviet Union; Shchelokov, the minister of internal affairs; and Georgadze, the secretary of the Presidium of the Supreme Soviet of the Soviet Union.

At this reception Andropov declared in the name of the government, "The opinion of the members of the Politburo on the question of the immediate rehabilitation of your people is unanimous. The opinions of the members of the Politburo on the question of the return of Crimean Tatars to Crimea, however, diverge."

As for my question, "Yurii Vladimirovich! Have I understood you correctly, that in the Politburo there are people for the return of Crimean Tatars to Crimea, and people against?" Andropov answered: "Yes, you have understood correctly."

In fact, on 5 September 1967, the edict of the Presidium of the Supreme Soviet of the Soviet Union, was published: "On Citizens of Tatar Nationality Who Lived in Crimea" (see chap. 12 in this volume).

But this edict legitimized the illegality of 1944, having declared Crimean Tatars settled in the places of exile.

In a word, the edict of 5 September 1967 granted "freedom to the dead and eternal exile to the living."

When we grasped the treacherous essence of the edict, we the initiators of the national movement began to prepare a universal people's protest in the name of women, children, and old people. Of course, the authorities did not expect such a sharp response. The Crimean Tatar people flatly declared to the government that the edict of 5 September 1967 was against the people, unconstitutional, and aimed at the destruction of Crimean Tatars as a nationality.[4]

In September 1967, I took the entrance exams to the Institute of History of the AN USSR for the fourth time. I passed all the exams, but in Moscow I was not accepted in the postgraduate program but rather sent off to Tashkent, to the Institute of History of the AN UZSSR, where I was admitted on 1 April 1968.

I was admitted into the postgraduate program for just one reason—to tear me away from the national movement and from the history of my people.

At the Institute of History of the AN UZSSR, I was supposed to study the history of Uzbekistan, not Crimea.

I did not live up to the expectations of the KGB, which had hoped that my postgraduate studies would be more important to me than the national movement for the return to the homeland.

On the contrary, I began to address myself to the problem of my people all the more.

In April 1968, I witnessed the assaults on Crimean Tatars in the city of Chirchik in the UZSSR, and I wrote the texts of telegrams and protests to the Soviet government about these events.

That same year I participated in the trials of activists in the Crimean Tatar national movement. For weeks and months I sat in the courtroom, taking notes on the judicial inquiry. At night friends and I prepared the "Bulletin from a Court of Law," which I distributed to Crimean Tatars.

For example, all the material for the book *Tashkent Trial* was gathered by me. In fact, I gathered the material for an unofficial dissertation called "The National Movement of Crimean Tatars."

Officially I was preparing a dissertation on the theme "The Growth of the Cultural and Technical Level of the Working Class in Uzbekistan, 1946–1956."

I was not able, however, to finish and preserve my dissertation because in

May 1971 I was arrested and sentenced to three years imprisonment in ordinary camps. I sat out my term in the Mordvin ASSR prison camps.

After my arrest my friends elaborated on the material for *Tashkent Trial*, and they managed to send it to the West, where it was published in Amsterdam by the Herzen Fund in 1976.

On account of my arrest I did not manage to empty my photo album either, which was called "Repressed Members of the National Movement." I had collected biographical data on almost all the sentenced members as well as photographs of them.

I collected copies of the prosecutor's conclusions and the verdicts of the court.[5]

The Uzbekistan KGB knew about all this because they followed me around day and night. I even knew the license numbers of their cars and recognized the faces of KGB collaborators who followed me.[6]

On my second arrest I refused to sign anything or to answer any questions. But I betrayed this principle once. One time an investigator gave me a question in written form (the interrogation protocol): "What role do you play in the national movement of Crimean Tatars?" "Oh, that question I'll be glad to answer," I said. "Write: 'A normal role. One of a Crimean Tatar who wants to return home to her native land, Crimea!'" Of course, the investigator did not write down such an answer.

I answered that question only because the very posing of it recognized the existence of the national movement of Crimean Tatars.

Neither the Soviet government nor the penal authorities wanted to recognize the existence of such a movement.

In 1974, I was released. I returned to Samarkand and again began to take an active part in the movement. I prepared material for samizdat publication on Crimean Tatars.

I drew up plans for several appeals: from participants in the war, from Communists, from young people. I was coauthor of the "Appeal to the Twenty-fourth Congress of the CPSU."

At the same time I struggled for the right to complete my postgraduate studies. But in 1976 I received the official answer that I would not be admitted (see chap. 12 in this volume).

Citing the United Nations conference of November 1962 on discrimination in education, I began to work toward emigrating from the Soviet Union so as to complete my education in the West. This struggle to emigrate lasted two years. I flew from Samarkand to Moscow several times with my petition to emigrate for the superior courts of the Soviet government (OVIR). But each time I was refused.

In June 1978, I again arrived in Moscow and addressed a declaration to the general secretary of the Central Committee of the CPSU, Leonid Brezhnev, with the request that I be allowed to leave the Soviet Union.

My declaration to Brezhnev ended in these words: "Since 18 May 1944 I have been constantly persecuted by the KGB; only death will save me from all the forms of persecution in the land of the Soviets." I made this statement to the Central Committee on 20 June, and on 23 June 1978 the Crimean Tatar Musa Mamut immolated himself in Crimea as a sign of protest against the repression of Crimean Tatars. And, when on 27 June I went to the Central Committee for a reply to my declaration, I was given right there and then a positive reply: "You may validate your documents for emigration. . . ."

Again I flew off to Crimea, and I will note that, before my arrival in Crimea, I did not know that Musa Mamut had immolated himself.

And so in Aqmesjit (Simferopol') I learned of Musa Mamut's self-immolation and death.

Naturally, I went right away to the village of Besh-Terek (Donskoy), where Mamut had lived with his family. And, in the course of two months, I collected documents about Musa Mamut and helped the family write declarations, letters, and protests. I went with his wife to the state prosecutor of Crimea with a demand to bring to justice the policemen and workers of the village council who for three years had taunted Musa Mamut.

What moved a forty-six-year-old worker, the father of three young children, to immolate himself before the eyes of his eleven-year-old son?

Musa Mamut was born on 20 February 1931 in the Bakhchesaray region of the Crimean ASSR. In that terrible year of 1944 he was thirteen years old, and so as not to die from hunger he had to go to work.

War and deportation closed the doors of school to him forever.

Musa Mamut reached at most the fourth grade.

After the edict of 5 September 1967 about the unjustified exile of an entire people from Crimea in 1944, thousands of Crimean Tatar families returned to the homeland. In April 1975, Musa Mamut and his family returned as well.

In the village of Besh-Terek in the Aqmesjit (Simferopol') region, Musa

Mamut bought a house and began petitioning to validate the purchase and to get a work permit.

But, acting on secret instructions, the authorities in Crimea continued to persecute Crimean Tatars. Musa Mamut did not escape this persecution. Validation was refused to him for the purchase of his house and for a work permit. All his requests were met by refusals and threats. Soon the penal authorities (the KGB, the state prosecutor, and the police) joined forces with the SELSOVIET (village council) and the court of Crimea and went from talk to deeds.

On 13 May 1976, Musa Mamut and his wife, Zekie Abdullaeva, were tried by the Aqmesjit (Simferopol') regional court for so-called infringement of the passport regime.

Musa Mamut was sentenced to two years' imprisonment and his wife (as the mother of three children) to two years' probation, according to article 196 of the Criminal Code of the Ukrayina SSR.

The decision of the Crimean district court from 3 June 1976 says plainly:

Musa Mamut and Abdullaeva Zekie have been found by the court guilty of and sentenced for traveling in April 1975 from the Tashkent district to the village of Donskoe in the Crimean district, and for transacting a purchase of house no. 136 on Komsomol Street.

In court Mamut and Abdullaeva did not acknowledge themselves guilty of the charges against them.

Thus Musa Mamut was imprisoned only because he traveled from the Tashkent district to the Crimean district. Such a fate has befallen hundreds of Crimean Tatars who were condemned only for traveling from Uzbekistan or Kazakstan to the Crimean district.

In the spring of 1978 his term was up, and Musa Mamut again returned to his house in Crimea.

And again he went to the authorities for a permit for his house, but everywhere he heard only threats: "We'll put you away, we'll put you away, get lost!"

Three days before he immolated himself, Musa Mamut declared to the chief of the regional police: "Crimea is my homeland! I returned to my homeland to live and to die. You won't take me alive. I've got some gasoline handy."

And, in fact, when a motorcycle policeman came to Musa's house on 23

June to run him in, Musa Mamut, telling the policeman that he was going to change his clothes, went into the barn, doused himself with gasoline, and, walking toward the policeman, set himself afire. Instead of saving the man, this policeman left his motorcycle and ran away.

But after him ran Musa Mamut, engulfed in flames.

Musa Mamut burned before the eyes of his eleven-year-old son. An inhabitant of the village of Besh-Terek brought Mamut to the city hospital of Aqmesjit (Simferopol'), where on 28 June 1978 he died.

The coroner's report said: "90 percent burns." I saw the coroner's report when I collected material on Musa Mamut in Crimea in the summer of 1978.

Henceforth, the Initiative Group of Crimean Tatars will go by the name of Musa Mamut.

As a memento of Crimea I took wormwood and a charred twig from the cherry tree under which Musa Mamut had burned. I have these with me to this very day.

In November 1978, I left the Soviet Union. On 20 November, I arrived in Vienna, and, on 25 April 1979, I arrived in New York, where I have been living until recently.

Here it has been years already that I have lived in the United States, and no one has called me on it and said, "We forbid you to think," as was said to me in Mordvin camp 26 by the chief of the regime, Krymenko. We forbid you "to travel the world and to speak at conferences," as the Soviet and Uzbek KGB constantly said to me.

Although I have found freedom and peace, new friends, and sympathetic American people here in the United States, I have not for a moment forgotten my homeland, Crimea, its long-suffering people, my relatives, or my friends.

For example, in a letter of September 1973 to the UN general secretary, Mamedi Chobanov writes:

I am already in my thirtieth year, and for not one day have I enjoyed the rights of a full citizen of the Soviet Union, since I have had the misfortune of being born of Crimean Tatar parents.

In my twentieth day of life, in May 1944, I was exiled from my homeland, Crimea, together with all my long-suffering people. Our family ended up in the northern Urals, where the very first winter my father froze and died, not fifty years old; and my older sister, from hunger and cold, fell ill with tuberculosis and died at the age of twenty-one.

And not only they, but thousands upon thousands of other Crimean Tatars perished from typhoid, hunger, frost, and various diseases. I spent my whole childhood in a foreign land, in exile, under the regime of the special settlements. We were not permitted to travel more than a few kilometers from the settlement. My whole generation of children—the Crimean Tatars of those years—grew up under prisonlike conditions. And we were forced to shout in schools and kindergartens: "Thank you comrade Stalin for our happy childhood."

Some twenty-four years of my life were impaired through no fault of my own. In the spring of 1968, setting my hopes on the edict [of September 1967], I went back to the homeland after a twenty-four-year hiatus. In the cities and villages of Crimea there was a great demand for workers, and settlers were brought in by railcar from Ukrayina and Russia. But everywhere I looked, when it was found out that I was a Crimean Tatar, I was right then categorically denied work and residence in Crimea.... On 26 June 1968, I was arrested in the reception room of the Oblast Ispolkom (OBLISPOLKOM: provincial executive committee) of Crimea, and, with the help of false evidence, I was sentenced to three years' imprisonment.

In prison I thought about whether loving the homeland and wanting to return there were crimes.

Are there many people in the Soviet Union who are forbidden to love their homeland and to live in it? Why is it forbidden to me? Who would it disturb? Having sat out my sentence, I again returned to the homeland, but I wasn't even able to get a passport, no matter where I tried.

The chief of the district passport office, Lieutenant Colonel Gaidamak, declared: "I'll put you in jail again and again and again until you stop loving your homeland and your mother."

And, in fact, Mamedi Chobanov was sentenced to prison three times—1968, 1972, and 1980—and three times he returned to Crimea. So Colonel Gaidamak did not succeed in stopping Chobanov, even with imprisonment, from loving his homeland and mother.

At this writing, Mamedi Chobanov lives in Crimea, in the village of Zhuravki, Kursk region.

I heard about Mamedi Chobanov for the first time in 1968 in the communiqué "Oppression of the Crimean Tatars in Crimea," a Crimean Tatar document that discusses the sentencing of those Crimean Tatars who returned to Crimea.

One of the sentenced men was Mamedi Chobanov.

Naturally, in collecting material on the repressed members of the Crimean Tatar national movement, I was interested in the trial of Mamedi Chobanov. However, we managed to meet in person only in 1974.

That is because from 1968 to 1971 Chobanov was in a camp and, as you know, I was sentenced to three years in 1971.

Afterward, in 1972, Chobanov was again sentenced, to one and a half years.

Thus, only in the spring of 1974 did we, for the first time, manage to meet, in Aqmesjit (Simferopol'), Crimea. Later, we met again. Mamedi Chobanov is a short, very simple, and rough man. His appearance is open and courageous.

The struggle has led me not only to Chobanov but to other bold and valiant sons and daughters of the people. Among them are Mustafa Jemiloglu, Yurii Osmanov, Gomer Baev, Elgar Shabanov, and hundreds of others.

About the steadfastness and valor of each of these men one could write a legend.

Verily, a time will come when the Crimean Tatar people shall write songs and legends about them.

It is very unfortunate that I cannot give the names of all the activists in the national movement; I do not have the moral right to write about everything openly, out of consideration for their safety. However, I will try to describe the general picture of the national movement.

Despite the fact that the Twentieth Congress empowered the Central Committee to "eliminate the consequences of the deviation from the Leninist principles of the nationality policy of the CPSU," not only were the "consequences of the cult of personality" regarding Crimean Tatars, Volga Germans, Caucasian Turks, and Khemshils not eliminated, but they were legitimized by edicts of the Supreme Soviet of the Soviet Union from 28 April 1956 and 5 September 1967.

For example, in the edict from 28 April 1956, article 2, it is plainly stated that "the lifting of restrictions [i.e., of the supervision of the special commandant] from the specified persons and members of their families does not entail a returning of their property that was confiscated during resettlement, and they do not have the right to return to the places from which they were removed."

Nonetheless, the Twentieth Congress of the CPSU stirred the Crimean Tatar people.

The initiators of the nascent movement were representatives of the older generation of Crimean Tatars—former Party and Soviet workers in the Crimea, participants in World War II and the partisan movement, and veterans of labor. They, citing the decision of the Twentieth Congress of the Party "to eliminate the consequences of the cult of personality," wrote individual and collective letters requesting the return of the Crimean Tatar people to their homeland.

Gradually, the national movement of Crimean Tatars for the reestablishment of their rights as a nationality became acknowledged.

Initially, I had divided the national movement into three stages in 1971 at the trial in Tashkent. Later, having studied the documents and spoken with the first representatives who had gone to Moscow in 1957, I came to the conclusion that the Crimean Tatar movement had four stages:

—The first stage was the period of the movement's coming into being, from 1956 to 1964.
—The second stage was the more active period, from 1964 to 1970.
—The third was the period of decline, from 1970 to 1977.
—The fourth is the activization of the struggle to get back to Crimea, from 1978 to the present.

## Old Communist Participants in the National Movement

In characterizing the first stage—the period of the movement's coming into being—I cannot but say a few words about the beloved and esteemed leaders (*Aksakals*) of the national movement. Nothing may threaten them. They have all passed away.

They are Abduraman Ibrahimov, Bekir Umerov, Jeppar Akimov, and Bekir Osmanov. All of them were active builders and defenders of Soviet authority in Crimea and the Crimean ASSR.

Abduraman Ibrahimov and Bekir Umerov were arrested for the first time in the years 1934–37 as "bourgeois nationalists" and sentenced to twenty-five years' imprisonment. Only after the death of Stalin (in 1953) were they released and rehabilitated with the reestablishment of their labor and Party service. But despite this they did not have the right to live in their homeland.

Although from 1918 on Ibrahimov and Umerov took active part in the establishment of Soviet authority in Crimea, the Soviet state itself in the 1930s declared them "enemies of the people" (or of the Soviet state).

Jeppar Akimov and Bekir Osmanov were not only builders of socialism in Crimea but also defenders of the Soviet state against fascism from 1941 to 1944. They were old Communists and defenders of the Crimean Tatar movement for the return to the homeland in Crimea.

They were my teachers in the national movement.

Although they were members of the Party, until the end of their lives they were against the elimination of the Crimean ASSR; they battled for and demanded the return of Crimean Tatars to the homeland.

Thus is my activity in the national movement bound up with these people, about whom I would like to say a few words.

Abduraman Ibrahimov worked (until his arrest) in the REVKOM (Revolutionary Committee) of Crimea and in other agencies. Not long before his death, for his active part in the national movement A. Ibrahimov was expelled from the Party, of which he had been a member for forty-six years.

Death spared Abduraman Ibrahimov a second arrest.

He died in 1968 in Samarkand, UZSSR.

It is well known that, not long before his death in November 1983, Bekir Umerov sent to the Central Committee of the CPSU a letter demanding that Crimean Tatars be returned to Crimea and that the Crimean ASSR be reestablished. Apparently, death saved him too from repression.

Bekir Umerov was born at the beginning of the century (1900–1901) in Crimea, in the city of Kezlev (Evpatoriia).

From the age of eighteen he took part in the struggle for the establishment of Soviet authority in Crimea. Bekir Umerov began his revolutionary activity as a Komsomol leader. Later he gradually moved up the Party ladder. He was secretary of the district committee of the Komsomol in the Crimean ASSR.

During the Ezhov period (1934–37), nearly all the intelligentsia and Party elite in Crimea were destroyed.

Not only was Bekir Umerov arrested, but also his wife Hatije; his young daughter was brought up by nonrelatives. And only after the death of Stalin could Bekir aga be reunited with his family, not in Crimea, but in exile in Uzbekistan.

In 1957, Umerov was fully rehabilitated with the reestablishment of his Party and labor service. Later he was granted a personal pension. Nonetheless, beginning in the 1960s, Bekir aga actively took part in his people's struggle. Bekir aga was active in the national movement and worked in research and journalism, studying the history of the Crimean Tatar people. In particular, he composed a list of Crimean Tatar intelligentsia who were killed from 1918 to the 1940s.

The list composed by Bekir Umerov bf repressed, executed, tortured, and maimed cultural and academic activists has more than two hundred names. Of course, the list is not complete.

Bekir aga strove to arouse in the young and adult Crimean Tatars a love for their history and culture while they were far away from their homeland. He collected and composed a list of the literature on Crimea and Crimean Tatars.

I was often his guest when I lived in Samarkand. We spoke at length about the past, present, and future of our people. For me Bekir aga was living history, history of the establishment of Soviet authority in Crimea, of the destruction of the Crimean Tatar intelligentsia, and of the Gulag (from 1934 to 1956 he was in Soviet prisons and camps).

In one of his articles for Crimean Tatar samizdat publication Bekir Umerov wrote: "One of the most refined and perfidious methods of the Party's policy toward the non-Russian people was and remains the almost complete destruction of the intelligentsia of these people. Poets, writers, workers in art and culture, being the carriers of Crimean Tatar culture, are considered by Moscow to be most dangerous enemies." That is the conclusion arrived at by the eldest member of the CPSU, pensioner Bekir Umerov.

This refined inquisitorial method of repressing the Crimean Tatar intelligentsia continues to this day, the only difference being that today our intelligentsia are destroyed, not physically, but mentally.

Those of the intelligentsia who are most active in the movement are thrown behind barbed wire and into prisons; others are deprived of work or the right to education or are not even allowed into archives. I will introduce the names of some activists who have been jailed for their part in the national movement:

—Enver Memetov—mathematician and postgraduate student of the AN USSR (1968), Moscow.
—Yurii Osmanov—physicist-engineer, twice jailed (1968, 1983), Moscow.

—Jelal Chelebiev—engineer, jailed three times (1967, 1984, . . .), Tashkent.
—Reshat Jemilev—engineer, jailed three times (1967, 1972, 1980), Tashkent.
—Mustafa Jemiloglu—expelled from the institute and jailed six times (1966, 1970, 1974, 1976, 1979, 1984). He sat out his sixth term in Magadan in the late 1980s.

I could cite a hundred names since I have collected data on every Crimean Tatar who has been arrested.

But these examples suffice to demonstrate eloquently the tragedy of Crimean Tatars.

Bekir Osmanov was another active elder member of the national movement. He entered the history of the partisan movement in Crimea as a famed intelligence officer, for whose head the German command posted an enormous reward.

For his heroism during the war, Bekir aga was awarded numerous medals and decorations, including the Decoration of Glory (all three degrees—that is equivalent to the award of Hero of the Soviet Union).

But, on 18 May 1944, he too was squeezed into a cattle car and sent to Central Asia for "treason against the motherland."

Bekir Osmanov and his family lived and worked in the city of Fergana in the Uzbek SSR.

In 1957, for the first time, a group of Crimean Tatars, mostly former Party and Soviet workers in Crimea, participants in the war and partisan movement and veterans of labor, requested the Central Committee of the CPSU to return Crimean Tatars to their homeland. Among them was Bekir Osmanov. He was also an initiator of the petition movement of Crimean Tatars.

More than once did Crimean Tatars send him to Moscow as their representative.

From Bekir Osmanov's pen came the article "Soviet Rule and the Fate of the Crimean Tatar People."

For his part in the national movement Bekir Osmanov endured numerous acts of repression. Searches, surveillance, and "talks" at the KGB office were nearly everyday phenomena.

In January 1968, his eldest son, Yurii (Yusup) Osmanov, was arrested and sentenced to two and a half years. His wife, Mariya Gushchinskaya, was of Belorussion nationality. She passed away in 1974.

Yurii Osmanov is the author of many articles, including one about Ismail Gaspirali. In honor of Gaspirali, Yurii named his son Ismail.

In 1969, Bekir Osmanov was expelled from the Party.

Bekir was by profession an agronomist and a very good one. In 1977, he and his younger son, Artem, returned to their homeland. In the village of Dmitrevo, in the Aqmesjit (Simferopol') region, he bought a house. Of course, for the authorities in Crimea, and especially for the KGB, Bekir aga was an undesirable person. However, they did not decide to evict him a second time and were obliged to give him a permit.

In 1982, Yurii was arrested a second time and sentenced to three years' imprisonment.

The second arrest of his eldest son ultimately broke the health of Bekir aga. He died on 26 May 1983, half a month after his son's trial.

Bekir Osmanov was interred next to the grave of Musa Mamut, who five years earlier immolated himself in protest against the persecution of Crimean Tatars in the Soviet Union.

I want to speak of yet another man, the dear and respected Jeppar Akimov, or, as he is known among the people, Jeppar aga.

Jeppar Akimov was one of the most visible and authoritative men not only among the activists of the national movement but among the whole people. He enjoyed the great respect of other peoples as well.

Jeppar Akimov was born in 1909 in the village of Tuak (Tubak) in the Tavricheskaya district (before the November Revolution, Crimea was called the Tavricheskaya district), not far from the city of Sudaq. Jeppar aga was a teacher by profession. He graduated from a pedagogical school and worked as a teacher in his native village.

In the 1930s, he was invited to work at the State Publishing House of the Crimean ASSR as head of the political department. He worked mostly on translations from Russian into the Crimean Tatar language.

He also translated the "classics of Marxism-Leninism." During the Ezhov period he was arrested as a "bourgeois nationalist," but the arrest of Ezhov himself saved Jeppar from death. The Akimov affair was cut short. And only in 1939 did Akimov join the Party. Before the beginning of the war Jeppar aga was made editor-in-chief of the newspaper *Qizil Qrim* (Red Crimea).

During the war years (1941–44), Jeppar aga took an active part in the partisan movement in Crimea.

He was the author of all the pamphlets and appeals to the population of Crimea that called on the people to do battle against the occupiers and to aid the partisans and intelligence officers.

In April 1944, after the liberation of Aqmesjit (Simferopol') by the Red Army, Jeppar Akimov was again chief of the newspaper *Qizil Qrim*.

However, on 18 May, Jeppar's editorial activities were cut short.

Once I asked Jeppar aga the question, "Jeppar aga, were you, too, pulled from your bed by soldiers carrying automatics?" He answered, "It was at dawn, 18 May 1944. We (that is, the writer Seitumer Emin and I) were on our way to the editing department of the paper *Qizil Qrim*, when suddenly we were taken by soldiers out of nowhere who had automatics in their hands. The writer Seitumer and I tried to explain to them who we were and where we were going. And that we had to put out a paper by morning. To that one of the soldiers said sneeringly: 'We'll put it out without you.' To the very last moment," Jeppar continued, "I thought it was some kind of mistake. And only when we were crammed into cattle cars and locked in did I understand that a terrible crime, unseen in history heretofore, was being perpetrated against my people."

Jeppar Akimov and his family ended up in the town of Bekabad, UZSSR, where he lived and worked to the end of his days.

For his active part in the national movement Jeppar aga was expelled from the Party in 1968. The Crimean Tatar people more than once authorized him to deliver appeals to congresses of the CPSU. Ultimately, the KGB could not allow Crimean Tatars to have a leader, so on 29 August 1972 Jeppar Akimov was arrested in Tashkent.

Akimov's trial took place from 21 to 29 November 1972.

At the trial Jeppar aga spoke of the tragic position of Crimean Tatars within the system of supervision at the special settlements and of the fact that most Crimean Tatar people remained at these special settlements after the Twentieth Congress of the CPSU. This is what he said in court: "The documents signed by me express the will and aspirations of Crimean Tatars; their content does not distort Soviet reality but merely reflects the real and actual situation of the national question. . . . This movement is legal and inevitable. Therefore, the charges against me I consider groundless and illegal." Thus in the course of the inquiry and the trial Jeppar Akimov's guilt was never proved. But, despite this, he was sentenced to three years' imprisonment in ordinary camps.

Even Akimov's lawyer, Luk'yanov, requested that the sentence be commuted and the case dropped, in light of the unproved charges, since correcting and considering already prepared documents do not imply authorship or coauthorship of them.

"The court's conclusions about the authorship of Akimov are built not on proof but on presumptions." This is what the lawyer Luk'yanov wrote in a plea for an appeal to the state prosecutor of the UZSSR.

I was not at the trial of Jeppar aga since I was myself in the Mordvin camp. We met only in 1975, after Jeppar aga's release. He advocated that I leave the Soviet Union.

I learned of Jeppar's death only after I was here in the United States. He passed away on 22 June 1983, in the city of Bekabad, at the age of seventy-four.

The memory of the homeland was being taken away. The Soviet government did everything to keep Crimean Tatars from their native land, Crimea.

The authorities in Crimea are still creating unbearable conditions for Crimean Tatar families. They do not approve the purchase of houses; they do not register Crimean Tatars in the passport department of the police; they cut off the lights and water; they plow under already cultivated kitchen gardens! Crimean pensioners cannot receive their pensions, so that non-registered mothers and mothers of many children cannot receive aid for their children; court cases are instituted against Crimean Tatars; and until recently sentenced to resettlement, exile, and imprisonment for "infringement of the passport regime."

And to legitimatize this lawlessness, the Council of Ministers of the Soviet Union issued a special edict, "On Additional Measures for Strengthening the Passport Regime in the Crimean District," from 15 August 1978.

On the basis of this edict in the winter of 1978–79 the authorities in Crimea repeated 1944 in regard to those families who returned to their homeland. On account of this lawlessness in Crimea, academician Sakharov wrote his "Open Letter" to the members of the Supreme Soviet of the Soviet Union.

The tragic situation gripping my people in Crimea today has improved very little.

## Notes

1. The periodical *Information* gives an account of work done in petitioning for the quickest possible resolution of the nationality question. The account is composed

by the representatives in Moscow of the Crimean Tatar people. The first issue of *Information* was issued in October 1964. From October 1964 through March 1979, 129 issues of *Information* were put together by the representatives of Crimean Tatars in Moscow. It is hard to believe, but it is a fact, that, from October 1964 to 1979, there were representatives of Crimean Tatars in the reception room of the Central Committee of the CPSU in Moscow every day. In Crimea repression and material difficulties have continued and today the people need to keep their representatives continually in Kyiv.

2. We were presented with people's documents, such as, e.g., the "Appeal to the Twenty-third Congress of the Party." Investigators from the Soviet KGB tried to accuse us of exaggerating the death rate of our people in 1944; they said that Crimean Tatars enjoy every right as citizens of the Soviet Union. In answer to our question, "Why are there no schools teaching in the Crimean Tatar language, and why can't we live in Crimea?" the investigators did not answer and did not enter our question in the protocol of the interrogation.

3. In *Information*, no. 50, there were questions and answers on the reception in the Kremlin. For example, R. Muzafarov asked Andropov: "Will the books be removed whose authors depict us as traitors?" To this Yurii V. Andropov replied: "Yes, many books will be removed from the libraries." The talk in the Kremlin lasted three hours and twenty-one minutes. During the talk I wrote down the Crimean Tatars' questions and the answers of the leaders of the Soviet government. And, from these notes, we, the Moscow representatives, put together the following *Information*, no. 50, in June 1967.

4. Why was the "Universal People's Protest" written in the name of women, children, and old people? On 18 May 1944, mostly women, children, and old people were exiled, for all the adult male population of Crimean Tatars was at the front. By the edict of 5 September 1967, participants in the war and the new generation, born in Uzbekistan, were rehabilitated, but not we who were exiled in 1944 for "treason against the motherland."

5. Thus, many data were collected about Crimean Tatars condemned in 1962 and 1965–70. On the whole, much had already been collected on eighty to one hundred people. I managed to bring to the West several photos of repressed Crimean Tatars. But much material fell into the hands of the Uzbekistan KGB, on account of the indiscretion of my acquaintances.

6. Mostly it was Russians following me. Only once did I notice a Tajik after me—that was in Samarkand—and only once—in Tashkent—was it an Uzbek.

# 9

## *Mass Exile, Ethnocide, Group Derogation: Anomaly or Norm in Soviet Nationality Policies?*

EDWARD A. ALLWORTH

The case of Crimean Tatars in the Union of Soviet Socialist Republics had its intrinsic importance as an instance of large-scale human difficulty and determination to overcome hardship. At the same time the case entailed certain types of political behavior and societal realities perhaps specific to the Soviet Union after World War II. The subject fell under what Communist Party of the Soviet Union (CPSU) leaders termed *the nationality question*. For analytic purposes *the nationality question* refers here to problems of group satisfaction or dissatisfaction experienced by a nationality in its immediate and extended environment. Such problems fundamentally affect the group's attitude toward its situation in the state. These kinds of dissatisfactions express themselves in events or developments that analysts call *nationality problems*. Nationality policies purport to deal with the nationality question and attempt to resolve it by correcting the conditions causing nationality problems. Evidence from visitors to Central Asia and other parts of the Soviet Union, from unofficial publications (samizdat) from the Soviet Union's Crimean Tatars received in the West, as well as from Soviet publications themselves testifies to this group's continuing unhappiness about its location half in Central Asia and half in Crimea, its status, treatment, and condition.[1] For that reason, this case perhaps illustrates the workings and some motives of those nationality policies and their makers in the Soviet Union. The CPSU and local officials could not seem to resolve the nationality question in respect to the Crimean Tatar group. Therefore, examining the developments within the group and the nationality policies affecting them in order to record and interpret both remains worthwhile.

As outgrowths of this situation, two features became prominent after World War II in the relations between the Crimean Tatar nationality and the Soviet Russian regime. The Communist Party made its own rules in the nationality question, and it conceived and directed nationality policies throughout the country, some of them drastic (fig. 9.1). The authorities would punish infractions of those unpublished and perhaps uncodified regulations in several ways. They applied sanctions against the nationality in general. Publicly, CPSU chiefs rarely charged individuals or groups with ethnic offenses. Instead, under charges of slandering the state or upsetting public order, CPSU functionaries took to court dissenters who openly aired grievances. (This treatment resembles the methods of white supremacists in the Republic of South Africa, who arrested black citizens for "disturbing the peace" if they attempted to exert the right of using public facilities or transportation reserved for whites.) Or in the Soviet Union the authorities undermined a group by persecuting and destroying its leadership. In some instances, CPSU officials acted to uproot and disperse a nationality over a wide area, thus effectively neutralizing or nullifying it as a corporate entity.

The officials of the CPSU held a view of the Crimean Tatar group and its status that differed remarkably from the perspective taken collectively by the members of the group itself and by many observers outside the Soviet Union. It may be a sign of the insecurity then felt by Soviet authorities over the nationality question that as late as 1986 the Party once more threatened every group in the Soviet Union with reprisal if any nationality seriously and openly tried to articulate ethnic group feelings. In the language of the third program of the CPSU promulgated in March 1986, "the CPSU henceforth also will consistently fight against any expressions of localism and national distinction."[2]

Nothing fresh sounded here either in the wording or the sentiment expressed in the official program. But the repetition of the warning at that late date evinced continuing intolerance by leaders in the privileged Communist Party political organization toward spontaneous ethnic expression. For Crimean Tatars this injunction meant that they could make no demands to recover the group prerogatives earlier taken away from their nationality without incurring censure and worse punishment for voicing "localism and national distinction." In the mid-1980s, the nationality still lacked the protections offered by even a low level of official group status and recognition, through no fault of its own. Nevertheless, because of this deficiency, CPSU officials denied Crimean Tatars recourse to exercising any right to the ethnic amenities available to a nationality in the Soviet Union

Figure 9.1. Facsimile of an *ukase* unpublished when promulgated 26 November 1948 by the Presidium of the Soviet Supreme Council, ordering that members of nationality groups such as Crimean Tatars and Chechens, deported during World War II, had been exiled "forever, without right of return to their former places of residence," and would suffer criminal penalties (five years' imprisonment) for leaving their place of exile. Persons aiding such criminals would also receive severe punishment. From a copy provided by the Crimean Tatar Mejlis.

that lived in a unit bearing the group's name. This impasse between CPSU officials and Crimean Tatars characterized their relations after the mid-1950s.

By the time of the Twenty-third CPSU Congress, some senior Crimean Tatar leaders had determined that their nationality could not regain its ethnic rights without taking political action. To that congress of the CPSU, held in Moscow between 29 March and 7 April 1966, they directed a detailed, carefully worded appeal for redress of ethnic wrongs. The basis for their approach to the CPSU congress lay in the appellants' correct understanding that nationality problems lay in the purview of the single political party. They addressed themselves to the issue of ethnic group parity under the Soviet regime. As it happened, they shared their condition of inequality, stemming from the recent removal of a namesake territory, with Soviet Germans. The Russian government had deported eight entire nationalities and fractions of others from their home territories in the Soviet Union to internal exile during the first half of the 1940s. By 1966, the Crimean Tatar group remained the only Eastern one to which the Russian authorities had not restored at least a part of its earlier administrative-territorial namesake unit. Nor had this nationality received official exoneration (in Russian terminology, *reabilitatsiia*) of false charges accusing it in 1944 of mass collaboration with the Soviet Union's enemy.

While Crimean Tatars remained in exile and under denunciation, in 1964 political leaders in Moscow withdrew the sweeping accusations placed against the good repute of the Soviet Union's Germans. In those emotional times that counted for much in group morale building. It also removed many individual disabilities—prohibitions against travel, schooling in the mother tongue, and the like. Therefore, at the outset, such was the despair of the Crimean Tatars that they declared to delegates at the Twenty-third Congress of the CPSU: "The sole unequal ethnic group in our country—the Crimean Tatar—appeals to you today. An ethnic group from whom the homeland, good name and all constitutional rights are taken away!"[3] Unlike any other nationality in the Soviet Union, Crimean Tatars then suffered under a serious double disability. They still lacked the namesake political-administrative territory they had cherished. And they experienced a continuing public disapprobation accompanying onerous sanctions. From similar government motives, ethnic groups that had originally lacked namesake political units in the Soviet Union likewise suffered unjustified punishment. Meskhetian Turks, some Azerbaijanians, Greeks, and several other nationalities also underwent exile deep into Soviet Asia and later encountered a categorical Russian refusal when they attempted to return home to the Transcaucasus region. Decisions announced by the Supreme Council, Ukrayina, but undoubtedly made secretly by the nationality sector at the heart of the CPSU, settled the matter officially.[4]

As a result, the Crimean Tatar nationality remained deprived of several obvious Soviet forms of group recognition that it had enjoyed earlier. The group possessed no direct, formal affiliation with its eponymous administrative territory (a Crimean unit, which Crimean Tatars may not entirely inhabit as a group, exists in Ukrayina). As a consequence of having no unit status, the group lacks both a recognized written constitution and official deliberative body, and it identifies with no branch of any broader political organization that might develop on the basis of such a territorial unit. The nationality cannot send most of its children to public schools taught in their language, for there are few. Nor has it suitable higher educational institutions to expand, nurture, and strengthen sufficiently a distinctive Crimean Tatar cultural intelligentsia. Moreover, officials avoid establishing within the societies and institutes, such as the state-sponsored Union of Writers of the Uzbekistan Republic (UZSSR), subdivisions named and effectively devoted specifically to Crimean Tatars. Until 1989, Soviet authorities omitted specific information distinguishing Crimean Tatars from other Tatars in the census reports and most public records of the Soviet Union. And the nationality lacked other customary forms of formal "sovereignty" (official flag, seal, capital city, national anthem, and the like). The obligatory domestic passports until 1994 designated a Crimean Tatar merely as "Tatar, formerly residing in Crimea."

Toward these problems Crimean Tatar initiators, as they called themselves to avoid the possibly incriminating term *underground/unofficial leader*, offered a view not quite diametrically opposed to the outlook of Soviet Russian officials. The explanation for this failure of exact opposition or direct contradiction is that the authorities refused to discuss the basic grievance raised by Crimean Tatar initiators. Documents that most clearly illustrate the tangential collision between Communist Party leadership and the Crimean Tatar nationality come from the main political prosecutions undertaken through the Soviet judiciary of the UZSSR. Party authorities staged the first extensive political trial of Crimean Tatar initiators in July 1969. The charge in that case rested explicitly on what the indictment, issued by UZSSR Attorney General K. R. Ruzmetov, termed "defamatory documents" compiled and distributed by those accused.

According to him, even if they were based carefully on accurate Soviet records and statements, those Crimean Tatar documents "did set forth the policy of the CPSU and Soviet government in a defamatory spirit . . . and asserted that individuals of Tatar nationality who earlier resided in Crimea [a circumlocution common in officialese to avoid affirming the group's viability through use of the group name *Crimean Tatars*] exist in a condition of terrible need, deprivation of rights, oppression, and the like." The attorney general typically charged a leading defendant in the case, Reshat Bayramov (b. 1943 in Kamishlik, Crimean Autonomous Soviet Socialist Republic [ASSR]), an electrician working in Melitopol', Ukraine SSR, with having illegally entered into the group of initiators formed in Chirchik, UZSSR. The authorities had settled many Crimean Tatar exiles in Chirchik. He accused Bayramov of taking an active part in activities intended to resolve "the so-called Crimean Tatar question." From the end of December 1967 to March 1968, Bayramov stayed in Moscow as a representative of Crimean Tatars, noted the indictment. "In January 1968," said the charge, "he personally compiled *Information*, no. 60 [*Informatsiia*, no. 60]. In this document Bayramov [allegedly] cast aspersions on the situation of the Crimean Tatars in the Soviet Union, declaring that this ethnic group ostensibly is in a situation of oppression and is unequal among other ethnic groups of the Soviet Union."[5]

In addition, the first lines of the indictment signed by the attorney general of the UZSSR had stated that "a defamatory document under the title *Funereal Information Document No. 69*, addressed to the Union of Writers of Uzbekistan by the accused, Reshat Bayramov, served as the basis for bringing the present criminal case." This accusatory emphasis on the public appeals that Bayramov and others were making on behalf of their Crimean Tatar countrymen gave a significant clue to one self-protective motive behind the prosecution. Crimean Tatars assiduously took their case for rectification in their status to every conceivable office, bureau, and organization in the UZSSR, Moscow, and elsewhere, openly calling for relief from ethnic group deprivation.

The authorities in the Soviet system could not tolerate the likelihood that these appeals would generate and sway a considerable amount of public opinion. Despite constitutional provisions for free speech and a free press, the CPSU and the Soviet government maintained a monopoly over the manipulation of public opinion, to the limited extent that such a phenomenon existed, throughout the Soviet Union. The second target of this political trial displayed two characteristics. Bayramov and his associates accused makers and executors of Soviet nationality policies of deliberate injustice. In this way, the accusers put the CPSU's virtue and infallibility, already suspect owing to acknowledged political crimes committed under Stalin's regime, in question once more. And they drew public attention to the deprivations generally affecting the lives of Crimean Tatars. Should Crimean Tatar complaints of this nature go unchecked, officials appeared to fear, a hundred other nationalities might consistently bring grievances to the Kremlin door and the mainly Russian CPSU Central Committee and Politburo seated behind it.[6] The tremendous effort expended in prosecuting this case evidenced the serious concern felt on both these issues by party leaders.

The *Funereal Information Document No. 69*, which ostensibly provoked this court proceeding, appeared sometime between 15 May and 1 June 1968. Its specific reference to "funereal" related to what its compilers considered a twofold tragedy. They timed its release to commemorate the twenty-second anniversary of the date when the Party ordered all Crimean Tatars uprooted from their homeland. In the second place, the document deplored the violent conduct of Soviet officials and their subordinates around the time of the commemoration in forcibly sweeping hundreds of Crimean Tatars from the streets and residential areas of Moscow, the capital of the Soviet Union and the Russian Soviet Federated Socialist Republic (RSFSR). The officials reacted harshly against the organized lobbying, peaceful protests, and petitioning undertaken there by representatives of Crimean Tatars. *Funereal Information Document No. 69* compared the Europeans' search for African slaves of the seventeenth century with the Russian hunt for Crimean Tatars on Moscow's streets during 16–18 May 1968. Vehemently, the authors spoke about the shame of what they called this "racial discrimination." They demanded what they termed a "Leninist" not a KGB solution to the Crimean Tatar question. And they gave some details about the violent Soviet police actions led by high-ranking officers in Moscow, especially on 17 May 1968. Compilers of *Funereal Information Document No. 69* outspokenly surveyed recent government abuses of Crimean Tatar human and ethnic rights. The compilers noted that the authorities had brought more than fifteen court cases against participants in the lawful Crimean Tatar drive for the group's rights between 1956 and 1968. The *Funereal Information Document* reproduced testimony from six eyewitnesses to those abuses in Moscow and included signatures from more than one hundred Crimean Tatars identifying themselves with places of residence ranging from Almaty, Osh, Tashkent, and Dushanbe to Azerbaijan and Crimea. It closed with a statement that compilers sent this *Funereal Information Document* to the Central Committee CPSU, the Supreme Council, and the Council of Ministers of the Soviet Union, editors of newspapers and journals, and public and political leaders of the country "in all populated areas and towns where Crimean Tatars reside."[7] The campaign and its written counterpart proceeded legally and openly. Essentially, these events manifested a confrontation between a political oligarchy that arrogated to itself all the state's rights and powers and a determined ethnic group working to repossess from the oligarchy some of those rights. That drive brought into the open matters of democratic rights and nationality policies so unsettling to the regime that it resorted to drastic means in order to suppress the subject rather than solve the problems that caused such dissatisfaction among Crimean Tatars.

In the indictment put forward against ten Crimean Tatars at the end of 1969 the attorney general of the UZSSR charged specifically that *Funereal Information Document No. 69* "cast aspersions on the nationality policy of the CPSU and Soviet government and on the situation of Crimean Tatars in the Soviet Union. Aiming to call forth dissatisfaction with the state system existing in the Soviet Union, [its authors] distortedly describe in this document the fact of the resettlement of Tatars from Crimea. Regions where Tatars reside in Uzbekistan are called 'reservations' and places of 'exile.'"[8] The prosecutor objected to accusations of genocide arising from the huge loss of human life suffered during the deportation of Crimean Tatars (Crimean Tatar initiators estimate carefully that more than 46 percent of their countrymen died). He especially rejected the *Funereal Information Document*'s comparing Soviet treatment of Crimean Tatars with Nazi atrocities against Jews.

A crucial difference of view over construing Soviet nationality policies lay at the foundation of the Crimean Tatar dissatisfaction. The court representing the official attitudes also questioned the purity of Crimean

Tatar motives in raising the question of nationality policies. How did the two opponents—the aggrieved nationality and the CPSU with its police powers—define the nationality policies of the Soviet Union over which they now disputed? Essentially, the Party officials maintained that people of all Soviet nationalities enjoyed equal rights. In persisting with that line of response the authorities intentionally avoided the main claim that Crimean Tatars were making—that their nationality as a corporate body had suffered grievous injuries from the post–World War II application of Soviet nationality policies.

While CPSU spokesmen at every level insisted that all Soviet citizens suffered the same deprivations or enjoyed the same benefits, as individuals, these politicians refuse to address the issue of ethnic group rights. Crimean Tatars in essence argued that deprivation of nationality group rights inevitably deprived such a group's individual members of precious spiritual as well as material benefits. The official spokesmen insisted that the prosecutions and predictable punishments had nothing to do with ethnic discrimination. Rather, they said, those cases related only to laws against defaming the Soviet Union. Crimean Tatars defamed the Soviet Union, the attorneys general and prosecutors asserted, when they publicly criticized the state's nationality policies and spoke about indignities suffered at the hands of Soviet authorities. The courts would accept no evidence that Crimean Tatars' complaints might be valid. The case dealt only with the alleged crime of slandering the Soviet Union. Soviet policymakers and enforcers thus implied that Soviet nationality policies consist of decisions taken to ensure equality of treatment for each individual member of every Soviet nationality. This differs noticeably from decisions that might accord nationalities certain rights as groups. That did not enter into the recorded policies of the CPSU toward ethnic groups. Rights of ethnic groups, as such, formed no known category in such policies that might have authorized concerted ethnic group initiatives. Rather, such policies provided only that membership within a nationality offered the possibility for an individual in it to write and read in his own language, for his or her child to attend a school where teachers would instruct it, usually at first in its own tongue, and similar provisions.

Under the circumstances, a great many policies of the authorities obviously touched members of all Soviet nationalities in one way or another. But only certain kinds of policies, rather few in number and seldom explicitly pronounced or designated by the authorities, specifically sought to affect nationalities as groups. Thus, scholars must inductively try to understand Soviet nationality policies as clearly as possible. A working definition of such policies then in effect, in six steps, follows:

1. Soviet nationality policies consist of courses of action or inaction, and methods of accomplishing them, deliberately (consciously) adopted.

2. Central (CPSU) authorities determine those courses of action or inaction and have the power to carry them out.

3. Such courses of action or inaction embody specific, long-range goals or purposes.

4. The courses of action or inaction mean effectively to change or to sustain unaltered the nationality question, as defined above, generally.

5. And they aim to affect to a noticeable extent at least a major category or number, if not all, of nationalities in certain ways.

6. But these courses of action perhaps will not touch the dominant group, which stands outside the category of *nationalities*, in the same manner or degree as it affects the nationalities. If the subject were *ethnic policies* as a whole, rather than nationality policies, it might include the dominant group as well. But, owing to the dominant position of the Russians, ethnic policies yet would inescapably have different effects on the dominant Russian population and on the non-Russians.

A variety of actions may affect nationalities. Poorly undertaken economic measures, mistakes, accidents, or inadvertence, all may broadly influence single groups, perhaps whole categories of nationalities, and resemble "policies." But they lack the conscious adoption and specific long-term purpose aimed at the nationality question that would be required to qualify them as nationality policies. Observers as well as Soviet ideologists usually categorized the decision to establish administrative-territorial units named for specific nationalities as one notable example of genuine nationality policies. The Presidium of the Supreme Council of the RSFSR restored the Kalmyk Autonomous Oblast to its condition as an autonomous Soviet socialist republic in the RSFSR in July 1958. Up to 1987, the political authorities neither restored nor raised the territorial-administrative unit status of any unit named for a nationality that they exiled internally during the early 1940s.[9] This policy of inaction particularly aroused consternation among Crimean Tatars.

In their view, Vladimir I. Lenin, then the chairman of the Russian Soviet government's Council of Commissars, gave a sacred, permanent commitment to Crimean Tatars when his government in Moscow established the Crimean Autonomous Soviet Socialist Republic (CASSR) in November 1921. They regarded any subsequent government action against the viability of that CASSR as illegal. Soviet nationality policies, in their view, stemmed from the Leninist proclamations in 1917 and 1918 concerning equality of nationalities and freedom of all religion, specifically Islam. They believed that Lenin's nationality policies protected Soviet nationalities from the deprivation of institutions such as local schools, from the loss of the practical possibility to participate effectively in the Communist Party of Crimea, of the rights to organize writers' groups, to publish periodicals and books, and the like.

A second defendant in the 1969 Tashkent trial, Rollan Kadyev, cited the Resolutions of the Tenth Congress of the Russian Communist Party (Bol'shevik), 1921, in his defense speech. Those resolutions, he told the court, promised the Party's help to the non-Russian ethnic groups to develop Soviet statehood (understood to mean administrative-territorial namesake units for each sizable, concentrated nationality). The resolutions also specified that the government would develop courts, administration, economic agencies, autonomous government, and the like made up of local people familiar with the life and psychology of the population; it would establish the press, schools, theater, and social and cultural institutions in the local language; it envisaged developing general and technical education in the local language.[10]

Given the conflicting attitudes, major contradictions emerged between these strong Crimean Tatar beliefs and those of the Moscow hierarchy. They became open through the confrontations and arguments heard in the political trials brought against selected Crimean Tatars. On the sixteenth day (28 July 1969) of the court proceedings in Tashkent against the ten Crimean Tatar initiators, Reshat Bayramov presented his defense statement. In it, he elaborated on the assertions made in *Funereal Information Document No. 69*, charging Soviet authorities with the serious crime of genocide. He remarked that in respect to his letter, "Genocide in the Policy of the Soviet State," the attorney general's indictment claimed that Bayramov "groundlessly, from a defamatory position, makes a parallel between the nationality policy of the Soviet government and the colonial policy of capitalistic states." Bayramov acknowledged that his letter said that "a policy of genocide is employed against the Crimean Tatar ethnic group." And in the defense speech he explained that charge through paraphrasing the United Nations' Genocide Convention dated 9 December 1948, accepted by the Soviet Union and dozens of other member countries:

Genocide is a crime. It represents a series of actions directed at the full or partial destruction of some ethnic, national, or religious group. For example, let us take autonomy. National autonomy is a means linking a definite group of people in one nation or ethnic group. With the very expulsion of our ethnic group and liquidation of the CASSR our ethnic group was deprived of further national development and found itself in conditions of annihilation. That is, we lost what I spoke about already when one of the forms of genocide is defined as destruction of whatever links defined the group of people in a single nation or ethnic group. And also deprivation of the possibility of developing the persecuted ethnic group, destruction of its language, literature, art, destruction of historic monuments of ancient culture, and the like. Proceeding from a series of concrete facts, which I cited above, it is possible to say that the current party-state leadership decided firmly and persistently to continue a policy of annihilating the Crimean Tatar nation, the remnants of our culture and life, literature [and] art, and that it wants not only to destroy it but to eradicate it from the roster of nations once inhabiting the territory of the Soviet Union. And the *ukase* of the Presidium of the Supreme Council of the Soviet Union promotes further application of a policy of genocide in whatever form it might be expressed. [This was] also the policy of czarism—Crimea without Crimean Tatars. As to responsibility for genocide, each state bears international political and material responsibility. Organizations pursuing the goal of genocide and in whose name crime is committed must be acknowledged as criminals and disbanded. Article [9] of the Statutes of the International Tribunal stipulates this. The conclusions, citizen judges, I leave to you.[11]

Reshat Bayramov here demanded that the Soviet authorities face a critical interpretation of their conduct and policies, an interpretation that they publicly disavowed. In this *Funereal Information Document*, citing the United Nations' 1948 Universal Declaration of Human Rights, article 19, adopted 10 December 1967 by the Soviet Union, and Leonid I. Brezhnev's speeches about the interests of people of the various nationalities, Bayramov applied both types of statements to the negative treatment of Crimean Tatars as a measure of Soviet conduct.

Bayramov's open letter, "Genocide in the Policy of the Government of the Soviet State," came out in samizdat form in May 1968. It furnished most of the passage in his court defense speech quoted above. Even more pointedly than in the defense statement, the letter charges the Soviet Union with genocide: "The ruling circles of the Soviet government, brutally breaking generally accepted standards of international law, in broad terms carries out genocide against the Crimean Tatar ethnic group." The greatest grievance, the destruction of human life, received first attention in Bayramov's discussion. But he turned to aspects of ethnocide that seemed equally outrageous to him: burning books and old manuscripts just because they appeared in the Crimean Tatar language, for example. The Communist authorities also destroyed books by Russian and foreign historians and literary authors about Crimea. "Soon, it was imperative to write 'a new history' of Crimea and literature about it [Crimea, in which] Tatars are traitors, disloyal, bandits, and, in the final analysis, not a full-fledged ethnic group. This was what the ethnic groups of the world must know about Crimean Tatars. [Their] diligence, honesty, loyalty—all this must be forgotten."[12]

In the end, after lengthy testimony and without a jury, court officials in Tashkent declared all ten Crimean Tatar defendants guilty, as charged, of political offenses (criticizing the Soviet government). Under RSFSR law they sentenced Reshat Bayramov and Rollan Kadyev to the longest sentences handed down in this case—three years' deprivation of liberty in an ordinary correctional facility.[13] Among the ten defendants, those two had thoroughly, specifically articulated the case condemning the contemporary application of Soviet nationality policies as un-Leninist, calling them coercive and discriminatory.

Soviet nationality policies received a second unusually extensive examination during a court case directed against another Crimean Tatar defendant whose name has become synonymous with his group's newer drive for ethnic rights. From 12 to 19 January 1970, again in Tashkent, the city court prosecuted Mustafa Jemiloglu (1943–) and a Jewish codefendant for "systematically preparing, duplicating and distributing documents in which are contained patently false fabrications that defame the Soviet social and state system." The Slavic councilor, B. Berezovskii, of the UZSSR prosecutor's department, charged Jemiloglu with criminal activity under articles 50, 59, and 60 of the Criminal Code, UZSSR. Article 50 of the UZSSR code does speak of evidence arising in connection with an "action harmful to society." Those articles prescribed the handling of material and other evidence in a case, but none bore specific relation to any kind of ethnic discrimination or nationality policies.[14] The close connection of the Committee for State Security (KGB) with this case revealed the political nature of the indictment as much as did the charges involved. The transmittal memorandum conveying the twenty volumes of evidence from S. Polatkhojayew, the president of the UZSSR Supreme Court, to T. A. Abdullayew, the president of the City Court of Tashkent, also went to the chief of the KGB unit in the Council of Ministers, UZSSR.[15]

During pretrial interrogation on 12 January 1970, Jemiloglu questioned the judge about the application of those articles in the codes under RSFSR and UZSSR criminal law.

*Jemiloglu:* "Please explain to me what articles 190-1 of the Criminal Code of the RSFSR and articles 191-4 of the Criminal Code of the UZSSR punish one for: for the distribution of false facts or the incorrect interpretation of them?"

*Judge:* "The articles punish one for compiling and distribution of false fabrications that defame the Soviet system."

*Jemiloglu:* "If for the distribution of false information, then why didn't the court forward the case for investigation? You see, from the indictment it is obvious that the inquiry did not investigate a single fact described in the documents that we are accused of compiling.... I consider the indictment patently false."[16]

The persistent refusal of the court to assess objectively and admit or refute the validity of the documents themselves constituted the crux of the disagreement between the judges and the Crimean Tatar defendant. It ensured that Jemiloglu could not persuade the court of his innocence, for he would not deny his role in developing and circulating the documents. The court's definition and charge of defamation did not turn on the accuracy of the facts and the justification Crimean Tatars might have for publicizing their group's deprivations. Instead, the defamation charge rested on the bad light in which Crimean Tatars cast the Soviet authorities by making the documents—true or untrue—widely available. The legal restrictions that stymied Jemiloglu's defense could not prevent him from making his case against mistreatment of the Crimean Tatar nationality as such under the application of Soviet nationality policies.

The Slavic prosecutor, Bocharov, spoke in his indictment speech to the court about "slanderous fabrications" in the documents compiled by Jemiloglu and others. The official summarized for the court what he called the four main complaints in the documents. They spoke of arbitrariness and illegality in the Soviet Union, about a policy of chauvinism ostensibly conducted in the Soviet Union, about intervention and occupation (references to Soviet invasion of Czechoslovakia in 1968), and the absence of democracy in the Soviet Union. Specifically, Bocharov rhetorically asked if there were any justification for these "slanders." Answering himself, he categorically denied their validity:

There are no sorts of bases for them. Not a single witness has cited any evidence giving a basis for these slanderous fabrications. Take even the slander on the nationality policy of the Soviet Union [claiming] that Tatars are ostensibly unequal. Now this is a completely deliberate fabrication that stains black the light and wise nationality policy of our government. The defendants are fully aware that national oppression was eliminated in the Soviet Union. A new historical community of persons was formed. The people, in the first place, the Soviet people, have a common motherland, common, most progressive Marxist-Leninist ideology, a common worldview, common goal, and even common traits, not to speak of spiritual makeup.... The defendants especially calumniate about the so-called Crimean Tatar question, trying to show that Tatars are somehow in an unequal situation. But this is a deliberate lie. All our ethnic groups enjoy identical rights. It must be added that representatives of the Crimean Tatar ethnic group are elected to the supreme agencies of power, there are deputies, there are representatives from the Crimean ethnic group among the *raion, oblast*, and supreme council deputies of the toilers. For example, there is the first secretary of the Aqqorghan committee of the Party, comrade Tairov. There is a mass of workers in many responsible positions. Even in the prosecutor's offices there are Crimean Tatars.... You heard exchanges here [to the effect that] they do not permit the Crimean Tatar ethnic group in Crimea. Witness Muratov said here that his countrymen live in various *raions* of Crimea. They did not refuse him a permit because of his nationality, but there are definite conditions generally applicable to all citizens of the Soviet Union for permits.

Or the matter of the lack of democracy in the Soviet Union. This is slander compounded.... Jemiloglu! You know that Soviet citizens have the right to labor, right to education, cost-free medical care, electoral rights.... The song goes: "Wide is my native land .../ I don't know another such land, / Where a person breathes so freely." These words testify to the fact that the most democratic democracy in the world exists in our country.[17]

Once again, the official in essence charged Crimean Tatars with the crime of exercising their right to free speech. Even more pointed, the prosecution set the stage for rebuttals from this defendant, Jemiloglu, about the unfairness or illegality of Soviet nationality policies and actions taken under them.

On the fifth day of the case, 16 January 1970, Mustafa Jemiloglu addressed at length the matter of Soviet nationality policies and his alleged slander of them and the leadership. He undertook this in a defense speech entitled "The Policy of the Leadership of the CPSU and Government in the Nationality Question of Crimean Tatars." Surveying the application of nationality policies first, he dealt with the forcible internal deportation of his people from Crimea in 1944. He labeled that a serious crime, a crime against humanity, under the Statute of the International Nuremburg Tribunal, article 3b, a tribunal in which the Soviet Union participated actively. The defendant then described a canvass conducted among exiled Crimean Tatars in the Soviet Union during 1966 in preparation for their appeal to the Twenty-third Congress of the CPSU, mentioned earlier. That survey, in which he took an active part, produced a seven-volume report, which Crimean Tatars submitted to the Central Committee, CPSU. Its general findings showed that, during the first two years of the expulsion from Crimea alone, about 46 percent of the nationality perished. "This was genocide—ethnocide," he said, "for which crime, according to the International Convention on Genocide adopted by the United Nations Organization in 1948 [including the Soviet Union], the criminals must most sternly be made to answer."[18] (For a translation of the section in Mustafa Jemiloglu's defense speech devoted to Soviet nationality policies, see chap. 12 in this volume.) As an eyewitness, he described the condition of rights among Crimean Tatars in the places of exile, subject to the arbitrariness and humiliation of the local commandants, as indistinguishable from that of medieval serfs in Russia.

In a second major discussion, Jemiloglu gave testimony showing that the authorities in various places in Central Asia fabricated letters in the names of Crimean Tatars and deceived some Crimean Tatars into signing them. These forgeries opposed the drive to return to the homeland in Crimea. The authorities later circulated these letters with the intention of discrediting the movement for repatriation. In addition, the same forgeries became part of the court evidence intended to counter charges by Jemiloglu and his colleagues that all Crimean Tatars wished to return to their homeland and suffered from illegal prohibitions against it.[19]

Jemiloglu's defense statement, after recounting many actions organized by Crimean Tatars in search of their rights and the measures taken against their efforts by the police, KGB, and other authorities, proceeded to analyze the *ukase* issued by the Presidium, Supreme Council of the Soviet Union, on 5 September 1967. In the *ukase* the Supreme Council's Presidium declared that appropriate ministries of the union republics would take measures for the development of the culture of the Tatars formerly residing in Crimea. The *ukase* indeed directed the councils of ministers in those constituent republics now hosts to the exiles "to render aid and assistance to citizens [not to the group as such] of the Tatar nationality in economic and cultural development with regard for their national interests and peculiarities."[20] Nikolay Podgornyi, chairman of the Presidium, and M. Georgadze, secretary of the Presidium, signed the decree. Mustafa Jemiloglu pointed out that, "no matter what conditions might be created in the places of exile, the national culture of an ethnic group torn from its homeland and without existing national statehood [meaning a namesake administrative-territorial unit] could not develop fully." In the second place, he commented, the promise of the government in this *ukase* turned out to be a lie. Noting that, in order to charge participants in the Crimean Tatar repatriation drive with defamation of the nationality policy of the CPSU as well as with nationalism, the state prosecutors would as a rule cite the existence of certain minimal group expressions. Those would come through references to the Crimean Tatar–language press, radio transmissions, and performances of ethnic song and dance groups, prosecutors noticed. In response to that assertion Jemiloglu remarked that the Crimean Tatar–language newspaper *Lenin bayraghi*, issued since May 1957 by the Central Committee of the UZSSR Communist Party, hardly reflected the interests of the ethnic group and even so at the time was the only paper in the Crimean Tatar tongue among 307 coming out in Uzbekistan.[21]

The defendant cited several examples of destruction by the Soviet authorities of monuments, graveyards, inscribed tombstones, and structures created by Crimean Tatars in Crimea. At the same time they replaced traditional Tatar street and place names with Russian and Soviet substitutes. He also pointed out that in Central Asia the song and dance ensemble Qaytarma lost a large part of its repertory through Soviet censorship. Censors declared some of the songs unacceptable on the ground that they resembled Turkish songs. They barred many others because they referred specifically to Crimea. "Therefore," said Jemiloglu, "with full justification I accuse the Soviet government of conducting a policy of national-cultural genocide, that is, of a policy directed at the destruction of the national culture and uniqueness of the Crimean Tatar ethnic group."[22]

Between 1965 and 1969, testified Jemiloglu, authorities encouraged officials to denigrate Crimean Tatars in public in Central Asia, Moscow, and elsewhere. He himself heard a presentation given by a lecturer for the Central Committee UZSSR Communist Party in 1965 in which the speaker falsely and slanderously declared that Crimean Tatars betrayed the country during World War II, destroyed Red partisans, and formed five divisions under the Germans to fight Soviet forces. In Uzbekistan's towns public officials made comparable statements with impunity. Anti-Tatar lectures also began to be heard in Moscow. According to him, the authorities converted museums in Crimea into anti-Tatar exhibitions attracting thousands of visitors. Guides generalized about how Crimean Tatars ostensibly lived in the past only by banditry and slave trade, how they betrayed Russians during the occupation of Crimea by foreign troops, and the like. In these and other ways at the level of the general public the authorities tried to discredit the nationality and justify Soviet deportation of Crimean Tatars from Crimea. Mustafa Jemiloglu concluded this section in his extensive defense summary by emphasizing two strong points. The authorities took actions, arranged provocations, and placed indictments against Crimean Tatar group organizers in order to intimidate and break the solidarity of the repatriation movement. The authorities worked energetically to turn other nationalities against Crimean Tatars. By taking this action they evidently meant to counter the public sympathy generated by the Crimean Tatar campaign for support. Finally, officials attempted to retard and minimize the revival of the national culture of the Crimean Tatar ethnic group, pushing it to the verge of complete disintegration. "Such is the policy of the Soviet party-government leadership in the nationality question of Crimean Tatars," said Mustafa Jemiloglu.[23]

The court had the last word. In the verdict, the judgment responded to Jemiloglu's declarations about Soviet nationality policies. The judge singled out Jemiloglu's letter personally composed and addressed to the editors of the (Russian-language) newspapers *Andizhanskaia pravda* and Moscow's *Izvestiia* as well as to the (Uzbek-language) *Sawet Ozbekistani*. The jurist asserted:

> In this document Jemiloglu, defaming the Soviet society and state, asserted that in the Soviet Union true friendship between ethnic groups [*druzhba narodov*] does not exist. "It is much more possible and necessary to speak," writes Jemiloglu, "about national enmity, which, unfortunately, has roots that defend themselves, I think, with the very powerful [means] of this state." . . . Defaming the nationality policy of the Soviet state, Jemiloglu, in that same document, writes that "the right of ethnic groups proclaimed by Lenin to determine their own fate themselves was trampled," . . . that allegedly "a political and national death was prepared" for Tatars who earlier resided in Crimea.[24]

At the end of April 1968, the court noted, Mustafa Jemiloglu and others compiled "a defamatory document" addressed to the Politburo, the Central Committee of the CPSU, and the Presidium of the Supreme Council, the chairman of the Council of Ministers, and the attorney general of the Soviet Union complaining of violent actions taken against Crimean Tatars by the authorities in Chirchik, Uzbekistan. In another document addressed to Soviet writers, scientists, artists, and cultural leaders as well as political and social figures, the supporters of the drive, including Jemiloglu, allegedly "defamed the nationality policy of the Communist Party and Soviet government." Supposedly, they did this by "asserting that ostensibly a policy has been instituted in regard to the Tatar ethnic group earlier residing in Crimea for infringing on its rights and dignity and that arbitrariness and illegality are employed against the representatives of this ethnic group." To punish the defendant for making all these critical statements about Soviet nationality policies and about the absence of democracy, as well as other subjects, the court, presided over by Pisarenko, found Mustafa Jemiloglu guilty. The court condemned him for "preparing, duplicating and distributing documents in which knowingly false fabrications are contained that defame the Soviet state and social system." The Slavic judge sentenced him to deprivation of freedom for three years on each charge, the sentences to be served concurrently in a harsh-regime labor colony.[25] To the end, the court insisted that Mustafa Jemiloglu should have considered his documents false because the Party authorities declared them untrue, although he knew them to be correct.

Notwithstanding the political rejections registered in those two cases,

Crimean Tatars continued the nonviolent campaign to regain their nationality's territory and other group rights. The 1970s and 1980s saw repeated public actions undertaken by the Crimean Tatar initiative group to bring its case to Soviet authorities emphatically. In one of the more recent episodes in that ongoing process, yet another, even younger generation of Crimean Tatars in Central Asia confronted the UZSSR authorities in a different forum over the issue of regaining their Crimean homeland.

For several years Uzbekistan's administration had pursued a policy of settling Crimean Tatars far to the southwest of Tashkent in areas new to any real concentration of that ethnic group. Under encouragement from the authorities, some Crimean Tatar families moved from elsewhere in the UZSSR to the settlements of Mubarek and Baharistan *raion* located in Qashqadarya (Kashka Darya) *oblast*, seventy kilometers northwest of the oblast capital, Qarshi, and ninety kilometers southeast of Bukhara. But administrative efforts to draw Crimean Tatars into that underpopulated district quickly led them to suspect that officials might regard the remote plains of Qashqadarya as a solution for the UZSSR's (and the Soviet Union's) Crimean Tatar problem.

This attitude came into the open when the UZSSR Ministry of Education attempted to assign Crimean Tatar graduates of Tashkent's Nizami Pedagogical Institute to teach in Mubarek and Baharistan *raions*. That institute housed a Department of Tatar Language and Literature, the only educational subunit in the Soviet Union devoted specifically to the training of Crimean Tatars. In it, the young people learned to teach Russian language and literature rather than their own culture. The department, established about 1970, meant to supply instructors to teach in Crimean Tatar primary and secondary schools. They expected these schools to open after the Supreme Council of the Soviet Union in 1967 issued its *ukase* exonerating the Crimean Tatar nationality from blanket charges of collaborating with the wartime enemy. Those Crimean Tatar schools never materialized. As a result, by 1979, the Nizami Pedagogical Institute graduated twenty to twenty-five teachers annually who found themselves obliged to teach the Russian language to mixed classrooms. Five or six Russian schools in the UZSSR instituted optional classes in the Crimean Tatar language for groups who studied there. But instructors had to perform at the most rudimentary level without the help of schoolbooks and other aids in the Crimean Tatar language.

Into that situation the authorities introduced an incentive unprecedented among Crimean Tatars since 1944. The authorities promised to open schools in the Mubarek and Baharistan *raions*. In them, all subjects would be taught in the Crimean Tatar language. Perhaps they would also organize a teachers' college there. This offer meant to attract the cooperation of the two dozen Crimean Tatars graduating each year from the Department of Tatar Language and Literature in Tashkent. Between March and April 1983, officials drafted this newest plan for developing a Crimean Tatar nucleus in Qashqadarya *oblast* and, most likely, aiding the UZSSR economy by shifting industrious Crimean Tatar farmers into that area. A little before April, administrators allocated the graduating class as usual to various posts throughout Uzbekistan. But, toward the end of April 1983, the dean of the Nizami Pedagogical Institute called in all the graduating students from the Department of Tatar Language and Literature and gave them new assignments. He allocated the entire class to Mubarek. In addition, educational authorities directed Crimean Tatar graduating seniors from other institutions of higher learning and vocational training schools in Tashkent to Mubarek.[26] In the face of a great deal of pressure openly and indirectly applied to them, the Crimean Tatar graduating students refused to become the vanguard of a resettlement project in Mubarek and Baharistan *raions*. In rebuffing attempts by officials from the Ministry of Education and the UZSSR Supreme Council to attract them to that target area, the students explained that they meant to settle down compactly only in the Crimean homeland.

This incident revealed very much about the cohesion of the Crimean Tatar community in Central Asia. At the same time it gave evidence in the mid-1980s concerning Soviet nationality policies. In this attempt to resettle Crimean Tatars in a rural area of the UZSSR, the authorities had shown that they accepted the wish for compact settlement. It is evident also that the politicians could, in the negotiations, offer Crimean Tatars approval to conduct primary and perhaps secondary education in their own language for Crimean Tatar children. This apparent flexibility in potential application of nationality policies suggested that the Crimean Tatars' resolute efforts had created possibilities for satisfying some of their demands. It also showed that official withholding of ethnic group recognition depended considerably on the actual political costs of adopting that approach to specific nationality problems. In this case, with great effort, Crimean

Tatars had found the way to exact some desired responses from the authorities. The fact that Crimean Tatars remained unwilling to accept only partial satisfaction of their demands left the Soviet leadership in the predicament it created for itself when it deported Crimean Tatars from the Black Sea littoral some forty years earlier.

In examining Soviet nationality policies directly, it is possible to restate that dilemma in the following way:

1. Taken in isolation, the forcible resettlement and exile of the entire Crimean Tatar nationality from its homeland in Crimea to the Urals region and Central Asia appears to represent an aberration from normal nationality policies of the CPSU rather than an example of the standard procedure.

2. Observers possibly may not regard as an expression of normal policy the continued refusal by Soviet authorities since 1944 to rectify completely what then seemed a distortion of nationality policies.

3. Additional uncertainty about official Soviet intentions arises from the fact that the authorities justify their current conduct by reliance on the situation created by their anomalous actions taken in May 1944. As a consequence, the original involuntary resettlement of the whole Crimean Tatar nationality would seem to compromise the legality or, at least, consistency of subsequent policies.

4. The CPSU's continuing denial of self-determination to Crimean Tatars who wish to revive their traditional cultural institutions and their political life and to return to the Crimean homeland may constitute evidence of a change in policies. That would reveal instability in Soviet nationality policies, something Soviet leaders deny. At the very least, the trait or pattern of changeability in such policies would give a different cast to the public reputation of Soviet nationality policies. Communist Party politicians might claim, as they do on most issues, that consistency in this sphere equates with policies and actions that strengthen the Party at any particular period, regardless of their inconsistency in other respects.

5. Under the circumstances, these decisions and actions taken by the political authorities toward the entire Crimean Tatar nationality now appear to the group's members to take a repressive, discriminatory direction. They seem to substitute, since World War II, for what party leaders once claimed was the CPSU's egalitarian approach to ethnic groups in the Soviet Union. But, with the leadership's ideology of relative justice and truth

(truth or fairness in all cases not being absolutes but existing only relative to the self-interest of the Party), CPSU leaders put themselves outside the reach of arguments from the standpoint of normal ethical consistency.

6. To allow that relativistic explanation to prevail in this instance would beg the question about the formulation and application of anomalous or standard policies in the Crimean Tatar case. Ignoring that interpretation then brings the discussion back to an examination of what actually happened in 1944 and thereafter. The record shows that, since 1957, Soviet officials have given some ground before the determined initiative of Crimean Tatars to regain certain minimal group rights (publishing in the Crimean Tatar language and alphabet, activation of a specific teacher-training section in the vocational educational system, approval for an ethnic song and dance troupe, e.g.). These give testimony that the authorities presently judge as unfair the actions that they took in 1944, thus acknowledging an anomaly in nationality policies at that time.

7. But the very minor concessions granted by the political authorities in this case suggest that they consciously meant this banishment of Crimean Tatars from their homeland as exemplary, knowing at the time that it would be a deviation from normal policies. With such action, not confined to Crimean Tatars, the leadership intended to intimidate other nationalities through the exercise of punitive powers. This made coercion and force a standard, recognized part of the repertory at the disposal of Soviet nationality policy makers. It linked arbitrary Russian policies of the Soviet period toward non-Russians with punitive Russian policies of the czarist era (physical and cultural actions taken against Jews, Kalmyks, Kazaks, Koreans, Ukrayinans, and many other nationalities under both regimes, e.g.). An exemplary action by its nature singles out a target group. The policy behind it did not have to aim at all nationalities in the state, nor did the leaders need to apply those policies regularly and consistently.

8. Nikita S. Khrushchev, first secretary of the CPSU, declared in his speech during a closed session of the Twentieth Congress of the CPSU, 24–25 February 1956, that "mass deportations from their native places of whole nations, together with all Communists and Komsomols [Communist Youth League] members . . . are rude violations of the basic Leninist principles of the nationality policy of the Soviet state."[27] In 1956, at least, the leading politicians in the Soviet Union agreed with the Crimean Tatar spokesmen in declaring the 1944 exiling of whole nationalities an anomaly in the nationality policies of the CPSU. Although a logical consequence of

that declaration by Mr. Khrushchev would seem to have been restoration to the homeland of the Crimean Tatar group, it did not occur.

From these considerations, the situation of Crimean Tatars from the 1960s to the 1980s argues that official decisions made and actions taken since 1944 followed a normal pattern in Soviet nationality policies. But, because CPSU leaders singled out Crimean Tatars for continuing special deprivation during the decades after the death of Stalin in 1953, analysts could classify the group exile as neither anomalous nor exemplary. They might see it as irrational, an expression of Russian bias against the Crimean Tatar nationality in particular. Perhaps that prejudice emanated from the antagonistic relations recorded between the two ethnic groups throughout their long history of interaction. Perhaps the policies applied to Crimean Tatars owe their origin to the general anti-Asian feeling not seldom expressed by some intolerant Russian leaders as well as ordinary Russians.

Taking another approach, for decades Marxist ideologists among Soviet Party leaders have advanced the notion that smaller ethnic groups in the Soviet Union, and elsewhere, lack the right benefiting larger ones to continue a full-fledged corporate existence. This attitude goes directly back to Karl Marx and especially to Friedrich Engels. In their "Democratic Panslavism" (1849), they declared that ethnic groups without what they called basic historic, geographic, political, and industrial prerequisites for independence and vitality had no future. In "Hungary and Panslavism" (1849) and other articles, they wrote scathingly about ethnic groups such as Jews, Saxons, or Slavs "that insist upon clinging to an absurd nationality in the midst of a foreign land." An attitude that focused on Europe could not fail to extend into Eastern lands as well. They referred to such ethnic groups as "remains of nations which have been mercilessly trampled down by the passage of history, as Hegel expressed it, . . . ethnic trash whose . . . entire existence is nothing more than a protest against a great historical revolution."[28] That ideological bias against smaller nationalities would signify serious problems for Crimean Tatars in another way, for they now lacked a namesake territory and seemed to number well under one million souls. Ideologists could use the notion of *historical necessity* against them.

In a country where component ethnic groups led their lives largely as they wished, through their own initiative Crimean Tatars might have overcome the disabilities they suffered earlier. Their inability to accomplish that in the Soviet Union evidently stemmed wholly from the actions taken against their efforts by the politicians of the CPSU and the state. A careful American scholar has suggested that foreign policy considerations determined Soviet leaders to deport Crimean Tatars from the Black Sea area and that the false charge of collaboration cynically facilitated the government's plans.[29] Thus, both practical political and ideological motivations led to the application of these measures against the group's wishes under guidelines supplied by Soviet nationality policies. The general message transmitted to Crimean Tatars and observers by this experience cannot be mistaken. For domestic and foreign audiences, spokesmen of the regime have long treated Soviet nationality policies as entirely positive decisions meant to ameliorate the conditions of life for every nationality in the Soviet Union. Now it became unmistakable that such policies might have their very negative functions, as well, so far as the survival of individual nationalities was concerned. In that respect, the conduct of the Crimean Tatar case showed destructive actions against ethnic groups to constitute a normal aspect of Soviet nationality policies.

## Notes

1. Edward Allworth, "Flexible Defenses of a Nationality," in *Nationality Group Survival in Multi-Ethnic States: Shifting Support Patterns in the Soviet Baltic Region*, ed. Edward Allworth (New York: Praeger, 1977), 2.
2. "Programma kommunisticheskoi partii Sovetskogo Soiuza: Novaia redaktsiia: Priniata XXVII s"ezdom KPSS," *Vodnyi transport*, 7 March 1986, 5.
3. "Obrashchenie krymskotatarskogo naroda k XXIII s"ezdu KPSS—mart 1966 g.," in *Tashkentskii protsess: Sud nad desiat'iu predstaviteliami krymskotatarskogo naroda (1 iiulia—5 augusta 1969 g.)* (Amsterdam: Fond imeni Gertsena, 1976), 9.
4. *Vedomosti Verkhovnogo Soveta SSSR*, no. 36 (5 September 1967): art. 493, pp. 531–32; "O poriadke primeneniia stat'i 2 Ukaza Prezidiuma Verkhovnogo Soveta SSSR ot 28 Aprelia 1956 goda," *Vedomosti Verkhovnogo Soveta SSSR*, no. 36 (8 September 1967): art. 494, p. 532; "O poriadke primeneniia v otnoshenii grazhdan SSSR—turok, kurdov, khemshilov i azerbaidzhantsev, prozhivavshikh ranee v Gruzinskoi SSR, stat'i 2 Ukaza Prezidiuma Verkhovnogo Soveta SSSR ot 28 aprelia 1956 goda i stat'i 2 Ukaza Prezidiuma Verkhovnogo Soveta SSSR ot 31 oktiabria 1957 goda," *Vedomosti Verkhovnogo Soveta SSSR*, no. 23 (5 June 1968): art. 188, pp. 311–12; both references also cited by Robert Conquest, *The Nation Killers: The Soviet Deportation of Nationalities* (London: Macmillan, 1970), 184–89.
5. *Tashkentskii protsess*, 205–6.

6. Ibid., 205.
7. *Traurnaia informatsiia no. 69*, Radio Svoboda, no. 396 (14 August 1970).
8. *Tashkentskii protsess*, 210.
9. "O preobrazovanii Kalmytskoi Avtonomnoi Oblasti v Kalmytskuiu Avtonomnuiu Sovetskuiu Sotsialisticheskuiu Respubliku," *Vedomosti Verkhovnogo Soveta RSFSR*, no. 8 (14 August 1958): art. 401, p. 339; Conquest, *The Nation Killers*, 210–11.
10. Rollan Kadyev, "Zashchititel'naia rech' Kadyeva Rollana," in *Tashkentskii protsess*, 597–98; Richard Pipes, *Formation of the Soviet Union: Communism and Nationalism, 1917–1923*, rev. ed. (New York: Atheneum, 1968), 190.
11. *Tashkentskii protsess*, 574–75; Leo Kuper, *Genocide* (New Haven, Conn.: Yale University Press, 1981), 210–11.
12. Reshat Bairamov, "Genotsid v politike pravitel'stva sovetskogo gosudarstva," in *Tashkentskii protsess*, 728–36.
13. *Tashkentskii protsess*, 680–81.
14. *Shest' dnei: "Belaia kniga"* (New York: Fond Krym, 1980), 121–22, 176; *Ozbekistan SSR jinayät-pratsessuäl Kadeksi: 1978 yil 1 yänwärgächä bolgän ozgärtish wä qoshimchälär bilän* (Tashkent: "Ozbekistan" Näshriyati, 1978), articles 50, 59, 60, pp. 27, 30.
15. *Shest' dnei*, 176.
16. Ibid., 187.
17. Ibid., 311–12.
18. Ibid., 333.
19. Ibid., 338–40.
20. *Vedomosti Verkhovnogo Soveta SSSR*, no. 36, art. 493, p. 532; *Shest'dnei*, 342.
21. *Shest' dnei*, 342–43.
22. Ibid., 334–45.
23. Ibid., 350.
24. Ibid., 394.
25. Ibid., 396, 400–401.
26. "Pressure on Graduating Students of Tatlit," *Materialy samizdat*, RFE-RL, issue no. 18/84 (8 June 1984), *Arkhiv samizdata*, no. 5224, 3:2, pp. 23–24.
27. Nikita S. Khrushchev, "Special Report to the 20th Congress of the Communist Party of the Soviet Union," in *Crimes of the Stalin Era* (New York: New Leader, 1962), S44.
28. Karl Marx and Friedrich Engels, "Hungary and Panslavism," in *The Russian Menace to Europe* (Glencoe, Ill.: Free Press, 1952), 61, 63, and "Democratic Panslavism," in ibid., 71–72.
29. Alan Fisher, *The Crimean Tatars* (Stanford, Calif.: Hoover Institution Press, 1978), 168–70.

# 10

## *Mustafa Jemiloglu, His Character and Convictions*

LUDMILLA ALEXEYEVA

Mustafa Jemiloglu is the national hero of Crimean Tatars. Given the conditions in the Soviet Union, heroism and readiness to sacrifice oneself were requisite qualities for an activist in any independent social movement. Anyone embarking on this path must, from the very start, demonstrate these qualities, for, if he does not, preservation of his independent social position is impossible. Therefore, all the national and religious movements in the Soviet Union, as well as the civil rights movement, possess their own heroes. Mustafa Jemiloglu's heroism still stands out among the pleiad of heroes in the Crimean Tatar movement for the return to Crimea: he alone among them sat out six terms of imprisonment. The policy of the authorities toward Mustafa Jemiloglu is obvious—he was condemned to be their perpetual prisoner. The especially cruel attitude of the penal authorities toward Mustafa Jemiloglu was brought on by his special role in the Crimean Tatar movement: he is the movement's acknowledged ideologue. He worked out a concept of the history of Crimean Tatars that ran contrary to the official Soviet version and on the basis of that concept established a platform for the Crimean Tatar movement, which, in turn, determined its strategy and tactics and influenced the moral principles of the movement's members. What does Mustafa Jemiloglu represent as an individual personality? What are his convictions? His character was formed by the tragedy of his people—the deportation of 18 May 1944 and the struggle of his whole people to return to their homeland. As an individual, he has left his mark on the ideology and character of the Crimean Tatar movement.

Mustafa Jemiloglu was born 13 November 1943 in the village of Ay-Serez (Boskoe) in the Sudaq region of Crimea. In May 1944, he was only seven months old. Of course, he has no personal recollection of the horrors of the road to persecution. But, from the moment he became conscious of himself, he was a deportee, sentenced, as it were, to the special regime on account of the fact that he had been born of Crimean Tatar parents.[1] All his childhood memories are about the special regime. During the first twelve years of his life, Mustafa saw and knew of nothing but the small settlement where he was registered by the special regime, and he could neither see nor know anyone but those special deportees. Most of these people were Crimean Tatars. Many people of other nationalities were either guards or foremen at work. The special settlements offered an ideal way to cultivate xenophobia.

From earliest childhood, Mustafa listened to countless stories about deportation. They were not legends but testimonies of people who had endured deportation. They mentioned the names of their friends who died on the grievous road to deportation, and they described the inhumane conditions of their death. Not infrequently did he hear other stories as well, from Crimean Tatars who had been at the battlefront at the moment of deportation. Their lot was to fight to the end. But those who managed to survive the war all underwent the same metamorphosis: from being soldiers and officers in the victorious Soviet Army (among whom many were decorated for bravery), they all became "traitors to the homeland" at the instant of demobilization, and as such they were sent to those special settlements where they were awaited by the very same sorts of traitors—their mothers, wives, and children. Mustafa's father, Abduljemal' Mustafaev, lived through such a metamorphosis. He was at the front when his wife, Makhfure, and their four young children were thrown out of their house after a fifteen-minute roll call and dispatched to a special settlement in Uzbekistan. Not only were Mustafa's mother, father, elder brothers and sisters, and he himself considered traitors, but even his sister who was born after the war: the stigma of *traitor* was indelibly stamped on every Crimean Tatar.

From birth, or perhaps from childhood, Mustafa sought an answer to the question, Why are we lepers? There are two mutually exclusive answers to that question.

In the Soviet newspapers and magazines, as well as in the elementary schoolbooks that Mustafa first read, Crimean Tatars were characterized as a sly, aggressive, and cruel people who had for ages lived on banditry and plundering and who had brought much hardship to their Russian neighbors. The "treachery" of Crimean Tatars during the war with the Nazis was not recounted in the written sources, but not infrequently did commandants of the special settlements and schoolteachers in their history classes speak of it: they all received the same instructions in secret sessions that Crimean Tatars often found out about. In 1965, Mustafa himself happened on such a session: in a hall for academic workers of the public library named for Navoy in Tashkent, Blok, a lecturer of the Central Committee of the Communist Party of Uzbekistan gave a lecture in which he said that Tatars would not be returned to Crimea, for they committed acts of treachery during the war, formed five divisions in aid to the Nazis, and destroyed nearly all the Soviet partisans who were active in Crimean territory.[2]

As far as the history of Crimean Tatars and their characterization as a people are concerned, the most complete publication on the history of Crimea, available only in the Soviet Union, is the four-volume *Notes on the History of Crimea*, edited by P. Nadinskii, Simferopol'. In volume 1, which was published in 1951, it says: "Crimean Tatars, accustomed to living on profits gained from plundering raids, have worked at productive labor little themselves, and unwillingly. For this reason Crimea was a poor and backward region until it was ceded (in 1783) to Russia." Nadinskii wrote that "only the union with Russia changed fundamentally the face of Crimea; it literally leapt out of the morass of three centuries of vegetation, and socially the economic life of the area 'struck oil.'"[3]

Why "three centuries of vegetation"? Because, in Nadinskii's estimation, before that Crimea was Russian territory: "The Crimean land has been from time immemorial Russian land, and the ceding of Crimea to Russia was not a capture of a foreign land."[4] Nadinskii was echoed by V. Vetlina, who wrote: "In 1783 an act of historical justice was accomplished—the Crimean isthmus was joined to Russia."[5] It is impossible to find any balanced evidence in Soviet sources on Crimean Tatars in Crimea.

Later, Mustafa learned that right after the war a grandiose endeavor had been carried out. Everything printed in the Crimean Tatar language was burned, even the "classics of Marxism-Leninism," and Russian books with other than Nadinskii's or Vetlina's view of the history of Crimea and Crimean Tatars. Mosques were destroyed, Muslim graves were leveled, and gravestones were used as construction material for new buildings. Tatar names of streets, villages, and cities were changed to Russian ones. As in Orwell, old works were rewritten and new ones written in which the history of Crimean Tatars from antiquity to the present day was distorted to correspond to the Party's positions, and one position was to root out of the people's consciousness the history of Crimea, which was indissolubly bound to Crimean Tatars, and to defame the people.

Mustafa got another answer from the older inhabitants of the special settlement, among whom were many educated people. They were the former Crimean Tatar elite, Party and Soviet workers, writers, teachers, artists, doctors, and engineers. Within the special settlements they were all demoted to the level of common factory worker in those small villages to which they were sent as deportees. They answered Mustafa's bitter question "in the spirit of the decisions of the Twentieth Congress of the CPSU": Crimean Tatars are the victims of a mistake from the period of the cult of personality, victims of a Stalinist deviation from the Leninist policy on nationalities, which was correct and quite beneficial to Crimean Tatars. According to a decree signed by Lenin in 1921, Crimea received the status of an autonomous republic within the Russian Soviet Federative Socialist Republic (RSFSR). Thanks to this status, Crimean Tatars had schools that taught in their native language as well as other cultural institutions, including theaters, clubs, newspapers, and publishing houses. During the war with the Nazis, Crimean Tatars together with Russians bravely battled against the occupiers at the front and in partisan detachments (Mustafa knew about this from a family chronicle since his father had been at the front). The "mistake" concerning Crimean Tatars was so clear that the present Soviet leaderships would no doubt rectify it.

However, this well-wrought depiction of deportation as the result of a mistake made "up above" in the distant Stalinist past did not flush with subsequent events.

In 1956, three years after Stalin's death, there was talk at the Twentieth Congress of "reestablishing the Leninist principles of democracy." It would seem that this would have been sufficient to make immediate amends for the hideous rise of the "cult" and to return Crimean Tatars from the special settlements to their homeland. But that action was not considered. True, soon after the Twentieth Congress of the Communist Party of the Soviet Union (CPSU), on 28 April 1956, the Presidium of the Supreme Council issued an edict (stamped "not for publication in the press") about releasing the deportees from the special settlements. But the edict did not absolve Crimean Tatars of blame for betraying the motherland, and it left in force a prohibition against their returning to Crimea. Crimean Tatars were given passports, but on issuance of a passport each recipient had to sign a form to relinquish any claim to property that was left in Crimea at the time of deportation. Passports were not issued unless such a form was signed.

In light of its utter failure to rectify the illegal measures taken against

Crimean Tatars, this edict was a blow to the Crimean Tatar movement to return to Crimea. This movement shaped the course of Mustafa Jemiloglu's entire life.

The initiators of the movement during its first period were Crimean Tatars—former Party and Soviet workers. They called on their countrymen to go to the superior Party and Soviet courts with requests that the fate of the Crimean Tatar people be decided as soon as possible. The movement manifested itself during this period solely in the form of petitions that were loyal and suppliant in tone. Usually the beneficence of the Soviet state toward Crimean Tatars before 1944 was recounted, and then there followed assurances of Crimean Tatars' devotion to the Soviet system, the Party, and the government. The firm conviction was also usually expressed that the authorities would correct the "mistakes from the period of the cult of the personality" and return Crimean Tatars to their homeland. The Crimean Tatar petition campaign was waged by truly all the people—some petitions carried more than 100,000 signatures. However, unlike the treatment of deportation as a "mistake from the period of the cult of personality," this expression of the people's will elicited no response from the new government. In the years 1961–62, the initiators of the petition campaign were given to understand from the authorities that their activity was not desirable and could well bode ill for them in the end. A significant segment of the movement resigned at this point. The movement, likewise, came to a dead end and, lacking any prospect, began to die out.

At this time, the eighteen-year-old Mustafa Jemiloglu, who in no way considered himself a leader and who had since his youth taken no active part in the petition movement, breathed new life into it by altering its fundamental conception.

An edict of the Presidium of the Supreme Council from 28 April 1956, which did not allow Crimean Tatars to return to Crimea, did give them the opportunity to leave the confines of the special settlements. Mustafa took advantage of this fact right after graduating from school. He left Gulistan (Uzbekistan), where he lived with his parents, and went to Tashkent, the capital of Uzbekistan. There he worked at an aviation factory but spent all his free time in the Tashkent public library, named for Navoy, in the rare and antique book department. There he buried himself in books and gathered heaps of evidence on the history and culture of Crimean

Tatars, which had somehow been preserved despite the vigilance of the revisers of history.

In trying to cast light on the grounds for deportation and on the manifest aversion of Stalin's successors to returning Crimean Tatars to Crimea, Mustafa Jemiloglu delved deeper and deeper into the centuries in his investigations at the library. He traced the history of the formation of their culture, their branching off from the other tribes and peoples that populated Crimea and the steppe around the Black Sea, and their relations with neighboring peoples and with the Russian state, all for the duration of the entire history of Crimean Tatars.

There in the library, Mustafa became acquainted with two young countrymen who were interested in the very same matter. They spoke with him and found out that he had managed to learn more in his investigations than his colleagues. Despite his modest appraisal of his own knowledge, he systematized the evidence that he gathered about his people and even worked out a conception of its history. One of Mustafa Jemiloglu's basic conclusions was that Khan Giray's refusal to be aligned with the Muslim world and to approach Russia in the eighteenth century was fateful for the future Crimean Tatars for this action put Crimea under Russian authority. When his new acquaintances had learned of Mustafa's concept, they proposed that he prepare a short lecture on the history of Crimean Tatars to be given before a small audience. An abstract of the lecture filled about eight pages of a school notebook. This is how Mustafa (in the spring of 1962) described his reading of the lecture in a letter to Petr Grigorenko:

> About twenty-five young men and women sat on long benches in a small room. They were mostly students and workers from the nearest city district. People had heated arguments and read poems in Russian and Tatar; they lamented the Crimean Tatars' position of inequality, and they discussed the problems of returning to their homeland.
> 
> The speakers criticized the existing system and let loose some utterly unflattering epithets for the "true Leninist" Khrushchev.
> 
> When I was given the floor, I read my speech. Dispensing with modesty, I must say that my speech was met with great enthusiasm. Up to that point, no one had ever listened to me so attentively in my entire life. They applauded me for a long time, and everyone asked me for the abstract.

Mustafa describes his success thus:

For young people who had always read about their ancestors in the official literature as if about some kinds of barbarians and betrayers who were always being vanquished by the heroic Russians, it was of course pleasant to hear the "news" that the glorious Russian Czar Petr I was soundly beaten in 1711 at the river Prut by the Turkic-Tatar forces, that Crimean Tatars had put things in order in Moscow more than once, and that Crimean Tatars had institutions of higher learning long ago.[6]

Judging from the motifs Mustafa put forth in his lecture, he did no injustice to truth, but he nonetheless concentrated attention on events that were flattering to Crimean Tatars' sense of national pride. And toward this end any evidence sufficed: both the creation of institutions of higher learning before the Russians and the successful attack on Moscow, which an objective historian would be loath to call a "putting in order."

Mustafa's characteristic acuteness of judgment in his assessment of events in Crimean Tatar history impressed his peers. Toward the beginning of the 1960s, Crimean Tatar youths (and not only the youths) began to grow dissatisfied with the strategy of the movement's leadership at that time. They were especially dissatisfied with the tone of the messages to the authorities (which made the messages sound as if addressed to good friends of the Crimean Tatar people). The authorities paid no attention to the messages and displayed no intention of resolving the Crimean Tatar question. In the Soviet Union, where the dominant nationality was Russian, dissatisfaction with the central authority spontaneously engendered an anti-Russian sentiment. In any case, the concept of Crimean Tatar history offered by Mustafa Jemiloglu did not run contrary to this sentiment. This approach was put forth by him in 1963 in "A Short Historical Note on Turkish Culture in Crimea from the Thirteenth to Eighteenth Century." This work was seized in a search and thus has not been widely disseminated in samizdat. However, Jemiloglu's concept, disseminated and elaborated by others as well, was later put forth in many Crimean Tatar documents, as, for example, in the "Address of 60,000 Crimean Tatars to the Twenty-fourth Congress of the CPSU," as the point of view of the entire Crimean Tatar people on its past and as the reestablished memory of the people. The fundamental idea is that Crimean Tatars are the descendants of Mongolian settlers of the plains around the Black Sea, who had since time immemorial lived there and later resettled in Crimea. Russians, on the other hand, first made their way into Crimea during the Russo-Turkish wars of 1736–39 and 1768–74. Tens of thousands of Tatars were killed in these invasions, and countless monuments of their culture were destroyed.

Beginning with Catherine, the emperors generously granted land in Crimea to their friends and gentry. Just one decade after Crimea was incorporated into Russia, more than 380,000 *desyatins* of land were meted out in this way. Formerly, this land had belonged to Crimean Tatar peasants. The wholesale expropriation of land and its exploitation gave rise to massive emigration. Suddenly, whole Crimean Tatar families and villages left their homes and workplaces and made their way to the sea, to Turkiye. In 136 years (1783–1917) of Crimean union with Russia before the Revolution, a dense population of four million Crimean Tatars in Crimea was reduced to 150,000 people.[7]

The young Mustafa did not agree with the older generation of the Crimean Tatar intelligentsia in his assessment of the Soviet period of Crimean Tatar history; he especially differed on the causes of deportation and on the attitude of Stalin's successors in the Soviet leadership toward the Crimean Tatar tragedy. He did not believe that the tragedy was caused by their "error" regarding the Crimean Tatar position in the war with Nazi Germany, nor did he believe that certain individual malefactors were guilty of this "error." Mustafa Jemiloglu and his adherents considered the Soviet leadership's policy toward Crimean Tatars to be a direct continuation of the imperial czarist policy, only more complete and ruthless. The creation of an autonomous Crimean republic was a short-lived departure from the chauvinistic policy of czarist times, but in 1944 the Kremlin completed a plan to create a Crimea without Crimean Tatars, a plan once entertained by the Russian emperors. Mustafa, however, did not come to this point of view right away. His final testimony at his trial on 12 May 1966 testifies to this. This trial, based on charges that he avoided conscription into the army, was the last link in the chain of persecution that had begun after Mustafa read his speech on Crimean Tatar history. Before this point, there had been summonses to the KGB, searches, short jail sentences, and dismissals from work and from the institute. Despite Mustafa's sharp tone at the time, that speech shows his firm adherence to the point of view of the elder leaders, namely, that the Crimean Tatar tragedy was brought about by the actions of malevolent persons. At that time, Mustafa held responsible for the slander only those who actually carried out the deportation and who were guardians in the regime of the special settlements—the KGB men. It was they, in Mustafa's opinion, who impeded the return of Crimean Tatars to Crimea after Stalin's death. In his final testimony at the trial of 1966, Mustafa Jemiloglu said, in part, that

> the KGB collaborators are furious that we are gathering statistical evidence about Crimean Tatars who perished in exile and that we are collecting materials against the sadist commandants who derided the people during the Stalin years and who, according to the precepts of the Nuremburg Tribunal, should be tried for crimes against humanity....
>
> As a result of the crime of 1944, I lost thousands upon thousands of my brothers and sisters. And this must be remembered! Remembered just like the crematoria of Auschwitz and Dachau. Remembered, so that it shall not be repeated. Remembered, so that the Nazi and chauvinistic vileness can be rooted out at the source from which these crimes arose. But this is not desired by someone....
>
> I hope that you, on hearing out the judgment in this matter, will be guided only by law and justice, will heap blame on the guilty parties without considering the positions they occupy, and will blame also the path of arbitrariness and baseness. If you display fear before the guilty people in the KGB, that will spell victory for them and will only encourage the evils embodied by these villains.[8]

Mustafa Jemiloglu's restoration of Crimean Tatar history and his brave and triumphant speeches, both on the Crimean Tatar problem and in defense of repressed activists in the Crimean Tatar movement, have made him the preeminent figure within the movement. He has become the most authoritative ideologist of the "new wave." At his following trial in October 1969, Mustafa Jemiloglu was charged with writing a number of documents, including letters to the editors of Soviet papers, the "Address to Soviet Writers, to Workers in Science, History, and Art, and to Political and Social Activists," as well as several pieces of *Information* (nos. 65, 79, etc.). An analysis of these documents will help trace the process by which a new assessment of the Crimean Tatar position was developed and illustrate how a strategy based on this new assessment was worked out for the struggle to return to the homeland. The fundamental characteristics of this evolution include an avoidance of anti-Russian sentiments and a much more uncompromising condemnation of the Soviet leadership, whose policy toward Crimean Tatars had begun, from 1968, to be described by the movement as one of "genocide."

It is possible that both these tendencies in the ideology of the Crimean

Tatar movement were directly connected to the rapprochement of the leaders of the "new wave," especially Mustafa Jemiloglu, with the Moscow civil rights activists Aleksei Kosterin, Petr Grigorenko, Il'ya Gabay, and Aleksandr Lavut and later with the academician Sakharov. The rapprochement of Crimean Tatars with the civil rights activists played an important role in the development of both the Crimean Tatar and the civil rights movements. It helped Crimean Tatars emerge from isolation and allowed them to acquaint public opinion within the country with their problems and to summon a response to the injustice of their treatment. It is interesting that, in samizdat archives at Radio Liberty and in the West in general, there are no documents on the Crimean Tatar movement from 1956 to 1966. The very earliest documents extant in the West concern the year 1967 since they managed to find their way there from Jemiloglu's adherents only via the Moscow civil rights activists—Crimean Tatars had no possibility of establishing ties with the West themselves. Former Crimean Tatar leaders not only had no ties with the civil rights activists, but they also did not want the "publicity" since they were afraid of upsetting the authorities in that way and of slowing the decision to return Crimean Tatars to Crimea.

In the "Appeal of the Representatives of the Crimean People to the World Public," dated 21 July 1968, the following characterization was given of the documents from the first decade of the Crimean Tatar movement for the return to Crimea: "From 1957 to 1967, we sent to the Central Committee of the CPSU and to the Presidium of the Supreme Soviet of the Soviet Union hundreds of thousands of collective and individual letters demanding an end to the injustice."[9]

The same is expressed in the "Appeal of the Crimean Tatar People to Free People, Democrats, and Communists" (1968): "Beginning in 1965, the Crimean Tatar people have been requesting the leadership of the Party and the government to return the people to their homeland and to re-establish the people's equality. Hundreds of collective appeals, supported by hundreds of thousands of Crimean Tatar signatures, were sent to the central Soviet and party organs."[10]

Mustafa Jemiloglu and other activists in the movement made the acquaintance of Petr Grigorenko on 17 March 1968 when representatives of Crimean Tatars held a party in Moscow in honor of a gifted friend and writer—Communist Aleksei Kosterin. Grigorenko's speech that evening made a great impression on Crimean Tatars. Said Grigorenko:

The law is on your side.... But, despite this, your rights are being trampled. Why? It seems to us that the main reason is that you underestimate your enemy.... You think that you are dealing with only honorable people. But this is not the case.... You are dealing with the leadership of the Party and government with conciliatory written requests . . . that ask only why no unconditional right exists. You must firmly seize what is offered by law, not request but demand! . . . Begin to demand. And demand not part, not a fraction, but all of what was illegally taken from you—the establishment of an autonomous Crimean Tatar Soviet Socialist Republic![11]

Grigorenko proposed that they not limit themselves to writing petitions but supplement them "with every means offered by the constitution—the freedom of speech and of the press, of meetings, street processions, and demonstrations." He called on Crimean Tatars, not to hole themselves up in a nationalistic eggshell, but to establish contacts with people of other nationalities in the Soviet Union who were sympathetic to them, with Russians and Ukrayinans, and also with nationalities that have endured and do still endure the denigration that Crimean Tatars have. He also said: "Don't consider your matter to be solely intranational. Look for help from progressive societies worldwide and from international organizations.... Genocide, from the perspective of international law, is a crime.... International law is also on your side."[12]

This speech repeatedly drew applause and enthusiastic exclamations from the Crimean Tatars present. It was in accord with their own thoughts and feelings, only more precisely formulated. Both psychologically and politically it was very important that this summons came from the Moscow civil rights movement. It lacked any trace of an anti-Russian sentiment.

Rapprochement with the Moscow civil rights activists, and acquaintance with their working methods and most important with their civil positions, changed the tone of Crimean Tatar documents. Their authors began to avoid the sharp epithets for the authorities, but at the same time they firmly insisted on the fulfillment of their demands and built their case on the legality of their demands, not on the loyalty of Crimean Tatars to the Soviet state. This change in style of the Crimean Tatar pronouncements can be investigated, in part, by comparing Mustafa's final testimony at his first trial (quoted above) with his defense testimony at the following trial in November 1969. If in 1966 Jemiloglu spoke about the underhanded dealings of the "villains from the KGB" as the cause of the Crimean Tatar tragedy, in 1969 he described the tragedy as resulting from the "policy of the Soviet Party and government leadership on the question of Crimean Tatars." He called their deportation from Crimea a "state-sanctioned crime," emphasizing that the post-Stalin leadership had done nothing to rectify the consequences of this crime. Quite to the contrary, all the might of the Soviet state and of the Party-state propaganda machine was marshaled, as in the past, to prevent Crimean Tatars from returning to Crimea. Jemiloglu sees the crimes of the Soviet state against Crimean Tatars as a problem extending far beyond the bounds of the interests of Crimean Tatars alone:

If the fate of the Crimean Tatar people is a model for deciding the nationality question and an experiment in the plans for Russifying the country, then let that fate be a clear warning beacon for other peoples, especially those from the developing countries of the Muslim East, when they choose their friends and their foreign-policy orientation at some point in history. To speak the truth for all to hear about the position of Crimean Tatars in the Soviet Union, I consider imperative not only the matter of saving the nationality from death, but also our duty before other peoples, before civilization.[13]

In that defense testimony, Mustafa Jemiloglu also spoke about the folly and even the danger of submitting to lawlessness, cruelty, and injustice, and he illustrated his position not only with facts from the history of Crimean Tatars but also with the tragic experience of the Stalinist terror, which cost all the peoples of the Soviet Union an enormous number of victims: "Life has shown that such qualities as obedience and silence have brought the country much suffering and have cost millions of human lives, among them people whose various talents will not be produced by the Soviet land for a long time to come."[14]

Judging by this statement of 1969, Jemiloglu had until that time staked the success of the Crimean Tatar movement directly on the degree of democratization of Soviet society as a whole. Hence, Jemiloglu's interest and that of his Crimean Tatar adherents in the events in Czechoslovakia: the victory there of "socialism with a human face" could have become a prologue to a long-awaited transition not only in the countries of Eastern Europe but also in the Soviet Union.

At his trial in November 1965, on answering the charges of "slander against the internal policies of the Soviet Union," Mustafa Jemiloglu expressed his view of the events in Czechoslovakia in 1968:

Here for the first time in the history of the socialist countries, the people were presented with authentic democratic freedoms. For the first time the press, radio, television, the screen, and the stage began to serve, not the government, but the people. And this fact elicited the sympathy of millions of people on all the continents for a new government of Czechoslovakia, with Dubček as the leader; it was sympathy for authentic socialism.

But this provoked the mad rage of those who held power through deceit and violence. And they used every means to suppress freedom in Czechoslovakia, resorting, in the final stage, to armed intervention.

In the document "A Review of Falsifications and Refuted Documents," which I am accused of writing, it is said that, at midnight on 21 August, Soviet armed forces and also the troops from four countries—members of the Warsaw Pact—crossed the borders of the sovereign Czechoslovakian Republic to establish there an order amenable to the Soviet leadership.[15]

As one can see, this "review" was written at the beginning of September 1968. Subsequent events affirmed fully these words.

Mustafa Jemiloglu asserted the right publicly to express his views on the events in Czechoslovakia and then repudiated the competence of the judicial prosecution:

As a citizen, and, what's more, as a representative of the people, I consider myself morally responsible for everything that happens in the world. Regarding any event that happens in any corner of the globe, I am in the right when I consider it an obligation to express and make known my views and convictions. This right of mine is upheld by the Constitution of the Soviet Union and is affirmed in the Universal Declaration of the Rights of Man, which the Soviet government signed and is obliged to honor.[16]

All the more did Mustafa Jemiloglu feel himself responsible for events within the Soviet Union. Such an ideological position explains his participation in the founding of an initiative group for the protection of human rights in the Soviet Union, which was created by the Moscow civil rights activists in May 1969 and which addressed a complaint to the United Nations about persecution in the Soviet Union for one's convictions. In that address, the problem of Crimean Tatars was accompanied by the problem of the psychiatric persecution of dissidents, the problem of the arrests and incarceration of participants in the Ukrayinan national movement, and the problem of repression against the Baltic people and against Jews who seek to emigrate to Israel.

In analyzing the causes of the Crimean Tatar tragedy, Mustafa Jemiloglu linked it directly to the absence of democracy in the Soviet Union. Agreeing with the leaders of the nationalistic period of the movement to return to Crimea—that deportation was a direct consequence of the "cult of personality," of the unbridled rule of a despot—Mustafa Jemiloglu concerned himself with why, in the Soviet Union, "in place of one despot another arose." He tied this, first of all, to the absence of freedom of speech and of the press, freedom of demonstration, freedom to criticize and check the activity of the government, to the absence of what comes under the term *democracy*. In support of this thesis, Mustafa introduced facts about the infringement by the authorities of the constitutional rights granted to the citizen. These examples concerned not only Crimean Tatars—he spoke of the illegality of the trial of Sinyavsky and Daniel and of Galanskovs, Ginzburg, and their comrades; of the court trial of the Ukrayinan Vyacheslav Chernovil and of the chairman of a *kolkhoz* in Latvia named Ivan Yakhimovich; of the sentencing of Anatoly Marchenko, who had written about post-Stalin camps for political prisoners, and of demonstrators who had protested the armed invasion of Soviet troops into Czechoslovakia.

Andrei Grigorenko (the son of Petr Grigorenko), well known to Mustafa Jemiloglu, later wrote about this period of Mustafa's life during the years 1968–69:

> He spends a lot of time in Moscow. He follows carefully the events in Czechoslovakia, signs letters in defense of those unjustly persecuted in the Soviet Union, and protests against the occupation of Czechoslovakia. Mustafa, for his part in the civil rights movement, goes far beyond the bounds of a purely national struggle for the interests of his people. He is occupied by all aspects of the problem of human rights, in the right of the individual, in the right of diverse groups, and in the right of diverse religious and ethnic minorities.
>
> His solid knowledge of the particularities of the position of ethnic minorities makes him a man who has played a significant role in finding a common language between the various ethnic groups and nationalities in the Soviet Union and bringing these groups together with the movement in defense of human rights in the Soviet Union; that is by no means very simple in the complex system of

centuries-old and ingrained mistrusts between so many ethnically diverse components of the Soviet empire.[17]

Jemiloglu's conviction that democratizing Soviet society was the only way to resolve the Crimean Tatar problem and, in turn, his conviction that a positive resolution of this problem would be a true indicator of a step by the Soviet Union toward democratization were shared by many of his comrades in the struggle to return Crimean Tatars to Crimea. It would be categorical to assert that the hope for democracy, the close cooperation with the civil rights activists, and the striving toward cooperation with the other nationalist movements in the Soviet Union were all introduced into the Crimean Tatar movement by Mustafa Jemiloglu alone, but one must not underrate his role in communication of these ideas to his countrymen and to foreigners as well (see fig. 10.1).

It is precisely here that lies Mustafa Jemiloglu's contribution to the efforts of Crimean Tatars to return to Crimea. Perhaps by adopting such an ideology the Crimean Tatar movement enabled itself to preserve and strengthen the absolutely peaceful character by which it has distinguished itself from its very inception.

The suppliant tone with which the petition campaign of the Crimean Tatar movement began offered by its very nature only peaceful methods toward the attainment of its goals. By refuting the use of loyal requests and changing the tone of the appeals to the Supreme Council and courts from suppliant to demanding, there existed the danger of changing the methods of attaining the goals from peaceful to violent. There was also the danger of violence at the settlements in Central Asia from participants in the mass demonstrations and meetings held by the leaders of the Crimean Tatar movement in support of the demands to return to Crimea. During the mass resettlement in Crimea that began in 1967, and during the implementation of the right to live in one's homeland without prior permission, acts of violence could have been the reply of the Tatar population when the authorities, and the population who settled there after the deportation of Crimean Tatars, hindered them from returning to Crimea. (That is how things happened in the northern Caucasus on the land of the Chechen, Ingush, and other peoples who were deported during the war and returned from the end of the 1950s to the beginning of the 1960s.)

The complete absence of violent elements among Crimean Tatars for

Figure 10.1. Mustafa Jemiloglu, president, Crimean Tatar Mejlis (*third from left*), main speaker in an international seminar about the status of Crimea, Columbia University, New York, 18 November 1996. Photo by Nermin Eren.

the entire thirty years of the movement's existence is truly astounding when one considers the vivacious, temperamental, forthright character of the people and the unceasing degradation, injustice, and direct acts of violence (during evictions and dispersals of demonstrations) that were perpetrated against Crimean Tatars by the authorities whose representatives were constantly trying to provoke an armed opposition, so as to have grounds for repression.[18]

The unendurable psychological pressure of a long and unequal battle has given rise to such acts of despair as the self-immolation of Musa Mamut and the suicide of Izzet Memedulaev, but not once, truly not even once, have the charges against Crimean Tatars of violence corresponded to reality. Of course, praise for this belongs to Mustafa Jemiloglu and to all the leaders of the Crimean Tatar movement in all of its stages, but this praise is due, not only to the leaders of the Crimean Tatar movement, but to all its members, to the entire Crimean Tatar population.

In the aforementioned appeal to the Twenty-fourth Congress of the CPSU by sixty thousand Crimean Tatars, the position of the Crimean Tatar people was compared to that of another people who were also without a real homeland—the Palestinians, for whom the Soviet government and Soviet propaganda continually expressed great sympathy and who received continuous generous aid from the Soviet Union. Crimean Tatars also expressed sympathy for the Palestinians but nonetheless posed a legitimate question about the ethical and moral norms of the Soviet internationalists who sympathized with the Palestinians but who waged a policy of genocide against one of their own Soviet nationalities.

Members of the Crimean Tatar movement could not find refuge in the territory of friendly foreign states but were always located in dangerous proximity to their powerful and merciless adversary. It is well known that Mustafa Jemiloglu had been jailed six times. From his first arrest at the age of twenty-three, until the age of forty-three, Mustafa spent only seven years unincarcerated.

It is also impossible to compare the attention paid by the international media to the Crimean Tatar problem with the continual publicity given to the Palestinian movement. One cannot equate the material and political support that the leaders of the Palestinian movement have at their disposal in their region and throughout the world (from both the public and governments) with the attitudes of governments and the general public of those countries toward the Crimean Tatar movement, which lives on the sacrifice of the movement's members, who are involuntarily poor.

It would seem, with the Palestinians in possession of such an enormous superiority, that there would be much greater hope for them to reach their goal by peaceful means. But it has so happened that the huge superiority at the disposal of the Palestinian movement, in comparison to that of Crimean Tatars, is put in the service of an entirely different ideology—the ideology of irreconcilable hostility toward Israel and toward all who support or even sympathize with Israel.

Yurii Orlov rightly concluded that constructive changes in the contemporary world can be successful only by means of nonviolent methods. Orlov asserts that

no sort of violence will be able to change the psychological situation for the better now . . . in today's world. Strong threats or violence can only increase the likelihood of totalitarianism. . . . It is necessary to try, without counting on quick success, but also without considering this program utopian, to change the moral atmosphere [in the world] gradually by sharply posing the question of violence in the sphere of man's spiritual life.[19]

In the broad ethical, antitotalitarian movement, Orlov sees a difficult and slow, not necessarily successful, drive. Yet it is the sole way to counter the use of violence against individuals and nations in the contemporary world. The nonviolent Crimean Tatar movement is already an essential part of another drive that will, perhaps, arise in the future and whose success may work toward the resolution of the Crimean Tatar problem as well.

One might object that Crimean Tatars' nonviolent struggle, in fact, has not returned their homeland to them despite years of heroic effort. The Crimean Tatar fight may not be entirely unsuccessful, but instead the strategy of Mustafa Jemiloglu and his adherents may be flawed.

The sacrifice and noble struggle of all the people acted to weld Crimean Tatars together and strengthened their national consciousness extraordinarily. This and only this helped Crimean Tatars to preserve themselves as a nationality, despite a Soviet policy of ethnic genocide. Moreover, the nobility of peaceful opposition, the acknowledgment of the leaders' righteousness, unbesmirched by violence and base politicking, has greatly raised civic consciousness not only among the activists in the Crimean Tatar movement but also among the Crimean Tatar public. The absence of nationalistic pride and xenophobia, the benevolence toward surrounding peoples, the patience toward other opinions, the readiness to consider the interests of neighboring individuals and people and to seek solutions of their problems that are acceptable to them, all are inherent in literally all the documents of the Crimean Tatar movement espousing return to Crimea. This has secured sympathy for the Crimean Tatar movement, not only from the civil rights activists, but also from a significant segment of the present-day inhabitants of Crimea. In the *Chronicle of Current Events*, there are many stories about those inhabitants' refusals to participate in the eviction of Crimean Tatars who had resettled in Crimea. Thus, in the village of Kursk in the Qarasuvbazar (Belogorsk) district of Crimea, where twenty-two Crimean Tatar families had lived, their persecution by the authorities greatly disturbed the local non-Tatar population. *Kolkhoz* electrician A. Isaev (judging from his name, a Russian) refused to cut off the lights in Crimean Tatar houses and for this received a Party reprimand and was made into a locksmith. Tractor operator Puzyrev (also a Russian name) refused to plow the personal tracts of land reappropriated from Crimean Tatars and was fired from his job. A tractor brigade of the *kolkhoz*, also made up of non-Tatars, refused to raze the home of a displaced

Crimean Tatar.[20] At the funeral of the Crimean Tatar Musa Mamut, who immolated himself in protest of discrimination against Crimean Tatars in Crimea, not just Crimean Tatars took part. One of the placards carried by the participants in the funeral procession said, "Musa is away from his tormented Russian brothers. Sleep, justice shall prevail."

For the leaders of the Soviet Union it was psychologically inconceivable to agree to settle Crimean Tatars in a strategically important border region like Crimea. The Tatars, on the one hand, have ancestral ties and a common religion with the Turkish population across the Black Sea (that, apparently, was the motive for deportation in 1944) and, on the other, have actively demonstrated for years the people's universal will to stand up for their rights. They have courageously presented to the authorities an account of all the human victims, the destruction of national culture, and the unending discrimination. Mustafa Jemiloglu and his adherents were right: a solution to the Crimean Tatar problem was possible only as a result of democratization of the system or as the result of its enfeeblement. In any case, having preserved their national self-awareness and dream of returning to Crimea, most Crimean Tatar people shall be able to make the dream reality, for the people are protected by the support of democratic forces in the country, some of the present population of Crimea, and, possibly, the greater part of world public opinion.

## Notes

1. Under the regime of the special settlements, inhabitants were forbidden to go beyond the confines of the special settlement. Crimean Tatars were settled in villages and small cities in Uzbekistan and other Central Asian republics. For dwellings, they had barracks, huts, and buildings belonging to the factory, where all the inhabitants had to work as simple workers, regardless of their specialty. Even responsible specialists were not allowed to hold management positions. The settlement of Crimean Tatars scattered into small villages was conducted without regard for family ties. Often parents and their adult children ended up in different villages and were not able to see each other or travel to a funeral—to leave the confines of the settlement threatened one with a lengthy prison camp sentence.

2. "Sudebnyi protsess Il'i Gabaya i Mustafy Dzhemileva," in *Shest' dnei* (New York: Fond Krym, 1980), 348.

3. Ibid.

4. Ibid., 168.
5. V. Vetlina, *Moscow Strolls* (Moscow, 1955).
6. Andrei Grigorenko, *A kogda my vernemsia* (New York: Fond Krym, 1977), 12.
7. *Arkhiv samizdata*, Radio Svoboda, no. 630, vol. 12, pp. 11–13.
8. Grigorenko, *A kogda my vernemsia*, 28–29.
9. *Tashkentskii protsess*, sbornik dokumentov (Amsterdam: Fond imeni Gertsena, 1976), 781–82.
10. *Arkhiv samizdata*, Radio Svoboda, no. 397, vol. 12, p. 1.
11. *Arkhiv samizdata*, Radio Svoboda, no. 76, vol. 7, p. 4.
12. Ibid., 4–5.
13. "Belaia kniga" in *Shest' dnei*, 350–51.
14. Ibid., 376.
15. Ibid., 364.
16. Ibid., 362.
17. Grigorenko, *A kogda my vernemsia*, 33.
18. *A Chronicle of Current Events*, no. 51 (London: Amnesty International, 1977), 120–23.
19. Yurii Orlov, "Vozmozhen li sotsializm ne totalitarnogo tipa?" in *Samosoznanie*, ed. P. Litvinov, M. Meerson-Aksenov, and B. Shragin (New York: Khronika, 1976), 298.
20. *A Chronicle of Current Events*, no. 53 (London: Amnesty International, 1977), 120–21.

# 11

## *The Crimean Tatar Drive for Repatriation: Some Comparisons with Other Movements of Dissent in the Soviet Union*

PETER REDDAWAY

The aim of this chapter is to describe, in summary fashion, the origins and development of the Crimean Tatar drive for repatriation to Crimea, the tactics of the movement, the countertactics of the Soviet authorities, and some foreign responses to the movement—while, as a counterpoint to lend perspective, making comparisons with similar aspects of other movements of dissent in the Soviet Union in the same period.

Although it was not the first movement of organized dissent to emerge in the post-Stalin Soviet Union, the Crimean Tatar drive was the one that had been the longest in continuous existence by 1987, for twenty-nine years.[1] Meskhetians, an Islamic people from South Georgia deported to Central Asia by Stalin in 1944 without any charges being brought against them, began campaigning in 1956 to return to their homeland. But their movement appears to have been weakened in the 1970s by certain factors, including some minor concessions by the authorities, and, as a result, to have run out of steam.[2]

It was the well-known law of February 1957, giving legal exculpation to most of the people deported by Stalin during World War II, but not to Crimean Tatars (or Soviet Germans), that brought the Tatar movement quickly into being. Mass petitions and group lobbying of official bodies in Moscow were its main tactics, the line being that the authorities must have made a mistake: Tatars had been overwhelmingly loyal in the war, the deportation of 1944 had been the work of malevolent forces in the security police, and there was no reason now not to exculpate the Tatars and allow them to return to Crimea. When intensive pressure on this basis over several years failed to produce results and the movement began to falter, in 1962 the young Mustafa Jemiloglu provided some new thinking[3] and also took part in creating in Tashkent the movement's first—and only—formal group, the League of Crimean Tatar Youth. This was instantly crushed by the KGB.[4] However, the fall of Communist Party of the Soviet Union (CPSU) General Secretary Nikita Khrushchev in 1964 gave new hope and vigor to Tatars, as it did to Meskhetians and dissident groups among Baptists and Ukrayinans.[5]

In this year, Crimean Tatars established—and maintained for several years—a permanent, rotating lobby in Moscow. This lobby had no formal name or structure. Its members, who usually stayed in the capital for a few weeks each, were delegates from local communities, who simply called themselves "representatives of the Crimean Tatar people in Moscow." As such, they compiled and circulated regular reports on their lobbying activities and also on the harassment and detention to which they were often subjected.

Persistent, systematic lobbying of this sort—which had never been sustained for long by any non-Muscovite group except Tatars—paid off in two different ways. First, senior members of the Party and state leadership agreed on three occasions to receive Tatar delegations, and out of the third meeting[6] came a partial concession: the decree of 1967, which, although it effectively denied Tatars their main demand—the right to return home—nonetheless exculpated them at last from the false charge of mass treason during the war.

Second, a mailing of letters to Moscow members of the Writers' Union elicited in 1966 a sympathetic response from an old writer, Aleksei Kosterin, who proceeded to connect Tatars with the incipient human rights movement.[7]

Either genuinely or deliberately, many Tatars misunderstood the words in the 1967 decree that claimed they had "put down roots" in their places of exile. About 100,000 of them set off from Central Asia for Crimea, but most of them were physically prevented from settling there. By the mid-1970s, only fourteen hundred families—chosen by the authorities for their political passivity—had been allowed to settle legally.[8] Other families would sometimes succeed in buying a house and living there without official registration for some time before, in the next wave of deportations, being forcibly evicted from the peninsula.

The combination of these simultaneous developments—the actual ban on free settlement and the linkup with the human rights movement—

produced in 1968–69 the most dramatic two years in the movement's history. Early in 1968, for the first time, a Tatar signed a collective appeal—to a conference of Communist parties—sponsored by Moscow intellectuals. A year later another Tatar, Jemiloglu, joined the first formal group set up by these intellectuals—the Initiative Group for the Defense of Civil Rights in the Soviet Union—as one of the fifteen founder members, some of whom, like Jemiloglu, represented particular national or religious groups. In 1968, the total number of signatures on Tatars' appeals over the preceding eleven years reached three million. This meant that, if, say, two-thirds out of roughly 300,000 Tatar adults signed petitions, they must have signed about fifteen each on average. And, in 1969, Tatars staged their first public demonstration on a Moscow square.

When the authorities caught their breath, they began to retaliate with arrests both of Tatars and of their Moscow supporters, who, led by General Petr Grigorenko, had been urging them to take a more militant stance and to widen their appeals to include bodies abroad.[9] While Tatars fought back, turning the trials of their activities into political demonstrations, nonetheless their movement incurred some heavy blows. By contrast, the crescendo of support from the human rights movement was only just beginning. This movement championed the Tatars' cause in appeals to the United Nations and other world bodies, made a special study of their position in Soviet law,[10] gave extensive space to their affairs in its main samizdat journal, *A Chronicle of Current Events*, and in 1973 devoted a whole issue to them.[11]

In 1975–76, the movement made a major (and successful) effort to publicize the plight both of the newly arrested Jemiloglu and of Tatars as a whole by campaigning on Jemiloglu's behalf. Among other things, Andrei Sakharov and his wife traveled to Omsk and were widely reported as they tried in vain to attend his trial.[12] Then, after the formation by Yury Orlov in 1976 of the Moscow "Helsinki group" for monitoring Soviet observance of the human rights provisions of the Helsinki Final Act, the group continued this type of assistance by compiling detailed reports on the Tatars' situation and delivering them to representatives in Moscow of the thirty-five signatory governments.[13]

The first determined offensive by the authorities that was aimed at suppressing organized public dissent of all sorts was launched in early 1977. When, however, it promptly provoked loud protests in the West, it was halted, to be relaunched only in late 1979.[14] But Tatars were a special case. For reasons that are not yet clear, large-scale action against them began earlier than against other groups, in 1978. The main focus was the seven hundred families who had in recent years managed to settle in Crimea and live there without official registration. Forcible deportations started again, accelerating after the issuing of an unpublished decree in August 1978. By containing provisions that violated Soviet laws and international agreements, this decree facilitated the process of deportation from the administrative viewpoint. Between November 1978 and February 1979, about sixty families were deported, and, in 1980, the point was reached where only sixty families (out of seven hundred) remained in Crimea. Indeed, the authorities would probably have gone further still, had it not been for two self-immolations in Crimea by Tatars protesting the systematic cruelty involved in the deportations and also a sharp intensification of the Tatars' "traditional" protest actions of mass petitioning and group lobbying in Moscow.[15]

Nonetheless—and again for reasons that are not yet fully clear—the Tatar movement now entered one of its quieter phases. Whereas fourteen Tatars arrested in 1978–79 received substantial jail terms, since that time the average rate of such jailings appears to have been only about two per year.[16] Without doubt, Tatars felt keenly the heavy blows suffered from 1979 on by their main ally and publicity agent, the human rights movement, as well as by all the other movements of national, religious, political, cultural, trade unionist, and social dissent around the country. But they must also have been weary after more than two decades of remarkable national exertion, with only rather meager tangible results to show for it. And they may, since 1979, have been considering a change in their tactics.

Today's situation in Crimea remains a stalemate. The authorities are apparently as opposed as ever to the administrative inconvenience that the return to Crimea of perhaps another 200,000 or 300,000 Tatars would involve; to the hypothetical strategic risk that some of the more alienated Tatars might pose in a militarily sensitive area; and to the potential political cost of yielding to one dissident group's demands and thus encouraging other groups to step up their struggle for official concessions to their particular concerns. On the other hand, there is no reason to doubt that, while Tatars resourcefully adapted to life in the scattered areas where they live, they have forged a strong national unity under difficult conditions, or that most of them would return to their homeland if given the chance, or that an active leadership will continue to express that national aspiration publicly through various forms of protest, whatever the level of control. As one leading dissident wrote, Tatars "showed us democrats the strength a movement gathers when it is supported by an entire people."[17]

## Tatars' Tactics in the Soviet Era

It is important to focus more narrowly on Crimean Tatars' tactics and make some comparisons with the tactics of other movements. Much of the summary assessment that follows relates to what has gone before, while other points have not previously been touched on.

The Tatars' main tactics of the late Soviet period can be summed up as follows:

1. Conduct a campaign based on appeals for the regime to return to the "correct nationality policy of Lenin" and to observe relevant UN covenants and conventions that it has signed.

2. Eschew references to our Islamic faith, even though it is an important part of our national identity, and do not demand the right to emigrate to Turkiye, that is, do not seek to follow the well-trodden path of our ancestors over the last two centuries.

These tactics—seemingly designed to ensure maximum Tatar unity—present a relatively moderate, "loyalist" image reminiscent of the images projected by some neo-Leninist political groups and, in the 1960s, by dissident Baptists. The latter praised Lenin's constitutional separation of church and state and his moderate policies toward Baptists.[18] By about 1970, however, the Baptists tired of constantly reiterating these points as their alienation deepened, and some—especially those of German stock—began to seek relief in emigration.

The Tatars' position of implicitly rejecting emigration contrasts sharply with the Meskhetians' decision, taken in 1969–70, to demand the right to emigrate to Turkiye.[19] This demand met with no success and may have divided and weakened the Meskhetian movement.

A similar, relatively "moderate," nonprovocative tinge is evident in the next tactics of Crimean Tatars to be considered. These have been the following:

3. Appeal primarily to official Soviet bodies, and, only when persecution is especially severe, turn to audiences abroad; in that case, address, not the governments of Islamic countries, but mostly UN bodies or "world public opinion." An exception here—significantly, the product of an individual—is Reshat Jemilev's appeal to Saudi king Khaled in 1978.[20]

4. Collaborate continuously with the human rights movement, but not, at least openly, with other persecuted nationalities—even those who, in the 1960s, were in a nearly analogous situation, namely, Meskhetians and Soviet Germans.[21]

5. While working closely with the human rights movement, avoid doing so—after Jemiloglu's bold experiment of 1969[22]—to the extent of actually joining its formal groups.

6. Act openly,[23] legally, and peacefully, resolutely rejecting—along with all other dissident movements (a few of which, however, notably in Georgia and Armenia, produced "rogue" exceptions)—any form of violence (fig. 11.1).

In case any of the above makes Tatars appear weak or irresolute, this further list of tactics should correct such an impression. Tatars consistently followed these principles:

7. Act on the advice of Tatars' ally General Grigorenko and use the weapon of legalism to the limit. (A dissident comments—regarding the tactics of some Tatars who were on trial in 1969—"Such utilization of Soviet laws was not new in the opposition movement, but Tatars carried it to its logical conclusion and exploited every possible point of law.")[24]

8. Minimize the vulnerability of the movement's leaders by doing without any formal leadership group (at least a publicly known one), yet at the same time maintain more democratic, informal, grassroots structures than other movements maintain by having representatives of local communities regularly elected—to lobby in Moscow or take part in informal regional conferences to discuss the movement's activities. (By eschewing formal leaders Tatars distinguished themselves from many nationalist, religious, and human rights groups[25] and may have benefited by preserving a significant continuity of leadership.)

9. Document Crimean Tatars' legal and moral case with extraordinarily detailed statistics, including some derived from a referendum of the whole group, and (by virtue of a sustained industriousness probably surpassing even that of Baptists and

Figure 11.1. Crimean Tatars demonstrating on the government square in the Crimean capital, Aqmesjit (Simferopol'), in July 1990 for the right to return to lands at Alushta and other places along the southern coast of Crimea. Three fully visible placards read (*left to right*): "In 1939 in Alushta lived 16,400 Crimean Tatars; in 1990 in Alushta lived 20 Crimean Tatars, we demand that plots of land be apportioned without obstruction"; "Cease disinformation and incitement of the populace against the return of Crimean Tatars"; "The southern shore of Crimea is not a resort, but the Homeland for deported Crimean Tatars." Photo courtesy of Mme Safinar Jemiloglu, wife of President Mustafa Jemiloglu.

Lithuanians) reinforce these statistics with continual mass petitions and group lobbying of official bodies.

## Tactics of the Soviet Authorities

The countertactics of the authorities can be more briefly summarized as follows:

1. For propaganda reasons, allow (after 1967) a small number of nonactivist Tatars to live legally in Crimea, but deport, at regular intervals, all others.

2. Allow Tatars in Central Asia some elements of cultural autonomy by sponsoring a newspaper and a folk ensemble for them. In 1974, the authorities seem to have tried to go beyond cultural autonomy and turn an administrative region of Uzbekistan into a quasihomeland for Tatars. The same official, Tairov, was appointed as Party first secretary in the region, and Tatars were installed in other important posts. But the attempt was abandoned in 1978, perhaps because the new KGB campaign against Tatars that year increased their sense of alienation.[26]

3. In view of the exceptional strength and unity of the Tatar movement, keep trials to a minimum and jail sentences down—usually to the relatively mild level of three years or less. In this way, only about three hundred Tatars received sentences between 1957 and 1987 (less than a fifth of the comparable Baptist figure), few large-scale demonstrations have been provoked, and major martyr figures have not been created. The nearest to such martyr figures have been Mustafa Jemiloglu, sentenced to jail terms repeatedly over twenty years, and Musa Mamut, whose self-immolation in 1978 aroused deep passions among Tatars.[27]

4. Try to obtain recantations from important Tatars after their arrest and aim to divide the people by sponsoring a countermovement of Tatars opposed to any return to Crimea.[28] The only notable success here occurred with the physicist Rollan Kadyev in 1984. The KGB regularly circulated anonymous documents urging this line, which, because of their anonymity, carried little or no weight. In 1978, it contrived one with the signatures of thirty-one Tatars in various official positions. These tactics met with minimal success.

## Responses to the Tatar Movement from Abroad

Unlike many other dissident movements, that of Crimean Tatars received little support from abroad. The Tatars have numerous kin in Turkiye, but before 1991 the Turkish government evidently ensured, for diplomatic reasons, that they remain passive. The tiny Tatar community in New York in fact did more than its cousins in Turkiye.[29] Predictably enough, the United Nations did nothing about a formal submission requesting that it take some action on the Tatars' behalf.[30]

Most prominent among the bodies that supported Tatars, at least on occasion, were the Tunisian government,[31] the Islamic Council of Europe,[32] and the Minority Rights Group of London.[33] And the humanitarian organization Amnesty International worked constantly for Tatars imprisoned for the peaceful expression of their views.[34]

## Conclusion

Despite the clear justice of their case, which impressed both dissidents in the Soviet Union and foreigners, Crimean Tatars probably could not realistically hope for powerful support from abroad. Their natural lobby was too small in the United States and too tightly controlled in Turkiye, and the key governments, the Turkish and the Soviet, both appeared to find the existing situation convenient.

Nonetheless, for the reasons listed above, the Tatar movement appears likely to continue indefinitely, probably until such time as its central demand is satisfied. Meanwhile, it will remain as a living example to other oppressed groups, of how to work for justice in difficult circumstances, with the moderation, dignity, self-discipline, and remarkable persistence that by 1994 had brought around half of its members back to Crimea.

## Notes

1. Reliable accounts of the movement, from various perspectives, appear in Ann Sheehy and Bohdan Nahaylo, *The Crimean Tatars, Volga Germans and Meskhetians* (London: Minority Rights Group, 1980); Aleksandr Nekrich, *The Punished Peoples* (New York: Norton, 1973); Robert Conquest, *The Nation Killers: The Soviet Deportation of Nationalities* (London: Macmillan, 1970), chaps. 12, 14; Peter Reddaway, *Uncensored Russia: The Human Rights Movement in the Soviet Union* (London: Cape, 1972), chap. 12; Petr Grigorenko, *Memoirs* (London: Collins, 1983), chap. 24 (this contains some minor errors), and *The Grigorenko Papers* (London: Hurst, 1976); Andrei Grigorenko, *A kogda my vernemsia* (Commack, N.Y.: Crimea Foundation, 1977); Leonid Plyusch, *History's Carnival* (New York: Harcourt Brace Jovanovich, 1979), chap. 13; Ludmilla Alexeyeva, *Soviet Dissent* (Middletown, Conn.: Wesleyan University Press, 1985), chap. 7.
2. Sheehy and Nahaylo, *The Crimean Tatars*; Reddaway, *Uncensored Russia*, chap. 13.
3. See chap. 10 in this volume.
4. A. Grigorenko, *A kogda my vernemsia*, 12–24.
5. Michael Bourdeaux, *Religious Ferment in Russia* (London: Macmillan, 1968); and Michael Browne, *Ferment in the Ukraine* (London: Macmillan, 1971).
6. See Ayshe Seytmuratova's firsthand account of this meeting in chap. 8 of this book and in Jonathan Steele and Eric Abraham, *Andropov in Power* (Oxford: Robertson, 1983), 100–102.
7. See Pavel Litvinov's account in the booklet *In Defense of Mustafa Dzhemilev*, ed.

P. Litvinov, R. Baraheni, R. Schoenman, and M. Sostre (New York: Mustafa Dzhemilev Defense Committee, 1976), 9.

8. *A Chronicle of Human Rights in the USSR* (hereafter *CHR*), no. 28 (1977): 11.

9. *Tashkentskii protsess* (Amsterdam: Herzen Foundation, 1976); *Shest' dnei: Sudebnyi protsess Ili Gabaya i Mustafy Dzhemileva* (Commack, N.Y.: Crimea Foundation, 1980); Reddaway, *Uncensored Russia*.

10. See the documents of the Human Rights Committee (Sakharov, Chalidze, and others) of 1972 in *CHR*, nos. 5–6 (1973): 57–61.

11. *Chronicle of Current Events*, no. 31 (May 1974). The *Chronicle of Current Events* (hereafter *CCE*) has been published in English translation by Amnesty International and is distributed in the United States by Routledge Journals (9 Park St., Boston MA 02108). An average issue contains five to ten pages of highly condensed material about the Tatars.

12. *CHR*, no. 16 (1975): 10–13; A. Grigorenko, *A kogda my vernemsia*.

13. *CHR*, no. 28 (1977): 11; Alexeyeva, *Soviet Dissent*, chaps. 7, 17.

14. Peter Reddaway, "Dissent in the Soviet Union," *Problems of Communism*, no. 6 (1983): 1–15.

15. *CHR*, no. 31 (1978): 27–28, and no. 33 (1979): 11; *CCE*, no. 51 (1979): 114, 120–26, no. 52 (1980): 79–95; and no. 57 (1981): 53.

16. Peter Reddaway, "Soviet Policies on Dissent and Emigration: The Radical Change of Course since 1979," Occasional Paper no. 192, Washington, D.C.: Kennan Institute for Advanced Russian Studies, 1984), 50.

17. Plyushch, *History's Carnival*, chap. 13.

18. Bourdeaux, *Religious Ferment in Russia*.

19. Sheehy and Nahaylo, *Crimean Tatars*, 25–26.

20. *CCE*, no. 51: 123.

21. About the Germans, see Sheehy and Nahaylo, *Crimean Tatars*.

22. Reddaway, *Uncensored Russia*, chap. 7.

23. A rare exception, arising from the severe conditions of 1979, is a Tatar appeal to President Giscard d'Estaing of France, which is anonymous and attributes its anonymity to these conditions (*CCE*, no. 53 [1980]: 123).

24. Plyushch, *History's Carnival*, 181.

25. For the most systematic material on this issue, see Alexeyeva, *Soviet Dissent*.

26. For a revealing document about the folk ensemble written by a Tatar official, S. Tairov, see *CHR*, nos. 5–6 (1973): 33–36; *CCE*, no. 51 (1979): 128.

27. About Jemiloglu, see chap. 10 in this volume. About Mamut, see *CCE*, no. 51 (1979): 120–24.

28. *CCE*, no. 51 (1979): 128.

29. By setting up the Crimea Foundation to publish, among others, two of the books listed in nn. 1 and 9.

30. V. Chalidze's submission of 1974 in *CHR*, no. 9 (1974): 38–56.
31. *CHR*, no. 35 (1979): 67.
32. *CHR*, no. 40 (1980): 43–50.
33. Sheehy and Nahaylo, *Crimean Tatars*.
34. By publishing the English translation of *CCE*.

# 12

## *Documents about the Ordeal of Forced Exile*

### Document 1

"Zapis' sudebnogo protsessa Il'i Gabaia i Mustafa Jemileva v g. Tashkente 12–19 ianvaria, 1970 p. . . . Den' pervyi . . ." (A record of the trial of Il'ya Gabay and Mustafa Jemilev in the city of Tashkent, 12–19 January 1970), in *Shest' dnei* (New York: Crimea Foundation, 1980), 179–87. Translated by William Spiegelberger. The name of Mustafa Jemiloglu appears here only as Dzhemilev or D., to distinguish it from J[udge].

#### *The First Day: Monday, 12 January 1970*

Judge: Dzhemilev (Jemiloglu) Mustafa. What is correct?

Dzhemilev: Correct, the Muslim way is Mustafa Abduldzhemil'. According to the documents, it is DZHEMILEV Mustafa.

J: Year, month, and date of birth?

D: 13 November 1943.

J: Place of birth?

D: Crimean Autonomous Soviet Socialist Republic (ASSR), Sudaq region, village of Ayserez.

J: In your passport it is ASSR?

D: The passport was issued after the ASSR was liquidated, so that there it says Crimean District of the Ukrayinan Soviet Socialist Republic (SSR). The village of Ayserez is also called something else now [Mezhdurech'e].

J: Nationality?

D: Crimean Tatar.

J: Education?

D: Unfinished higher education. Three terms at the Tashkent Irrigation Institute.

J: Married?

D: Yes.

J: Where did you work before your arrest?

D: In the city of Gulistan.

J: Have you been sentenced for any crime?

D: Yes, twice. On 12 May 1966 for my active role in the nationalist movement of Crimean Tatars I was sentenced by the Tashkent court to one and a half years of imprisonment on trumped-up charges of infringing article 70, section 1, of the Criminal Code of the Uzbek Soviet Socialist Republic (UZSSR). I was released after the conclusion of my sentence on 12 November 1967.

J: And the second time? You said you were sentenced twice?

D: That *was* the second time. The first time was on 18 May 1944, when I was sentenced to exile from my homeland for "treason against the motherland" at the age of seven months. True, the sentence was carried out by the government, without trial.

J: But that was an administrative resettlement.

D: Why, then, in the governmental edict, was there mention of the heinous crime of the Crimean Tatars, of collaboration with the Germans, of treas....

J: When did you receive a copy of the prosecutor's conclusion?

D: On 5 January 1970.

J: Are you in command of the Russian language?

D: I wish, of course, that the trial were conducted in my native Crimean Tatar language and that among the judges there were at least one Crimean Tatar. But for the past twenty-five years not a single one of my countrymen has merited such an honor, for there are no Crimean Tatars in the judicial agencies of the Soviet Union. Therefore, I should reconcile myself to the fact I will be judged by citizens of another nationality and not in my native language.

J: The composition of the court: chairman Pisarenko, people's deputies Usmanova and Orlova, defense attorney Kaminskaia. According to article 253 of the Criminal Code (UK) of the UZSSR, the defendants and other participants in the trial have the right to object to the judge, the prosecutor, the people's deputies, and the court secretary.

D: I will defend myself without counsel. You spoke as if attorney Kaminskaia is to defend me.

J: We guarantee you defense in the person of attorney Kaminskaia. If you have an objection, you may make it later. Do you have faith in the composition of the court? There are no objections?

D: To express my faith or distrust, I should have some sort of information about the participants in the trial. I ask to know the Party status of the members of the court, their work status, the position of the judge, and the place of employment of the people's deputies. I also ask to know whether these judges and the prosecutor Bocharov have taken part in the trials of participants in the Crimean Tatar nationalist movement.

J: I, for example, have been working in the judicial agencies for seventeen years. The people's deputies: Usmanova. . . .

Usmanova: I worked at a tram depot.

J: Orlova works at [he names some organization]. I have not yet taken part in the trials of Crimean Tatars.

D: And the prosecutor?

J: I haven't the right to ask him.

Prosecutor: [Very softly.] I took part in the trial of the Chirchiks.

D: I object to prosecutor Bocharov. The case involves a universal protest of the Crimean Tatar people in which all the participants in the trials of members of the nationalist movement are subjected to sharp criticism. Therefore, Bocharov cannot be impartial.

J: Did you know Bocharov personally before that time?

D: Personally, no.

Kaminskaia: Please tell me, Mustafa, does this document implicate you?

D: Yes, in its dissemination.

Gabay: I second Dzhemilev's statement and voice my objection to the prosecutor.

J: And why do you object?

G: I am also implicated in the dissemination of that document.

J: Does the name Bocharov figure here?

D: All the participants in the trials of Crimean Tatars are recounted there. What's more, Bocharov has a direct relation to the Chirchik events in April 1968, events that are reflected in the many documents that implicate us.

J: Even if prosecutor Bocharov did take part in the trials of the Chirchiks, that still does not mean anything. That trial was of a different character, and the prosecutor can behave differently.

G: You must not dissuade us.

Prosecutor: In the document of the case it is said that a certain prosecutor Bochagov presided over the trial of a peaceful group of Crimean Tatars in Chirchik. But then I am not Bochagov, but Bocharov. And in Chirchik I was nothing more than an eyewitness. And the police did not disperse a peaceful gathering of Crimean Tatars, as the document claims; rather, they restored public order, which was destroyed by certain persons of Tatar nationality.

Attorney: This is the first time in my legal experience that a prosecutor has given testimonial evidence about facts that implicate the accused. The defendants did not give substantial grounds for their objection to the prosecutor, but inasmuch as the prosecutor himself stated that he was an eyewitness to the Chirchik events, this constitutes sufficient grounds for an objection. He cannot be a plaintiff since he is a witness as well.

D: If it please the court, I may request the comrades to present to the court for inclusion in the case some photographs that were taken during the events in Chirchik. In one of the photos you can see prosecutor Bocharov. You can draw your own conclusions whether he was a mere eyewitness there. That's a henchman.

J: The court will retire for a meeting. A ten-minute intermission.

After the intermission the presiding judge Pisarenko stated that the court, having conferred, had decided that the statements of the defendants and of the attorney Kaminskaia concerning their objection to prosecutor Bocharov were groundless; the objection was therefore denied.

D: The decision of the court about the groundlessness of our objections is an unfounded assertion. You did not even trouble yourselves to introduce some kind of even hollow evidence on which your decision was founded. I still consider my objection to the prosecutor to be grounded, and, therefore, I will not answer any of his questions. From your decision it is completely clear that you are working according to a prearranged program and are not prepared to uncover the truth or judge in the full sense of the word.

G: I support Dzhemilev's statement and will not answer the prosecutor's questions.

Attorney: Had the prosecutor himself not stated that he had been an eyewitness to the events in Chirchik, and had he not evaluated those events, I would not support the petition of my client and of Dzhemilev. But, since the prosecutor himself made a statement about it in his polemic with Dzhemilev, then, being a witness, he cannot be a prosecutor. Therefore the court should decide on this matter once more.

J: The court will not retire twice to confer on one and the same question.

But your opinion, as the special opinion of the attorney, may be set down in the court record.

D: I request that my opinion be included in the court records as well, as that of the defendant and attorney, since I speak without defense counsel.

J: According to Soviet law you have the right to defense counsel, and the court guarantees you defense in the person of attorney Kaminskaia. If you do not agree with that, then you should make a statement in written or oral form and give grounds for your objection.

D: First of all, it is not the court that guarantees me a defense in the person of attorney Kaminskaia, but rather my relatives and friends by my request, and only for the period of familiarization with the materials of the case. I informed the attorney of this before she began to familiarize herself with the materials of the case in the capacity of my attorney. And I did this not at all because I consider myself better qualified to carry out my legal defense than attorney Kaminskaia would have been able. . . .

Attorney: I knew that Dzhemilev would refuse defense counsel.

Prosecutor: Did you take part in the preliminary investigation?

Attorney: Yes, that is, after the preliminary investigation had concluded and the materials of the case were given over for our familiarization.

J: [To Dzhemilev.] Why do you refuse defense counsel?

D: Because there are very few attorneys who make truly defensive cases in trials where political questions that are unpleasant to the government are dragged out. And speaking at such trials they subject their legal position to serious danger. I myself was a witness when prosecutor Erykalov, at the trial of ten representatives of Crimean Tatars in August 1969 in Tashkent, requested the board of the Supreme Court of the UZSSR to issue a confidential decision with a petition to exclude attorney Monakhov from the Moscow board of attorneys and to forbid him henceforth from practicing law for his "un-Party-like method of defense" in court. As a result, Monakhov was removed from his position. I can introduce several such examples.

Considering that the case against me is not so very complex and does not demand special juridical knowledge, and also that the sentence that will be handed down is almost well known to me already, I decided not to risk even once the job of a decent attorney, but to make use of article 45 of the Criminal Code of the UZSSR and to avail myself of the right to defend myself.

J: Write down an explanation where you show that the court guaranteed you a real defense in the person of an attorney but that you refused defense counsel. [He gives Dzhemilev a blank sheet of paper. Dzhemilev writes something and hands back the paper. The presiding judge Pisarenko reads it aloud.]

J: "I inform the board of the Tashkent city court that I refuse defense counsel and will defend myself." I requested that it be written in a different form.

D: I wrote it as I saw fit.

J: You should write it as the court sees fit.

This argument continues for several minutes. The presiding judge insists that Dzhemilev add to his statement the words "the court guaranteed me a real defense in the person of an attorney . . . ," but Dzhemilev refuses to make such an addition. Finally, Dzhemilev says:

D: Give me my paper. I am not at all obliged to give you written statements. I refuse the services of attorney; that is my right, as provided by the Criminal Code. It suffices that I inform you of this orally.

J: Well, fine then! How picky you are, Dzhemilev. What did it cost you to write a couple of words? It is a completely insubstantial question that does not pin you down in any way.

D: So it isn't necessary to quibble over such a bit of nonsense.

Judge Pisarenko whispers something to the deputies, who nod their heads, and then Pisarenko declares:

J: The court, having conferred, has decided in light of the fact that the defendant Dzhemilev is actually defended by the person of attorney Kaminskaia, and since he refuses defense counsel by declaring that he will defend himself, to sustain Dzhemilev's petition. Attorney Kaminskaia is relieved from the defense of Dzhemilev.

Further on, the question of witnesses is raised.

J: At most three witnesses have come. But I hope that in the meantime we will get to question the witnesses; all of them will be here. I propose that we continue our investigation into the case. Your opinion, comrade prosecutor?

Prosecutor: I leave that question to the consideration of the court.

Attorney: I doubt that all the witnesses will arrive on time. Up to the moment of my departure from Moscow the witnesses from Moscow had not yet received notice. From Moscow there is only one witness, Gabay's wife, who has arrived in court, and she doesn't know that she is to participate at the trial in the capacity of a witness.

Judge Pisarenko begins to whisper with the deputies.

D: Doesn't my opinion on this question interest you?

J: Fine, fine. Do you think that it is possible to continue the trial in the absence of the remaining witnesses?

D: No, I don't think so. As is well known, the Criminal Code does not stipulate any kind of mandatory order for the consideration of evidence. The court determines this order, considering both sides and guided by the interests of justice. I think that at first it is appropriate to confirm the facts that are described in the documents, of whose composition and dissemination we are being accused. For this it is proper that each document be announced in order and that the witnesses be questioned on the facts and events whose authenticity is open to doubt in the court. Therefore, from my point of view, the question of witnesses has a great significance. The number of witnesses, as recounted in the prosecutor's conclusion and, no doubt, summoned to court, is clearly insufficient. . . .

J: If you have a petition to summon additional witnesses, you may state it later. Right now that is not the issue.

D: The petition is one thing. I want to say that, if the witnesses named in the prosecutor's conclusion do not appear, then this trial will be quite strange. I think that it is appropriate to postpone the trial until the witnesses appear, even if according to the list of the prosecutor's conclusion.

J: The court, having conferred, has decided to continue the investigation into the case in the presence of those witnesses who have arrived. Does anyone have any kind of petition?

Attorney: I want to ask you to grant me time to familiarize myself with the case and to speak with my client. I received the telegram on the evening of 7 January and managed to buy an airplane ticket only today. I came here straight from the airport. I request to be granted some time, even if only the rest of today and all of tomorrow.

J: Your opinions?

G: I support the petition of the attorney. Have all the witnesses been summoned?

J: All have been sent notices. [To Dzhemilev.] Do you have a petition?

D: I have many petitions, but I will abstain from making them as long as the attorney's petition is not sustained.

J: Your opinion, comrade prosecutor?

Prosecutor: I leave it to the consideration of the court.

At this time a note is given over from somewhere. The judge reads the note and puts it in his pocket.

D: I request that the note you were just given be made public.

J: Why should I make it public?

D: Because you don't have the right to receive notes during the trial out of nowhere and, what's more, to tuck them away in your pocket. Show it.

J: Fine, I'll read it out. [He reads the note, which says that it is necessary to grant the attorney time to familiarize herself with the case and to settle into a hotel.] As you see, it's about your attorney's petition. Are you satisfied? What tactlessness on your part. You know, I'm not just a judge, but a man too. I also have a family, children, and personal affairs. The note could have been addressed to me personally, and not as a judge. Should I read those notes out as well? Shame on you, Dzhemilev!

D: You should deal with your personal and family affairs at home and not within the confines of the court. I'm very sorry that it has been necessary to remind you of such simple things. And your lesson in morality concerning tact you should read to your children. You must decide on the petitions of both sides not guided by notes. For receiving instructions from the KGB chiefs it is sufficient, and intermissions. . . .

J: [Irritatedly.] Enough, sit down! [He repeats.] KGB, KGB. . . . [To the side of the hall.] Do not give me any more papers! [Pause.] The court, on conferring, has decided to sustain the petition of attorney Kaminskaia and to grant her the opportunity to familiarize herself with the case for the remainder of the day and the first half of tomorrow.

Then the judge bids the defendants to stand, and he reads them their rights as stipulated in the Criminal Code of the UzSSR. The witnesses present are allowed to leave. Among those who leave is Il'ya Gabay's wife. Then the prosecutor's conclusion and the resolution part of the determination of the dispensation session concerning the handing over of the court is read out.

J: [To Gabay.] Do you understand the charge?

G: Yes, that is, I understand what the prosecutor's conclusion was about.

J: Do you acknowledge your guilt?

G: No!

J: Maybe you acknowledge it in part?

G: No, not in part, not at all.

J: [To Dzhemilev.] Do you understand the charge?

D: Tell me, does article 190-91 stipulate a punishment for the dissemination of false evidence or for an incorrect evaluation of facts?

J: In general you do not have the right to ask questions of the judge. But fine, as an exception. . . .

D: Good, no exceptions are necessary. I'll put it another way. I ask you to explain for what article 190-91 of the UK RSFSR (Russian Soviet Federative Socialist Republic) and article 191-94 of the UK UZSSR stipulate punishments: for the dissemination of false facts or for the improper handling of facts?

J: The article stipulates a punishment for the composition and dissemination of false fabrications that besmirch the Soviet order.

D: So is it for information or its assessment?

J: For information and its corresponding slanderous assessment.

G: Strange expression, "slanderous assessment."

D: If it is for the dissemination of false information, then why did the court not get to the bottom of the case? For it is clear from the prosecutor's conclusion that the proceedings did not call into question a single fact in the documents of whose composition I am accused.

J: You are putting questions to the court again. We are prepared to get to the bottom of the case. Do you acknowledge your guilt?

D: No. I consider the charge to be knowingly false.

J: Sit down! Court is adjourned until 2:00 P.M. tomorrow. . . .

## Document 2

*Edict of the Presidium of the Supreme Council of the Soviet Union.*

493. On citizens of Tatar nationality who lived in Crimea.

After the liberation of Crimea in 1944 from fascist occupation, the facts of active complicity of a certain segment of the inhabitants of Crimea with the German aggressors were groundlessly extended to the whole Tatar population of Crimea. These groundless charges against all the citizens of

Figure 12.1. Crimean Tatars in their tent city just outside Alushta, 1990, shortly before its destruction by town authorities. Photo courtesy of Mme Safinar Jemiloglu and the Crimean Tatar Mejlis.

Tatar nationality who had lived in Crimea should be dismissed, all the more because a new generation of people has entered into the working and political life of society.

The Presidium of the Supreme Council of the Soviet Union decrees:

1. To record the corresponding decisions of the state agencies in the section that contains the groundless charges against citizens of Tatar nationality who had lived in Crimea.

2. To record that Tatars, who had once lived in Crimea and who have now settled in the territory of the Uzbek and other republics of the Union, shall participate in social and political life, shall be elected as deputies in the Supreme Councils and local Councils of Workers' Deputies, shall hold responsible posts in Soviet, economic, and Party organs, and shall have radio broadcasts and newspapers in their native language, as well as other cultural institutions.

The Councils of Ministers of the Union Republics are empowered with the goal of developing further the regions possessing a Tatar population and are to offer assistance and cooperation to the citizens of Tatar nationality in economic and cultural building with due regard for their national interests and distinctions.

Chairman of the Presidium of<br>
the Supreme Soviet of the Soviet Union, N. Podgornyi.<br>
Secretary of the Presidium of<br>
the Supreme Soviet of the Soviet Union, M. Georgadze.<br>
Moscow, Kremlin. 5 September 1967.<br>
No. 1861-VII.

## Document 3

*Disposition of the Presidium of the Supreme Council of the Soviet Union.*

494. On the order of adaptation of article 2 of the edict of the Supreme Council of the Soviet Union from 28 April 1956.

The Presidium of the Supreme Council of the Soviet Union decrees:

To make known that the citizens of Tatar nationality who formerly lived in Crimea and members of their families shall enjoy the right of every citizen of the Soviet Union to reside in every territory of the Soviet Union in accordance with the pertinent legislation concerning employment and the passport regime.

Chairman of the Presidium of<br>
the Supreme Council of the Soviet Union, N. Podgornyi.<br>
Secretary of the Presidium of<br>
the Supreme Council of the Soviet Union, M. Georgadze.<br>
Moscow, Kremlin. 5 September 1967.<br>
No. 1862-VII.

## Document 4

Uzbekistan SSR
Academy SI
Academy of Sciences
Uzbek SSR
23.02.76
No. 40-91

city of Tashkent, Gogol St., no. 70
tel. 386847

To: The Ministry of Higher and Middle Education of the UZSSR t. ABDURAKHMANOV G. A.
Copy: Seytmuratova, Ayshe, Samarkand, Superfosfatnyi village, Teatral'naya St., House 8, Apt. 1.

Postgraduate student of the history of the AN UZSSR Seytmuratova, Ayshe was dismissed from the degree program on 18 June 1971, in connection with her arrest and sentencing to a three-year prison term, all in connection with her irresolute moral and political behavior. A little more than three months remains until the end of her term of study.

At the present time Seytmuratova Ayshe may not be reinstated in the postgraduate program, according to the new Statute "On the Granting of Scholarly Degrees and Scholarly Positions," declared by the Council of Ministers of the Soviet Union on 29 December 1975; under heading 1067, point 24 of section III, it is said that "Scholarly degrees may be granted to those persons who have a thorough professional knowledge of and academic achievement in a certain branch of study, who have a broad academic and cultural horizon, who have a mastery of Marxist-Leninist theory, who have positively applied themselves to academic, industrial, and social work, who adhere to the norms of Communist morality, and who are guided in their actions by the principles of patriotism and proletarian internationalism."

Academician-Secretary of the Department of<br>History, Linguistics, and Literary Studies of the AN UZSSR,<br>Academician AN UZSSR, Sh. Sh. Shaabdurakhmanov

# III

Returning to Crimea

# 13

## *The Elusive Homeland*

EDWARD A. ALLWORTH

Crimean Tatars focused international attention on the idea and problems of homeland most intensely during the decades of the 1970s–1990s, as they had, less broadly, within the Russian state during 1917–18. Recently, through actions and words, they have projected a postmodern vision of the native land. It displays special nuances in the current period, an era characterized even more unmistakably by immigrant and other societies abandoning traditional ways while evolving into post-communist ethnic heterogeneity.

### Foreigners' Understanding of Homeland

Under these circumstances, whether a homeland serves its people better as an idealized vision or as a certain piece of ground remains a question of perspective or of cultural philosophy. Several analysts foreign to Crimea have reached valuable insights concerning place and territory, sometimes seeing them as surrogates for homeland. One thoughtful scholar suggests that for a specific group of people the homeland consists, not of a particular point on the earth's surface, but of a mythical concept. That enables people's great powers of recuperation to build a subsequent homeland, even in another location, if the first has been destroyed or denied them. At the same time, he argues that strong attachment to homeland does not necessarily have to arise explicitly from a notion of its sacredness but may originate modestly in a sense of familiarity, ease, or security.[1]

These views fly in the face of some conventional theory about homeland and diverge tangentially from much of the interpretation of homeland articulated in politics and the related social sciences of the late twentieth century. Rather than grapple with the term *homeland* as such, geographic research usually focuses more intently on the characteristic functions of place and territory generally. The author of one such study sees place as a discrete, elastic area in which social relations can occur and help develop a sense of place and with which humans can identify. To some extent, that makes *place* sound like a surrogate for *homeland*, but he specifies that such a pattern emerges from home, work, school, church, and similar nodes around which people's lives revolve,[2] rather than from the locus of homeland in the human imagination or personal longing.

Disagreeing with the idea of an intangible homeland, a British sociologist states his belief that, when an ethnic community loses touch with the original habitat, in order to revive it must possess some territory of its own, that is, have "a recognized 'homeland' to which it rightfully belongs and which belongs to it by virtue of an historic association and origin." As examples, he cites the Turks in Anatolia and the Jews of Israel; others might add the Armenians in Transcaucasia. This, he asserts, responds to the necessity for a nation, which, like a modern state, is territorial.[3]

His requirement that a substitute homeland hold previous historic and ethnic meaning for the group of new inhabitants contradicts the idea, presented at the outset, that groups may build entirely new homelands, but it also obliges an inquirer to tie the question of a modern homeland to problems of nationality. That injects geography and politics, perhaps unnecessarily, into any attempt to understand the pure meaning of *homeland*. Emphasizing that matter of ethnic identity leads the analysis in the direction of investigating nationality and nationalism and away from the central question of homeland itself. Such an emphasis entails a conventional method in social science of insisting on generalization at the expense of the particular experience valued in the research of some anthropologists or humanists. Thus, a Welsh geographer writes: "Nationalities typically over-emphasise the particular uniqueness of their own territory and history. . . . Territory is nationalized by its treatment as a distinctive land. . . . The symbolic attributes of land and landscape . . . [play] role[s] in the construction and mobilization of national identity."[4]

The same preoccupation with depersonalization finds its expression in the focus on what some call *territoriality*. This approach claims to regard space with historical sensitivity in order to reveal how space and society are interconnected. Treated in that way, territories require the assiduous care and boundaries used to influence and control behavior. But, unlike a tangible homeland, says the theorist, those who exercise control over it need reside neither inside that territory nor anywhere near it.[5]

Into that discussion of homeland, an American geographer brings the volatile concept of inhabitant population, as contrasted with immigrant communities. In a carefully reasoned study and survey of the pertinent literature, he makes the related point that, when socially and politically mobilized, people he calls *indigenes* serve as strong catalysts in activating what he calls *national-territoriality* in the process of modernization. The main motivation driving indigenes, he argues, comes not from any instinctual need but from "a desire to control their own lives in order to fulfill their national destiny." Like comparable generalizations, this contention sidesteps the basic problems of understanding homeland, which others may insist has nothing to do with instinct or destiny. He passes over the distinct nature and function of homeland in favor of focusing on the nationality question, which an analysis of homeland might justifiably avoid.[6]

In a well-informed account specifically concerning Crimea, a contemporary Russian historian adds to the examination of the meaning of *homeland* by avoiding explicit discussion of it while describing a basic change that occurred in it. First, throughout a full-length study, he documents the prevalence of ethnic heterogeneity from the beginning of Crimea's history through its period of relatively short Crimean Tatar political hegemony to the first two decades of the twentieth century. This pluralism bears on all subsequent developments there. In the course of describing the main events in the long history of the peninsula, the historian reveals that, beginning almost from the time of the first powerful khans of the Giray dynasty in the fifteenth century, the status and identity of the region have gradually undergone a transformation from a presumptive homeland for Crimean Tatars into a territory that retains little necessary physical identification with Crimea's heterogeneous population.[7]

## Development of a Pragmatic Policy

Ambiguities in both regional identity and the link between populace and territory demanded clarification from people who cared deeply about maintaining such a significant connection. Inside the complex arena within which public opinion is formed among Crimean Tatars themselves has emerged in very recent times an unusually effective group of persons taking initiatives meant to accomplish that preservation. That group organized especially strong nonviolent public action, beginning no later than the autumn of 1967, when a decree issued by the Supreme Council of the Soviet Union granted Tatars the right, in effect, to live anywhere in the country except Crimea. This in spite of the fact that the decree exonerated exiled Crimean Tatars of false charges that during World War II they had collectively betrayed what Communist propagandists called the Soviet fatherland. (For the chronology of the movement to return to Crimea, see chap. 8 of the 1988 ed. of this volume.)

Those leaders faced a complex of several closely interdependent tasks. If their people were to survive as a group against organized and popular Soviet opposition, they shared the basic requirement, before all else, of reviving the terribly battered sense of awareness, identity, and unity of their people. Regaining the group's self-confidence, name, and honor, the elders felt, should play a crucial role in that drive. Countering discrimination and achieving ethnic parity with other Soviet nationalities deserved attention next. Most important, and, perhaps, even more difficult, would come the mobilization of the dispersed Crimean Tatars around some unifying theme. For several reasons, discussed below, the leadership settled on the idea of returning to the Crimean homeland, a major decision that required people to agree on both means and ends. Gaining essential recognition for the group as a whole from surrounding people, Russians in particular, then might become possible.

How wholeheartedly did everyone accept the aim of abandoning the homes, lives, cultural institutions, and employment so arduously rebuilt in Central Asia? Under the relatively stable conditions obtaining in Central Asia in the 1980s, why would they favor, after the murderous deportation in 1944, yet another perilous journey back into the inhospitable situation in Crimea? The subsequent behavior of the nationality would give the answers. Some of the attitudes expressed in conversations and in poetry give an indirect response to those queries (see chap. 1 in this volume).

Decisions and actions by the politicians in Moscow and Uzbekistan that discriminated harshly against the nationality converted several of those options into necessities. If Crimean Tatar "initiators" cared devoutly, as they did, about the survival of their nationality, they would have to act soon to hold it together. Whether to stay in Central Asia was the question. Whatever their decision, the painstaking steps toward recapturing a sustaining knowledge of Crimean Tatar history and culture for contemporary and future generations had to receive priority. (About steps in this effort, see chaps. 3 and 4, and esp. p. 68 of the latter, in the 1988 ed. of this volume.)

One circumstance alone, among many, strongly justified the precedence accorded by the group's leaders to self-reeducation concerning the history of Crimea and Crimean Tatars. Among the delegates (89.8 percent males) sent to Simferopol' for the Second Qurultay in June 1991, 116 participants making up a young plurality of those 226 voting representatives (65.5 percent under fifty years of age) accredited to the meetings listed their birthplace as one locality or another in Central Asia, not Crimea.[8]

The leadership also spoke and acted to forward Tatar migration to Crimea, not a return so much as a journey into the unknown for most children and adults forty years of age and under. Their urgency increased with an awareness of how quickly members of a dispersed community can integrate themselves individually into the population of a host country through natural interaction with neighbors and inclusion in institutions. The first decades of exile exposed Crimean Tatars in Central Asia to extremes of discrimination and deprivation, enforced isolation from coreligionists and Turkic-speaking nationalities. After 28 April 1956, when the central authorities lifted the special settlement regime (see chap. 4, p. 54, in the 1988 ed. of this volume), many Crimean Tatars gradually gained sympathy and friendship from surrounding Kazaks, Tajiks, Uzbeks, and others.

Although the possibility of assimilation into related populations in Central Asia posed a threat to the Crimean Tatar community, the decision to urge a migration from Central Asia to Crimea created risks almost as serious for the group's survival. As indigenous inhabitants, along with Crimean Tatars (204,000 counted or 255, 000 estimated in Crimea's population of 2.61 million in 1993) came the tiny groups of Tatar-speaking Jews—Qaraims (2,602 in the Soviet Union and 1,404 in the Ukrayina Soviet Socialist Republic (SSR) in 1989) and Qrymchaqs (900 in the Soviet Union in 1989)—who survived the Nazi invasion and then the Soviet reoccupation. The Crimean Tatar definition of *indigenous* did not include Russians, European Jews, or most of the numbers of other Slavs and Europeans living there (a recent source reports fractions of 110 different nationalities present in Crimea in 1993).[9] Although Crimean Tatars made up but 7.7 percent of the people in Crimea in that same year, their numbers ranked them third largest of its ethnic groups, followed by Germans with about 1.7 percent of the total.[10]

In 1995, as in 1993–94, the leaders estimated that at least half the Crimean Tatars of the former Soviet Union exiled in 1944, and their offspring, remained dispersed outside Crimea. The high commissioner on national minorities of the Organization for Security and Cooperation in Europe (OSCE), Max van der Stoel, also noted that some 250,000 deported Crimean Tatars, about half their core population, still hoped to return to Crimea.[11] When reliable numbers confirm that estimate, (see table 1.1), statisticians probably will show that three-quarters or more of the remaining Crimean Tatar population of the former Soviet Union still outside Crimea reside in Central Asia. A considerable proportion of the 47,000 counted in Ukrayina proper before the massive return may now have migrated into the Crimean part of Ukrayina itself. According to the census conducted in the Soviet Union at the start of 1989—its adequacy concerning Crimean Tatar numbers doubted by many specialists, including the editors of the source cited here—25.1 percent of the reported 271,715 Crimean Tatars lived in the three Slavic union republics, 74 percent in Central Asia's SSRs, including Kazakhstan, fewer than 1 percent in Transcaucasia, and far fewer than 0.05 percent in the Baltic SSRs.[12]

The westward displacement now under way of Crimean Tatars to Crimea from Tajikistan and Uzbekistan could result in segregating the more energetic, mobile, and perhaps younger adults, notably the males, from those less inclined to move, less vigorous, to some degree disabled, or economically unprepared to face the expenses. That would leave the body not only demographically and socially divided but virtually cut in half by physical segregation and an imperfect communication and transport system.

In 1995–96, that became the predicament for the Crimean Tatar people and their leaders. In Crimea, perhaps time and the hostility of Russian settlers toward them stood on the side of the returning exiles in the struggle to preserve group identity. But, in Central Asia, they faced the attrition of numbers implied in factors relating to age, economic viability, and tendencies encouraging integration and assimilation, such as the weakening and loss of the native language.

Immersion in a much more numerous populace speaking largely understandable, related languages and sharing a belief system (Communism overlaid on Islam) and certain elements of culture assured that many deported individuals would find some friends, protectors, even spouses, especially among young people in educational and cultural institutions and from the kinder families of the longtime residents with offspring in their age cohorts.

Speaking whatever tongue they chose, before their deportation in 1944, Crimean Tatars had rightly deserved a reputation as industrious, disciplined working people. Around a century earlier, during an equally devastating outflow of Tatars from Crimea, Russian eyewitnesses recorded what that fruitful, skilled labor had meant to Crimea. One with the perspective of earlier experience in the region, Russian princess Elena S. Gorchakova, in her *Memoirs about Crimea* (*Vospominaniia o Krymie*), wrote in 1881 about the main cause of the devastation she observed during visits to Crimea:

If one judges impartially, one is obliged to acknowledge that Russian colonization of the Taurida Peninsula did not bring it great benefit and did not provide its inhabitants either happiness or wealth.... Russian culture, if it touched a Tatar, ruined him, as in Yalta, Bakhchesaray, and other cities of Crimea, where, at each step, the charm and poetry of the East gives way to the banality and moral damage of our trade centers, and where a Tatar forfeits with each passing day his patriarchal customs, form of life, hospitality, courtesy, noble pride and awareness of personal dignity.... The land, ever generous, rewarded the labors of the agriculturalist, trade flowered, and even under the hegemony of the Turks, Crimea continued to be rich and populous. Only from the time of its incorporation into Russia did it begin visibly to be deserted.[13]

Nonetheless, in the 1920s, experience showed that Crimean Tatar husbandry could revive the productive land when given the chance. In the early decades of the twentieth century, the records showed that the "culture and life style of Crimean Tatars were found to be on a high level, [and] in Crimea the domestic artisan industries were developed broadly enough to play their positive role in filling the market with the most varied goods over a broad spectrum and in ensuring the population's employment."[14]

The horticulturalists and municipal employees ultimately earned a similar regard in the places of Central Asian exile in the twentieth century. This meant that employment patterns outside the home also sometimes constructively threw the deported people together with Koreans, Russians, or Uzbeks, for example, in the bureaucracy and agencies of municipal and republic government, in service centers, on the farms, and in professional work and cultural organizations. In time, when the others began to understand the predicament of Crimean Tatars, attitudes started to change. An eyewitness from among them later commented: "And Uzbeks then, recognizing that a monstrous injustice had been committed, began to share with Crimean Tatars the last crust of flat bread, the last handful of *kishmish* [raisins] or walnuts."[15]

## Obstacles to Disunity

Those several demographic conditions tended to overwhelm the unity and distinctiveness of the exiled people in Central Asia. There, in 1989, statistics also recorded 977,352 Tatars from Kazan or Astrakhan, rather than Crimea, settled throughout almost all *oblasts* and towns of Central Asia. Potentially, this posed an even greater threat of amalgamation than Tajiks or Uzbeks themselves to the maintenance of group integrity among Crimean Tatar exiles.[16] As one of many measures meant to dissolve Crimean Tatar group and personal identity, Soviet officials had merged data regarding the fewer Crimean Tatars into the large body of Kazan and Astrakhan Tatars living throughout the Soviet Union in post–World War II census reports preceding the final compilation in 1989. The comprehensive population reports from 1979 listed no "Crimean" Tatars at all, although they registered 15,078 Tatars and 1,151 Qaraims as residents of the Crimean Province (Krymskaia *oblast*) in the Ukrayina SSR at that time.[17] But such conditions proved insufficient to assimilate significant numbers of Crimean Tatars into the population of the Tajikistan and Uzbekistan SSRs because other developments mattered more. In those places with the greatest concentration of deportees, certain violent events that occurred only six months after the State Statistical Committee took the decennial census in 1989 might explain why.

An outbreak of ugly ethnocentrism in Uzbekistan and Kyrgyzstan shocked outsiders like Crimean Tatars living nonviolently in those SSRs. The young Uzbeks in the Farghana Valley who went on a rampage lasting for days in early June 1989 and the Kyrgyz who erupted in ethnic conflict just a year later gave the deported Meskhetian Turks and Crimean Tatars, involuntarily resettled there, a savage demonstration of the reality that identifiable aliens faced additional serious hazards in Central Asia. This happened to these exiles notwithstanding their Turkic and at least nominal religious kinship with the local people.[18]

These warning signs appeared as another generation of leaders coalesced among Crimean Tatars. The public statements and expressions of attitudes from these spokesmen and -women took on at first an earnest, formal tone and then acquired almost official weight. This developed despite the fact that Crimean Tatars had not achieved independence and that no higher Soviet government authority had given the activists lasting political recognition.

From the first, the new leadership body simply assumed a public authority conferred on it through acceptance by members of Crimean Tatar families and by few others. Publicly undaunted, the leaders proclaimed their positions widely, beginning audaciously, even before the last gasp of the Soviet state. As the components making up that ponderous political unit rapidly disassembled, Crimean Tatar delegates met in Aqmesjit (Simferopol') from 26 to 30 June 1991 to lay out their course openly.

For the present inquiry, most important became the efforts in the course of that Second Qurultay to define its constituency and the people's location and recognized identity both internally and internationally. For that purpose, the tenets outlined in the statutes of the Organization of the Crimean Tatar National Movement (Organizatsiia Krymskotatarskogo Natsional'nogo Dvizheniia, or OKND), drawn up between May 1989 and May 1990 and first published in the spring of 1991,[19] provided revealing guidelines. In the opening sentence of the preamble, the statutes declare the movement's reason for existence as "the return of Crimean Tatars to their own historic Homeland—Crimea—and the restoration of the national statehood that existed prior to the deportation of 1944."

That exact order of priority no longer received expression in the documents issued from the Second Qurultay held in late June 1991. Although a key statement makes reference to "the historic Homeland," emphasis had shifted. Now, the leadership stressed national statehood over the specific problems of identity and homeland. In the Qurultay's important "Declaration about National Sovereignty of the Crimean Tatar People" (28 June 1991), the text and its title immediately refer to the ideas of politics—national sovereignty, self-determination, and the right to reestablish a government on and control the resources of the peninsula of Crimea. (See the full translation of the declaration in chapter 16.)[20] The statement laid claim to a certain "national territory," of course, but did not find it necessary to explore the implications of the notion of a homeland for a dispersed, severely beleaguered nationality in the late twentieth century.

Again during that Second Qurultay, the delegates called on Crimean Tatars specifically to accept a political goal as their primary task. The "Appeal of the Qurultay to the Crimean Tatar People" of 29 June 1991 defines the first of three main self-imposed obligations as "restoring the statehood of the Crimean Tatar people on all the territory of its Homeland—the Crimea . . . on the basis of the right of each nationality [*narod*] to self-determination on its national territory."[21]

This declaration and the appeal reveal that the leadership of Crimean Tatars now felt pressed to take a second step. The initiators evidently believed either that events would not allow them to delay entering the political contest directly or that the earlier, urgent need to reawaken the group self-consciousness and strengthen the collective historical memory needed for cohesiveness among them had received adequate attention. They decided to concentrate on public political action or, rather, on political declaration, for, although Crimean Tatars felt themselves morally strong, they scarcely possessed the power to accomplish extensive political aims quickly by themselves. By the time of the Third Qurultay, June–July 1996, the policies of the leadership aimed even more specifically at the group's interrelations with outside authorities and nationalities. In the words of an official commentator: "The Mejlis considers itself the sole authentic representative body of Crimean Tatars, formulating its strategic program in the following terms: full and unobstructed return of Crimean Tatars to the homeland; compensation for the damage inflicted on them by the deportation; restoration of national statehood of the Crimean Tatar people in Crimea with full guarantee of civil rights and freedoms for all inhabitants of the peninsula and free development of national cultures, faiths, languages, and traditions of all ethnic groups and nationalities represented in Crimea."[22]

## Redefining Crimeans

Despite the well-focused drive forwarded by these leaders, the general conception of *homeland* lacked one crucial link with the object of their "return" strategy. In contrast with the learned discussions conducted among foreigners and surveyed in the first section of this chapter, the usual definitions of *homeland* current in Crimean Tatar, Soviet Russian, or Western usage avoid including the stipulation that a homeland must relate to a specific nationality group. Rather, almost uniformly, they define the word *homeland* in personal terms. Whether termed *rodina*, *vatan*, *heimat*, or *homeland*, it is a place where someone was born and raised, a country of origin, a native land, or a country of which a person is a citizen. The noticeable exception to this consistent approach to the concept occurred at a moment that might exert strong influence on the thinking of Crimean Tatars. The accepted definition of the Russian *rodina* circulated in the standard reference work of the era and state, the first edition of the *Great Soviet Encyclopedia* (*Bol'shaia sovetskaia entsiklopediia*), read quite differently. Equating the term *rodina* with Russian *otchizna*, "native country," and *otechestvo*, "fatherland," the work goes beyond a personal to a collective version, defining *rodina* as "a country [*strana*] historically belonging to a given ethnic group [*narod*] that this ethnic group populates, developing its own culture and defending its own independence and freedom."[23] Pre-Soviet reference works omitted that meaning for *rodina*. The patriotic solidarity expressed in 1941, when that source appeared, very likely reflected the sense of peril acutely felt by Russian and European people then gravely threatened by the military forces and ideologies of authoritarianism in the West and the East.

On incorporation of Crimea into the Russia-wide empire, a differing concept of *homeland* settled over the peninsula, an all-embracing one. For Crimean Tatars, the imposition of Russian rule hardly seemed conducive to a love of the broad new homeland. In time of peril, however, prominent members of the Tatar community rather soon expressed the Russian attitude toward the empire and shared a concern for the survival of the Russia-wide fatherland. With the outbreak of the Crimean War in 1853, the forces of Britain, France, the Ottoman Empire, and Sardinia opposed those of imperial Russia. On 19 January (o.s.) 1854, the mufti of Tavricheskaia *guberniia*, Seyyid Jelil Efendi, called on his Muslim *katibs* (clerks) and *imams* to disseminate his message to all Tatar coreligionists to support the Russian side in the war (in Crimea, the mufti served as foremost Muslim legal arbiter and chief of the Muslim community there recognized and appointed by the czarist court): "And all of us Muslims, small and large, must be sincerely loyal to the Czar and to the Homeland [*Otechestvo*] and begrudge neither life nor blood for them if it is demanded of us for their defense; also, [we] must not say and think reprehensibly and adversely [toward] the Russian homeland."[24] From its content and rhetoric, the letter seemingly had been composed by Russian advisers to the mufti quite sensitive to the natural sympathies of Muslim Tatars favoring the cause of Russia's Turkish enemy in the conflict. A public testimonial directed to Czar Nicholas Pavlovich, from certain Crimean noblemen (*beys*) and princes (*murzas*), published somewhat earlier, sounded a similar, fervid tone of unqualified support for Russia in the Crimean War.

That same vision of a broader homeland encompassing all constituent nationalities and individual homelands of the multiethnic state surely lay behind the actions of Soviet political and military leaders. The inclusive concept rationalized the action that uprooted Crimean Tatars from their peninsula and tore so many other nationalities from the places where they and their predecessors had long spent their lives in another time of peril—the fight with Nazi German military might during World War II.

In the aftermath of the traumas inflicted by the inhumanity of the Communist regime and the losses of what official statements always referred to as "the Great Fatherland War," the broad, patriotic definition of *homeland* (seen in Crimean Tatar as *Ulu Vatan*) continued to prevail in Soviet usage for about thirty years. That was exactly the period during which the majority of adults and of the younger generation of Crimean Tatars so greatly affected by the official deportation of 1944 received schooling in the Soviet Union. The second edition of the *Great Soviet Encyclopedia*, issued beginning in the 1950s, shifted priority slightly by offering as a first meaning for *rodina* the more general, and personal, "a country in which a person was born and of which he is a citizen." Only in second place comes the repetition of the terminology used in 1941 attaching ethnic group to territory.[25]

In a very significant change, the third edition of the *Great Soviet Encyclopedia* deliberately returned to the concept of prewar Soviet dictionaries. It repeated only the 1955 volume's personal definition of *homeland* (in a terse entry omitting the wartime passage that emphasized the link between country and ethnic group). In making this alteration, the editors again adopted the individual meaning for *homeland* found in the recognized and unabridged Russian-language dictionary of 1939. It had presented no group link with land but cited several Marxist usages, especially V. I. Lenin's antinationalist and class-conscious dictum, "The Soviet Union is the second homeland of the workers and the oppressed of the entire world." In that respect, the version offered in the *Great Soviet Encyclopedia*, likewise in 1939, echoes Lenin under the heading *Fatherland (Otechestvo)*: "The Soviet Union is the homeland [*rodina*] of the workers of the Soviet Union, of the international proletariat, the genuine fatherland of all the oppressed, of all advanced and progressive humanity."[26] Soviet authorities had arbitrarily modulated the concept of the embattled homeland asserted under universal peril from the Axis powers to the ideology of Marxism, which in principle, if not in practice, denied the existence of limited ethnic or national homelands in favor of world Communism.

By December 1991, the leaders of the Crimean Tatar Mejlis, the core body or executive committee selected by the Second Qurultay, had slightly modified their position concerning homeland. They, too, connected the idea of homeland somewhat less tightly than before with the question of ethnicity. Toward the end of that eventful year, hoping to deflect ethnocentric opposition, they issued a draft constitution for a proposed Crimean Republic whose name significantly avoided the word *Tatar*. Furthermore, the wording given in the preamble included two categories of people as valid participants in the life of that hypothetical republic: indigenous inhabitants and "citizens of other nationalities for whom, on the strength of historical circumstances [left unspecified], Crimea became the Homeland."[27]

## Qualifications of a Homeland

Regardless of numbers, this specification of indigenous inhabitants raised but did not settle the question of how a place qualifies as a human group's homeland in the postmodern era, one of the central problems framed by the situation of Crimean Tatars. A promising, partial answer offered in the documents from the period leading up to the demise of the Soviet Union came from a conference held in the village of Musa Ajji Eli, Crimea, 7–8 October 1989. Singling out Crimean Tatars, representatives from "national democratic independence movements" spoke of them as "a nationality formed on the territory of Crimea and one that had its independent state there for centuries."[28] Such a claim founded on statehood (hardly *national* in the modern sense) might resolve the dispute over which of the people—

Figure 13.1. Front page of newspaper carrying the "Declaration of National Sovereignty of the Crimean Tatar People," 28 June 1991 (fully translated in chap. 16). From *Avdet* nos. 15/16 (26/27) (11 July 1991): 1.

Russian, Tatar, or Ukrayinan—dominated the peninsula politically before the others. It seems doubtful that a claim of exclusive right to territory based on the existence of a remote period of previous "national statehood" can strengthen the argument of group origin. No living nationalities besides Crimean Tatars, Qaraims (called *Karaites* in the census data from 1989 published in the Ukrayina SSR in 1991), and Qrymchaqs could seriously assert a right, on the basis of group origin or name, to that peninsula in the late twentieth century.

These ideas seemed to contradict the position taken in the 1991 declaration of the Crimean Tatar Mejlis (fig. 13.1), discussed above, which furiously rejected restoration of the Crimean Autonomous Soviet Socialist Republic (ASSR) as a national-territorial formation by the Crimean (not Crimean Tatar) administration of the *oblast*.[29] By insisting on an ethnic, but not a territorial, qualification for a claim to the place, the Crimean Tatar theorists evidently meant to base their argument on the principle of cultural identity in order to establish legal jurisdiction over the entire land of Crimea. Such an approach suggested a belief in the possibility of holding an exclusive cultural-ethnic right to the homeland.

Few, if any, nationalities in the world so dominate their countries culturally, demographically, socially, and politically that they can fairly claim exclusive right to the entire land where they live. That includes those nationalities with a very high proportion of the population in their countries—Finns (94 percent) in Finland; Han Chinese (94 percent) in the Peoples' Republic of China; Hungarians (Magyars; 92 percent) in Hungary; or Japanese (99.4 percent) in Japan, for example.[30] In the final decade of the twentieth century, Crimea gave homes to people of more than a hundred different nationalities, two of them many times more numerous than Crimean Tatars. A broad ethnic mixture had characterized the demography of Crimea virtually throughout its history—and certainly since the arrival of the Tatar horsemen of the Golden Horde in the region during the thirteenth century.

## Partial Homelands

Argument from precedent in the case of claims to territory layered with civilizations from ancient to modern times harbors an intrinsic weakness. Since medieval times, rulers of the Golden Horde, Crimean Tatars, Ottoman Turks, czarist Russians, Soviet Russians, and Ukrayinans have, at different stages, held sway in Crimea for considerable periods of time. Why would a season or a century of military or political hegemony by one dynasty or another in history, by itself, retrospectively entitle its tribes or its followers to exclusive right to a former territory? Claims to territory not based strictly on power or physical possession required a complex of different, related bases.

If extended earlier periods of political dominion by one Communist Party secretary, khan, sultan, or emperor over territory in the past cannot substantiate an indisputable claim by one group of followers to the same land in the present, does that nevertheless negate the possibility that descendants can claim at least a partial hereditary homeland amid the ethnic conglomeration interspersed within a certain political unit? Frequently, in the present era, regions and independent countries house great mixtures of individuals quite without formal salients of discrete territory or political recognition as subgroups in the general population. Take, for example, the Commonwealth of Australia, except in preserves for aborigines; the French Republic; the Republic of Kazakstan; the Republic of Latvia; the United States, except in reservations for Native Americans; and many other countries.

By recording the existence of many imperfect or incomplete homelands—that is, ethnically unhomogeneous ones—those examples pose a further problem in qualifying homelands for specific nationality groups, or the reverse. Among the inhabitants living in a country, which resident nationality group deserves the right to govern and name the place, and which may rightfully develop the dominant culture for a shared homeland and why? What sorts of traits must the naming group display, for example? Crimean Tatar spokesmen and -women assert, with justification, they believe, that Crimea belongs to them because they have no other homeland,[31] whereas each of the three large Slavic segments in the population of the peninsula can relate to a namesake home country outside Crimea. But, when Crimean Tatar leaders acknowledge the fact that even one other nationality lives legally with them in Crimea—as do official statements, cited above, by including Qrymchaqs and Qaraims among the indigenous people of the peninsula—they recognize the principle of shared and partial homeland.

This version of partial homeland implies mixing in demography and sharing space in common, rather than subdividing territory according to ethnic unit. Building on this idea of ties to a partial homeland suggests another sort of link to a certain region—exclusion as a common experience. Certainly, this feature of life in Crimea distinguishes recent Slavic immigrants from the people who previously put down roots there. Crimean Tatar documents reject the notion of sharing Crimea with such immigrants.

Should a territorial style of partial homeland arise there today, it would find most of the largely rural or suburban Crimean Tatars excluded from cities and from the southern littoral, where a preponderance of the group formerly lived. Foreign travel writers have applied the term *landless*, perhaps unconsciously meaning *homeless*, to Crimean Tatars in Crimea. One such report relating to the second half of the nineteenth century records that "a large part of Crimean Tatars are landless, living on estates of landlords, and thus fully dependent on the landlords." An official commission learned in 1872 that, of the 140,000 rural Crimean Tatars living in the *guberniia*, about half remained landless.[32] Documents filed in the government archives in 1884 refer to grants of plots to twenty-eight thousand peasants. Again in 1897 an official Russian report discusses Crimean Tatar landlessness, verifying that their condition remained a perennial problem.[33] That situation finds an echo in the complaint heard in the czarist Imperial Second State Duma (1907), when a petition prepared by the head of the "Young [Crimean] Tatars" raised the troubling question of fifty thousand "landless farmers" yet languishing in their poverty-stricken, predominantly agricultural economy.[34]

This opinion, that homelessness entitles people to a refuge, now seems to receive general, if sometimes unenthusiastic, acceptance in internal and international relations. The distribution of populations and political forces almost invariably denies the displaced nationality exclusive right to the land of its dreams. The recent history of Armenia and Azerbaijan, Bosnia-Herzegovina and Serbia, Israel and Palestine, Kashmir, or Liberia—all regions where many believe that might has made wrong—testifies to that. Leading political opponents of an exclusive Crimean Tatar right to Crimea heatedly insisted in 1991, as they often had and would again, that the peninsula also "is the motherland of the Crimean-Ukrainian, the Crimean-Russian, and the Crimean-Jewish people."[35] The Crimean dilemma illustrates the truism that what seems fair to the homesick seldom proves decisive in political resolution of major problems involving homelands.

The drive of uprooted people to return to the land they regard as home cannot everywhere reward them with immediate satisfaction. The American idea that, when separated even by a moderate amount of time and social distance from their origins, individuals or groups cannot return to them[36] suggests that, in the modern or postmodern era, a remembered homeland surely changes into an increasingly unfamiliar place just as people distanced from it inexorably change. In other words, as the attitudes and behavior of individuals and groups evolve especially rapidly after great upheavals such as World War II, so does the imagined homeland undergo significant alteration. In the interim, not only has Crimea absorbed outsiders in large quantities, but it has also become greatly urbanized, shifted from the political jurisdiction of one state to another, and reorganized its economy and culture tremendously during the half century of Crimean Tatar absence. This gives credence to the idea that, after sufficient years and experience abroad, no one can really go back where he or she came from, for *back* implies sameness. In a speedily postmodernizing era, that traditional home place no longer exists.

Observers both East and West readily discern that urban development and degradation of the countryside now emerge as the principal man-made instruments, aside from warfare, that bring about highly visible change with its attendant social disruption in most regions today, as they did from the beginning of this century. A contemporary American author who visited the Middle East, Central Asia, and other non-European regions in recent travels, felt that he observed there a crumbling of social mortar, so to speak, a growing imbalance between man and nature resulting in ecological disaster and, significant in this discussion, the alienation of the regions' peoples: "Drunken, violent, disoriented Uzbeks, Tajiks and Uighurs, . . . having lost a land to love, have lost their own identities."[37] Here, the writer describes the appalling spectacle of a homeland ruined by the economic and social abuses inflicted in the name of progress and ideology by an authoritarian regime. The destruction of the Aral Sea in Central Asia killed all life in and around it. The same government that wreaked havoc there ruled and ruined Crimea. His reflections pose a sharp question: To what extent can a physically despoiled, unlovable, and coldly inhospitable motherland serve the crucial purpose of nourishing the spirit either of residents or of inhabitants exiled from it? How can a drastically altered place enhance the unity in a scattered group of former residents? By noticing the negative impact of a degraded country on its own people, the observer in principle demands consideration of the dilemma faced by Crimean Tatars as well as the attitude they express regarding the return to Crimea.

A factor probably even more striking than the degradation of the environment emerges from the human metamorphosis. The greatest change confronting those who would return to Crimea has resulted from the wholesale repopulation of the region by Slavic outsiders since 1944. That demographic invasion brings about a certain amount of heterogeneity there, but members of the three Slavic nations—Belarussian, Russian, and Ukrayinan—dominated the society so strongly (constituting 95 percent of Crimea's entire population in 1989) that a blending or merging among ethnic groups hardly matters. The Russian population of Crimea (1,629,542 in 1989) alone numbered more than six times the Crimean Tatars in Crimea as recently as 1993.[38]

Momentarily disregarding the effect of those huge discrepancies, with ethnic mixing a common feature of most postmodern societies and territories outside as well as inside the former Soviet Union, the phenomena of ethnically divided, fractional, and otherwise incomplete homelands generally prevail. Current affairs offer many examples of divided nations, each fragment with its notion of homeland—Armenia, Azerbaijan, Buryatia, Germany long after World War II, Korea, Taiwan, and others. Numerous

Figure 13.2. Crimean Tatar women in rural Crimea distraught over attacks on their settlements by Russian vigilantes. Photo courtesy of Mme Safinar Jemiloglu and the Crimean Tatar Mejlis.

instances exist of ethnic groups in one state closely neighboring ethnically distinctive neighbors—in Belgium, Canada, India, the People's Republic of China, Switzerland, the United Kingdom, and the like. That effectively counters assertions of priority stemming from a period of medieval statehood or even from the fairly recent history of the proclaiming new governments. For this reason and several already discussed above, attempts to establish indisputable land claims today through appeals to technical factors such as political coups and military conquest hardly can prove conclusive.

## The Power of Intangibility

Enemies possessing superior physical strength cannot obliterate the idea of homeland from the minds and culture of defeated foreigners short of annihilating them all. Conquerors may seize terrain and capture populations, but the very intangibility of homeland seems to confer on it the greatest strength and durability. Abstract symbols provide signal features in the complicated aspect of immaterial power.

Communist political leaders instituted a second sort of subversion of name, even more destructive than the physical replacement of familiar designations discussed in chapter 1 of this book. Starting in the mid-1940s, as they implemented policies aimed at erasing cultural landmarks and traditional names from the landscape and cartography, they energetically exploited the networks of media and propagandists to undermine Crimean Tatars' good name.

Especially in wartime, Soviet leaders expected every subject nationality, however badly abused by the regime, to remain loyal to the Soviet-wide homeland and its oppressive government and Communist Party ideology. When the non-Slavic nationalities such as Crimean Tatars failed to understand and accept completely that unfamiliar corporate concept of homeland, the authorities and the Russian majority in the Soviet Union accused them of treason to a state coextensive with the Soviet concept of homeland. No Slavic nationality at that time suffered such comprehensive public condemnation or humiliation for its hostility to the Soviet Union or to the Russians, although many Belarussians, Russians (under General Andrei A. Vlasov, e.g.), and Ukrayinans actively resisted the Moscow dictatorship when opportunities arose during World War II. The state's formulation referring to a wider homeland (*Ulu Vatan*) particularly confused non-Russian, self-aware people in the East, such as Crimean Tatars. The concept instilled in them a profound ambivalence toward identification with the primary homeland, whatever it was, and uncertainty over the degree of fealty owed either the primary or the secondary, the broader or the narrower, the official or the ideal identity.

The vicious invective projected from the policy makers in the Kremlin against Crimean Tatars during the war made them the target of hatred and abuse by a large part of the Soviet population. While Nazi forces continued to occupy Crimea, internal documents circulated within the Soviet Union's highest agencies of government, including the Peoples' Commissariat for Internal Affairs, the Peoples' Commissariat for State Security, and others, articulating a hostility against Crimean Tatars, especially, through guilt by association, that would become general in the country.

The Soviet Russian government of the Soviet Union, in its wholesale condemnation of scapegoats, independent-minded small nationalities, and other categories of victims, originated nothing new in that region when it defamed whole populations. Many centuries earlier, confrontations between ancient Greeks and nomadic Scythians along those same northern shores of the Black Sea had prompted the sedentary people, who considered themselves civilized, to call *barbarians* everyone in the mobile population of the plains whose ideology or lifestyle differed strongly from their own.[39] *Barbarian* bore a comprehensive (pejorative) thrust then, no doubt just as *anti-Soviet* or *traitor* did in the mid-twentieth century.

In April 1944, officials of Soviet agencies composed a secret directive that described their immediate goals and attitudes as "cleansing the territory of the Crimean *oblast* of resident agents of German and Rumanian intelligence and counterintelligence, betrayers of the homeland and traitors, active accomplices and henchmen of the German fascist occupiers, participants in anti-Soviet organizations, bandit formations, and other anti-Soviet types who rendered aid to the occupiers."[40]

Within a month, an even more damning order circulated within the top level of government and crystallized the official view castigating Crimean Tatars in general for perpetrating wartime acts of which, in 1967, the Soviet government officially exonerated the nationality when it was already too late to spare them decades of anguish, mistreatment, and violence. Although the order from the State Committee of Defense, headed by Joseph Stalin himself, dated 11 May 1944, remained secret for decades, state-controlled journalists and other propagandists quickly broadcast the tone of malice against Crimean Tatars sounded in the order's pronouncements (see fig. 8.1):

In the period of the Fatherland war, many Crimean Tatars betrayed the Homeland [*Rodina*], deserted units of the Red Army defending Crimea, and went over to the side of the enemy. They joined volunteer Tatar military units, formed by the Germans, battling against the Red Army; in the period of the occupation in Crimea, taking part in German punitive detachments with German fascist troops, Crimean Tatars were especially distinguished by their beastly reprisals in regard to Soviet partisans and also aided the German occupiers in organizing the business of forcibly driving Soviet citizens into German slavery and that of the mass execution of Soviet individuals.[41]

Here again, the notion of corporate Soviet homeland, rather than the nationality's singular place, became the measure of loyalty exacted by the Soviet leadership.

Hatred, fueled by such prejudice against the Crimean Tatars, only grew in ferocity over the period 1967–94, when the group decided to go beyond appeals for equal treatment and recognition and chose to make a concerted move back to Crimea. Among the most visible anti-Crimean Tatar acts, described above in chapter 1, were the destructive attacks against housing, tent cities, and settlements (see fig. 12.1) by Slavic vigilantes and militia members who had immigrated into Crimea in place of the Tatars following the deportation in 1944. The long record of their mistreatment of Crimean Tatars shows such blatant, repeated actions against the returnees by Slavic officials and ordinary non-Tatar citizens that outsiders can only wonder how the victims endured it and clung to their determination to remain nonviolent.[42] Nevertheless, they did.

This overt bias amounted to contempt for good repute. It grew into one of the most painful assaults made on the Crimean Tatar group identity. People cannot restore their group's good name quickly through devices such as substituting an untainted label. In the surrounding community of nationalities, they must reearn their unjustly blackened good character. This takes a long time, probably generations, regardless of the publicly acknowledged fact that evil politicians stole it from them. Such bad publicity led many in the Tatar group to feel ashamed of themselves and their people. It especially hurt children. In their Russian-language schools, the official anti-Tatar propaganda and its popular voice led both pupils and teachers to single out Crimean Tatars as bandits, barbarians, and traitors to the (Soviet) fatherland. (See chap. 3, pp. 29–30, in the 1988 ed. of this volume.) Before the cattle cars loaded with starving deportees reached the places of exile, the authorities dispatched teams of agitators from various republic-, *oblast*-, and *raion*-level agencies and offices spread throughout the republics to many parts of Central Asia in order to explain that the local population should despise the deportees who would soon reach the area. These spokesmen and -women called the exiles traitors, betrayers, and venal turncoats. When Crimean Tatar war veterans reached Central Asia after VE day, they too heard themselves automatically called traitors to the homeland, solely on the basis of their ethnic identity.[43]

Besides permanently hurt pride, the invective aimed against the good name of this small nationality would produce other important consequences, not all of them entirely negative, in the period ahead. The response to that diatribe showed that Crimean Tatars took seriously these threats of permanent damage to their good repute. Most directly, anti-

Tatar measures and prejudice stimulated the victims to defend their image in the larger community. Crimean Tatar activists launched a strong effort to earn public and government support for their cause in 1966 with an appeal to the Twenty-third Congress of the Communist Party of the Soviet Union (CPSU). The message stressed the two themes under scrutiny here, their deprivation of access to the homeland and the right to the restoration of their good name.[44]

That preoccupation with the group's reputation stemmed not merely from the sullying of it orchestrated by CPSU ideologists and publicists during and after World World II. Crimean Tatars, Turks, Central Asians, and other people of the East placed extraordinary emphasis on the values of honor, honesty, and fairness, that is, on their good name. The small colony of Qrymchaqs in Crimea, for example, had enjoyed wide regard as people of honesty, of good name, years before the Bolshevik coup d'état of 1917. The premium placed on those qualities by Crimean Tatars again became clear during a defense argument made by Mustafa Jemiloglu at his trial in Tashkent in 1969 for ostensibly slandering the Soviet Union (by speaking the truth about abuses) and repeated by him in another court 15 February 1984: "I swore . . . that no one would ever, under any circumstances, force me to refuse to fulfill my obligation and the duties laid on me by honor, conscience, and national dignity."[45]

Given that background, neither friend nor foe could have felt astonished when, in Aqmesjit (Simferopol') on 30 June 1991, during the Second Qurultay, that subject arose once again. The meeting approved and issued the "Appeal from the Qurultay of the Crimean Tatar Ethnic Group [*Narod*] to All the Inhabitants of Crimea," which returned to this powerful theme. In it, the Qurultay spoke to other residents of the peninsula about its constituency's good qualities, among other things: "Finding ourselves in exile [starting in 1944, we] Crimean Tatar people confirmed our good name [*dobroe imia*], proving ourselves exceptionally hard-working and peaceful people, ready to share our experience, knowledge, [and] the results of our labor with all amicable ethnic groups [*narody*]."[46] Individuals expressed these feelings separately and in widely divergent places. A small scattering of Crimean Tatars lived in the Transcaucasus among the Muslim Abkhazians in the Republic of Georgia, for instance. When the terrible civil war of the 1990s that overtook that region forced Crimean Tatars to flee and they made their way to Crimea, they emphasized that "Abkhazians always regarded us Crimean Tatars as good neighbors."[47]

Foreign scholars' ideas of homeland, a place that some contend requires a necessary connection with ethnicity, have but peripheral relevance here. Crimea's transformation from a presumptive homeland for a certain nationality has little connection with the region's multiethnicity. Although the unifying concept of homeland may seem out of date in the postmodern era of immigrant countries or places, the behavior and ideas of displaced groups engaged in reimmigrating to a certain spot on the globe perhaps does not comply with that general rule. For the Tatars, Crimea had to function as the personally, culturally, and socially legitimizing homeland. Because of its name and history, for them, no other place could serve. Rejoining it would bring the redemption for which they hungered in international affairs.

Despite the fragmentation of the nationality, renewed Tatar residence in Crimea expresses deeply significant emotional and intellectual feelings and values. Good name, love, moral certainty, give Crimean Tatars their main strength for attaining the goal of a happy home in Crimea. After the widespread Soviet vilification, reclaiming the homeland meant vindication, honor, and justice as much as anything else. And the Crimean Tatar definition of *homeland*—based on a certain remembered and labeled piece of terrain—nevertheless resonates above simple possession of land, with a meaning that emanates from the intangible qualities of fairness and justification, dignity and respect, values most highly revered among living as well as long-deceased Crimean Tatars.

In view of that, the pertinent formulation in this case, and probably others, would define *homeland* as an idealized environment promising emotionally nurturing social and material surroundings felt to sustain, protect, and satisfy members of the specific community in question.

Earlier in the twentieth century, poets used to sing fervently about a sacred or eternal homeland. In verses entitled "My Homeland" ("Vetanim menim"), Osman Amit (1910–42) plays off the figure of passing time against the permanence of his delight with the homeland:

| | |
|---|---|
| A new year overtakes years past, | Yil ote yillarni yangi yil quva, |
| Victorious, the clock hand passes them by, | Ghalebe kosterip ote yelquvan, |
| A happy life this is, my son, | Bakhitli omyur bu, oghlum, |
|     smile, go on! |     kul', quvan! |
| How beautiful is this homeland | Ne qadar guzel' bu vetanim |
|     of mine! |     menim![48] |

Lilia Budzhurova's short verse "What Is the Homeland's Scent?" (translated in chap. 1) exemplifies the more sensual evocation of native place.

Praise of Crimea not only takes a lyric or a didactic approach such as these aimed at youngsters or at the mature self but also finds expression through many special epithets (or pet names) for Crimea. Sometimes these stand in place of the toponym and convey respect and affection. Shamil' Alyadin (born in 1912 in Makhul'dyur village, Crimea), novelist and former editor of the journal *Yïldïz*, long the only literary periodical in the Crimean Tatar language, returned to Crimea from Tashkent on his eighty-second birthday in 1994, after decades in exile. When members of the Crimean Tatar literati met him, they used a decorative style reaching beyond the single word *vatan*. Welcoming him, in various expressions they evoked "the native Land, Mother Country, or Motherland" (*tuvghan Vatan, Ana-Yurt* or *Ana-Vatan*).[49]

Frequently, the expression *sacred homeland* (*muqaddes vatan*), or variants of it, appears in signed articles in the press and in statements ordinary people make about Crimea. Sometimes those who use it refer to the spiritual, possibly physical, presence of revered predecessors. Before the centennial of the birth of the poet and scholar Bekir Chobanzade in 1993 (see the section devoted to him in chap. 4 above), the jubilee committee made elaborate plans for a commemoration. Reporters announcing the coming of this celebration singled out the area of the villages Argin, Efendikoy, and Baqsan in the Qarasuvbazar (Belogorskii) district as "sacred soil" (*muqaddes topraq*) because, they wrote, Chobanzade and his forefathers (*baba-dedeleri*) had at one time walked that ground.[50]

A prominent living Uzbek poet, acutely cognizant of the trauma inflicted on men and women by physical alienation from their personal world, has very recently written lines that can pertain most appropriately to the situation of today's Crimean Tatars remaining in Central Asia as well as to those trying to gain a new foothold in the Crimean peninsula after an involuntary absence of five decades: "You and I do not deeply comprehend what the Homeland may be. And pray God that we don't understand it. For only wanderers cut off from the Homeland fully understand what Homeland may be. . . . That is the reason why those who write the greatest verses concerning the Homeland are the poets who possess a powerful desire to see the Homeland."[51]

No court of last resort, wherever it may sit, can render a verdict resolving these few, key questions, for they concern physical rights involved in unresolvable disputes: Why does a nationality making an exclusive claim to the territory of a region retain a right to assert it in perpetuity, if it does? To what extent do intervening events and conquests, no matter how unfair or illegal under national or international law, alter the basis for such a claim? How many decades or centuries can such a right persist, if at all? One response may answer all three queries, near the close of the twentieth century, because it does not rest on a material basis. Military reconquest and politics aside, the eligibility of absent groups to regain a lost homeland probably survives no longer than the living memory of one or two generations, in other words, around fifty years at most, in developed countries of the postmodern era. This timetable offers Crimean Tatars a fleeting chance before the new millenium to secure some greater stake in the contemporary Crimea or to create some new place in the present peninsula. In this, they may, without abandoning memories of the past, savor the compelling, intangible aspects of homeland, rather than focusing solely on erosion of the tangible.

## Notes

1. Yi-Fu Tuan, *Space and Place: The Perspective of Experience* (London: Edward Arnold, 1977), 150, 159.

2. John A. Agnew, *Place and Politics: The Geographical Mediation of State and Society* (Boston: Allen & Unwin, 1987), 28, 35.

3. A. D. Smith, "States and Homelands: The Social and Geopolitical Implications of National Territory," *Millennium* 10, no. 3 (1981): 197, 188.

4. Pyrs Gruffudd, "Remaking Wales: Nation-Building and the Geographical Imagination, 1925–1950," *Political Geography* 14, no. 3 (April 1995): 219–20.

5. Robert David Sack, *Human Territoriality: Its Theory and History* (Cambridge: Cambridge University Press, 1986), 3, 19.

6. Robert J. Kaiser, *The Geography of Nationalism in Russia and the USSR* (Princeton, N.J.: Princeton University Press, 1994), 22, 25.

7. Valerii Vozgrin, *Istoricheskie sud'by krymskikh tatar* (Moscow: "Mysl'," 1992), 3–4, 13–14, 125–26, 134–35.

8. "Po dannym mandatnoi komissii," *Avdet*, nos. 15/16 (26/27) (11 July 1991): 8; cited also in Andrew Wilson, *The Crimean Tatars: A Situation Report on the Crimean Tatars for International Alert* (London: International Alert, 1994), 13.

9. Boris L. Finogeev, Eskender M. Liumanov, and Galina D. Bodner, *Problemy*

*zaniatosti krymskotatarskogo naseleniia Kryma (analiticheskii obzor)* (Simferopol': "Tavrida," 1994), 8, 14 (table 1.3); *Natsional'nyi sklad naselennia Ukraïny* (Kyiv: Ministerstvo Statystyky Ukraïny, 1991), pt. 1, pp. 4–5, cited in Maria Drohobycky, ed., *Crimea: Dynamics, Challenges, and Prospects* (Lanham, Md.: Rowman & Littlefield, for the American Association for the Advancement of Science, 1995), table 4.1, p. 71; "Vsesoiuznaia perepis' naseleniia 1989 goda," *Vestnik statistiki*, no. 10 (1990): 71.

10. Wilson, *The Crimean Tatars*, app. 4, p. 36.

11. Sh. Qïrïmlï, "Meraba, 1994-ndzhi sene!" *Qïrïm*, no. 1 (1 January 1994): 1; Saulius Girnius, "OSCE Conference on Deported Peoples in Yalta," *OMRI Daily Digest*, no. 186, pt. 2 (25 September 1995).

12. "Tatary Krymskie: Rasselenie i iazyk (po dannym perepisi 1989 goda)," in *Krymskotatarskoe natsional'noe dvizhenie*, ed. M. H. Guboglo and S. M. Chervonnaia (Moscow: TsIMO. Rossiiskaia Akademiia Nauk. Tsentr po Izucheniiu Mezhnatsional'nykh Otnoshenii, Institut Etnologii i Antropologii im. N. N. Miklukho-Maklaia, 1992–96), 1:12–13, 85 (table 2).

13. E. G., *Vospominaniia o Krymie: Sakskiia griazi* (Moscow: Tipografiia Obshchestva Rasprostraneniia Poleznykh Knig, 1881), 141–43. The copy consulted for this reference, from Moscow's Russian State Library, shows on its title page a bold counterstamp with the single word SUPPRESSED (POGASHENO). Both Czarist and Soviet Russian censors refused to pass for publication criticism of Russia for its abuse of Crimea's ethnic minorities and their lands.

14. Finogeev, Liumanov, and Bodner, *Problemy zaniatosti krymskotatarskogo naseleniia Kryma*, 91.

15. Emil' Amit, "Nikto ne zabyt, nichto ne zabyto . . . Vospominaniia," in Svetlana Alieva, comp., *Tak eto bylo Natsional'nye repressii v SSSR 1919–1952 gody. Repressirovannye narody segodnia* (Moscow: Rossiiskii Mezhdunarodnyi Fond Kul'tury "Insan," 1993), 3:93.

16. *Natsional'nyi sostav naseleniia SSSR* (Moscow: Finansy i Statistika, 1990), 88, 98, 122, 126, 132 in page proof of a compilation prepared by Goskomstat.

17. *Chislennost' i sostav naseleniia SSSR: Po dannym vsesoiuznoi perepisi naseleniia 1979 goda* (Moscow: Finansy i Statistika, 1984), 104.

18. Edward Allworth, "The Hunger for New Leadership," in *Central Asia: 130 Years of Russian Dominance: A Historical Overview*, ed. Edward Allworth, Central Asia Book Series (Durham, N.C.: Duke University Press, 1994), 574–76, 590.

19. "Ustav Organizatsii Krymskotatarskogo Natsional'nogo Dvizheniia," *Vatan* (Feodosiia), no. 4 (1991): 3–15, cited in *Krymskotatarskoe natsional'noe dvizhenie*, 2:60–68.

20. "Deklaratsiia o natsional'nom suverinitete krymskotatarskogo naroda," *Avdet*, nos. 15/16 (26/27) (11 July 1991): 1.

21. "Obrashchenie Kurultaia krymskotatarskomu narodu," *Avdet*, nos. 15/16 (26/27) (11 July 1991): 2.
22. S. M. Chervonnaia, "Krymskotatarskoe natsional'noe dvizhenie v kontekste etnopoliticheskoi situatsii v Krymu (avgust 1991–mart 1995 gg.)," in *Krymskotatarskoe natsional'noe dvizhenie*, 3:74.
23. P. Vyshinskii, "Rodina," in *Bol'shaia sovetskaia entsiklopediia* (Moscow: OGIZ RSFSR, Gosudarstvennyi Institut "Sovetskaia Entsiklopediia," 1941), vol. 49, col. 49.
24. N. Dubrovin, ed., *Materialy dlia istorii krymskoi voiny i oborony Sevastopolia: Sbornik, izdavaemyi Komitetom po Ustroistvu Sevastopolskago Muzeiia* (St. Petersburg: V Tipografii Departamenta Udielov, 1871), 1:252; reprinted from the periodicals *Russkii Invalid* (no. 60 [1854]) and *Sievernaia Pchela* (no. 60 [1854]); also cited in Vozgrin, *Istoricheskie sud'by krymskikh tatar*, 323.
25. "Rodina," in *Bol'shaia sovetskaia entsiklopediia* (n.p.: Gosudarstvennoe Nauchnoe Izdatel'stvo, "Bol'shaia Sovietskaia Entsiklopediia," 1955), 36:599. Here, the editors have greatly shortened the entry, by comparison with the one published in the first edition (vol. 49, 1941), which devoted eight and a half long columns (cols. 49–58) to Marxist interpretation and historiography related to *homeland/rodina*.
26. "Rodina," in *Bol'shaia sovetskaia entsiklopediia* (Moscow: Izdatel'stvo "Sovetskaia Entsiklopediia," 1975), 22:162; "Rodina," in *Tolkovyi slovar' russkogo iazyka*, ed. D. N. Ushakov (Moscow: Gosudarstvennoe Izdatel'stvo Inostrannykh i Natsional'nykh Slovarei, 1939), 3:1370; "Otechestvo," in *Bol'shaia sovetskaia entsiklopediia* (1939), vol. 43, col. 569.
27. "Konstitutsiia Krymskoi Respubliki, razrabotannaia Medzhlisom krymskotatarskogo naroda (proekt), dekabr' 1991 g.," in Guboglo and Chervonnaia, eds., *Krymskotatarskoe natsional'noe dvizhenie*, 2:144.
28. "Dokumenty soveshchaniia predstavitelei natsional'no-demokraticheskikh nezavisimykh dvizhenii (7–8 oktiabria 1989 g.)," in ibid., 2:70; regarding the following statistics, see ibid., 1:85.
29. "Deklaratsiia o natsional'nom suvernitete," 1.
30. *The World Almanac and Book of Facts, 1993*, ed. Mark S. Hoffman (New York: World Almanac/Pharos Books, 1992), 742, 753, 761, 768.
31. Urszula Doroszewska, "Crimea: Whose Country?" *Uncaptive Minds* 5, no. 3 (21) (Fall 1992): 47, citing Servir Kerimov, a Mejlis deputy.
32. O. Voroponov, "Sredi krymskikh Tatar (Iz 'Putevykh zametok')," in *Zabveniiu ne podlezhit . . . (Iz istorii krymskotatarskoi gosudarstvennosti i Kryma)*, comp. Nariman Ibadullaev (Kazan: Tatarskoe Knizhnoe Izdatel'stvo, 1992), 165–67.
33. "Rusya Devlet Tarih Arshivi (Rossiiskii gosudarstvennyi istoricheskii arkhiv)," Document Collection, subject 95, folios 28–29; "Rusya Ichishleri Bakanï'nïn Tavrida Gubernatoruna Hükümdar Hazretleri'nin Tavrida Guberniyasïnïn 1897

Yïlïna Ait Durum Raporuna Düshtügü Notlar Hakkïndaki Maktubu," in Central State Archive of the Autonomous Republic of Crimea, file 26, register 1, subject 2815, folio 38; both documents translated and printed in Denis Y. Zolotaryov, "Tavrida Gubernatorlarïnïn yïllïk raporlarïnïn Kïrïm Tarihinin kaynaklarï olarak önemi," *Emel. Iki aylik fikir-kültür dergisi*, no. 213 (March–April 1996): 24–26.

34. A. K. Bochagov, *Milli Firka—natsional'naia kontrrevoliutsiia v Krymu* (Simferopol', 1930), 22, citing 'Abdurrashid Mehdi's appeal to the Duma, *V Gosudarstvennuiu Dumu ot tatarskago naroda krymskago poluostrova* (Qarasubazar, 1907), which is mentioned in Alexandre Bennigsen and Chantal Lemercier-Quelquejay, *La presse et le mouvement national chez les musulmans de Russie avant 1920* (Paris: Mouton, 1964), 140–41.

35. Yuriy O. Meshkov, leader of the RDK (the Republican Movement of Crimea), interviewed in December 1991, cited from *Molod' Ukrainy*, 12 December 1991, 1, in David R. Marples and David F. Duke, "Ukraine, Russia and the Question of Crimea," *Nationalities Papers* 23, no. 2 (1995): 274.

36. Although preoccupied with introspection, Thomas Wolfe's novel *You Can't Go Home Again* (1940) popularized the view and expressed a nostalgia peculiarly appropriate in a country settled largely by people whom economic deprivation, religion, and government oppression had strongly pushed to uproot themselves forever from their homelands.

37. Michael Ignatieff, review of *The Ends of the Earth: A Journey at the Dawn of the 21st Century*, by Robert D. Kaplan, *New York Times Book Review*, 31 March 1996, 7.

38. "Tatary Krymskie," table 2, p. 72; Drohobycky, ed., *Crimea*, table 4.2, p. 72.

39. Neal Ascherson, *Black Sea* (New York: Hill & Wang, 1995); Richard Bernstein, review of *Black Sea*, by Neal Ascherson, *New York Times*, 6 December 1995, C21.

40. "O merakh po ochistke territorii Krymskoi ASSR ot antisovetskikh elementov," in *Prikaz Narodnogo Komissara Vnutrennikh Del, Soiuza SSR i Narodnogo Komissara Gosudarstvennoi Bezopasnosti*, N 00419/00137 (13 April 1944), published in *Avdet*, no. 11 (22) (16 May 1991): 2.

41. *O krymskikh tatarakh*, Postanovlenie Gosudarstvennyi Komitet Oborony (GOKO) no. 5859cc, 11 maia 1944 goda, Moskva, Kreml', Sovershenno Sekretno, Predsedatel' Gosudarstvennogo Komiteta Oborony, I. Stalin. Poslano t.t. Molotov, Beriia, Malenkov, Mikoian, Voznesenskii, Andreev, Kosygin, Gritsenko, Yusupov, Abdurakhmanov, Kobulov (NKVD UzSSR), Chadaev—vse; Shatalin, Gorkin, Pevant At [the preceding two words or names were inserted in unclear hand], Smirnov, Subbotin, Benediktov, Lobanov, Zverev, Kaganovich, Miterev, Liubimov, Kravtsov, Khrulev, Zhukov, Shirokov, Lopukhov—sootvetsvenno [end of document], 6 pp., typewritten, bearing official stamp of GOKO on signature page 6 (cited from a xerographic copy of the original document); "Ukaz Pre-

zidiuma Verkhovnogo Soveta SSSR o grazhdanakh tatarskoi natsional'nosti, prozhivavshikh v Krymu," in *Vedomosti Verkhovnogo Soveta Soiuza Sovetskikh Sotsialisticheskikh Respublik* (8 September 1967), reprinted in *Krymskotatarskoe natsional'noe dvizhenie*, 2:51.

42. See *Materialy samizdata*, RFE/RL, issue no. 18/84 (6 June 1984), *Arkhiv samizdata* no. 5224 1:2; *Krymskotatarskoe natsional'noe dvizhenie*, 2:310–24.

43. Emil' Amit, "Nikto ne zabyt, nichto ne zabyto . . . Vospominaniia," excerpted in Alieva, comp., *Tak eto bylo*, 3:92–93.

44. "Obrashchenie krymskotatarskogo naroda k XXIII s'ezdu KPSS—mart 1966 g.," cited in *Tashkentskii protsess: Sud nad desiat'iu predstaviteliami krymskotatarskogo naroda (1 iiulia–5 avgusta 1969 g.)* (Amsterdam: Fond imeni Gertsena, 1976), 9.

45. *Materialy samizdata*, RFE/RL, issue no. 20/85 (10 June 1985), *Arkhiv samizdata* no. 5453; "The Sixth Trial"—no. 25050.

46. "Obrashchenie Kurultaia krymskotatarskogo naroda," 1.

47. E. Khairullaeva, "My vyzhili v etom adu," *Avdet*, no. 2 (93) (27 January 1994): 3.

48. Osman Amit, "Vetanim menim," in *Qïrïmtatar edebiyati: 7-indji sïnïf ichyun derslik-khrestomatiia*, comp. A. Veluilaeva and L. Alieva (Aqmesjit: Qïrïm Devlet Oquv-Pedagogik Neshriyati, 1993), 87; translated by Edward Allworth with Seyit Ahmet Kirimca.

49. "Aqsaqal yazïdjïmïz vatangha qayttï," *Qïrïm*, no. 30 (30 July 1994): 1; "Shamil' Alyadin," in *Qirimtatar edebiyati*, 122–33.

50. Sh. Buyuk-Asli, "Muqaddes topraqqa ziyaret," *Dostluq*, no. 23 (30 May 1992): 4.

51. [Erkin Ä'zäm?] "Pak yuräklär niyät qilsä . . . Ozbekistan khälq shairi Erkin Wahidaw bilän suhbät," *Täfäkkur*, no. 2 (1995): 9.

## 14

## Politics in and around Crimea: A Difficult Homecoming

ANDREW WILSON

Return: The Revival of the Qurultay and the Politics of
National Homeland, 1989–91

*The Late Soviet Period*

The campaign by Crimean Tatars first to restore their good name and then to reclaim and return to their homeland has been going on ever since 1956, when Khrushchev's momentous "secret speech" to the Twentieth Congress of the Communist Party of the Soviet Union (CPSU) rehabilitated Chechens, Kalmyks, and other deported peoples and authorized their organized return home but failed even to mention Tatars.[1] Without significant rehabilitation, the outcast Tatars had little to lose from a more or less permanent campaign of mass protest once political conditions were liberalized in the late 1950s and early 1960s. Nor did the 1967 decree that absolved them from accusations of wartime collaboration with the Germans and granted them the right to "reside in every territory of the Soviet Union" do much to deter their campaign. It was not widely publicized, and the authorities claimed that, as "citizens of the Tatar nationality formerly resident in Crimea" had "settled in the Uzbek and other Union republics," there was therefore no need for them to return to Crimea.[2] Although thousands attempted to make the journey in 1967–68, nearly all were turned back.

It was only the authorities' increasing resort to coercion that caused the movement to subside in the late 1970s (see chaps. 9 and 11 in this volume). However, the long-standing protest campaign at least allowed Crimean Tatars to develop a well-defined agenda and habits of organization that would serve them well in later years. It was therefore no surprise that they were one of the first groups to take advantage of renewed liberalization under perestroika. Once again, Tatars were at the forefront of dissent,

Table 14.1  The Number of Crimean Tatars in Crimea, 1979–94

| | | | |
|---|---|---|---|
| 1979 (Soviet census) | 5,400 | July 1991 | 132,000 |
| Spring 1988 | 17,500 | August 1991 | 142,200 |
| 1989 (Soviet census) | 38,000 | May 1993 | 250,000 |
| May 1990 | 83,000 | September 1993 | 257,000[a] |
| January 1991 | 100,000 | 1994 | 260,000 |

*Sources:* Adapted from Andrew Wilson, *The Crimean Tatars* (London: International Alert, 1994), 37; Mikhail Guboglo and Svetlana Chervonnaia, eds., *Krymskotatarskoe natsional'noe dvizhenie*, 3 vols. (Moscow: Tsentr po izucheniiu mezhnatsional'nykh otnoshenii, 1992–96), 1:153, 2:254; and Svetlana Chervonnaia, "Kryms'kotatars'kyi natsional'nyi rukh i suchasna sytuatsiia v Respublitsi Krym (do chervnia 1993 r.)," in *Etnichni menshyny Skhidnoï ta Tsentral'noï Yevropy: Komparatyvnyi analiz stanovyshcha ta perspektyv rozvytku*, ed. Volodymyr Yevtukh and Arnol'd Zuppan (Kyiv: INTEL, 1994), 103–4.

[a]Tatar leaders claimed that 227,000 Crimean Tatars were officially registered on the peninsula in late 1993 and that a further 30,000 were living there unofficially. The rest of the population consisted of 626,000 Ukrayinans, 1,461,000 Russians, and 119,000 others. The Ukrayinan population was heavily Russified; 81.4 percent of the non-Tatar population was Russophone. (F. D. Zastavnyi, *Heohrafiia Ukraïny* [L'viv: Svit, 1994], 413; Volodymyr Tevtoukh, "The Dynamics of Interethnic Relations in Crimea," in *Crimea: Dynamics, Challenges, Prospects*, ed. Maria Drohobycky [Lanham, Md.: American Association for the Advancement of Science/Rowman & Littlefield, 1995], 69–85.) See also table 1.1, where somewhat different figures emerge from other sources for 1993.

constantly testing the limits of permissible protest after breaking the Soviet taboo on public demonstrations in Moscow in June 1987.

The response of the authorities was more defensive than in the 1960s and 1970s but always remained one step behind the Tatars' demands. Although the new Soviet leadership was undoubtedly embarrassed by what had been done to Tatars in 1944, it could not conceive of any way of settling their grievances without alienating the Slavic population in Crimea. Gorbachev set up a commission under Andrei Gromyko to study the Tatars' problem, but, although his report in June 1988 recommended removing "unjustified obstacles to changes of residence" by Tatars (i.e., returning to Crimea), it did nothing to meet any of their key political demands. It failed to provide an unequivocal condemnation of the 1944 deportation and made no mention of restoring the designation *Crimean Tatar*. Nor did it take a position on the Tatars' demand for the revival of some form of national-territorial autonomy along the lines of the 1921–45 Crimean Autonomous Soviet Socialist Republic (CASSR) (see below).

The path-breaking semidemocratic elections to the Soviet Congress of People's Deputies in March 1989 produced a certain change of mood. In November 1989, the new Soviet parliament finally decided formally to condemn the deportation, but by then Tatars were increasingly taking matters into their own hands as the declining powers of the Soviet state opened the floodgates to mass return to Crimea. Table 14.1 records how the number of new arrivals peaked during 1990–92, before rapidly rising travel costs slowed the flow to a trickle after 1993. The frontispiece map and table 1.1 show how the returnees (approximately 260,000 in all) were concentrated in their traditional homelands on the northern side of the Crimean mountains (Bakhchesaray, Aqmesjit [Simferopol'], Qarasuvbazar [Belogorsk], and Islam-Terek [Kirovskoe] *raion*, formerly "Old Crimea").[3] In July 1991, a decree of the Soviet Council of Ministers finally proposed limited material assistance to help the Tatars' organized return, but by then few Tatars had any confidence in Soviet institutions to deliver the goods.

### *The Establishment of Crimean Tatar Parties*

The failure to obtain real redress of grievance from the Soviet authorities in the late 1980s led Crimean Tatars to create their own organizations and develop their own political strategies. The original parent organization, the National Movement of Crimean Tatars (in Russian, Natsional'noe Dvizhenie Krymskikh Tatar, or NDKT), first appeared in April 1987, although its leaders had initially worked together during the protest campaigns of the 1960s.[4] The NDKT was therefore to an extent old-fashioned in its approach, and its faith in policies of peaceful protest and loyal petition to the authorities soon seemed outmoded. More radical Tatars therefore founded the breakaway Organization of the Crimean Tatar National Movement (in Russian, Organizatsiia Krymskotatarskogo Natsional'nogo Dvizheniia, or OKND) in May 1989.[5]

### The NDKT

After 1989, the NDKT continued to exist and grew increasingly hostile to the OKND. Its first leader, the veteran dissident Yurii Osmanov, was murdered in November 1993; he was succeeded by Vasvi Abduraimov, a former official in the Crimean ministry of education. The NDKT was a much looser organization than the OKND and could not be considered a political party as such, but it expressed a consistent political philosophy, the basis for which was its opposition to any "attempt to divide the people of Crimea into two antagonistic, irreconcilable camps." "In Crimea," argued Abduraimov, "the Slavo-Turks (Crimean Tatars, Russians, and Ukrayinans) have a real possibility to create and perfect a micro-model for a Slavo-Turkic 'superunion'"[6] and by the example of their cooperation help prevent the historical fault line of confrontation between the Orthodox and Islamic worlds reemerging in Crimea. In fact, Abduraimov liked to quote the views of "Eurasianists" such as Nikolai Trubetskoi and Lev Gumilev to argue that cooperation between Slavs and Turks had laid the basis for Russia's unique culture and the foundations of its geopolitical strength.[7] The NDKT therefore attacked the "anti-Slavic and pan-Turkic policy" of the OKND[8] and even after 1991 tended to regret the disappearance of the Soviet Union as an overarching institution preventing open confrontation between Slavs and Tatars, calling for a "Eurasian union" to take its place.[9] Abduraimov even talked of the possible future "creation of a single Slavo-Turkic ethnos . . . on the territory of the former Soviet Union."[10]

Just before the collapse of the Soviet Union, the NDKT prepared a detailed constitutional blueprint for Crimea. Its preferred model was a restored Crimean ASSR, albeit one idealized as embodying "the national statehood of the Crimean Tatar people" in which their rights would not be "held hostage to the artificial (criminal) diminution of the Crimean Tatar people on their national territory" but protected by the oversight of then all-Soviet institutions.[11] The NDKT was therefore never as tame and conformist an organization as its opponents liked to suggest, although it continued to stress the importance of working with existing authorities and rejecting radical methods.

In the early 1990s the Crimean authorities attempted to bolster support for the NDKT by recognizing it ahead of the politically more awkward OKND.[12] However, the NDKT's poor showing in the 1994 Crimean elections (see below) destroyed the pretense that the Crimean Tatar community was represented by a plurality of equally legitimate voices, and the organization slipped from center stage.

## The OKND

The OKND was undoubtedly the stronger of the two organizations. Whereas the NDKT could be dismissed as something of a one-man band, the OKND had around six hundred members and, after its founding congress in August 1991, most of the accoutrements of a normal political party. In essence, the OKND was a radical nationalist party, which, although strictly nonviolent, preferred a more direct approach to the cautious tactics of the NDKT. Its guiding principle was "the return of [all] the Crimean Tatar people to their historic homeland and the restoration [*vosstanovlenie*] of their national statehood." The party's blueprint for a future Crimean state promised to "guarantee the observance of the rights and freedoms of all individuals, regardless of their race, nationality, political opinions, and religion," but at the same time argued that "without ensuring the freedom and rights of the nation it is impossible to ensure the freedom and rights of the individual." Therefore, although the OKND supported a secular and multiethnic state, it would be one in which "the unity and uninterrupted development of the national culture" and language of Crimean Tatars would be given priority. The OKND accepted that, "on the basis of an agreement with" Kyiv, the future Crimean state "would be a part of Ukrayina,"[13] but it also sought to develop links with Turkiye and other Black Sea states, and many of its members expressed support for the Chechen side in the war with Russia.[14]

The centerpiece of the OKND's political strategy was the election of a Crimean Tatar assembly (Qurultay) in June 1991 (see below). Thereafter, the two worked in parallel, with the OKND continuing to operate as a political party and the Qurultay as the would-be sovereign assembly of the Crimean Tatar people. Seventeen of thirty-three members of the Mejlis (plenipotentiary committee) elected by the 1991 Qurultay belonged to the OKND,[15] and the first two leaders of the OKND, Mustafa Jemiloglu (1989–91) and Refat Chubarov (1991–93), were elected head and deputy head of the Mejlis in 1991 (the leader of the OKND since 1993 has been Rejep Khairedinov). In fact, some OKND members went so far as to argue that it was no longer necessary to maintain the party as a separate organization after 1991 and that it should be dissolved into the Qurultay.[16] However, a basic division of functions justified their continued separate existence. Whereas the Qurultay and Mejlis were deliberative bodies that were ultimately answerable to an electorate (see figs. 14.1 and 14.2), the OKND saw itself as a radical ginger group and the conscience of the Mejlis, acting as guardian of the key principles decided on in 1991. Nevertheless, after the departure of Chubarov as leader in 1993,

Figure 14.1. Nine of the thirty-three member Crimean Tatar Mejlis (beneath a portrait of Numan Chelebi Jihan, first president, Crimean National Government, 1917–18), during a July 1993 session of the Second Qurultay (*left to right*): Server Omerof, Julvern Ablamitov, President Mustafa Jemiloglu, Vice President Refat Chubarov, Refat Appazov, Remzi Ablaev, Refat Kurtiyev, Server Kerimov, and Nadir Bekirov. Omerof, Appazov, and Kurtiyev did not serve in the next Mejlis, starting June 1996. Photo courtesy of Vice President Chubarov, and Abdurrahim Demirayak.

the party lost much of its original dynamism and ability to shape the political agenda.

### The Qurultay

The defining moment in modern Crimean Tatar politics came in June 1991, when the Second Qurultay, or national assembly of the Crimean Tatar people, convened in the Crimean capital of Aqmesjit (Simferopol') (the assembly was called the *Second* Qurultay in order to emphasize continuity with the body first established in December 1917). As stated above, the organization of the assembly was entirely the work of the OKND, which had begun laying plans as early as March 1990. The NDKT in contrast attacked

Figure 14.2. Five leading members of the Crimean Tatar Mejlis on stage in June 1996 during the Third Qurultay (*front, left to right*): Server Kerimov, Vice President Refat Chubarov, President Mustafa Jemiloglu, *Avdet* editor Lilia Budzhurova, and Lenur Arifov. Photo courtesy of Abdurrahim Demirayak.

"the formation of 'proto-state' forms such as the 'Qurultay-Mejlis'" as a form of self-isolation from mainstream political life in the peninsula that could only help perpetuate the "1944 policy of Crimea without Crimean Tatars" and, in any case, considered such action as equivalent to "the inmates of a prison camp proclaiming 'self-rule.'"[17]

The Qurultay claimed to represent almost all the 272,000 Crimean Tatars recorded by the 1989 Soviet census as resident in the Soviet Union, both in Crimea and in Russia and Central Asia (at the time, only 130,000 Tatars had returned to the peninsula).[18] Although the organizers claimed that the true number of their compatriots was at least twice as high, it was decided to work with the official Soviet figure "in order to avoid future speculation from the authorities about the legitimacy of the Qurultay."[19] The 262 delegates therefore supposedly each represented one thousand Crimean Tatars, including those too young to vote, and were elected in two stages between October 1990 and May 1991. First, Crimean Tatars gathered in groups of thirty in open meetings throughout the Soviet Union to choose "electors,"[20] who then traveled in blocks of thirty-three to thirty-four to regional conferences, where delegates to the Qurultay proper were elected by secret ballot. The largest number of delegates was elected in Crimea (127); nine were from elsewhere in Ukrayina, eighty-eight from Uzbekistan, twelve from other Central Asia republics, and sixteen from the Russian Soviet Federative Socialist Republic (RSFSR). Most were men (90 percent) of elderly middle age, veterans of the 1960s protest movement. A plurality were actually born in Central Asia (116).[21]

The organizers of the Qurultay claimed that a total of 86,360 Crimean Tatars voted in Crimea and that a similar number voted in Russia and Central Asia,[22] although the author has no independent information with which to assess this claim. Nevertheless, the Qurultay was able to assert that the electoral process gave the assembly "the right to elect the sole legitimate representative body of the Crimean Tatar people,"[23] that is, the thirty-three-strong Mejlis, which would act on behalf of the Qurultay between sessions. Mustafa Jemiloglu was elected head and Refat Chubarov his deputy. By mid-1993, some three hundred "mini-Mejlises" had been set up at the local level in Crimea and some four hundred by 1996.[24]

The Qurultay adopted a national flag, incorporating the family emblem of the Giray dynasty, rulers of Crimea before 1783, and a national hymn, *My Pledge [Ant etkenmen]* (see chap. 4), and passed the "Declaration of National Sovereignty of the Crimean Tatar People" (see the full translation in chap. 16), which soon acquired the status of a founding document and statement of fundamental principle. The Declaration was based on the absolutist theories of national self-determination favored by the OKND, its two key statements being the claims that "Crimea is the national territory of the Crimean Tatar people, on which they alone possess the right to self-determination," and that "the political, economic, spiritual, and cultural rebirth of the Crimean Tatar people is possible only in their own sovereign national state." Moreover, the Declaration asserted that all "the land and natural resources of Crimea, including its spa and recreational potential, is the basis of the national wealth of the Crimean Tatar people," albeit subject to the qualification that it was also "a source of well-being for all the inhabitants of Crimea." The Declaration concluded by raising the possibility that, "in the event of [any attempt] by state agencies or any other source to resist the aims proclaimed by the Qurultay and the present Declaration, the Qurultay will entrust the Mejlis with securing recognition of the Crimean Tatars' status as a people engaged in a struggle for national liberation and act in accordance with this status"—a not particularly veiled threat to use direct action in support of their aims.[25]

The general thrust of the Declaration was therefore uncompromising and the claim to national statehood unqualified, despite appearing in the general context of soothing promises that "relations between Crimean Tatars and national and ethnic groups living in Crimea must be organized on the basis of mutual respect and the recognition of human and civil rights" and the declaration by Tatars to their new neighbors that they had "no intention to inflict any harm or encroach on your property, spiritual, cultural, religious, political, and other rights. We will respect the national sentiments and human dignity of all people" in Crimea.[26] The Qurultay repeatedly referred to Crimea as "the [sole] historical homeland [*rodina*]" of the Crimean Tatar people, to which they were tied by history and the rights of an indigenous (*korennoe*) people. Clearly, however, an absolute claim to sovereignty based on principles of original settlement and the claim to be the sole indigenous people on the peninsula would be difficult to implement in a situation where Crimean Tatars still made up only 5–6 percent of the local population.

### The Mejlis's Constitutional Project

However, from the very beginning, there was an inherent tension between the absolutist doctrine of national self-determination that inspired the Declaration of Sovereignty and the practical demands of everyday politics. Although the OKND repeatedly insisted that the policies of the Mejlis should be kept "as close as possible to the principles of the declaration of sovereignty,"[27] the latter's leaders were in practice prepared to be flexible and act in a spirit of consociational compromise (Jemiloglu stayed closer to the OKND, while Refat Chubarov was more of a pragmatist). The contrast was reflected in a second key text, the draft constitution of the Crimean Republic drawn up by the Mejlis in December 1991.

In contrast to the declaration, the draft constitution used a carefully worded formula to define sovereign power in a future Crimean state as resting with "the people of Crimea—Crimean Tatars, Qrymchaq and Qaraïm, who make up the indigenous population of the republic, and citizens of other nationalities, for whom by virtue of historical circumstances Crimea has become their homeland" (the last phrase was significant for avoiding any reference to "occupation" or to the "settler population"). In order to balance the interests of the two groups, it was proposed to introduce a system of "dual power." At a local level, representation would work through two parallel networks: local councils for the general population and in "areas of compact settlement of the indigenous population corresponding [mini-]Mejlises." As the councils and Mejlises would overlap territorially (only in isolated areas were Tatars a majority community; otherwise, they tended to settle on the outskirts of the main urban areas), an Austro-Marxist system of national-personal autonomy seemed to be envisaged, whereby a local Mejlis would cater for all the "social, economic, cultural, national, and ecological" needs of Tatars within its jurisdiction (and presumably also for the Qrymchaq and Qaraïm)—education in particular—and the councils would serve the general population in a similar fashion.[28]

The Mejlis proposed that this parallel or consociational system would also operate at a national level. The Crimean parliament would have two chambers of equal powers elected simultaneously (changes to the constitution would have to be by referendum or by "a two-thirds majority in both houses"). A Council of People's Representatives of one hundred deputies would be elected by the general Crimean electorate from territorial constituencies, and a Mejlis of fifty would be elected by the Qurultay to serve as the upper house.[29] A Crimean president would also be introduced, but in order to be elected he or she would need the support of "more than half the electors taking part in the voting, including more than half the voters representing the indigenous population of the republic" (or "more than one-third" in any second round).[30] In effect, therefore, Crimean Tatars would have a veto over who was elected. Moreover, "in order to better express the will of the indigenous population," the power of the president would be balanced by a vice-president elected by the Qurultay (there was no indication of any division of functions between the two posts).[31]

Taken together, these measures amounted to an essentially pragmatic power-sharing agenda, although, when combined with the absolutist principles laid out in the Declaration of Sovereignty, they tended to lead the Mejlis to demand veto powers in any future constitutional arrangement that it would be difficult for the majority population to accept. None of the proposed changes was implemented. Nevertheless, they provided a useful guide to the kind of ideal type of system that Crimean Tatars wanted to see develop, against which future changes could be judged (it is important to bear in mind that the constitutional arrangements worked out in 1994 fell considerably short of the Tatars' original demands—see below).

## The Wrong Republic: Independent Ukrayina and Autonomous Crimea, 1991–93

### The 1991 Referendum

By the time the Qurultay assembled in June 1991, however, Tatars had been beaten to the punch with their plans for a future Crimean republic. The accelerating pace of Crimean Tatar return and the growing influence of the Ukrayinan nationalist movement in Kyiv prompted the Crimean leadership to rush forward with their own plans to hold a referendum on the peninsula's status. Rather than create an ethnic Tatar republic, however, the Communist-dominated Crimean leadership proposed to restore the interwar Crimean ASSR.

As noted above, ironically, many Crimean Tatars looked back on the period of the original Crimean ASSR as an era of relative freedom and Tatar preeminence, but only the NDKT could now overlook the preference of the Crimean Communist Party for the very same constitutional model. In historical fact, the Crimean ASSR was not an ethnic republic as such. As in other Soviet republics, a "nativization" policy was adopted in the 1920s, but the Crimean ASSR was always a "Crimean," rather than a "Crimean Tatar," republic. Under the leadership of Veli Ibrahimov from 1923–28, a positive discrimination policy built up Tatar representation to a position of rough equality with local Russians,[32] but no further (Crimean Tatars made up only 25.1 percent of the local population in 1926 and 19.4 percent in 1939, Russians accounted for 49.6 percent of the population in 1939, and Ukrayinans 13.7 percent).[33] Moreover, nativization policies were often merely declarative. Slavs continued to predominate in the main urban centers, and Crimean Tatars lost ground substantially in the 1930s. Nevertheless, Tatars would demand the return of a similar quota system in the mid-1990s (see below).[34]

Without the element of positive discrimination, the restoration of a Crimean rather than a Crimean Tatar ASSR in the circumstances of early

1991 would clearly not favor Tatars. At the time, only 100,000 had returned to the peninsula; Tatars therefore made up only 4 percent of the total local population (see table 14.1).[35] Only one Tatar (Iksander Memetov, a local businessman close to the centrist establishment party PEVK)[36] had been elected to the Crimean council in the 1990 elections, only sixty Tatars were to be found among the twelve thousand employees of the Crimean interior ministry, and none at all were in the local security services.[37] The OKND therefore urged a boycott of the poll organized by the Crimean authorities in January 1991, which asked the question, "Are you in favor of the recreation of the Crimean Autonomous Soviet Socialist Republic as a subject of the Soviet Union and a party to [Gorbachev's proposed] Union Treaty?"[38] Nevertheless, turnout across Crimea was an impressive 81 percent, of which 93 percent voted in favor.[39] When the decision was swiftly endorsed by the Ukrayinan Supreme Council, Tatars found themselves having to deal with a distinctly unfriendly regime in Crimea as well as with the Soviet and Ukrayinan authorities.

### Geopolitics: Russia, Ukrayina, or Turkiye?

The problem was thrown into unexpectedly sharp focus by the sudden disappearance of the Soviet Union and the emergence of Ukrayina as an independent state with legal sovereignty over Crimea. At first glance, Tatars had little cause for celebration. Unlike either the Soviet Union or the Russian Federation, Ukrayina was not a federal state and therefore arguably offered fewer possibilities for accommodating Tatar demands. Moreover, although the Ukrayinan nationalist movement had been a keen supporter of the Crimean Tatar cause before 1991,[40] the national Communists who dominated the leadership of the new Ukrayinan state had shown no interest whatsoever in the Tatars' plight. Their instant ratification of the January 1991 poll demonstrated that their primary concern was containing the growth of the Russian separatist movement on the peninsula. Kyiv therefore continued to allow the Crimean authorities a virtual free hand in relations with Crimean Tatars.

Nevertheless, Crimean Tatars were compelled to make a choice of sorts. As Refat Chubarov later argued, "any idea of an independent Crimea in whatever form, whether as a Crimean Tatar state . . . or [simply] independent, is absurd. . . . Given the strength of geopolitical constraints in the region, Crimea must be in the orbit of one of the great states of the area—whether that is Ukrayina, Russia, or Turkiye."[41] In practice, after 1991 the choice narrowed to one—Ukrayina.

Siding with Russia would have meant an inconceivable alliance with the local separatist movement. Moreover, it was extremely unlikely that nationalists in the Russian Duma would allow the Russian government to antagonize the Russophile movement in Crimea by doing anything more than express general sympathy for the Tatars' predicament.[42] Finally, most Tatars still regarded Russia de facto as the party responsible for the 1944 deportation.

A pan-Turkic orientation was simply not practical geopolitics and would have played into the hands of the local Russophile propaganda machine and its focus on the chimerical "Islamic threat." Nevertheless, most leaders of the Qurultay continued to view Turkiye as a natural ally.[43] Negotiations with Turkish president Suleyman Demirel in May 1994 and May 1996 produced promises of assistance in building a thousand homes in Crimea, along with the necessary "sociocultural infrastructure." The leaders of the Qurultay were also keen to develop links with the estimated two to five million Turkish citizens of Crimean Tatar descent (see chap. 15), who were able to provide substantial practical assistance, if not a strong lobbying presence in Ankara.[44] Tatars also demonstrated a certain sympathy for the Chechen cause after the war with Russia began in December 1994, although reports that they had sent anything more than humanitarian aid remained unsubstantiated.[45]

Acceptance of Crimea's status within an independent Ukrayina was therefore the only feasible short-term option. In November 1991, on the eve of the crucial referendum on Ukrayinan independence, a special session of delegates to the Qurultay declared its "support for Ukrayina's efforts to become an independent democratic state" and recommended that all Crimean Tatars vote yes in recognition of the fact that "Ukrayina and Crimea have been and will continue to be historical neighbors [*sic*]." Tatars were also urged "to vote for a candidate from the democratic block [i.e., one of the three nationalist candidates who unsuccessfully opposed Leonid Kravchuk] in the simultaneous presidential election."[46]

Only a bare majority of Crimean voters voted yes in the referendum, 54.2 percent of a turnout of 67.5 percent, compared to 90.3 percent of a turnout of 84.2 percent in Ukrayina as a whole (Crimea was the only region in

Ukrayina that came anywhere near to voting no). In a calculated appeal to the authorities in Kyiv, the Mejlis therefore claimed that "it was only the vote of Crimean Tatars . . . that produced a majority in Crimea for the supporters of Ukrayinan independence."[47] The Mejlis's argument was plausible. Around 140,000 Crimean Tatars had returned to the peninsula by late 1991 (although not all were registered voters), and they could just have tipped the balance between the 561,500 Crimeans who backed Ukrayinan independence and the 437,500 who were against.[48]

The Qurultay therefore hoped that Ukrayinan independence would usher in a new era in relations with Kyiv. Their preferred model for future relations was set out in an appeal submitted to the Ukrayinan parliament and the new president, Kravchuk, that envisaged a rolling six-stage program leading up to the year 2000:

– *Stage 1:* First was "the study of the history of the [Crimean Tatar] problem in its legal, political, historical, ethnographic, and culturological aspects" and meetings and initial negotiations with "representative bodies of the Crimean Tatar people," in other words, the Mejlis.
– *Stage 2:* The Ukrayinan parliament was "to pass an act granting de jure recognition of the Mejlis as the sole higher plenipotentiary representative body of the Crimean Tatar people."
– *Stage 3:* A program of "technical-economic" development for Crimea would be begun.
– *Stage 4:* The Ukrayinan parliament was to pass a law "on the restoration [*vosstanovlenie*] of the rights of the Crimean Tatar people (nation) in Ukrayina," along with corresponding amendments to the Ukrayinan constitution; a bicameral Crimean council would be introduced with the Mejlis "as the basis for the upper house" (decisions would be taken "by the agreement of both houses"); "the jurisdiction of Ukrayina over Crimea in international law" would be confirmed simultaneously with "the restoration of the statehood of the Crimean Tatar people in the form of national-territorial autonomy on the territory of Crimea as a part of Ukrayina" (it was unclear whether such statehood had to be recognized in some institutional form).
– *Stage 5:* Then came "the reorganization of state power in Crimea," along with the "reform of the system of local government in the Republic of Crimea."
– *Stage 6:* Finally would come "the realization of a socioeconomic and cultural program" over three to five years; "a program of organized repatriation" of those Crimean Tatars remaining in Central Asia and elsewhere; the "social defense [of

Tatars] during the period of transition to a market economy and a guarantee of [their] privatization rights"; and "the creation of the necessary national-cultural infrastructure" for Crimean Tatars (schools in particular). The Crimean Tatars would then enjoy the same rights as "existing Ukrayinan citizens."[49]

However, at this stage, the Qurultay was to be disappointed.[50] Its overtures to Kyiv were rebuffed, with President Kravchuk in particular remaining lukewarm (as with the Mejlis's model constitution, however, the program nevertheless provides a useful outline of how Tatars would ideally like the future to develop, and most of its key elements have been raised in subsequent negotiations with Kyiv). Only once, in the aftermath of Crimea's temporary declaration of independence in May 1992, did Kyiv contemplate establishing links with the Mejlis, but the feelers tentatively put out were withdrawn as soon as the crisis subsided.[51] Kravchuk's priority was to provide more or less uncritical support for the relatively moderate chairman of the Crimean council, Mykola Bagrov, in order to bolster his position against the separatist opposition (Yurii Meshkov's Republican Movement of Crimea).[52] Therefore, if only for tactical reasons, Kyiv was prepared to support the line of the Crimean authorities that the claim by the Qurultay/Mejlis to "parallel sovereignty" in Crimea ruled it out as an acceptable negotiating partner.[53] It was only the crisis provoked by Meshkov's decisive victory over Bagrov in the January 1994 presidential election in Crimea that finally forced Kyiv to change its mind (see below).

There were also several practical problems between the Mejlis and Kyiv. In 1992, the Mejlis encouraged all Crimean Tatars to apply for citizenship in the new Ukrayinan state.[54] However, although the Ukrayinan citizenship law of November 1991 took the apparently generous step of automatically granting citizenship to all those then resident on Ukrayinan territory (in contrast to Latvia and Estonia, there was no attempt to exclude Russian immigrants), the law was not so generous to Crimean Tatars, only around 140,000 of whom had returned by August 1991 (see table 14.1). According to the 1991 law, those who arrived later than 1 November 1991 had to wait five years before becoming eligible for citizenship. Tatar leaders therefore appealed to the Ukrayinan authorities to bypass this process, but procedures remained slow and cumbersome, and, in late 1995, some seventy thousand later arrivals still lacked Ukrayinan citizenship. Under Ukrayinan law, they were therefore denied the right to vote and access to most welfare benefits and had no right to participate in the privatization program.[55]

Two other sore points were military service and the mechanics of Tatar resettlement. The first was partially settled after the Mejlis declared in January 1992 that Crimean Tatars should refuse to take the oath of loyalty in the new Ukrayinan army, when most Tatars were offered the right to confine their period of service to Crimea.[56] Resettlement, on the other hand, was a more intractable issue. As the Crimean authorities were extremely reluctant to allow Tatars to make claims on the property they had lost in 1944, they were compelled to build elsewhere (70 percent of Tatars lived in new rural settlements). Moreover, Tatars were largely prevented from settling in the southern coastal region. However, although Kyiv provided the only significant sums to aid new building and the provision of utilities and services (see below), the Mejlis was aggrieved that the money passed to the Crimean authorities. Tatar settlements were frequently attacked by local thugs, while the authorities turned a blind eye.[57]

Therefore, although circumstances forced the leadership of the Mejlis to remain loyal to Ukrayina, many radicals, particularly in the OKND, grew increasingly frustrated with Kyiv's position. According to Ilmy Umerov, head of the Bakhchesaray Mejlis, speaking at the 1993 Qurultay, for example, "in voting for the independence of Ukrayina on 1 December [1991], we voted for the rebirth of the Ukrayinan people in their own homeland. But it seems we voted for new oppressors, for a new tyranny over the Crimean Tatar people. . . . Ukrayina today is in both form and content in practice a colonial state."[58] Tatar radicals who sought to establish a separate radical party in 1993 (named after the main Crimean Tatar party in 1918–20, the Milli Firqa—see below) declared that "the attitude of Milli Firqa toward the Ukrayinan state depends on the attitude of the Ukrayinan state toward the problem of restoring Crimean Tatar rights. As long as [Ukrayina] fails to recognize and create the conditions for the free self-determination of the Crimean Tatar nation, Milli Firqa will consider it to be a foreign colonial state."[59] The Mejlis was able to prevent too many Tatars from breaking ranks, but the strain was increasingly evident so long as Kyiv continued to reject the Mejlis's overtures.

*Local Politics: No Welcome Home*

Strains within the Tatar movement were also produced by the extremely tense relations between the Qurultay/Mejlis and the local Crimean authorities throughout the period 1991–93. The possibility of Crimea's taking forcible measures against Tatars first arose during the July 1991 Qurultay. Under its last leader, Leonid Grach, the local Communist Party circulated instructions on means of counteracting its influence and spreading dissension within its ranks, and the Crimean council passed a resolution condemning the "illegality" and "nationalist character" of the Qurultay. The council also declared that "the proclamation of Crimea as the national territory of the Crimean Tatar people, with the symbols and attributes of statehood, together with exclusive property rights over land and natural resources, and also the attempt to create parallel structures of power and illegal administration, is in contradiction to the constitution of the Ukrayinan SSR and Soviet and [all] existing law." Therefore, the Qurultay "could not represent the Crimean Tatar people in relations with state agencies."[60] During the attempted coup in Moscow in August 1991, the Crimean authorities briefly contemplated following up the decree with measures to suppress all the "structures formed by the Qurultay."[61]

Nor did relations improve much after the ban on the Communist Party in August 1991. Mykola Bagrov's tentative attempts at a rapprochement with the Tatars were blocked by a strong opposition movement consisting of a revived Communist Party of Crimea (KPK) and Yurii Meshkov's republican movement (later the Republican Party of Crimea).[62] In October 1992, during a series of violent demonstrations outside the Crimean council, the Crimean authorities instructed the militia "to take measures to put a stop to the anticonstitutional activity of the Mejlis and OKND and also [to seek] legal compensation for any material losses" caused by Tatar demonstrators[63] and contemplated an outright ban on the two bodies and a roundup of Tatar leaders. It seems that they were dissuaded by Kravchuk, but at the price of Kyiv's continuing to keep the Mejlis at arm's length.

### The Growth of Crimean Tatar Radicalism

Growing frustration with the authorities in both Kyiv and Aqmesjit (Simferopol') therefore tended to fuel the growth of a new radical fringe movement among Crimean Tatars. Although the leaders of the Mejlis have had considerable success in upholding their traditions of nonviolent protest, Crimean Tatars have periodically resorted to direct action in defense of their rights, usually, it must be said, in response to threats from other quarters. In October 1992, a public demonstration spilled over into an attempt to sack the Crimean council; railway lines were blocked in October 1993 in protests over the proposed election law (see below); and large-scale confrontations with militia erupted in June 1995 after Tatar traders organized rallies to denounce alleged collusion between local authorities and racketeers. Moreover, claims that Crimean Tatar radicals have considered establishing (or have already established) *Asker* (soldier) self-defense units have periodically appeared in the press.[64] Although Refat Chubarov carefully denied that the Qurultay/Mejlis had anything to do with such plans,[65] fears grew through 1993–96 that radical activists might be taking the task on themselves.

Radicals within the Qurultay and the OKND have several times considered establishing a separate party. A draft program for a revived Milli Firqa (National Party) appeared in September 1993 under the sponsorship of Ilmy Umerov, which, using language rather more colorful than that of the Mejlis, described the primary tasks of the would-be party as "defending Crimean Tatars from the threat of annihilation, coercion, and assimilation and liquidating the colonial oppression of [all] foreign states against Crimea and Crimean Tatars." Nevertheless, its broad political aim, "the full, all-around development of national self-rule as a step toward the establishment of a sovereign national state," was no different from that of the Qurultay, as defined by the 1991 Declaration of Sovereignty. However, Milli Firqa differed markedly in its attitude toward Ukrayina (see above) and clearly envisaged a future Crimean republic as a more narrowly ethnic state. The draft program declared that "the only state language [in Crimea] will be Crimean Tatar" and promised that "preferential citizenship rights will belong to those who lived in Crimea before 1944 and their descendants."[66]

However, on all occasions to date, the Mejlis has proved able to maintain formal unity within the Crimean Tatar movement (the NDKT excepted), a considerable achievement in itself, especially in comparison to the fissiparous tendencies common to party politics in most post-Communist states. The would-be Milli Firqa failed to make the break in 1993–95 and faded away after Umerov accepted the number 4 position on the Qurultay list for the Crimean elections (see below) and was duly elected. An organizing committee for an *Adalet* (Justice) "Crimean Tatar nationalist party" appeared in 1995 under Mejlis member Server Kerimov, as did a shadowy

Islamic Party of Crimea, but once again both preferred to operate as informal groups within the Mejlis.[67]

## The 1994 Elections: Quota and Participation Controversy

### Election Quotas

The Crimean authorities dismissed out of hand all the constitutional suggestions put forth by the Mejlis in 1991. The only possible form of consociational arrangement they were prepared to discuss was deliberate over-representation for Tatars in the elections to the Crimean council due to be held in 1994, although not on the scale of the (ultimately unsuccessful) Abkhazian or Crimean ASSR model envisaged by some in the Qurultay.[68]

As the slowdown in the pace of the Crimean Tatar return seemed likely to cap their numbers at around 10 percent of the local population (see tables 1.1 and 14.1), it was unlikely that Tatars would be able to win any individual constituency if the traditional majoritarian voting system were maintained. Even a proportional system would entitle Tatars to only nine or ten seats in the proposed ninety-eight-seat council (the Mejlis had summarily dismissed an offer of seven seats back in March 1991).[69] Moreover, many Tatars had fundamental doubts about participating in Crimean elections at all, as it would leave them far short of the aims laid out in the Declaration of Sovereignty and in the eyes of many would simply serve to legitimate an "occupying regime."

In March 1993, Bagrov offered the Qurultay fourteen seats out of ninety-eight, overruling strong opposition from Meshkov's republican movement and the KPK (their alternative project sought to swamp the Tatar vote by electing all Crimean deputies from one large all-Crimean multimandate constituency on a party list system).[70] Tatars were initially unsure how to respond. The OKND argued that the offer should be rejected outright because it failed "to stipulate the right of the Crimean Tatar people to a veto" in the council.[71] The second session of the Second Qurultay in July 1993 demanded one-third of the seats,[72] later refining this to a formula of twenty-two of eighty, along with six further seats for the other deported and/or indigenous peoples (Greeks, Germans, Armenians, Bulgarians, Qrymchaq, and Qaraïm).[73]

However, when the issue was put to a vote in the Crimean council in September 1993, only forty-six deputies (out of just under two hundred) were prepared to support even Bagrov's plan. The majority backed an alternative proposal to revert to the majority system throughout Crimea.[74] The decision sparked the largest Tatar protests since their return. Mass demonstrations were organized, railway lines blocked, and a permanent picket of the council threatened. The Crimean council duly backed down a month later and reverted to the fourteen plus four formula (fourteen for Tatars and four for the other deported peoples—the tiny Qrymchaq and Qaraïm populations were deemed too small to warrant separate representation). The general Crimean electorate would also elect fourteen seats from a parallel party list, and the remaining sixty-six seats were to be territorial constituencies in which anyone could stand. However, the arrangement was for one election only, and Crimean Tatars received no guarantee of permanent representation.

The proposal was discussed at a special session of the Qurultay in November 1993.[75] The OKND again wanted to reject the offer, acceptance of which would "legitimize the Crimean parliament" and "deprive the Mejlis of its status as the sole representative organ" of the Crimean Tatar people. The quota would neither "allow effective defense of Crimean Tatar interests nor guarantee their participation in state [i.e., Crimean] administration."[76] The events of September and October supposedly showed that only direct action produced results, and Rejep Khairedinov, leader of the OKND, called on the Mejlis to form a Crimean Tatar national government that could act as an alternative center of power.[77] Mustafa Jemiloglu, the leader of the Mejlis, remained lukewarm about the quota proposal and decided not to stand in the elections, possibly because his main concern was to prevent a radical faction from splitting away from the Tatar movement, while Refat Chubarov led the pragmatic argument in favor. (Vasvi Abduraimov for the NDKT was arguing outside the Qurultay that "not to take part in the elections would mean voluntary capitulation before the 1944 strategy of 'Crimea without Crimean Tatars'").[78]

Delegates to the Qurultay voted 167 to 16 in favor of participation[79] but attempted to keep any future Tatar faction under their control by insisting that all candidates promise to "implement strictly and unswervingly the Declaration of National Sovereignty of the Crimean Tatar people, the election platform, and other decisions of the Qurultay and Mejlis." Deputies would be subject to recall if they refused to do so.[80] The OKND fell into line at its fourth congress in January 1994.[81]

### The Election Results

Four different sets of elections were held in Crimea in 1994, followed by local elections in 1995.[82] In some, Crimean Tatars were able to make a considerable impact; in others, their relative impotence was cruelly exposed, especially in elections where the quota system did not operate. Although the elections provided the Qurultay/Mejlis with a foothold in the local council and helped persuade Kyiv to provide Crimean Tatars with greater political and economic assistance, they also demonstrated the difficulties of exercising real political influence on the peninsula with only slightly over 10 percent of the local population.

### The Crimean Presidential Election

Although the quota issue had been rumbling for some time, Tatars were suddenly confronted with an extra issue when Crimean presidential elections were scheduled for January 1994. Whereas the argument about the elections to the Crimean council was finely poised, Tatars were understandably fundamentally hostile to the very idea of a Crimean presidency. It was not a post any of their leaders could aspire to (in addition to the Tatars' minority position, only those who had been resident in Crimea for ten years were to be allowed to stand), it contradicted the positions laid out in the Mejlis's 1991 draft constitution, and, in the words of a resolution passed by the November 1993 session of the Qurultay, the "possible election of a candidate from one of the Crimean parties espousing a chauvinist ideology" could lead to a dangerous "attempt to reexamine existing state borders in the region."[83]

The NDKT initially had no qualms about running its own candidate, Rustem Khalilov. Ironically, however, his campaign was stopped in its tracks by an electoral commission ruling that half the seven thousand signatures collected in his favor were invalid.[84] In January 1994, the NDKT therefore reversed its decision and called for a boycott.[85] Members of the Mejlis, by contrast, had always been inclined toward a boycott and on 2 January decided by eighteen votes to eight to recommend that Tatars stay at home. However, rising support for Yurii Meshkov, now head of the separatist "Russia" bloc,[86] and the consequent threat "to stability in Crimea" led them to reverse the decision a week later by declaring that support for Mykola Bagrov, the relatively moderate chairman of the Crimean council and Kyiv's preferred candidate, was the lesser of two evils, although Mustafa Jemiloglu indicated that he went along with the decision reluctantly.[87] However, the Mejlis insisted that "participation in the elections did not imply in any way the recognition by the Mejlis of the institution of a Crimean presidency" as such and was simply an attempt to block Meshkov's path to power.[88]

The leaders of the Mejlis claimed that some 119,000 Crimean Tatars voted in the first round and 116,000 in the second (out of a maximum Tatar voting strength of approximately 134,000),[89] with over 90 percent supposedly following their instructions to support Bagrov.[90] If this were indeed true, then Crimean Tatars provided almost half Bagrov's first round vote of 245,042 (333,243 in the second round) and, as in December 1991, provided the cornerstone of the pro-Kyiv vote (the elections having demonstrated the relative passivity and deep-seated "Russification" of Crimea's 626,000 Ukrayinans). Limited indirect support for the Mejlis's claim can be drawn from the official results, as Bagrov's first-round vote rose well above his average of 16.9 percent in areas of concentrated Crimean Tatar settlement, such as Qarasuvbazar (Belogorsk) (26.1 percent) and Bakhchesaray (21.3 percent). Nevertheless, however impressive Crimean Tatar voting solidarity, it did little to affect the overall result. Bagrov trailed well behind Meshkov in both the first (16.9 to 38.5 percent) and second (23.4 to 72.9 percent) rounds.[91] (For an explanation of Crimean regions and place names, see tables 1.1 and 14.1.) The Mejlis was unable to prevent the election of the most openly anti-Tatar candidate, placing into sharp focus the problem of returning to a homeland dominated by a distinctly unfriendly Slav majority.[92]

## The Elections to the Crimean Council

Crimean Tatars made a more successful impact on the March–April 1994 elections to the local Crimean council, although once again they could do little to affect the overall result.[93] The separate contest for the fourteen seats on the Crimean Tatar list not surprisingly resolved itself into a straight fight between the Qurultay and the NDKT.[94] The Qurultay's election platform called for the recognition of "the Mejlis as the supreme plenipotentiary representative organ of the Crimean Tatar people" and repeated the demand made in the 1991 Declaration of Sovereignty for "the restoration of Crimean Tatar national statehood" in Crimea (a full translation of the platform can be found in chapter 16). The Qurultay also demanded the recognition of Russia's "primary responsibility for the genocide of Crimean Tatars" and its "financing of the process of return, rehabilitation, and compensation for damages brought on the Crimean Tatar people" and called on the Central Asian states "to participate" in the same process.[95]

By contrast, the NDKT also called for the rebirth of Crimean Tatar statehood but stressed the importance of Tatars' entering "the structures of [existing] state power" during the transition period and, unlike the skeptical Qurultay, argued that the quota system provided a sufficient constitutional basis for resolving most foreseeable problems.[96]

The Qurultay/Mejlis again demonstrated the voting discipline of its supporters, winning 90,959 votes on the special Crimean Tatar list (89.3 percent of the total) against a mere 5,566 for the NDKT (5.5 percent). Support for the Qurultay was consistent throughout Crimea, its lowest level being 81 percent in Jankoy (Dzhankoi). The Qurultay therefore won all fourteen seats available, as the NDKT failed to win one-fourteenth of the vote. Chubarov headed the list. Turnout was 75.8 percent (101,808 of a total registered Crimean Tatar electorate of 134,834).[97]

However, in the sixty-six single-member constituencies, Crimean Tatars were unable to elect a deputy. Local branches of the Mejlis put forward thirty-five candidates in thirty-two of the constituencies, ten of whom made it through to the second round. The Mejlis's candidates won 78,860 votes in the first round and 54,538 in the second,[98] but none were elected, indicating how reliant Crimean Tatars were on the quota system.[99] Moreover, all ten were standing in rural constituencies, where 70 percent of Crimean Tatars lived. In the big cities such as Aqmesjit (Simferopol') (1.4 percent) of Kezlev (Evpatoriia) (3.4 percent), Tatar candidates trailed badly or were not on the ballot at all (Alushta, Yalta, Kefe [Feodosiia], Kerch').[100] The best results for the Mejlis appeared in Qarasuvbazar (Belogorsk), where two candidates, including Abdureshit Jepparov, one of the founders of the OKND, won 26 percent of the vote, Islam-Terek (Kirovskoe) *raion* (23.4 percent), and Bakhchesaray (18.2 percent).

Overall results of the elections were even more disappointing (see table 14.2 below). The Crimean Tatars' potential allies in the local Ukrayinan

Table 14.2  Original Results of the 1994 Elections to the Crimean Council

|  | Lists | | | Single Mandate | Total |
|---|---|---|---|---|---|
|  | Tatar | Other | General | | |
| Qurultay | 14 | — | — | — | 14 |
| "Russia" bloc | — | — | 11 | 43 (+ 4) | 54 (58) |
| KPK | — | — | 2 | — | 2 |
| PEVK | — | 1 (+ 2) | 1 | (4) | 2 (8) |
| RusPK | — | — | — | 1 | 1 |
| Independents | — | 1 | — | 10 | 11 |
| Total | 14 | 4 | 14 | 62/66[a] | 94/98 |

*Source:* Andrew Wilson, "The Elections in Crimea," *RFE/RL Research Reports* 3, no. 25 (24 June 1994): 18, slightly revised in the light of subsequent information supplied by the Crimean council.

[a] Four seats were not filled at the first attempt.

community failed to elect a single deputy,[101] and the centrist parties who had proved sympathetic to the Qurultay in the past polled poorly, with only PEVK securing any seats at all (two, plus six supporters). The four other minority seats were taken by sympathetic moderates, but the separatist and Tatarphobic "Russia" bloc established by Yurii Meshkov triumphed elsewhere. In the all-Crimean party list, the "Russia" bloc won 66.8 percent of the vote, trouncing both center parties such as PEVK (7.1 percent) and the Union in Support of the Republic of Crimea (2.6 percent) and the Communist KPK (11.6 percent). The "Russia" bloc therefore won eleven seats, the KPK two, and PEVK one. Moreover, the "Russia" block also swept the board in the single-member constituencies, although fourteen independents were also elected (four were close to PEVK), along with one deputy from the hardline Russian Party of Crimea (RusPK). Overall, the "Russia" bloc won fifty-four of ninety-four seats (four seats remained empty until repeat elections in the summer), and a further four independents were close allies. Table 14.2 shows the results in detail.

### The Ukrayinan Parliamentary Elections

In the elections to the Ukrayinan parliament, also held in March and April, the contrast between the Crimean Tatars' voting discipline and the difficulty of making progress under the majoritarian electoral system was again sharply exposed. The Qurultay recommended that Tatars support a list of ten candidates in the second round of the elections (a mixture of Tatars, prominent Ukrayinans including Serhii Lytvyn, head of the main Ukrayinophile organization the Ukrayinan Civic Congress of Crimea, and centrist moderates such as Tat'iana Orezhova of the Union in Support of the Republic of Crimea).[102] None were successful; in fact none managed to win more than 38 percent of the vote (as the "Russia" bloc boycotted the poll, most seats were won by independents or by the KPK).[103] Of the three Crimean Tatars on the Qurultay list, Ava Azamatova won 15,625 votes (25.1 percent of the total) in Bakhchesaray, Abdulla Abdullaev 11,955 (23 percent) in Islam-Terek (Kirovskoe) *raion*, and Bekir Kurtosmanov 13,949 (25.5 percent) in Bakhchi-Eli (Leninsk) *raion*.[104] The Qurultay has therefore pressed the Ukrayinan authorities to introduce a quota arrangement similar to that used for the Crimean council for the parliamentary elections due in 1998 (or perhaps to make special provision for the Qurultay on a party list system), but Kyiv has been reluctant to set a precedent for Ukrayina's other national minorities.

The Ukrayinan Presidential Election

In the summer 1994 election for the Ukrayinan presidency, the leaders of the Mejlis felt honor bound to oppose the candidacy of Leonid Kuchma, as they accepted the caricature put forward by their Ukrayinan nationalist allies that he was excessively pro-Russian. On the other hand, they could raise little enthusiasm for Kravchuk, who had done so little to advance their cause since 1991, despite his speech at the May 1994 commemoration of the 1944 deportation belatedly referring to their "right to self-government."[105] However, the vast majority of political forces in Crimea, including centrists, Communists, and even several leaders of the "Russia" bloc, stood firmly behind Kuchma. Only the tiny Ukrayinan parties backed Kravchuk.[106] Therefore, the Tatars could do little to prevent Kuchma from sweeping Crimea with an impressive 89.7 percent of the total vote in the second round (91.9 percent in Aqyar [Sevastopol]). Even in areas of concentrated Tatar settlement such as Qarasuvbazar (Belogorsk), support for Kuchma was still 81.3 percent (17.2 percent for Kravchuk). The low vote for Kravchuk in areas such as Bakhchesaray (6,092) and Aqmesjit (Simferopol') (11,756) suggested that many Tatars stayed at home.[107]

## After the Elections: An End to Isolation?

### Crimea: Local Elections

Despite the seeming success of the 1994 quota agreement in drawing Crimean Tatars into public political life on the peninsula, the fragility of the arrangement was immediately demonstrated by the Crimean local elections in June 1995. In theory, the elections could have ushered in the kind of power-sharing arrangement proposed by the Qurultay back in 1991, but, under the rules drafted by the Crimean council, there was no provision either for special Crimean Tatar constituencies or quotas, let alone for separate Crimean Tatar councils, and participation was to be limited to those who had returned to Crimea before November 1991 (in other words, the Crimean authorities were seeking to take advantage of the Ukrayinan citizenship law to minimize the Tatar vote). Tatars protested to the Ukrayinan parliament, but the Crimean council ignored its instructions to make special provision for all the "deported peoples."[108]

The Mejlis therefore called on Crimean Tatars to boycott the poll.[109] Turnout was low (53 percent), but this probably reflected general voter apathy as much as the Mejlis's instructions. Moreover, the main winners from the partial results were the Communist KPK, no friend of the Qurultay.[110] Local structures of power in Crimea (and it was local councils that were responsible for practical measures such as providing water and electricity to new Tatar settlements) were therefore no better disposed toward Tatars than before.

The insecurity of the Crimean Tatars' position was further demonstrated when the new Crimean constitution adopted by the Crimean council in November 1995 failed even to mention the quota system, despite a prolonged hunger strike by several Tatar deputies in protest.[111] The perceived indifference of the Kyiv authorities, despite the advice of Max van der Stoel, the OSCE commissioner for national minorities, that the quota system be retained,[112] added to rising Tatar disillusionment, and the debate began to polarize once again between local Russophile parties, which wished to withdraw all special provision for Tatars, and Tatar radicals, who returned to demanding 33 percent of seats at all levels.

### Crimea: Political Realignment

Furthermore, although in the immediate aftermath of the 1994 elections the Qurultay could take some pride in its rout of the NDKT, with only

Table 14.3  Development of Factions in the Crimean Council, 1994–95

|  | Spring 1994 | Summer 1994 | Winter 1994/95 | Summer 1995 |
| --- | --- | --- | --- | --- |
| Russia | 54 | 44 | 22 | 22 |
| Republic | — | 11 | 10 | 10 |
| Russia/unity | — | — | 18 | 14 |
| Crimea | — | — | 10 | 10 |
| Agrarians/KPK | — | 10 | 11 | 5 |
| Agrarians/Crimea | — | — | — | 6 |
| Reform/PEVK | 2 | 9 | 10 | 10 |
| Qurultay | 14 | 14 | 14 | 14 |

*Sources:* List of deputies supplied by Crimean council in August 1994; UNIAN, 24 September 1994; UNIAN, 19 October 1994; *Krymskie izvestiia*, 7 March 1995.

*Note:* Numbers do not always add up to ninety-eight owing to frequent changes of allegiance and the variable number of independents.

fourteen deputies of ninety-four in the Crimean council the Tatar faction seemed to be in the powerless position radicals had predicted it would be back in 1993. The leaders of the victorious "Russia" bloc, Yurii Meshkov and Sergei Tsekov (the chairman of the council), maintained their anti-Tatar rhetoric and used the fact that the Tatar faction took the name of a rival assembly rather than a political party to freeze the Qurultay out of all influence in local administration (they had not, after all, negotiated the quota agreement). The OKND, on the other hand, responded by demanding that Tatar deputies be granted a right of veto over legislation in areas of immediate concern or else withdraw from the council, while even the more moderate Mejlis predicted that the policies of "the parliamentary majority based on the 'Russia' bloc" could lead to "armed civil strife and international conflict."[113]

However, the "Russia" bloc's apparent dominance of Crimean politics did not last long, and factional infighting and the shifting balance of power between Kyiv, Moscow, and Aqmesjit (Simferopol') soon began to break the political logjam, to the Tatars' advantage. Moreover, the failure of the "Russia" bloc to win the expected support from Moscow or take practical measures to improve the Crimean economy allowed centrist parties more friendly to Tatars to regroup and make a partial comeback.

Table 14.3 shows how the council was soon plagued by divisions between "Muscovites" and locals, between rural and city deputies, and between economic reformers and conservatives.[114] Rural independents formed an agrarian faction in mid-1994, along with a handful of deputies from the KPK, which in turn split in March 1995—the more moderate agrarian faction tending to vote with the Qurultay. A second moderate faction was a reform group, formed by PEVK with the help of the Armenian, Bulgarian, and Greek deputies. In September–October 1994, a Ruritanian factional and personal struggle between Meshkov and the Crimean council split the "Russia" bloc in three: "Russia" itself, the "Russia-unity" faction initially made up of the rapidly diminishing band of Meshkov's supporters, and the "Crimea" group led by local businessman Aleksandr Korotko, previously close to PEVK. The conflict was essentially clannish, but the "Crimea" group represented relative moderates who were prepared to compromise with the new Ukrayinan president Leonid Kuchma, especially after he launched Ukrayina's first serious program of economic reform in October. As a signal of their newfound willingness to build bridges with Kyiv, Kuchma's ally and son-in-law Anatolii Franchuk was appointed as Crimean prime minister (although he was temporarily deposed in the spring).

The breakup of the "Russia" bloc and the growing desire among more moderate local politicians to reach an accommodation with Kyiv helped shift the center of political gravity toward the Qurultay. In October 1994, Ilmy Umerov became the first member of the Qurultay to be appointed to a major government post, deputy prime minister responsible for health, social security, and ethnic affairs.[115] The following February, a reshuffle of the powerful presidium of the Crimean council gave the Qurultay two of fourteen seats, including Refat Chubarov as head of the committee for nationalities policy and deported nations.[116] However, the decisive change in the political climate came in March, when the Ukrayinan parliament took advantage of the Crimean *guerre des chefs* and Russia's preoccupation with the Chechen war to abolish both the 1992 Crimean constitution and the post of Crimean president. Two weeks later, Leonid Kuchma imposed direct presidential control over the Crimean government.[117] The "Russia" bloc was unable to organize an effective response, and a Crimean "loyal opposition" began to coalesce around the Qurultay and the various centrist groups. By early April, it could count on thirty-five deputies, who issued an appeal to Kuchma in support of his moves to bring the republic's Russophile leaders to heel; by late April, their numbers had risen to forty-two.[118]

A potential alternative governing majority was now in place. Significantly, despite strong pressure from nationalists in Kyiv to crack down harder on Crimea, Kuchma deliberately chose not to abolish the Crimean council and refrained from altering Crimea's formal position within the Ukrayinan constitution, indicating that Kyiv's problem was with Crimea's then leaders rather than with Crimea itself. Kuchma also held out the prospect that he would rescind his earlier decrees if Franchuk were to be formally reinstated as Crimean prime minister. The Crimeans duly obliged, and, in July, Tsekov was deposed and replaced by Yevhen Supruniuk, one of the leaders of the relatively pragmatic agrarian faction (by fifty-eight votes to thirty-one). Refat Chubarov's pivotal role as leader of the Qurultay faction was reflected in his election as one of Supruniuk's three vice-chairmen.

Although short-term political alignments would no doubt prove ephemeral, the political maneuvering suggested that Tatars could build pragmatic alliances with centrist Crimean politicians, to the extent of assembling a fragile governing majority, albeit one that probably lacked long-term coherence.[119] The possibility of open conflict between Tatar radicals and hard-line Russian nationalists that seemed to be looming in early 1994 had faded away, if only temporarily. Second, the change of local regime granted the Tatars their first real influence on the governance of the peninsula. Third, it showed that Tatars could work productively with Kyiv and, by helping oust Kyiv's opponents from power, demonstrated to the Ukrayinan authorities the political benefits of working with the Qurultay/Mejlis. As Mustafa Jemiloglu commented in 1993, "We appear to be better representatives of the Ukrayinan state [in Crimea] than the Ukrayinans themselves."[120] The crisis therefore encouraged the Tatars' hesitant orientation toward Kyiv, to the extent that they could even be accused of being "too pro-Ukrayinan" and "too anti-Russian."[121]

### *The Tatars and Kyiv: A Growing Coincidence of Interests?*

Kyiv, for its part, had first shown signs of changing its attitude toward Crimean Tatars in 1993–94. A ministry for nationalities and migration was established in April 1993, and it lobbied energetically on the Tatars' behalf, especially after the academic Volodymyr Yevtukh was appointed minister in 1995.[122] A draft law "On the Restoration of the Rights of the Deported" was prepared by the ministry, although it made slow progress in the Ukrayinan parliament in the face of opposition from Russophiles and conservatives.[123] The fiftieth anniversary of the 1944 deportation in May 1994 was marked with respect, if not mutual understanding, and by an academic conference in Kyiv that did much to publicize the Tatars' cause.[124]

However, the real change in Kyiv came after the 1994 Crimean elections. The Ukrayinan authorities had expected their candidate Bagrov to win the presidential poll but were now forced to realize that their proxy forces on the peninsula were no match for the local Russophiles. As briefly in May 1992, Kyiv now began to consider using the Qurultay as an alternative bulwark against the local separatists. In December 1994, Kyiv sent its first real high-level delegation concerned with the Tatar situation to Crimea under deputy prime minister Ivan Kuras.[125] The visit resulted in a promised increase in budgetary aid for deported peoples (80 percent of which was to go to assist Crimean Tatars) from 1.048 trillion karbovantsi in 1994 to 3.753 trillion karbovantsi in 1995,[126] although the eventual amount proved to be nearer 2 trillion karbovantsi ($11 million). The 1996 budget allocated 2.8 trillion.[127] According to Viktor Yakovlev, head of the deported peoples' department in the minorities ministry, the equivalent amount allocated by the Crimean authorities for 1995 was only 40 billion karbovantsi.[128] Moreover, Ukrayina's relative generosity was in sharp contrast to other, arguably more culpable, states. Despite two agreements signed between Ukrayina and Uzbekistan in October 1992 and November 1994, the lack of real money from either Central Asia or Russia to aid resettlement was a constant source of Crimean Tatar complaint.[129] Moreover, cash-strapped Ukrayinan politicians such as Yurii Karmazyn, head of the Ukrayinan parliament's temporary commission on Crimea, increasingly tended to agree.[130]

Kyiv's newfound closeness to the Qurultay was seemingly demonstrated by its swift response to the June 1995 riots in which Crimean Tatar protests at insufficient protection against local "Mafiosi" left four dead and many more injured in Kefe (Feodosiia), Sudaq (Sudak), and the nearby village of Shchebetovka. Kuchma met Mustafa Jemiloglu and Refat Chubarov for the first time and issued a decree promising a government commission to investigate the affair, draft in more police, and allow local councils to "appoint people directly responsible for implementing concerted measures to prevent criminal encroachment and to uncover organized criminal groupings."[131] The possibility of finally endorsing the official status of the Mejlis was also raised in the Ukrayinan Cabinet of Ministers.[132]

## The Third Qurultay

Nevertheless, Kyiv refused to rush into any new arrangement, as its primary concern remained preserving the delicate coalition of relatively friendly forces that had emerged in Crimea. Jemiloglu was soon once again expressing his disappointment as Kyiv continued to drag its heels and the investigation of the June 1995 events produced no concrete results. The sense of disillusion was evident when the Third Qurultay convened (a year late) in Aqmesjit (Simferopol') in June 1996.[133] Reelection of the delegates revealed a more radical mood, with an estimated 80 of 157 of those elected supporting the radical politics of the OKND.[134] (Most delegates, 134 in all, were now from Crimea, given "the objective difficulties of organizing elections in the [Central Asian] states"; only two were under the age of thirty.)[135] Ten of the thirty-three members of the 1991 Mejlis were reelected, with radicals such as Umerov and Kerimov prominent.

Jemiloglu's keynote speech struck a radical note, attacking the "chauvinist and . . . semifascist parliament" in Crimea and "Ukrayina's indifference to our plight" and bemoaning the general "loss of faith" in the authorities in both Aqmesjit (Simferopol') and Kyiv after their inadequate response to the June 1995 events. Kyiv's failure to reimpose the quota agreement was attacked as "sanctioning . . . discrimination against our people and the denial of their legal rights." "It is sad," he continued, "that, in our struggle with chauvinism and sometimes with outright Russian fascism in Crimea, we have not received the necessary support from Ukrayina, although Crimean Tatars and their representative body—the Mejlis—have always been the main and the most consistent supporters of the integrity and independence of Ukrayina. [It seems that] there are sufficient forces [in Kyiv], above all, those of a Communist and pro-Soviet orientation, to consciously torpedo the restoration of our rights."[136]

Radical delegates led by the OKND circulated an unsanctioned policy document, entitled "On the Struggle with the Colonial Regime," which called for "the complete liquidation of the Russian colonial regime in Crimea," the establishment of real national autonomy, and the withdrawal of all Tatar deputies from representative bodies "within two weeks" unless

Tatars were guaranteed 33 percent representation at all levels and called on the Mejlis to "make the necessary preparations for a mass, ongoing campaign of civil disobedience." "The possibilities for searching for agreement through parliamentary political activity are exhausted," it declared; "the time has come to talk to political barbarians in a language they will understand."[137]

The document was not put to a vote, but the Qurultay passed an appeal to the United Nations that used similar language, attacking "the Ukrayinan state [for] encouraging a system of apartheid in relation to Crimean Tatars" and behaving "no differently from the previous [Soviet] regime."[138] Even Chubarov accused the authorities of backsliding over the citizenship issue.[139] Although the existing leadership (Jemiloglu and Chubarov) was reelected and confirmed the basic principles of nonviolence and constitutional protest,[140] it was clearly finding it difficult to hold the line.

## The Crimean Tatar Dilemma

Since their mass return began in the late 1980s, the political situation of Crimean Tatars has been marked by three awkward conundrums. First, once their numbers peaked at around 250,000–260,000 (10 percent of the local population), there were too many Tatars to be ignored but too few seriously to challenge the power of the Russophone majority in Crimea. Second, there was the contrast between the radical agenda contained in the 1991 Declaration of Sovereignty and draft constitution and the pragmatic politics pursued by the Mejlis from day to day. Given the nature of Crimean Tatar history on the peninsula before 1944 (and especially before 1783), the rhetoric of "sovereignty" and "indigenous rights" was understandable, but it fitted ill with the realities of the Tatars' minority position in the 1990s. Third, Crimean Tatars had little practical choice but to side with Ukrayina in local geopolitical conflicts, but the very unconditionality of the alignment too often had Kyiv offering little practical support in return. The turnaround in local Crimean politics in 1994–95 left Kyiv better disposed toward the Tatars, but it was unlikely to rush into any formal alliance with the Qurultay/Mejlis. Many Tatars were therefore increasingly prepared to attack Ukrayina, like Russia, as a "colonial power." Working through the paradoxes and creating workable political arrangements was therefore likely to test all political forces on the peninsula, those of the returning Crimean Tatars most of all.

## Notes

1. On Crimean Tatar politics in the late Soviet period, see Edward J. Lazzerini, "The Crimean Tatars," in *The Nationalities Question in the Post-Soviet States*, ed. Graham Smith, 2d ed. (London: Longman, 1995), 412–35; Andrew Wilson, *The Crimean Tatars* (London: International Alert, 1994); Mustafa Cemiloglu (Jemiloglu), "A History of the Crimean Tatar National Liberation Movement: A Sociological Perspective," in *Crimea: Dynamics, Challenges, Prospects*, ed. Maria Drohobycky (New York: American Association for the Advancement of Science/Rowman and Littlefield, 1995), 87–105; Mikhail Guboglo and Svetlana Chervonnaia, "The Crimean Tatar Question and the Present Ethnopolitical Situation in Crimea," *Russian Politics and Law* 33, no. 6 (November–December 1995): 31–60; Mikhail Gobuglo and Svetlana Chervonnaia, eds., *Krymskotatarskoe natsional'noe dvizhenie*, 3 vols. (Moscow: Tsentr po izucheniiu mezhnatsional'nykh otnoshenii, 1992–96); Svetlana Chervonnaia, "Krymskotatarskoe natsional'noe dvizhenie v kontekste etnopoliticheskoi situatsii v Krymu (avgust 1991–mart 1995 gg.)," in *Krymskotatarskoe natsional'noe dvizhenie*, 3:26–101; and David R. Marples and David F. Duke, "Ukraine, Russia, and the Question of Crimea," *Nationalities Papers* 23, no. 2 (Summer 1995): 261–90. This chapter always seeks to refer to *Crimean* Tatars, but *Crimean* is dropped if it occurs too many times in a sentence and there is no risk of ambiguity.

2. Edward Allworth, ed., *Tatars of the Crimea: Their Struggle for Survival*, 1st ed. (Durham, N.C.: Duke University Press, 1988), 145–46; and *Krymskotatarskoe natsional'noe dvizhenie*, 1:105–17.

3. Most Crimean place names have been rendered in both Crimean Tatar and Russian.

4. *Krymskotatarskoe natsional'noe dvizhenie*, 1:133, 152.

5. Ibid., 154.

6. Vasvi Abduraimov, "Geopoliticheskie aspekty krymskogo uzla," *Areket* (the paper of the NDKT), no. 3 (28 February 1994): 1.

7. Vasvi Abduraimov, "Ia—storonnik slaviano-tiurkskogo edinstva," *Tavricheskie vedomosti*, no. 27 (5 July 1996): 2.

8. Abduraimov interviewed in *Vseukrainskie vedomosti*, 22 June 1995. See also Yurii Osmanov, "Strategicheskaia zadacha: 'Obzhuliverit' krymskotatarskii narod,'" *Areket*, no. 8 (18 August 1993): 3.

9. "Obrashchenie NDKT," *Tavricheskie vedomosti*, no. 16 (29 April 1994): 1.

10. Abduraimov, "Ia—storonnik slaviano-tiurkskogo edinstva," 2.

11. "Proekt kontseptsii Konstitutsii Krymskoi ASSR, predlozhennyi NDKT (1990 g.–1991 g.)," in *Krymskotatarskoe natsional'noe dvizhenie*, 2:99, 98, 102.

12. *Holos Ukraïny*, 12 August 1993, 4. The NDKT was actually registered as a movement rather than a political party.

13. "Programma OKND," in *Organizatsiia krymskotatarskogo natsional'nogo dvizheniia* (Simferopol', 1993), 5, 6, 7.

14. Shevket Kaibullaev, "Kontseptsiia vneshnepoliticheskoi deiatel'nosti OKND" (party document in the author's possession dated 15 December 1993); *Demokratychna Ukraïna*, 14 January 1995, 1.

15. Interview with Refat Chubarov, then leader of the OKND, in *Avdet* (the main paper of the Mejlis), no. 23 (12 November 1992): 2.

16. Alim Suleimanov, "Krizis v OKND—eto real'nost," *Avdet*, no. 23 (12 November 1992): 2. Compare Nadir Bekirov, "Ot OKND k 'Milli Firka,'" *Avdet*, no. 12 (11 June 1992): 2.

17. Statement by the NDKT, in *Areket*, no. 8 (18 August 1993): 4.

18. A. I. Kliachin ("Dinamika etnicheskikh sistem rasseleniia v Krymu [v sviazi s problemoi vozvrashcheniia krymskikh tatar]," *Etnograficheskoe obozrenie*, no. 2 [1992]: 33) cites 132,000 Tatars as of July 1991.

19. All information about the election process, including the quotation given, is derived from a document dated 1993, "Medzhlis krymskotatarskogo naroda, formirovanie i kompetentsiia (kratkaia spravka)," supplied to the author by the Mejlis. It seems that the organizers of the election may have divided a putative population of 272,000 into groups of 1,000 and worked backward, rather than beginning with actual voter turnout.

20. Voting was secret if an "observer" was present.

21. Only 2.6 percent were under thirty, 35.4 percent were thirty to thirty-nine, 27.5 percent forty to fifty, and 24.5 percent fifty to sixty ("Po dannym mandatnoi komissii," *Avdet*, nos. 15–16 [1 July 1991]: 8).

22. "Raschet chislennosti izbiratelei—krymskikh tatar, priniavshykh uchastie v izbranii delegatov natsional'nogo s"ezda krymskotatarskogo naroda—Kurultaia" (document supplied to the author by Nadir Bekirov). (The Mejlis claimed that the 137 delegates to the second session of the Second Qurultay in 1993 represented 93,160 Crimean Tatar electors in Crimea, or 60 percent of all adult electors.)

23. "Medzhlis krymskotatarskogo naroda," 3.

24. *Avdet*, nos. 16–17 (9 August 1993): 5; "Otchetnyi doklad predsedatelia Medzhlisa Mustafy Dzhemileva na pervoi sessii 3-go Kurultaia krymskotatarskogo naroda" (Simferopol', 26 June 1996), 10.

25. *Avdet*, nos. 15–16 (1 July 1991): 1; and *Krymskotatarskoe natsional'noe dvizhenie*, 2:109–11.

26. Ibid.; and "Obrashchenie Kurultaia krymskotatarskogo naroda k vsem zhiteliam Kryma," *Avdet*, nos. 15–16 (11 July 1991): 1.

27. Rejep Khairedinov speaking at the special session of the Qurultay in November 1993 (*Qïrïm*, no. 50 [11 December 1993]: 3).

28. "Konstitutsiia Krymskoi respubliki, razrabotannaia Medzhlisom krymskotatarskogo naroda (proekt)" (December 1991), in *Krymskotatarskoe natsional'noe dvizhenie*, 2:144, 160, 167.

29. Ibid., 162. It was unclear whether Crimean Tatars would also vote for the Council of People's Representatives. Functions were allocated to the parliament in general, without any indication of separate spheres of competence. Legislation required the agreement of both houses; in its absence, bills would go to a conciliation commission. Joint sessions were also possible (ibid., 162–64).

30. Ibid., 165. The formulation was slightly ambiguous. The second half of the sentence fails to make clear whether more than half of all "indigenous" electors is required or simply more than half those taking part.

31. Ibid., 166.

32. In 1927, Crimean Tatars and Russians each accounted for just over a third (each at 34.7 percent) of the seats on the Crimean central committee (Heorhii Kas'ianov, "Kryms'ka ARSR: 1920–30-ti roky," *Filosofs'ka i sotsiolohichna dumka*, no. 7 [1990]: 76).

33. Ibid., 80; and Kliachin, "Dinamika etnicheskikh sistem rasseleniia," 26. Some Crimean Tatars have claimed that an informal "40 percent rule" was used to build up their strength in the 1920s. See, e.g., the comments by Nadir Bekirov in *Avdet*, no. 6 (15 March 1991), as quoted in *Krymskotatarskoe natsional'noe dvizhenie*, 3:59.

34. *Krymskotatarskoe natsional'noe dvizhenie*, 3:40.

35. Svetlana Chervonnaia, "Kryms'kotatars'kyi natsional'nyi rukh i suchasna sytuatsiia v Respublitsi Krym (do chervnia 1993 r.)," in *Etnichni menshyny Skhidnoï ta Tsentral'noï Yevropy: Komparatyvnyi analiz stanovyshcha ta perspectyv rozvytku*, ed. Volodymyr Yevtukh and Arnol'd Zuppan (Kyiv: INTEL, 1994), 104.

36. PEVK is the Russian acronym for the Party of Economic Renaissance of Crimea.

37. "Otchetnyi doklad predsedatelia Medzhlisa," 17.

38. *Molod' Ukraïny*, 26 January 1991. According to official figures, only fifteen hundred Tatars "took ballot papers" with which to vote (*Krymskotatarskoe natsional'noe dvizhenie*, 1:290).

39. Kathleen Mihalisko, "The Other Side of Separatism: Crimea Votes for Autonomy," *Report on the USSR* 3, no. 5 (1 February 1991): 36–38. Detailed results are in *Izvestiia*, 21 January 1991. Crimean Russophiles also argued that the phrase "as a party to the Union Treaty" provided a mandate for the continued existence of the Soviet Union that took precedence over any Ukrayinan vote, especially when two months later 87.6 percent of Crimeans voted yes in the Soviet-wide referendum

called by Gorbachev in March 1991 on the preservation of the Soviet Union, compared to 70.5 percent in Ukrayina as a whole.

40. For examples of Ukrayinan nationalist support, see "Do parlamentu i narodu Ukraïny shchodo sytuatsiï v Krymu," in *Druhi Vseukraïns'ki zbory Narodnoho Rukhu Ukraïny: Dokumenty* (Newark, N.J.: Proloh, 1991), 64–65; and "Zaiava III Vseukraïns'kykh zboriv Narodnoho Rukhu Ukraïny pro stanovyshche v Krymu" (declaration of the third Rukh congress in 1992, in the author's files).

41. Chubarov interviewed in *Nezavisimost'*, 30 June 1995, 2.

42. "Postanovlenie Verkhovnogo Soveta Rossiiskoi Federatsii 'O reabilitatsii krymskikh tatar' (proekt)," reprinted in *Avdet*, no. 18 (9 September 1993): 3.

43. See, e.g., the remark by Mustafa Jemiloglu that, "if union with Turkiye were to come about some day, the inhabitants of Crimea would probably be no worse off than during the days of Russian rule" (interview in *Uncaptive Minds* 5, no. 3 [Fall 1992]): 57. See also Duygu Bazoglu Sezer, "Balance of Power in the Black Sea in the Post–Cold War Era: Russia, Turkey and Ukraine," in *Crimea*, 157–94; and Oles M. Smolansky, "Ukrainian-Turkish Relations," *Ukrainian Quarterly* 51, no. 1 (Spring 1995): 5–34.

44. The Turkish aid was worth an estimated $87 million. In addition, fifty young Tatars a year were offered places in Turkish universities, and two Turkish lycées were opened in Crimea. Akhmeta Ukhsana Kyrymly headed a union of Tatar groups in Turkiye.

45. For reports of demonstrations in support of the Chechens and the organization of humanitarian aid, see *Kratkaia khronika deiatel'nosti Medzhlisa krymskotatarskogo naroda: Iiul' 1991 g.–iiun' 1996 g.'* (Simferopol': Mejlis, 1996), 67, 74, 107.

46. "Rezoliutsiia o predstoiashchem vseukrainskom referendume i vyborakh prezidenta Ukrainy," in *Krymskotatarskoe natsional'noe dvizhenie*, 2:139–40; and *Avdet* (29 November 1991): 3.

47. "Programma vosstanovleniia prav krymskotatarskogo naroda v Ukraine (Vozmozhnyi variant)" (document submitted to the Ukrayinan president and parliament dated 19 September 1993 and supplied to the author by the Mejlis), 1.

48. *Krymskotatarskoe natsional'noe dvizhenie*, 1:222, cites a figure of 142,200 Crimean Tatars as of 1 August 1991. Detailed referendum results can be found in F. D. Zastavnyi, *Heohrafiia Ukraïny* (L'viv: Svit, 1994), 394 (percentage calculations are rounded up to the nearest hundred).

49. "Programma vosstanovleniia prav krymskotatarskogo naroda v Ukraine" (document supplied to the author by the Mejlis).

50. See also Susan Stewart, "The Tatar Dimension," *RFE/RL Research Report* 3, no. 19 (13 May 1994): 22–26.

51. Author's interview with Mustafa Jemiloglu, 29 September 1993; *Avdet*, nos. 16–17 (9 August 1993): 4.

52. For an analysis of Crimean politics in 1992–93, see Andrew Wilson, "Crimea's Political Cauldron," *RFE/RL Research Report* 2, no. 45 (12 November 1993): 1–8.
53. *Nezavisimaia gazeta*, 10 October 1992; *Holos Ukraïny*, 21 October 1993. See also the comments by Mustafa Jemiloglu in *Stolitsa*; no. 26 (1994): 15–16.
54. "Postanovlenie Medzhlisa krymskotatarskogo naroda 'O priobretenii (podtverzhdenii) krymskimi tatarami grazhdanstva Ukrainy,'" *Avdet*, no. 23 (12 November 1992): 1.
55. *Ukrainian Weekly*, no. 44 (29 October 1995): 2.
56. *Avdet*, no. 15 (22 July 1993): 4.
57. A chronology of public attacks on Crimean Tatars is provided in *Qïrïm* (25 September 1993): 3. See also "Kratkaia khronika deiatel'nosti Medzhlisa krymskotatarskogo naroda (iiun' 1991 g.–iiul' 1993 g.),"*Avdet*, no. 15 (22 July 1993): 1–10.
58. Cited by Volodymyr Prytula, "Ne takyi strashnyi Kurultai, yak ioho chekaly," *Post-postup*, no. 28 (2–9 August 1993): 3. See also Ksenia Niushkina, "Ekhali tatary na svoiu istoricheskuiu rodinu," *Nezavisimost'*, 4 August 1993, 2.
59. "Krymskotatarskaia partiia natsional'nogo vozrozhdeniia 'Milli Firka': Programmnye tezisy (Proekt)," *Avdet*, no. 18 (9 September 1993): 2.
60. *Avdet*, no. 15 (22 July 1993); "Postanovlenie Verkhovnogo Soveta Krymskoi ASSR o s″ezde (kurultae) predstavitelei krymskikh tatar (29 July 1991)," in *Krymskotatarskoe natsional'noe dvizhenie*, 2:122–24; author's interview with Leonid Grach, 30 September 1993.
61. Guboglo and Chervonnaia, "The Crimean Tatar Question," 39; Guboglo and Chervonnaia, *Krymskotatarskoe natsional'noe dvizhenie*, 3:33–34.
62. The KPK was formally revived in June 1992 and later became a constituent part of the Communist Party of Ukrayina (Wilson, "Crimea's Political Cauldron," 1–2; *Avdet*, no. 1 [12 January 1992]).
63. "O situatsii v Krymu v sviazi s antikonstitutsionnoi deiatel'nost'iu 'Medzhlisa krymskotatarskogo naroda' i organizatsii OKND," session of Sept.–Dec. 1992, *Vedomosti verkhovnogo soveta Kryma*, no. 1 (22 March 1993): 40.
64. Such calls were heard at two rallies in January and May 1995 (OKND leader Khairedinov, reported in *FBIS/SOV* 95-070 [31 January 1995]; *Novaia ezhednevnaia gazeta*, 31 January 1995; *Holos Ukraïny*, 13 May 1995; *Izvestiia*, 16 May 1995; *Segodnia*, 17 May 1995).
65. Chubarov interviewed in *Nezavisimost'*, 30 June 1995, 2.
66. "Krymskotatarskaia partiia natsional'nogo vozrozhdeniia 'Milli Firka,'" 2.
67. "Ustav Krymskotatarskoi Natsionalisticheskoi Partii 'Adalet' Qïrïmtatar Milletchi 'Adalet' (KMF)," *Avdet*, no. 5 (3 March 1995): 2; *Holos Ukraïny*, 13 May 1995, 1; *Segodnia*, 1 September 1995, 8.
68. Although Abkhazians made up only 17 percent of the population of Abkhazian

ASSR, a positive discrimination policy under Soviet rule gave them a majority of local leadership positions.

69. Chervonnaia, "Kryms'kotatars'kyi natsional'nyi rukh," 104.

70. Author's interview with Mykola Bagrov, 29 September 1993. See also Nariman Abdureshidov, "Ne otvergaia i bor'bu v parlamente," *Qïrïm*, no. 50 (11 December 1993): 3.

71. "Zaiavlenie TsK OKND po voporosu o vlasti v Krymu" (OKND document dated 27 July 1993).

72. The 1993 session is reported in *Avdet*, nos. 16–17 (9 August 1993): 1–8.

73. "Zaiavlenie Medzhlisa krymskotatarskogo naroda 'O vyborakh Verkhovnogo Soveta Kryma'" (Mejlis document dated 19 September 1993); author's interview with Refat Chubarov, 29 September 1993. See also *Holos Ukraïny*, 2 June 1993, 2; and *Demokratychna Ukraïna*, 6 July 1993, 1.

74. *Post-postup*, no. 34 (22–29 September 1993): 5.

75. See the detailed report in *Avdet*, no. 24 (2 December 1993): 2–6; *Holos Ukraïny*, 1 December 1993, p. 4; and Oleg Khomenok, "Na kogo postavit Medzhlis?" *Tavricheskie vedomosti*, no. 48 (3 December 1993): 1.

76. "Zaiavlenie tsentral'nogo soveta OKND" (party document supplied to the author dated 29 October 1993).

77. *Avdet*, no. 24 (2 December 1993): 2.

78. Vasvi Abduraimov, "Kakoi Prezident nuzhen 'Medzhlisu'?" *Areket*, no. 1 (14 January 1994): 2; Ukrayinan Independent Information Agency (UNIAN), 5 January 1994.

79. *Avdet*, no. 24 (2 December 1993), 5.

80. Khomenok, "Na kogo postavit Medzhlis?" 1. The form of the words was published in *Avdet*, no. 5 (10 March 1994): 3.

81. *Tavricheskie vedomosti*, no. 4 (4 February 1994): 1.

82. Andrew Wilson, "Parliamentary and Presidential Elections in Ukraine: The Issue of Crimea," in *Crimea*, 107–31, covers all the 1994 elections in Crimea in detail.

83. "Postanovlenie tret'ei (vneocherednoi) sessii II Kurultaia krymskotatarskogo naroda 'Ob institute prezidentstva v Krymu,'" *Avdet*, no. 24 (2 December 1993): 2. Similar points were made by the OKND ("Zaiavlenie tsentral'nogo soveta OKND po povodu priniatiia verkhovnym sovetom respubliki Krym zakona 'O vyborakh Prezidenta respubliki Krym'" [party document dated 22 October 1993]), 1.

84. *Areket*, no. 1 (14 January 1994): 4.

85. *Areket*, no. 3 (28 February 1994): 1.

86. The "Russia" bloc was an alliance between Meshkov's republican movement and the smaller People's Party of Crimea. Most of its members were strongly anti-Tatar and anti-Ukrayinan, but they were tactically divided on the best means of

returning Crimea to the Russian orbit—independence, some kind of Slavic union, or reunion with Russia pure and simple (*Tavricheskie vedomosti*, no. 46 [19 November]: 1 and no. 49 [10 December 1993]: 1–2).

87. Interview with Jemiloglu in *Kyïvs'ka pravda*, 8 January 1994, 2.

88. "Postanovlenie Medzhlisa krymskotatarskogo naroda 'Ob otnoshenii k prezidentskim vyboram v Krymu,'" *Avdet*, no. 1 (13 January 1994): 1. See also *Krymskaia pravda*, 5 January 1994, 1. The "majority of the 28 members present" at the session of the Mejlis on 25 January recommended continued support for Bagrov in the second round ("Zasedanie Medzhlisa," *Avdet*, no. 2 [27 January 1994]: 1).

89. The total number of electors on the official list for the Crimean Tatar roster in the spring elections was 134,384 ("Itogi golosovaniia po mnogomandatnomu izbiratel'nomu okrugu" [document supplied by the Crimean electoral commission]: 8). Nariman Abdureshitov of the Mejlis's political department calculated a maximum strength of 140,000 (*Avdet*, no. 4 [24 February 1994]: 2).

90. Information supplied to the author by the Mejlis.

91. In all Crimean elections, a second round was necessary if no candidate won over 50 percent of the vote in the first round.

92. See the Mejlis's pessimistic assessment of the likely consequences of the victory of Meshkov, "one of the most consistent opponents of the realization of Crimean Tatar rights," in "Zaiavlenie Medzhlisa krymskotatarskogo naroda v sviazi s itogami prezidentskikh vyborov v Krymu," *Avdet*, no. 4 (24 February 1994): 1.

93. A more detailed analysis can be found in Andrew Wilson, "The Elections in Crimea," *RFE/RL Research Report* 3, no. 25 (24 June 1994): 7–19.

94. The Crimean authorities almost sabotaged the election when they considered ruling that the Qurultay was not a registered political party and therefore ineligible to stand.

95. "Predvybornaia platforma Kurultaia krymskotatarskogo naroda," *Avdet*, no. 5 (10 March 1994): 3; also in *Krymskie izvestiia*, 22 March 1994, 2.

96. Z. Mutalupova, "Golosa—dostoinym," *Krymskie izvestiia*, 25 March 1994.

97. "Itogi golosovaniia po mnogomandatnomu izbiratel'nomu okrugu," 6. A further 1,320 votes (1.3 percent) went to the "Crimean Republican Cultural Center of the Crimean Tatars," a front organization of the Qurultay (at least four of its candidates were members of the Mejlis), and 980 (1.0 percent) to the "Crimean Tatar Cultural Fund of the Crimean Republic," a sibling organization to the NDKT.

98. Author's calculations from information provided by the Mejlis and from the official results in *Krymskaia gazeta*, 5 April 1994, 2–3; and *Krymskie izvestiia*, 12 April 1994, 1 (the shortfall from the 101,808 who voted for the Crimean Tatar list most probably is explained by the fact that the Qurultay/Mejlis was unable to put forward candidates in several areas, especially Or Qalu [Krasnoperokopsk], Kerch [Kerch'], and the southern coastal region).

99. Author's interviews with Refat Chubarov and Nadir Bekirov, 28 April 1994.
100. Author's calculations from the classification of constituencies in *Mieshchanskaia gazeta*, no. 10 (February 1994), 2.
101. To be fair, many Ukrayinan groups boycotted the poll or were not allowed to participate. On the other hand, the lack of Ukrayinan voting strength was ably demonstrated by the Ukrayinan Civic Congress of Crimea's demand that the peninsula's 626,000 Ukrayinans be granted a quota agreement similar to that for Tatars (*Kryms'ka svitlytsia*, 4 February 1995, 2).
102. *Avdet*, no. 7 (7 April 1994), 3.
103. Eleven of twenty-three seats in Crimea were filled at the first attempt (four went to the KPK, seven to centrist independents). In subsequent repeat elections, eleven more seats were filled: six went to the KPK (although one of their deputies subsequently died), four to independents, and one to PEVK. Once again, no Tatars were elected.
104. Azamatova worked on the Qurultay paper *Avdet*, Kurtosmanov with the Crimean committee on deported peoples.
105. Jemiloglu indicated that Kravchuk had belatedly made an effort to win the Tatars' support ("Otchetnyi doklad predsedatelia Medzhlisa," 6; see also L. Takosh, "Leonid II: Prognoz dlia Kryma," *Avdet*, no. 14 [22 July 1994]: 2).
106. "Partii Kryma privetstvuiut izbranie novogo prezidenta Ukrainy," *Krymskie izvestiia*, 19 July 1994, 1–2. See also *Tavricheskie vedomosti*, 1, 8 July 1994, 1–2.
107. Source: the author's calculations from official results supplied by the Crimean election commission.
108. See the interviews with Refat Chubarov in *Golos Kryma*, 7 April 1995, 2; and *Molod' Ukraïny*, 27 April 1995, 3. Even the NDKT felt compelled to protest (see *Krymskaia pravda*, 22 April 1995, 2).
109. *Novosti*, 25 June 1995, 1.
110. Significantly, the Communists were the main beneficiaries of declining support for the "Russia" bloc and claimed 290 deputies at all levels. PEVK won thirty-seven seats and the Republican Party set up by Meshkov a derisory five (UNIAN, 30 June 1995, 2). See also the opinion poll in *Krymskaia pravda*, 8 January 1995, 2.
111. *OMRI Daily Digest*, pt. 2, nos. 216, 221, and 224 (6, 13, and 16 November 1995). At the time of writing (August 1996), Crimeans were under pressure to rewrite their constitution to bring it into line with the new Ukrayinan constitution adopted in June 1996.
112. *OMRI Daily Digest*, pt. 2, no. 231 (29 November 1995).
113. Ukrayinan Radio, 28 May 1994; "Postanovlenie Medzhlisa krymskotatarskogo naroda v sviazi s opasnost'iu vozniknoveniia vooruzhennogo konflikta v Krymu" (Mejlis document dated 22 May 1994).
114. *Stolitsa*, no. 26 (1994): 15–16.

115. UNIAN, 13 October 1995.
116. *Krymskie izvestiia*, 11 March 1995, 1.
117. Chrystyna Lapychak, "Crackdown on Crimean Separatism," *Transition* 1, no. 8 (26 May 1995); Tor Bukkvoll, "A Fall from Grace for Crimean Separatists," *Transition* 1, no. 22 (17 November 1995): 46–49.
118. The thirty-five were made up of the Qurultay, reform, and agrarian factions plus independents (Interfax; *Nezavisimaia gazeta*, 7 April 1995).
119. Because it excluded the Communists and relied on the "Republic" group, whose support for the opposition was largely tactical. Although the "Russia" bloc imploded in late 1994, the underlying factors that produced its stunning electoral victories in 1994 remained largely unchanged, and separatist and anti-Tatar sentiment remained strong. See, e.g., Tsekov's interview in *Krymskoe vremia*, 29 June 1996, 2.
120. *Avdet*, no. 24 (2 December 1993): 4.
121. Interview with Refat Chubarov, *Nezavisimost'*, 30 June 1995, 2.
122. Author's interviews with deputy minister Oleksandr Piskun, 27 September 1993, and with Yevtukh, 9 February 1996 (the ministry became a state commission in August 1996).
123. "Zakon Ukraïny: Pro vidnovlennia prav deportovanykh (proekt)" (document in author's possession).
124. *Holos Ukraïny*, 17 May 1994. A historical conference organized by various civic groups to mark the anniversary appeal to the Ukrayinan president and parliament to do more to help Crimean Tatars ("Zvernennia mizhnarodnoï naukovoï konferentsiï 'Kryms'ki tatary: istoriia i suchasnist' [do 50-richchia deportatsiï kryms'kotatars'koho narodu],' 13–14 travnia 1994 roku do Prezydenta i Verkhovnoï Rady Ukraïny" [document dated 23 May 1994]).
125. *Krymskaia pravda*, 24 December 1994, 1.
126. *Krymskaia gazeta*, 3 February 1995, 1.
127. *Holos Ukraïny*, 18 August 1995, 1; *Zerkalo nedeli*, 29 June–5 July 1996, 2.
128. INTELNEWS, 1 June 1995.
129. See the appeal to the Uzbek president, Islam Karimov, and the resolution "O neotlozhnykh merakh po okazaniiu sodeistviia v vozvrashchenii i obustrouistve krymskikh tatar, vynuzhdenno prozhivaiushchikh v mestakh vysylki," passed by the third session of the Second Qurultay in November 1993 (*Qïrïm*, no. 50 [11 December 1993], 1).
130. Radio Ukrayina, 28 June 1995; *Segodnia*, 19 November 1994.
131. The decree is in *Uriadovyi kur''ier*, 29 June 1995, 4.
132. "Otchetnyi doklad predsedatelia Medzhlisa," 15; *Segodnia*, 1 September 1995, 8.
133. *Kryms'ka svitlytsia*, 29 June 1996, 1; *Tavricheskie vedomosti*, 5 July 1996, 2; and *Vseukrainskie vedomosti*, 2 July 1996, 3.

134. O. Egorova, "Radikaly v atake," *Krymskie izvestiia*, 29 June 1996, 1.

135. *Avdet*, no. 12 (24 June 1996), 2. Each of the 134 delegates from Crimea supposedly represented one thousand electors. Three delegates came from elsewhere in Ukrayina (the neighboring *oblasts* of Kherson and Zaporizhzhia), nineteen from "areas of compact settlement" in Uzbekistan, and one from Tajikistan. Sixty-nine percent of the delegates had higher education.

136. "Otchetnyi doklad predsedatelia Medzhlisa," 5, 7, 9, 10, 17.

137. The document, "O bor'be s kolonial'nym rezhimom (proekt)," was published in *Krymskoe vremia*, 4 July 1996, 8.

138. Ibid.; *Tavricheskie vedomosti*, no. 27 (5 July 1996), 2; and *Pravda Ukrainy*, 2 July 1996, 1.

139. *Yuzhnii kur'er*, 5 July 1996, 2.

140. See the interview with Jemiloglu, "Kurultai ne pidtrymav krainí tochky zoru," *Kryms'ka svitlytsia*, 6 July 1996, 1.

# 15

## *Crimean Tatar Communities Abroad*

NERMIN EREN

| | |
|---|---|
| The *umma* of Mohammed bore my soul | Ruhumï Muhammed ummeti dogurdï |
| My nation—is my father, | Milletim—babamdïr |
| My homeland—is my mother | Vatanïm—anam |
| The Green Land has mingled my blood in hers | Eshil yurt kanïmï kanïnda yogurdï, |
| If she smiles I'm happy, if she cries I'm sad. | O kulse sevinem, aglasa— yanam. |

This verse describes the past and present feelings of émigré Crimean Tatars toward their nation and homeland.[1] These patriotic feelings help people understand the relentless struggle of all Crimean Tatars for survival, revival, and the consolidation of Crimean Tatar culture in the center of the Crimean Tatar world, the Crimean peninsula.

After five decades in Soviet exile, Crimean Tatars began returning to their historic homeland in 1989. The first voluntary massive inmigration of Crimean Tatars in history occurred during the following three years. By 1993, 260,000 Crimean Tatars had made that journey. According to Crimean Tatar leaders, half the Crimean Tatar population living in the former Soviet Union is still in exile and awaits its day of return.[2] However, Crimean Tatars' return to their homeland is today at a standstill. Economic conditions, in addition to political obstacles in Crimea, are the primary reason for the present condition. The new independent states of the former Soviet Union are gradually consolidating their sovereignty and enforcing new border rules and tariff regulations that further complicate the return of Crimean Tatars still in exile. Presently, Crimean Tatar communities exist in the Central Asian republics of Kazakstan, Kyrgyzstan, Uzbekistan, and Tajikistan. Even though many Crimean Tatars were born in Central Asia, adapted to the local conditions, and became fluent in local languages, and even though many remain there, the vast majority regard themselves as alien to the dominant culture and to the people of Central

Asia. To some extent, this sentiment explains their decades-long struggle for repatriation and their struggle for survival as a nation.

Today, Crimean Tatars face another challenging task, different from and more complicated than their previous struggle for repatriation: rebuilding Crimean Tatar social life and cultural and political institutions in Crimea. Those Crimean Tatars who have returned have already begun that process. Moreover, émigré Crimean Tatar communities have also begun participating in this activity. In 1989, when Crimean Tatars started returning to their homeland, émigré Crimean Tatar communities immediately mobilized to provide financial and humanitarian aid to the returnees. Meanwhile, for a short period of time, émigré Crimean Tatars thought that an autonomous Crimean Tatar republic administered by Crimean Tatars themselves was imminent. However, they then assessed their situation more realistically, on the basis of current political events, and revised their expectations accordingly.

This inquiry seeks to provide an understanding of and shed some light on the life of émigré Crimean Tatar communities. Furthermore, this study provides brief background information on how these communities came into existence, how they have survived, and what their present conditions are in the countries in which they live as well as on recent cooperation with the Tatar parent group in the Crimea.

The underlying proposition of this inquiry is that the Crimean Tatar experience within the Russian Empire and the former Soviet Union must have provided the basis for sustaining a national Crimean Tatar consciousness among the émigré communities. Furthermore, collective memory and religious beliefs surely contributed to and reinforced the émigré communities' national identity.

In this study, the term *parent* refers to the main group of Crimean Tatars living in Crimea and within the borders of the now defunct Soviet Union. *Émigré* refers to Crimean Tatars living outside those areas who have maintained a real or an imagined relation with the parent group and the homeland, Crimea. This inquiry uses these terms instead of the designation *diaspora* because, unlike Jews or Armenians, émigré Crimean Tatar groups lack the strong, worldwide umbrella organizations to coordinate intergroup activity and provide an international platform for advocating the Crimean Tatar cause.

Although by and large Crimean Tatar émigré groups exist in a number of countries, this inquiry focuses only on those groups living in Bulgaria, Romania, Turkiye, and the United States. These are the areas where the most numerous, culturally and politically active émigré groups reside and maintain close contacts with the parent group.

## The Foundation of the Émigré Crimean Tatar Communities

The émigré Crimean Tatar groups evolved as a consequence of the Russian conquest and the resulting involuntary outmigrations beginning at the end of the eighteenth century and continuing throughout the nineteenth. A study of Crimean Tatar migrations, however, poses several difficulties for researchers, the most important being the lack of reliable statistical data. Tracking migration patterns is further complicated by the fact that the initial migration of a group was often followed by further migrations to the shrinking Ottoman Empire. Some of these migrations resulted directly from the Ottoman retreat, whereas some resulted from population exchange agreements between Turkiye, Bulgaria, and Romania. Some Tatars who had settled in Bulgaria and Romania remigrated to Turkiye along with the larger Turkish populations in these areas and blended in with the mainstream population in Turkiye. Notwithstanding these difficulties, some numerical estimates and settlement patterns given in Ottoman, Russian, and Tatar sources provide a general picture of Crimean Tatar emigration.

Émigré communities living in Bulgaria, Romania, and Turkiye and the majority of those in the United States are descendants of immigrants who left their homeland in massive waves shortly before and after the Russian annexation of the Crimean khanate in 1783. Large-scale migrations continued periodically during the nineteenth century and finally diminished at the beginning of the twentieth. Most émigrés left their homeland for political, economic, and religious reasons or because they were forced out. The ambiguous policies of the Russian Empire vis-à-vis the Tatars, mismanagement by local Russian officials, and distrust of Russian rule by Tatars contributed to the devastation of economic and social life in Crimea. Along with Crimean Tatars, small numbers of Bulgarians and Qaraims (Tatar-speaking Jews) living in Crimea also abandoned their homes for the same reasons.

## The Beginning of Crimean Tatar Migrations

Internal struggles among the Crimean Tatar ruling elite and the several Russian invasions during the independence period (1774–83) prompted the beginning of Crimean Tatar migrations, which took the form of exile, limited in scope and number.[3] Deposed khans, religious officials, *mirzas* (high-ranking members of clans), and their servants left Crimea and formed communities in Istanbul and Thrace during this period.[4] Their presence in the Ottoman Empire and the nature of their positions in Tatar society played an important role in Ottoman relations with Russia and Crimea. This group of Tatar dignitaries and conservative officials within the Ottoman government constantly pressured the Ottoman sultan to attempt to retake Crimea, which proved to be disastrous to both the Tatars and the Ottomans.

However, ordinary people began abandoning their homeland on a large scale shortly after the Russian conquest of Crimea in 1783. Individual decisions to leave rather than to stay under foreign domination, or in probable Russo-Ottoman war zones, were the primary reasons for these migrations, according to one source.[5] In general, Crimean Tatars preferred to stay and live in their homeland, but hardships imposed on them by the local Russian administration in Crimea further stimulated waves of large-scale migrations, one after another. The Crimean Tatar populace lacked knowledge of the Russian language and the Russian administrative and legal systems. Any pretext, such as insufficient documentation of ownership, was used to confiscate personal and institutional property. Such practices deprived the Crimean Tatar population of its traditional lands and social life. The distribution of Crimean Tatar lands among the Russian nobility and incoming Slavic settlers caused resentment among ordinary people and affected their decision to leave.[6] Exactly how many Crimean Tatars abandoned their homeland is difficult to determine, but Crimean Tatar and Russian sources provide some estimates that help quantify the extent of the early period (1783–1853) of migrations.

A Crimean Tatar Turkologist provides three different sources with estimates ranging from 80,000 to 500,000 people.[7] Another Crimean Tatar scholar estimates that as many as half a million Crimean Tatars migrated.[8] A Crimean Tatar researcher compares the Russian and Tatar estimates and concludes that the 500,000 figure estimated by Tatar sources is likely to be accurate.[9] Russian sources estimate this number to be 300,000.[10]

## Migrations after the Crimean War (1853–56)

The migrations after the Crimean War (1853–56) differ from previous outflows in certain ways. Contrary to the previous patterns of individual or collective involuntary outflows, increasing fear of forced eviction and Russification or Christianization triggered the mass migrations after the Crimean War. Despite the absence of reliable statistical data on earlier migrations, information on Crimean Tatar resettlement areas within the Ottoman Empire exists for this period.[11]

The Crimean Tatar exodus to the Ottoman Empire between 1855 and 1862 amounted to 230,000 people.[12] This figure is based on the number of passports issued to migrants. However, Crimean Tatar sources argue that the number should be more than 300,000 because migrants leaving in the immediate aftermath of the Crimean War were not included in the statistics since passports were not issued to them.[13] Crimean Tatars coming into the Ottoman lands settled mostly in Dobruja, forming large communities there.[14] However, the Russo-Ottoman War of 1877 caused another period of hardship for Tatars who had settled in the Dobruja area. Around eighty to ninety thousand Tatars remigrated, first to the Varna and Shumen (in today's Bulgaria) provinces of the Ottoman Empire. After a period of temporary settlement there, some returned to the Dobruja area, with a majority moving further and settling in the Edirne, Bursa, Eskishehir, Ankara, Izmir, Adana, and Konya provinces of modern Turkiye.[15]

Limited Crimean Tatar migrations continued until the end of the nineteenth century. Ismail Bey Gaspirali, the foremost Crimean Tatar reformer and educator, estimated that Crimean Tatar migration beginning from the Russian annexation to the turn of the twentieth century totaled between 1 and 1.2 million persons.[16]

Notwithstanding the ambiguous numerical estimates or the lack of reliable data, it is certain that a very substantial number of people abandoned their homeland, causing devastation to the social and economic life in Crimea as well as depriving the Russian administration of taxation revenues. In addition to the mass migrations during the late eighteenth and nineteenth centuries, a small number of Crimean Tatars left their homeland for political reasons during and after the First and the Second World Wars. World War I–era émigrés settled mostly in Turkiye; World War II–era émigrés lived several years in refugee camps set up by the allies in Europe and later immigrated mainly to Turkiye and the United States.

## Émigré Tatar Communities

Activists believe that the population of émigré Tatar communities is far greater than that of the parent group itself. This belief derives from the estimates of the Crimean khanate's population and the subsequent out-migrations.[17] Whether or not this statement is accurate, it reflects the self-image of émigré Tatars.

### Crimean Tatars in the Republic of Turkiye

Among the émigré communities, the largest group resides in the Republic of Turkiye. Émigré Tatars are largely concentrated in the following provinces of Turkiye: Adana, Ankara, Balïkesir, Bursa, Chorum, Eskishehir, Istanbul, Konya, Kutahya, and Tekirdagh.[18]

Activists estimate the size of the community in Turkiye to be more than five million people.[19] However, there are no census data to verify this figure. Even though gradual integration with the mainstream population took place over the course of the last two centuries, there is no doubt that the largest émigré community resides in Turkiye. Nevertheless, the concern is how many in this community identify themselves as Crimean Tatar and actively participate in the Crimean Tatar cause. Activists estimate that less than 5 percent of that number identify themselves as such and participate in the activities of Crimean Tatar organizations.[20] The growing number of Tatar organizations in Turkiye suggests that presently the émigré community is very dynamic and that the number of those in the young generation discovering their background and involved in the Tatar cause is increasing (especially after the collapse of the Soviet Union).

The majority of the Tatar community is well integrated into the mainstream population of Turkiye. Over the last several decades, the community in Turkiye produced many celebrities and high-ranking public and political figures, such as Esin Engin and Nesrin Sipahi (singers), Aziz Nesin (a writer), Ahmet Ihsan Kïrïmlï (the former minister of tourism), and Safa Giray (the former state minister). However, many members of the community, especially some of the public figures, have no sense of or interest in being Crimean Tatars, even though in some cases their names clearly imply a Tatar background.[21]

Intermarriage is common in urban centers; however, it is otherwise in rural areas, where Tatars sometimes constitute the majority. The Tatar language is almost forgotten in urban areas owing to close social interactions, intermarriage, and the educational system, but it is still spoken in rural areas. In urban centers, the modern Turkish language is the mother tongue for many Crimean Tatars and is often perceived as the same as the Tatar language, just with a slightly different pronunciation.[22]

Presently, Tatar communities in Turkiye face a leadership problem. The eminent leader Mustejip Ulkusal (1899–1996) recently passed away. His leadership role is being assumed by Ahmet Ihsan Kirïmlï, but so far Kirïmlï has been unable to unite émigré Tatar communities and implement his leadership. Some groups (especially the large community in Eskishehir) do not accept his leadership role. Other than the leadership problem, the most serious issue dividing the young activists is the representation of the Crimean Tatar Mejlis in Turkiye. Presently, Zafer Karatay, a longtime activist, represents the Crimean Tatar national Mejlis in Turkiye. Some groups oppose this kind of representation and advocate an institutional form instead. Other issues are minor and largely stem from different points of view between older and younger generations, such as the use of terms for identity. Many in the older generation prefer the name *Crimean Turkish* and insist that it be used as such, whereas much of the younger generation prefers and aggressively uses *Crimean Tatar*. (See documents 4–6 in chap. 16.)

### *Émigré Tatar Organizations in Turkiye*

The first Tatar organization in the Ottoman Empire, Kïrïm Talebe Jemiyeti (the Crimean Students' Society) was established in Istanbul by Numan Chelebi Jihan, Jafer Seydahmet (Kïrïmer), and several other students in 1908. At the end of the following year, a row between students regarding the activities of the organization led to the establishment of Vatan Jemiyeti (the Fatherland Society) by Jafer Seydahmet (Kïrïmer), Numan Chelebi Jihan, Yakub Kerchi, and Ahmet Shukru.[23] The former organization primarily aimed at cultural enlightenment, whereas the latter took a more aggressive stand and worked for the awakening of Crimean Tatars by spreading nationalist literature in Crimea. The importance of these two organizations stems from the fact that the founders later played an active role in establishing a Crimean Tatar government in December 1917.

After the establishment of the Republic of Turkiye (1923), the first Crimean Tatar organization, Kïrïm Turk Kultur Derneghi (the Cultural Association of Crimean Turks), was established in Istanbul in 1952. The second Tatar organization, Kïrïm Turkleri Yardïmlashma Jemiyeti (the Aid Society of Crimean Turks), was founded at the initiative of Mustejip Ulkusal in Istanbul in 1954. This organization began to reissue the Tatar journal *Emel* in 1960. Originally, *Emel* had begun publication in Constanta/Romania in 1930 and ceased publication at the beginning of World War II. The third organization, Kïrïm Turk Folklor ve Yardïmlashma Derneghi (the Folklore and Aid Association of Crimean Turks), was established by the initiative of Emin Bektore in Eskishehir in 1972. These organizations dominated émigré cultural life in Turkiye until 1985. In 1986, a larger, nonprofit organization, Emel Turk Kulturunu Arashtïrma ve Tanïtma Vakfï (the Emel Endowment for Research and Spread of Crimean Turkish Culture), was established in Ankara. This organization coordinated the activities of Ankara, Bursa, Eskishehir, and Istanbul émigré communities. It also initiated the establishment of a Crimean Tatar library in Ankara. The increase of émigré Tatar associations after 1990, however, undermined the activities of the Emel Endowment.

At present, the number of Crimean Tatar associations in Turkiye has reached twenty-four, and that number is likely to increase in the near future. The majority of these associations publish monthly newsletters (usually named after a Crimean Tatar city, like *Bakhchesaray*, or a symbol of Crimean Tatarness, such as *Kalgay* and *Tarak Tamga*) and inform their members of local Tatar community activities as well as developments in Crimea. There are two nonprofit umbrella organizations at present: Kïrïm Turkleri Kultur ve Yardïmlashma Derneghi Genel Merkezi (the Main Center for Cultural and Aid Associations of Crimean Turks), and Kïrïm ve Kafkasya Arashtïrmalarï Enstitusu (the Institute for Research on Crimea and Caucasus), which coordinate the activities of these twenty-four associations. The former publishes the bimonthly *Emel* and the latter *Kïrïm*.

Among the Crimean Tatar communities in Turkiye, it is possible to find anywhere from first- to fifth-generation émigrés, whereas in Bulgaria and Romania the majority of Crimean Tatar communities consist of third-, fourth-, or later-generation émigrés.

### *Crimean Tatars in the Republic of Bulgaria*

The émigré community in the Republic of Bulgaria is the least known, probably because of the size and the place of the group within the neighboring Turkish community. Tatars in Bulgaria are mainly the remnants of the nineteenth-century outmigrations, and, today, the majority have no sense of being Crimean Tatars. The statistical data available indicate that there were 18,228 Tatars living in Bulgaria in 1910, 4,905 in 1920, and 6,191 in 1926.[24] The decrease of the Tatar population in Bulgaria between 1910 and 1920 resulted from migrations to the Ottoman Empire following the formal independence of Bulgaria in 1908. No data are available for the period after 1926. In 1940, Bulgaria regained from Romania the southern Dobruja, with its Turkish and Tatar population. However, following World War II, a group of Tatars, along with the Turkish population in Bulgaria, immigrated to Turkiye in 1951, in 1968–74, and in 1978 as a result of a population exchange agreement between Turkiye and Bulgaria. Many of those Tatars settled in the Gazi Osman Pasha district of Istanbul and in the city of Bursa. A version of the Tatar language mixed with a Balkan dialect of Turkish is still spoken among the older generation of these immigrant Tatars, but they have no connection with the parent group in Crimea or with émigré Tatars in Turkiye.

Presently, the number of Tatars making up the community in Bulgaria is estimated to be under twenty thousand. The main Tatar population is concentrated in southern Dobruja (in the northeast part of Bulgaria), the traditional settlement area of Tatars during the migrations. After the collapse of the socialist system in 1989, the conditions among minorities began to improve with the democratization processes in Bulgaria. With this development, the Tatar community seems to have revitalized itself by organizing such social activities as the traditional Tatar *tepresh* (a gathering usually held at the end of May to celebrate the beginning of spring). In May 1994, the Tatar community in Bulgaria organized the first known demonstration commemorating the fiftieth anniversary of the Soviet deportation, which took place simultaneously in the cities of Silistre (Silistra), Akkadïnlar (Dulovo), and Vetva (Vyatovo), all in southern Dobruja and Pazarjïk, in central Bulgaria. Preparations for these activities began in 1991. A journalist, Ziya Selamet, and two teachers, Fikret Muzaffer and Nevzat Yakub Deniz, initiated the establishment of a Tatar cultural and educational organization. As a result, the Tatar association Asabay (Relatives) was founded on 1 April 1993.[25] The name of the association implies a Nogay background, for the word *asabay* is commonly used by Nogay Tatars.

## Crimean Tatars in the Republic of Romania

The Tatar community in Romania is little larger than that in Bulgaria and is primarily settled in northern Dobruja, the southeast part of Romania. According to one activist, the Tatar community in Romania numbers more than forty thousand today.[26] However, on the basis of exponential estimates, this number is likely to be around thirty thousand. Romanian census data list the Tatar population as 20,469 in 1956, 22,151 in 1966, and 23,107 in 1977.[27] Historically, Tatars in Romania constitute the most active community among all émigré Tatar groups, including that in Turkiye. The eminent émigré-born leaders and personalities such as Mustejip Ulkusal, Emin Bektore, and Mehmet Niyazi are the products of the Tatar community in Romania.

## The Tatar Organization in Romania

After the collapse of its socialist system in 1989, Romania's émigré Tatar community immediately established an organization in Constanta called Romanya Musluman Tatar Turklerinin Demokratik Birlighi (the Democratic Union of Tatar-Turkish Muslims of Romania). It has published a monthly newspaper, *Black Sea* (*Karadeniz*), since 1990 (see fig. 15.1) and an annual literary journal, *Colors* (*Renkler*), since 1992. The organization maintains close contacts with the Kriterion publishing house in Bucharest. So far, the journal *Renkler* and two books—the folkloric study *A Hero with Bear-Like Ears* (*Ayuw Kulak Batïr*, 1991) and the collection of poems *Toy* (a wedding celebration, 1992) have been published in Crimean Tatar by Kriterion. The organization has been sponsoring cultural meetings, religious ceremonies, the publication of books and journals about Crimean Tatar culture, and similar activities since its establishment.

In 1994, in Bucharest, the family of Hamdi Giraybay published a book of his poetry written in the 1920s in Crimean Tatar, entitled *To Young Tatars: Verses* (*Yash Tatarlarga: Menzumelev*). That was especially significant because the émigré community in Romania seems to have lost the Tatar language. While it could also be that the use of modern Turkish is deliberately being promoted, that is unlikely. In the first issues of the monthly newspaper *Karadeniz*, a grammatically corrupt version of modern Turkish was used with some Tatar words. In later issues, the use of Turkish became more correct and is improving with every issue. The use of Turkish is better in the literary journal *Renkler*. However, it is clear that the Tatar

Figure 15.1. Romanian Turk-Tatar monthly newspaper *Karadeniz* 4, no. 2 (1994): 1.

language has survived and is still spoken by the older generation. This fact is evident in the oral literature of the community. Nedret Mahmut and Enver Mahmut collected around fifty fairy tales and published them in their original spoken form in *Ayuw Kulak Batïr*.[28]

### Crimean Tatars in the United States

While it is much smaller than those described above, the most vociferous émigré Crimean Tatar community exists in the United States, where it is largely concentrated in the metropolitan New York area and is composed of five to eight hundred families.[29] Around two hundred families are World War II refugees, who immigrated to the United States during the 1960s. In the 1970s, families from Turkiye who claim to have Tatar background joined the community, and this latter group constitutes the majority and dominates all activities. In 1991, a small group of Tatars from Romania (around twenty families) immigrated to the United States for political and economic reasons. Their participation in the community activities, however, is limited. Today, Kïrïm Turkleri Amerikan Birlighi (the American Association of Crimean Turks), based in Brooklyn, has around five hundred registered family members. Activists in the community believe that the Tatar population in the United States includes some six to eight thousand people.

## Tatar Organizations in the United States

Kïrïm Turkleri Amerikan Birlighi serves as a social and religious center. This organization plays an important role in the social and cultural life of émigré Tatars in the United States. The social status of a member within the community is determined by his or her participation and position in the association. Generally, except where business matters are concerned, elders of the community hesitate to associate with outsiders. For that reason, their world is confined to the limits of their community. The younger generation is more open to outsiders, and the majority do not participate in the activities of the association. Elders of the organization are trying to attract younger Crimean Tatars to the association's activities by sponsoring soccer tournaments, parties, picnics, folk dance groups, and similar activities. Such efforts have, however, been largely unsuccessful. On the surface, it sems that the elders' tenacious hold on traditional ways drives away the younger generation. But the actual dilemma is the gap in education and mentality between the generations. The elders fear assimilation, whereas the younger generation is more receptive to the contemporary American lifestyle. The organization runs a part-time elementary school named after the eminent Crimean Tatar leader Ismail Gaspirali. The school follows the curriculum of the Ministry for Education of the Republic of Turkiye. The American Association of Crimean Turks supports academic activities in the United States. The Ismail Gaspirali Fund of Columbia University's Center for the Study of Central Asia was established with the active support of the association. Also, the association provided financial assistance for the establishment of the Association of Central Asian Studies at the University of Wisconsin, Madison.

Besides this larger association, there is also the National Center of Crimean Tatars, commonly known as the Crimean Foundation, which was established by Fikret Yurter and his associates. This organization actively deals with the political aspects of the Crimean Tatar cause and disseminates information through its outlet the *Crimean Review*, edited by Mübeyyin Batu Altan.[30]

### Other Groups

Aside from the émigré Tatar groups mentioned above, a small community composed of World War II refugees lives in Germany. Yet another Tatar community lives in Poland. The Polish Muslim-Tatars, as they call themselves, numbered 5,500 in 1939.[31] This community, however, is made up of the remnants of Tatar soldiers who settled in the territory of the Lithuanian Grand Duchy in the fourteenth century.

## Émigré Identity

During the course of the last two centuries, these émigré Crimean Tatar communities have sustained certain aspects of their distinct culture and identity in their respective countries. Émigré Tatar identity differs slightly in form from that of the parent group. Over the last hundred years, the traditional "Muslim Tatar" identity evolved into a national form as "Crimean Tatar" among the parent group and has no other religious or ideological dimension. In contrast, the form of national identity among émigré communities has several dimensions in formal use such as Crimean Turkish (*Kïrïm Turku*), Tatar-Turkish (*Tatar-Turku*), and Muslim Tatar-Turkish (*Musluman Tatar-Turku*). These forms arose from social and political conditions under which émigré groups reside. These forms of self-definition should be perceived as local identities and should not be viewed as constituting a division between émigré and parent groups. Moreover, it should also be understood that these local forms are used by those who are conscious of their ethnic background. (See documents 4–6 in chap. 16 in this volume.)

The *Turkish* component of the local identity, used by almost all émigré groups except some of the refugees of World War II, carries the sense of "Turkic" and should be understood as such. There is no word for *Turkic* in the modern Turkish language, except *Turki* (with the Arabic suffix *-i*), which means "Turk-like." For the Crimean Tatars, it is not suitable to substitute such a component of identity, for example, *Kïrïm Turki* (Crimean Turk-like).

However, the lack of an equivalent word in modern Turkish is not the only reason for this limitation; political and social aspects should also be kept in mind. Émigré Tatar communities live side by side within or with large groups of Turkish people, who exhibit great similarity in religion (Sunni Muslim, belonging to the Hanafi sect) and language (mutually understandable, but not the same). In non-Muslim environments such as Bulgaria and Romania, minority Tatar groups tend to associate and identify themselves with the larger Turkish groups in order to prevent real or imagined assimilation threats. In fact, this tendency resulted in gradual integration or voluntary assimilation with the Turkish groups. Intermarriages constitute the main trend of integration. Both sides belong to the *umma* of Mohammed (the community of the prophet Mohammed) and to the Turkic family.

In some areas of Turkiye and Bulgaria, the use of the name *Tatar* could be derogatory, a circumstance stemming from ordinary intercommunal conflicts and other alleged events that have supposedly taken place in history. This social pressure, however minor, has led to the preference for a Turkish identity among younger generations.

From a political standpoint, the *Turkish* component emerged mainly in response to the state policy of creating a homogeneous nation in Turkiye, a condition that existed in Bulgaria as well. The official use of any ethnic or national identity other than Turkish was restricted in Turkiye not only for Tatars but also for other groups. The local Crimean Turkish identity emerged, to some extent, as a response to this policy. Furthermore, émigré Tatar leaders favored this self-definition as such because their orientation was cultural, and for a period of time they favored political unity among all Turkic peoples. In this respect, the use of *Crimean Turkish* did not indicate any essential difference because Tatars constitute part of the Turkic family.

The situation of the Tatar community in Bulgaria, however, differs from that of their kin in Romania, in terms of population size and the extreme assimilationist policy applied to minority groups there.[32] The *Turkish* component there resulted from the policy of forced assimilation pursued by the Bulgarian Communist Party before the 1990s. The process began with smaller groups such as the Pomaks, a small group of Bulgarian-speaking Muslims, toward the end of the 1950s. When the Tatar community perceived this threat, it identified itself as *Tatar-Turkish* in relation to the Turkish community and *Turkish* in relation to the rest of the Bulgarian population.[33] The assimilation policy aimed at Tatars clearly demonstrated itself in the primary educational system of Bulgaria. Students of Tatar background could not attend optional Turkish language courses on the grounds that Tatars were a different nationality.[34] However, this policy was counterproductive and drove the Tatar community closer to the larger Turkish population in Bulgaria.

In Romania, the Tatar community maintains a Muslim identity along with the Tatar-Turkish one in formal use, even though *Tatar* or *Romanian Tatar* forms occur more commonly in daily speech. The community remains very conscious of its background and maintains strong relations with the parent core and with émigré groups in Turkiye. In fact, as already noted, the second generation of émigré leaders and the Crimean Tatar publication *Emel* are the products of the Romanian Tatar community.

In the United States, the form used for the local identity is split into two: *Crimean Turkish* and *Crimean Tatar*. The former is used by the majority who immigrated from Turkiye and the latter by the refugees of the Second World War. This situation, however, has created an often unpleasant debate among members of the community. The majority argue that *Crimean Turkish* is more appropriate because all belong to the Turkic family and have close ties with the Turkish community in the United States and Turkiye. Furthermore, the use of *Crimean Tatar* is perceived as a version of separatism by this group.

## *Sustaining the Émigré Identity*

The émigré Tatar identity long subsisted on the collective memory deriving from both Tatar culture and recent history. The parent group's dramatic experience and the struggle for repatriation in the former Soviet Union provided the bases for a strong Crimean Tatar consciousness among the émigré communities. Chapters 13–15 in the present volume allude to the reasons for that rising awareness. Also, a quick glance through the issues of *Emel* will substantiate this statement.[35] Almost all the editorials relate to the parent group's condition and the injustice inflicted on them in the Soviet Union. In every issue, at least one or two articles relate to the struggle in exile. Furthermore, the underground Soviet dissident samizdat publications monitored by the émigré Tatar activists were immediately translated from Russian into Turkish and published in *Emel* if they contained information regarding Crimean Tatar dissidents. Scholarly works on Crimean Tatars, published in German and in English, were also translated into Turkish and published in installments in the journal.[36] Such activists as Zafer Karatay, Hakan Kïrïmlï, Unsal Aktash, and Unver Sel closely monitored the Crimean Tatar newspaper *Lenin Bayraghï* and the literary journal *Yïldïz* (both published in Tashkent) and transliterated some important literary articles to republish them in *Emel*. Thus, these articles provided insight into the parent group's condition in exile and kept the émigré communities aware of and updated with regard to each other. The struggle of the parent group in the Soviet Union served to strengthen the loyalty of the émigrés to their communities. Émigré groups persistently supported the struggle by organizing demonstrations, lectures, and publications and circulating petitions to the leaders of their respective countries and to international organizations.[37] Activities of the émigré communities regarding the 1944 deportation are well documented and can be found throughout the pages of *Emel* and the *Crimean Review*. Furthermore, the annual commemoration of the deportation on 18 May (*kara gun*, the dark day, as it is referred to by Tatars) preserved and nurtured the consciousness of the émigré communities. Yearly demonstrations in front of international organizations, conferences, and religious ceremonies (*mevlit*) for the victims reminded the communities of the hardships that their kin endured in the Soviet Union.

Beside the parent group's experience in the Soviet Union, émigré Tatar identity survived on powerful symbols deriving from Crimean Tatar culture and history. Symbols such as territory, flag, leadership, and specific aspects of Tatar heritage, among many others, provided the necessary collective memory for the émigré communities to identify themselves as a nation and a people with a distinct culture.

The concept of homeland, discussed at length in chapter 13 above, served as one of the fundamental symbols for émigré identity. As with other émigré communities, attachment to a particular locality and reminiscences deriving from that place ensure continuation of an identity. Similarly, the "homeland Crimea" (*Vatan Kïrïm*) in the collective memory of émigré communities kept Tatar identity alive. This is evident in the form of the émigré identity whether the component is Tatar or Turkish. It is also reflected in such Tatar songs as *Guzel Kïrïm* ("Beautiful Crimea") as well as in émigré poetry, where reference to the homeland as *Yeshil Ada* (green island), *Yeshil Toprak* (green soil), and *Vatan* (homeland) occurs.[38]

The word *vatan* is reserved only for Crimea among émigré communities, even though many of the individuals making up those communities were born elsewhere and are citizens of another country. Furthermore, the names of émigré Tatar organizations such as the Cultural Association of Crimean Turks (Kïrïm Turk Kultur Derneghi), the Aid Society of Crimean Turks (Kïrïm Turkleri Yardïmlashma Jemiyeti), and the American

Association of Crimean Turks (Kïrïm Turkleri Amerikan Birlighi) reflect the concept of the homeland in émigré identity.

The Crimean Tatar flag with its sky-blue field and golden scale (*tamga*) on the right corner, as used by the First Qurultay (peoples' congress), was redesigned and standardized by Fikret Yurter, a first-generation émigré, further contributing to the émigré national consciousness.

Certain social practices peculiar to Crimean Tatars play a significant role in émigré social life, such as the annual *tepresh* mentioned above. This event strengthens the ties among members of a Tatar émigré community. It has been preserved in densely populated rural areas by Tatars and, recently, seems to have been revitalized among urban populations of Tatar origin.

Commemorating certain events in the history of a nation provides powerful bases and symbols for the emergence and continuation of an identity. The reform-oriented *jadid* program of Ismail Bey Gaspirali and the accomplishments of leaders emerging as a direct result of that program in the recent history of the Crimean Tatars provide vital symbols of leadership and bases for national pride. Young Tatar intellectuals, active in the Young Tatar movement (1905–9), whose members were strongly influenced by the Russian revolutionaries, organized Crimean Tatars through a network of effective communication systems reaching remote villages in Crimea. This group also held an election and convened the first popularly elected Qurultay, which declared the self-determination of Crimean Tatars and, as noted earlier, established the short-lived Crimean national government in December 1917. Numan Chelebi Jihan presided over the government, while Jafer Seydahmet served as defense and foreign minister in the cabinet. On 23 February 1918, Russian navy revolutionaries killed Numan Chelebi Jihan, and thus he became one of the most important national heroes and martyrs in the Crimean Tatar collective memory. Numan Chelebi Jihan's poem "I Pledge" ("And Ätkämän") later became the national anthem of the Crimean Tatar people (see chap. 4 in this volume). Jafer Seydahmet was able to escape and subsequently served his people as an émigré leader in Turkiye until his death in 1960. Both parent and émigré Crimean groups hold each of these leaders in esteem. The establishment of the short-lived Crimean Tatar government and the martyrdom of its president, Numan Chelebi Jihan, provided powerful symbols of a modern state and intensified national pride for the Crimean Tatar collective memory.

Tatar intellectuals among the parent and émigré groups have used this collective memory in constructing a modern Crimean Tatar/Turkish identity.

## *Émigré Leadership*

Leaders and intellectuals played the most important role in sustaining that émigré Crimean Tatar identity, through advocating the cause of the parent group in the Soviet Union and through transmitting the Crimean Tatar culture and heritage to younger generations. Among many intellectual figures, several leaders stand at the heart of the émigré Tatar communities. Jafer Seydahmet Kïrïmer, Mustejip Ulkusal, Abdullah Zihni Soysal, Shevki Bektore, Edige Kïrïmal, and the Ibrahim and Ismail Otar brothers are the most eminent leaders of the émigré Tatar communities. They ensured the continuation of Crimean Tatar culture in exile by establishing associations and archives, publishing journals, books, articles, and the like. These leaders have written extensively on the history, the culture, and the national struggle of the Crimean Tatars.

Jafer Seydahmet Kïrïmer was born on 1 September 1889 in the village of Qïzïltash in the vicinity of Yalta. After receiving his primary education in Crimea, he completed his formal education in Istanbul and later went to Paris and studied law in the Sorbonne. Kïrïmer took an active part in organizing Crimean Tatars for national self-determination in Crimea, a goal that was realized for a short time at the end of 1917. He drafted the election by-laws and the constitution of the Crimean national government, in which he served as minister. Before the immediate Bolshevik takeover in Crimea, Kïrïmer was authorized as a minister plenipotentiary by the Crimean national parliament and was on his way to Europe on a diplomatic mission. He spent the rest of his life as an émigré leader, actively participating in cultural and political activities among émigré Crimean Tatar groups. He was also an active leader in the anti-Bolshevik/Communist movement, Prométhée, established and financed by the foreign ministry of Marshal Pilsudski's Poland in 1927.[39] He died on 3 April 1960 in Istanbul.[40]

Beside many articles published in *Emel* and other journals, he is the author of the following materials: *Yirminji Asïrda Tatar Millet-i Mazlumesi* (Istanbul, 1911); *La Crimeé* (Lausanne, 1921); *Krym* (Warsaw, 1921); "Wschod i Tiurkowie" (The East and the Turks), *Wschod* (Warsaw), no. 2 (July 1931): 22–26; *Rus Inkilabï* (Istanbul, 1930); *Gaspïralï Ismail Bey* (Istanbul, 1934); *Rus Inkilabïnïn Bolshevizme ve Jihan Inkilabïna Suruklenmesi*

(Istanbul, 1948) (a collection of five conference papers); *Mefkure ve Turkchuluk* (Istanbul, 1965) (a collection of conference papers); *Unutulmaz Goz Yashlarï* (Istanbul, 1975); and *Nurlu Kabirler* (Istanbul, 1992) (the last two are collections of didactic stories based on actual Crimean Tatar personalities, published in various issues of *Emel*).

Mustejip Ulkusal was born in 1899 in the village of Azaplar, near Costanza/Romania. His family had migrated from Crimea and settled in Dobruja in 1862. After receiving his primary schooling in Dobruja, he went abroad to continue his education. At the beginning of World War I, Ulkusal went back to Dobruja and attended the Mejidiye Muslim Seminary. During the war, he tried to raise the educational level of his people by teaching in a school in his native town. After the war, Ulkusal completed his high school education in Istanbul and then attended law school at Bucharest University, Romania, and graduated in 1926. He established the cultural organization Tonguch for educational purposes in his native town. With his colleagues in Dobruja, he began publishing the journal *Emel* in 1930 and wrote numerous articles on the cultural and political life of Crimean Tatars. In 1940, Ulkusal immigrated to Turkiye and continued relentlessly to advocate the Crimean Tatar cause until his death. After Jafer Seydahmet Kïrïmer's death in 1960, Mustejip Ulkusal had assumed his leadership role among émigré communities. Mustejip Ulkusal died in October 1996.

Some major publications other than articles in *Emel* include *Dobruja ve Türkler*, 2d ed. (Ankara: Turk Kulturunu Arashtïrma Enstitusu, 1987); *Dobruja'daki Kïrïm Türklerinde Ata Sozleri* (Ankara: Turk Dil Kurumu, 1970); *Ikinci Dunya Savashïnda, 1941–1942: Berlin Hatïralarï ve Kïrïm'in Kurtulush Davasï* (Istanbul: Kurtulush Matbaasï, 1976); and *Kïrïm Turk-Tatarlarï (Dunu, Bugunu, Yarïni)* (Istanbul: Baha Matbaasï, 1980).

Abdullah Zihni Soysal was born in Kerch, Crimea, in 1905. As a first-generation émigré, he received his primary schooling in Crimea and immigrated to Turkiye in 1920. After graduating from Istanbul University, he went to Poland and received his Ph.D. in Turkology from Krakow University. In 1939, Soysal returned to Istanbul and then in 1941 went to Berlin, where he worked with Edige Kïrïmal and Huseyin Balich providing aid to Crimean Tatar POWs. In 1955, he returned to Istanbul, where he died in 1983.[41]

Some major publications by Soysal include *Z Dziejów Krymu Polityka-Kultura Emigracja* (Warsaw: Wydawnictwo Kwartalnika "Wschód,"

(1938); "XX recznica smierci Czelebi Dzihana," *Zycie Tatarskie*, no. 3 (March 1938): 16–19; "Mengli Giray," *Emel*, no. 8 (Jan. 1962): 5–7, no. 9 (March 1962): 8–12, and no. 13 (Kasïm 1962): 5–10; "Birinji Mehmet Giray Han," *Emel*, no. 14 (Jan.–Feb. 1963): 17–19, no. 15 (March–April 1963): 4–6, and no. 16 (May–June 1963): 4–6; "Saadet Giray Handan Sahib Giray Han devrine kadar," *Emel*, no. 18 (Sept.–Oct. 1963): 5–6; "Halim Giray Sultan," *Emel*, no. 19 (Kasim–Aralïk 1963): 5–7; "Kïrïmi Ibrahim Efendi," *Emel*, no. 23 (July–Aug. 1964): 5–6; "Gazi Giray," *Emel*, no. 46 (May–June 1968): 6–10; "Kïrïmda Yetishen Buyukler," *Emel*, no. 48 (Sept.–Oct. 1968): 32–33; "Habibullah bin Devlet Shah Kïrïmi," *Emel*, no. 50 (Jan.–Feb. 1969): 13–14; "Kïrïm'ïn ilk Turk Ahalisi," *Yeni Turk* (Istanbul), 9 (1941): 584–86, 611; "Buyuk Milletlerin Lisan Kongresi," *Emel*, no. 7 (1936); "Lisanlarïmïzïn Ruslashtïrïlmasï Siyaseti," *Emel*, no. 12 (1939); and "Kïrïm Buyuklerinden: Kefevi Abdulbaki Efendi, Abdulbaki Hijabi Efendi," *Emel*, no. 63 (March–April 1971): 5–7.

Edige Mustafa Kïrïmal was born in Bakhchesaray in 1911. His family had moved to Crimea from Poland in the first decade of the twentieth century. He received his primary schooling in a Tatar school in the town of Derekoy, finished the Russian high school in Yalta, and continued his education in the Pedagogical Institute in Akmesjit (Simferopol'). After the execution of Veli Ibrahimov (the head of the Crimean Soviet Socialist Republic) and fearing prosecution, Kïrïmal escaped to Turkiye via Azerbaijan and Iran. After a short time in Istanbul, in 1932 he went to Vilnius, where his uncle, Yakup Shinkiyevich, the mufti of Polish Muslims, was living. In 1934, he began to study at the Vilnius University School of Political Science, graduating in 1939. During World War II, Kïrïmal assisted Crimean Tatar POWs in Berlin and settled there after the war. He received his doctorate from Munster University in 1952. Kïrïmal worked in the Institute for Study of the Soviet Union and was the editor of the journal *Dergi*. Kïrïmal died in Munich on 22 April 1980.[42]

Some major publications other than articles published in *Emel* and *Dergi* include *Der Nationale Kampf der Krimtürken* (Emsdetten, 1942); "The Crimean Tatar," *Studies on the Soviet Union* 10, no. 1 (1970): 70–97; and "Mass Deportations and Massacres in the Crimea," *Cultura Turcica*, no. 1 (1964): 253–65.

Ibrahim and Ismail Otar are second-generation émigrés born in Bursa, Turkiye. The brothers' last name derives from the village Otar in the vicinity of Bahchesaray, Crimea. In order to preserve Crimean Tatar culture, the late Ibrahim Otar (1913–86), a lawyer by profession, and Ismail Otar began collecting materials relating to the culture and history of the Crimean Tatars and formed a library in Istanbul. Since his brother's death, Ismail Otar continues to gather materials and enrich the library. Ismail Otar published numerous articles in *Emel* and presently writes for *Kïrïm*. In order to bridge the gap between generations, Ismail Otar is transliterating books and articles regarding the Crimean Tatars from Arabic script into modern Turkish. Presently Ismail Otar is preparing a book on Bekir Sïtkï Chobanzadé (for more about him, see chap. 4 in this volume). Otar's poem entitled "Chigborek" (a Crimean Tatar dish) is widely known and circulated among émigré Tatars.[43]

Shevki Bektore, a second-generation émigré, was born in the town of Kavlaklar, Dobruja, Romania, in 1888. His family immigrated to Turkiye and settled in the town of Karakaya in the vicinity of Eskishehir. After completing his primary schooling in Eskishehir, he went to Istanbul, where he met Tatar students and became an active member of their organization, the Crimean Student Society (Kïrïm Talebe Jemiyeti). He served as a teacher and principal in various schools of the Crimean Autonomous Soviet Socialist Republic and Turkmen Soviet Socialist Republic during the 1920s. He was arrested on 18 March 1932 and spent twenty-five years of his life in Soviet prisons. In 1957, Bektore was allowed to return to Turkiye and reunite with his family.[44] His memoirs were published by Eroghlu Matbaasi in 1965 under the title *Red Flows the Volga* (*Volga kïzïl akarken*).

Emin Bektore was born in Pazarjïk, Romania, in 1906. A second-generation émigré, he received his primary and secondary schooling in Romania. He organized several Crimean Tatar folk dance ensembles and wrote and staged such didactic plays as *Shahin Giray Han*, *Atilla*, *Bora*, *Kïrïm*, and *Kok-koz Bayar*. Emin Bektore immigrated to Turkiye in 1940 and settled in Eskishehir. There he continued teaching Crimean Tatar folk dance and music until his death on 15 April 1995. Crimean Tatar folk dance and music have been included in the educational curriculum in the province of Eskishehir, thanks to his activities.[45]

## Cooperation between Émigré and Parent Groups

Cooperation and relations between émigré and parent groups began to increase in 1990, when members of the parent group began to return in large numbers to Crimea. Geographic proximity and better communication drove the parent and émigré communities closer together. After the demise of the Soviet Union, hopes among émigré communities that the parent group would take control of Crimea and establish a Crimean Tatar Autonomous Republic led many émigré Tatars to take active part in providing aid to the returning members of the parent group. These high hopes gradually faded as the émigré groups became more aware of the real political and social conditions prevailing in Crimea and Ukrayina. Nevertheless, émigré groups continued to provide assistance and relief to the parent group.

Non-Tatar organizations in Turkiye and in Germany are also providing help to the Crimean Tatar parent group. The Ministry of Education and the Department of Religious Affairs of Turkiye and a nonprofit organization, Turk Dunyasï Arashtïrmalarï Vakfï (the Turkic World Research Endowment), provide continuous help and material for educational purposes. The Red Crescent Society of Turkiye sends food and medical supplies to Crimean Tatars annually.[46] The daily newspaper *Turkiye gazetesi* has shown particular interest in the situation in Crimea and has organized several fund-raising campaigns among its readers to build or renovate religious institutions there. The Federation of Turkish Associations in Germany regularly provides technical and humanitarian assistance to Crimean Tatars. In addition, the Turkish government undertook a project of building one thousand houses for Crimean Tatars. The building process is under way, and the Turk Ish Birlighi ve Kalkïnma Ajansï (TIKA) is overseeing the project.[47]

In general, aid from the émigré communities is largely carried out on collective and individual bases. Collective activities occur in joint and local fund-raising campaigns. Members are invited to donate their contributions to a bank account opened for that purpose. Crimean Tatar associations in Turkiye collectively undertook a fund-raising campaign in 1992 in order to assist returning Crimean Tatars in building their houses in Crimea.[48] Another campaign was organized, at the initiative of Ali Faik Ichil, to buy a building for the Crimean Tatar National Mejlis in 1993.[49] Émigré Tatars in Romania organized a similar campaign in 1993.[50] The community in the United States provided financial support in several instances for buying buildings and transportation and communication equipment between 1991 and 1993.[51]

In addition to financial support, émigré communities in Turkiye provide help to Crimean Tatar students who are studying at Turkish universities. At present, around two hundred Crimean Tatar students study in Turkiye. The Center of Cultural and Aid Associations of Crimean Turks, in Ankara, one of the nonprofit umbrella organizations, provides stipends to Tatar students in Turkiye.[52] The center is also running an exchange program intended to harmonize young generations of émigré and parent groups. Forty-five Crimean Tatar teenagers were invited to visit Turkiye in July 1991. The visit was jointly organized by the Rebirth of Crimea Foundation in Crimea and the *Emel* Foundation in Ankara. The teenagers spent approximately a month with émigré Tatar families.[53] The émigré association in Eskishehir has been running a vocational program for adults, intended to improve their technical skills and their knowledge of how to establish and operate businesses in various fields in Crimea. Toward that end, in 1993, ten Crimean Tatar adults were trained for three months in Eskishehir.[54] The members of the same association provided financial help for circumcision rituals for eighty Tatar children in 1994.[55]

Cooperation other than planned campaigns and projects usually takes place on certain religious holidays, particularly during the month of Ramazan and the second religious holiday, Kurban bayramï (the Muslim festival of sacrifice). Muslims who are financially able are obliged by religious code to pay *zekat* (alms; one-fortieth of one's annual income) and sacrifice a *kurban* (a ram). A great number of Crimean Tatars fulfill their religious obligations by sending in the required amount of *zekat* and the cost of a *kurban* (approximately $40.00) to Crimea. Émigré Tatar associations in the United States and Turkiye jointly undertake the organization of observances and fulfill their members' religious duties.

Individual cooperation occurs between relatives and is very common, especially among the refugee families of World War II living in the West and their relatives in Crimea. Usually, a member of a family—father, brother, or sister—had been taken prisoner or used as forced labor in Germany and separated from the core family. After the war, if the possibility for reunification with the core family faded away, those individuals rebuilt their lives in their new home countries, especially Turkiye and the United States. During the five decades of separation, some were able to get in touch with their relatives, although many hesitated to even if they knew where their relatives were. Behind this behavior and thinking lay the fear that their relatives might be harassed or deprived of certain rights if the Soviet authorities learned that they communicated with their relatives in the West. After the collapse of the Soviet Union, that fear has disappeared, and many members of dispersed families were reunited or were at least able to communicate with each other. At every opportunity, gifts were exchanged, and financial help flowed from family members living in the West. Considering the value of hard currency in impoverished Crimea, even a small amount gave considerable help. Some émigrés, although not many, speak of plans to spend the rest of their lives in Crimea after retiring. The number of retired people wishing to live in Crimea may increase if the political, social, and health services improve in their ancestral homeland. However, second- or later generation émigré Crimean Tatars express no intention of living permanently in Crimea.

## Current Status of Relations

Overall relations between the parent and the émigré Crimean Tatar groups have been mostly smooth and productive since the end of 1989. The parent group in Crimea needs assistance of all kinds. Émigré groups have conscientiously provided as much financial and humanitarian relief as they could for half a decade, and this aid still continues, although to a lesser extent. Discussions among members of émigré communities suggest that émigré groups have grown tired of fund-raising campaigns and similar activities for the parent group. Many of them would like to see some tangible evidence that their assistance is being properly utilized for the well-being of the Crimean Tatar population, not just for certain groups or individuals. One particular incident led to the wide emergence of this attitude. The Imdat Bank, which was established by financial contributions from émigré Crimean Tatar groups in 1994 and owned by Qïrïm Fond in Crimea, had lent a large sum of credit to a Crimean Tatar businessman who has since disappeared. In addition, some members of the parent group visited several émigré communities in Turkiye and in the United States and collected donations, promising to put the money toward the common good of impoverished Crimean Tatar people in Crimea. Moreover, some émigrés also engaged in similar activities. However, while some established beneficial organizations such as the Dushkunler Yurtu (Shelter for Elderly and Needy People), others disappeared. Today, émigré Crimean Tatars would like to see some accountability and no longer want to be perceived simply as diaspora-dollar-dummies (DDD). On the other hand, many in the parent group think that it remains the obligation of the émigrés to provide financial and humanitarian relief because they, the parent group, have suffered the most in the struggle for repatriation.

Besides financial and humanitarian relief, one service that is being provided by the émigré communities that has great importance for the parent group is the preservation of traditional Crimean Tatar culture and the materials regarding Crimean Tatar history. Considering the loss or destruction of Crimean Tatars' cultural heritage in Crimea after the May 1944 deportation, the service provided by the émigré Tatars is of great importance in reconstructing the nation's cultural and social life in Crimea. In this respect, Ismail Otar and the late Mustejip Ulkusal, among others, probably provided one of the most important services to all the Crimean Tatar people. In addition, Fikret Yurter in the United States also contributed to this cause by collecting material important for Crimean Tatar history.

In general, émigré Crimean Tatar groups succeeded in providing valuable services in terms of financial and cultural help to the parent group shortly after 1989. Before that date, émigré communities did not have sufficient means of communication with the parent group in Central Asia, with the exception of reading the Crimean Tatar newspaper *Lenin Bayraghï* and literary journal *Yïldïz* published there. Today, émigré groups and the parent core in Crimea and Central Asia communicate and cooperate in a much better way than previously. Émigré assistance now has become much more multifaceted and specific with regard to financial assistance.

The Crimean Tatars are certainly not the only people with a history full of adversity, migration, deportation, persecution, and the like, but they are one of the most dispersed peoples in the world, their numbers being found from Central Asia to the East Coast of the United States. The Crimean Tatars are nearly unique in the sense that their numbers abroad outnumber the parent core in the homeland. The majority of Crimean Tatars abroad do not contemplate rejoining the parent group in Crimea. However, many of them increasingly continue to involve themselves in the affairs of Crimea and strengthen their ties and cooperation with their kin there. Whether the Crimean Tatars as a nation will be able to flourish under these circumstances depends on the parent group's ability to pull together its people abroad and direct their assistance to rebuild the Crimean Tatar social, cultural, and political life in Crimea.

## Notes

1. Memet Sevdiyar, "O kulse sevinem, aglasa—yanam." *Qïrïm*, 1 January 1994, 3. Sevdiyar was born in Crimea and became a refugee at the end of World War II. He has been living in the United States since the 1960s.

2. The information was given by Mustafa Jemiloglu, President of the Crimean Tatar Mejlis (the executive body of the parliament), in New York in November 1994. However, 1989 Soviet Union census data suggest otherwise. The total Crimean Tatar population in the former Soviet Union numbered 271,715. Crimean Tatars dispute that number for various reasons and argue that their population was undercounted.

3. The Russo-Ottoman War of 1769 ended with the Kuchuk Kaynarja treaty in 1774, which also ended the Ottoman protectorate over the Crimean Khanate. Until the Russian annexation of 1783, the khanate nominally survived as an independent state. For a detailed account of this period, see Alan W. Fisher, *The Russian Annexation of the Crimea, 1772–1783* (Cambridge: Cambridge University Press, 1970).

4. Ibid., 51.

5. Kemal H. Karpat, *Ottoman Population, 1830–1914: Demographic and Social Characteristics* (Madison, Wis.: University of Wisconsin Press, 1985), 65.

6. Sïrrï Hakan Kïrïmlï, "National Movements and National Identity among the Crimean Tatars" (Ph.D. diss., University of Wisconsin, 1990), 6–7.

7. Abdullah Zihni Soysal, *Z Dziejów Krymu Polityka-Kultura Emigracja* (Warsaw: Wydawnictwo Kwartalnika "Wschód," 1938), 75–76.

8. Ethem Feyzi Gozaydïn, *Kïrïm: Kïrïm Turklerinin Yerleshme ve Göchmenleri* (Istanbul: Vakit Matbaasï, 1948), 71.

9. Ahmed Ozenbashlï, *Charlïq Hakimiyetinde Qïrïm Faji'asï yakhud Tatar Hijretleri* (Aqmesjit, 1925), 65.

10. A.U., "O zaselenii Kryma novymi poselentsami," *Russkii Viestnik* 63 (1866): 257; and Peter J. Potichnyj, "The Struggle of the Crimean Tatars," *Canadian Slavonic Papers* 17, nos. 2/3 (1975): 302, citing *Bol'shaia Sovetskaia Entsiklopediia*, 1st ed. (1937), 35:279–324.

11. For a full account of this period of migrations, see Mark Pinson, "Russian Policy and the Emigration of the Crimean Tatars to the Ottoman Empire, 1854–1862," *Guney Dogu Avrupa Arashtïrmalarï Dergisi*, no. 1 (1972): 37–56, and nos. 2/3 (1973–74): 101–14.

12. Ibid., 109.

13. Gozaydïn, *Kïrïm*, 84; Kemal H. Karpat, "Ottoman Urbanism: The Crimean Emigration to Dobruja and the Founding of Mejidiye, 1856–1878," *International Journal of Turkish Studies* 3, no. 1 (Winter 1984–85): 8.

14. Karpat, *Ottoman Population*, 66.

15. Mustejip Ulkusal, *Dobruja ve Turkler*, 2d ed., Turk Kulturunu Arashtïrma Enstitusu Yayïnlarï 64 (Ankara, 1987), 39.

16. Ismail Bey Gaspïralï, "Muhajeret-i Muntazama," cited in Mirza Bala, "Kïrïm," in *Islam Ansiklopedisi* (1967), 6:757.

17. Émigré activists calculate that, of an estimated two to five million people of the khanate in the second half of the eighteenth century, more than one million Tatars migrated to the Ottoman Empire. Over the course of two centuries, this number must have grown to more than five million. The estimate of the khanate's population is based on the statement of Baron de Tott, who accompanied the khan Kïrïm Giray (r. 1758–64, 1768–69) as an adviser during the 1768–69 Russo-Ottoman War. He states that three horsemen were demanded from every eight families for the campaign and that a total of 200,000 men were recruited in 1768. Presuming four people per family, the calculation adds up to two million. Crimean sources presuming six or more people per family estimate a population of beween three and five million. See Baron de Tott, *Memoirs of the Baron de Tott on the Turks and the Tartars* (Paris: J. Jarvis, 1785), 441; Gozaydïn, *Kïrïm*, 27; Ozenbashlï, *Charlïq Hakimiyetinde*, 22.

18. Peter Alford Andrews, ed., *Ethnic Groups in the Republic of Turkey* (Wiesbaden: Ludwig Reichert, 1989), 304–8.

19. Lowell Bezanis, "Soviet Muslim Emigrés in the Republic of Turkey," *Central Asian Survey* 13, no. 1 (1994): 106.

20. Conversation with Ismail Otar in New York, November 1994.

21. For example, Safa Giray, former state minister in Turgut Ozal's cabinet, has shown no interest in the Crimean Tatar cause even though acknowledging a Crimean Tatar background. (This information was given by Mustejip Ulkusal during a conversation in Istanbul in 1987.)

22. Some members of émigré communities in Turkiye and the United States often complain that the visiting children of the members of the parent group speak Russian instead of Tatar. The members of the parent group reply that the emigrants' children do not speak Tatar either but Turkish and often get the incorrect response that the Turkish and Tatar languages are the same.

23. Jafer Seydahmet Kïrïmer, *Bazï Hatïralar* (Istanbul: Emel Turk Kulturunu Arashtïrma ve Tanïtma Vakfï, 1993), 59–60.

24. Huey Louis Kostanick, *Turkish Resettlement of Bulgarian Turks, 1950–1953* (Berkeley and Los Angeles: University of California Press, 1957), 6, no. 2:75; Feroze Yasemee, "The Turkic Peoples of Bulgaria," in *The Turkic Peoples of the World*, ed.

Margaret Bainbridge (London: Kegan Paul International, 1993), 43, 45; *International Studies Conference Danubian Study*, statistical annex, table 10.

25. *Emel*, no. 195 (March–April 1993): 45–46.

26. Conversation with Tahsin Jemil, Tatar representative in the Romanian parliament, New York, May 1994.

27. Elemér Illyés, *National Minorities in Romania Change in Transylvania* East European Monographs, no. 112 (Boulder, Colo., 1982), 34–35, 40, 42, 44, 52.

28. See Nedret Mahmut and Enver Mahmut, comps., *Ayuw Kulak Batïr* (Bucharest: Kriterion, 1991).

29. Alexander Bennigsen, "Tatars," in *Harvard Encyclopedia of American Ethnic Groups*, ed. Stephan Thernstrom (Cambridge, Mass.: Harvard University Press, 1980), 988–89.

30. The *Crimean Review* is an irregular publication of the Crimea Foundation. The Crimea Foundation has also published the following books: *Shest Dnei*, ed. M. Serdar (New York: Fond Krym, 1980); Andrei Grigorenko, *A Kogda My Vernemsia* (New York: Fond Krym, 1977); and Reshat Jemilev, comp., *Musa Mamut—Human Torch: List of Documents*, Publication no. 8 (New York: Crimea Foundation, 1986).

31. Selim Chazbijewics, "Muslims in Poland," *Islamic Life*, no. 12, reprinted in *Crimean Review* 6, nos. 1–2 (1991): 33–36.

32. The Turkish community in Bulgaria is estimated to be somewhere between one and two million, and Tatars constitute a tiny part of it (fewer than twenty thousand). However, in Romania, the number of Tatar and Turkish groups is estimated to be around seventy thousand, out of which the Tatar community constitutes around thirty thousand.

33. See Yasemee, "Turkic Peoples of Bulgaria," 45.

34. I know this from personal experience.

35. Readers should keep in mind that *Emel* has approximately three thousand subscribers and a considerable free distribution list that mainly includes institutional libraries and scholars concerned with the Crimean Tatar cause.

36. Alan Fisher's *The Crimean Tatars* (Stanford: Hoover Institution Press, 1987), and the works of Edige Kïrïmal such as *The Crimean Tatars* (Munich: Institute for the Study of the USSR, 1971), translated from English and German respectively by Eshref Bengi Ozbilen, are some examples. See the issues between 1980 and 1990.

37. These activities are largely carried out by the émigré communities in Turkey and the United States. For obvious reasons, there was not any activity by the groups in Bulgaria and Romania until the end of the 1980s.

38. See, e.g., "Amerika'daki Kïrïm Turkleri," *Emel*, no. 20 (Jan.–Feb. 1964): 21–22.

39. Lowell Biezanis (*sic*), "Volga-Ural Tatars in Emigration," *Central Asian Survey* 11, no. 4 (December 1992): 39–40.

40. For a full account of his life, see *Bazi Hatiralar* (Istanbul: Emel Turk Kulturunu Arashtirma ve Tanitma Vakfi, 1993). This book is a collection of his memoirs published in various numbers of *Emel*.

41. Mustejip Ulkusal, "Dr. Abdullah Zihni Soysal (1905–1983)," *Emel*, no. 137 (July–Aug. 1983): 1–3.

42. Mustejip Ulkusal, "Dr. Edige Mustafa Kirimal'i Kaybettik," *Emel*, no. 118 (May–June 1980): 1–5.

43. Ismail Otar, "Chigborek," *Emel*, no. 62 (Jan.–Feb. 1971): 25–30.

44. For a short account of his life, see Tezjan Ergen, "Milli yolbaschilarimiz: Shevki Bektore (1888–1961)," *Kirim*, no. 4 (July–Aug.–Sept. 1993): 12–13.

45. "Muhajeretteki aktivist, mefkureji, folklorju buyugumuz Emin Bektore," *Kirim*, no. 11 (April–May–June 1995): 12–13.

46. The first shipment of relief supplies worth $700,000 was sent to Crimea in May 1993 (see *Emel*, no. 196 [May–June 1993]: 39–40).

47. The information provided here is gathered from various issues of the journals *Emel* and *Kirim*. Both journals publish such information under the section titled "Haberler" (News).

48. Approximately $200,000 was raised for that purpose (see *Emel*, no. 189 [Jan.–Feb. 1992]: 41–49).

49. During the campaign, $52,800 was raised (see *Emel*, no. 196 [May–June 1993]: 49).

50. The community raised $3,000. Considering the economic situation in Romania, the amount is very significant. Information was provided by Tahsin Jemil during his visit to New York in May 1994.

51. The financial support was worth around $70,000 and was taken directly from the association's account. Information was provided by Remziye Molbayli, treasurer of American Association of Crimean Turks during 1991–93.

52. Conversation with Ahmet Ihsan Kirimli in New York, August 1995.

53. *Emel*, no. 185 (July–Aug. 1991): 45–46.

54. "Meslek edindirme kurslari," *Kirim*, no. 2 (Jan.–Feb.–March 1993): 46.

55. *Kirim*, no. 8 (July–Aug.–Sept. 1994): 46–58.

# 16

## *Documents about Returning to Crimea*

### Document 1

"Deklaratsiia o natsional'nom suvernitete krymskotatarskogo naroda, 28 iiuni 1991 g." (Declaration of national sovereignty of the Crimean Tatar people, 28 June 1991), *Avdet*, nos. 15/16 (26/27) (11 July 1991): 1. Translated by Edward A. Allworth.

The Crimean Tatar people/ethnic group, deprived of its national statehood as a result of Russia's conquest of Crimea at the end of the eighteenth century, for a period of more than two centuries underwent military, political, economic, cultural, and religious oppression. In 1917, convening its congress [*Kurultay*, or Qurultay], the Crimean Tatar people declared the restoration of its sovereign state—the Crimean Republic [i.e., the Crimean national government]. This bold attempt to realize the sacred will of the people was stifled by military force. However, the Soviet government, obliged to take account of the stubborn fight of our people, and also wanting to appear as an ally of Muslims of the foreign East in their fight with European colonialism, found a way out of the situation that had been created in the proclamation of the Crimean Autonomous Soviet Socialist Republic (ASSR).

After a relatively brief period of the Crimean ASSR's existence—with the requisite attributes of national-territorial sovereignty of Crimean Tatars on the territory of the Crimean peninsula—Crimean Tatars were subjected to wholesale genocide that continued from 1944 to 1956. The policy of discrimination according to the feature of nationality and the denial of the right to self-determination continues even at the present time. Despite the declaration adopted by the Supreme Council of the Soviet Union on 14 November 1989, "Regarding the Acknowledgement of the Illegality of the Criminal, Repressive Acts against Peoples Who Underwent Forcible Deportation, and the Securing of Their Rights," and despite several state measures for restoring the rights, so declared, of these people, the actual condition of the Crimean Tatar people has approached a critical point.

The situation is intensified by the absence of a unified structure, among the Crimean Tatar people, empowered to represent the interest of the entire ethnic group/people. In the setting that developed, a Qurultay of plenipotentiary representatives of the Crimean Tatar people, elected by democratic means throughout the territory of the [Soviet] Union and coming forward in the name of all Crimean Tatar people:

–proceeding from the principle of equality and self-determination of peoples, their inalienable right freely to establish their political status and freely to secure their own economic, social, and cultural development;

–worried by the actual condition of the people, compelled still in large part to be located beyond the boundaries of their historic Homeland;

–considering that the process of restoring their rights even of returning to the Homeland drags on with intolerable slowness;

–being conscious of the fact that further delay in unifying the people on their national territory will bring about its total destruction as an ethnos;

–striving to draw the entire potential of the people themselves and all progressive forces of society into the resolution of the problem of the Crimean Tatar people;

–acknowledging and fully supporting international acts/statements about the rights of man;

–placing before itself a basic goal—to achieve the fulfillment of the sacred will of its people to live in its own Homeland and to determine its own fate itself;

PROPOSES

the formation of a Mejlis as the highest plenipotentiary representative agency of the Crimean Tatar people and instructs it to act in accord with the will of the people, expressed in the documents of the Qurultay.

The Qurultay of the Crimean Tatar people

DECLARES

1. That Crimea is the national territory of the Crimean Tatar people, on which they alone possess the right to self-determination, because it is set forth in international legal acts/documents acknowledged by the world community. The political, economic, spiritual, and cultural rebirth of the Crimean Tatar people is possible only in their sovereign national state. Toward this goal, the Crimean Tatar people will strive, utilizing all means envisaged by international law.

2. The relations between Crimean Tatars and the national and ethnic groups residing in Crimea must be built on a base of mutual respect,

recognition of human and civil rights and interests, must ensure strict adherence to political, economic, cultural, religious, and other legal rights of all persons, regardless of their ethnic affiliation.

3. Any action against the realization of the inalienable rights of the Crimean Tatar people to self-determination on their own national territory runs counter to the regulations of the statutes of the United Nations and of other generally accepted international legal acts/laws. The Crimean ASSR, restored not as a national-territorial formation, is viewed as an attempt at juridical reinforcement of the results of the deportation of Crimean Tatars in 1944 and is not acknowledged in such form by the Qurultay.

4. The land and natural resources of Crimea, including its potential for health and recreation, is the fundamental national asset of the Crimean Tatar people and the source of well-being for all inhabitants of Crimea. They cannot be exploited against the will and without the consent of the Crimean Tatar people. Any actions that worsen the ecological condition and disturb the historical landscape of Crimea, including the adjacent waters of the Black and Azov Seas, must cease. Harm inflicted on the nature and resources of Crimea must be made good by the perpetrators.

5. In the event of [hostile] action taken by state agencies, or some other parties, against the attainment of the goals proclaimed by the Qurultay and the present declaration, the Qurultay charges the Mejlis with securing recognition of the status of a [namesake] people [*narod*] for the Crimean Tatar people engaged in a struggle for its own national liberation and to act in accordance with this status.

THE QURULTAY APPEALS

to the United Nations Organization, to the peoples, parliaments, and governments of states, [and] to international organizations, with a request to support the aspirations of the Crimean Tatar people for self-determination.

Adopted by the Qurultay of the Crimean Tatar people, City of Simferopol', 28 June 1991.

# Document 2

"The Election Program of the Qurultay of the Crimean Tatar People," *Avdet*, no. 5 (10 March 1994): 3. Translated by Andrew Wilson. The program was approved at the third session of the Second Qurultay, held in Simferopol' from 27 to 29 November 1993.

The third session of the Second Qurultay confirms its adherence to the ideas laid out in the "Declaration of National Sovereignty of the Crimean Tatar People" and views the participation of the Crimean Tatar people in the elections to the Supreme Soviet of the Crimean Republic as a step toward realizing the aims put forward in the declaration. The actions of those deputies elected on the Qurultay list must be guided by the decisions of the Qurultay—the tribune of the will and interests of the Crimean Tatar people and of the Mejlis—the supreme plenipotentiary representative organ of the Crimean Tatar people. Their efforts in the Supreme Soviet will be directed toward achieving the following aims.

### *In the Sphere of Political-Legal Activity and State Building*

The elaboration and realization of urgent systemic measures to create an organizational-legal and a material-financial basis for the return and reestablishment of Crimean Tatars on their historic homeland.

The reformation of the state structure of the Republic of Crimea in the direction of democratization, securing the full observance of the rights of man and of the indigenous [*korennoi*] people in accordance with international norms. The establishment between the Supreme Soviet and Council of Ministers of the Republic of Crimea, on the one hand, and the Mejlis, on the other hand, of relations that recognize the proper status of the Mejlis as the supreme plenipotentiary representative organ of the Crimean Tatar people.

The use of deputies' mandates to secure the effective participation of the representatives of the Crimean Tatar people in the most important branches of government-administrative and juridical-prosecuting power. Taking an active part in the formation of the higher echelons of executive power in Crimea.

The elaboration of constitutional and state-legal norms for the restoration of the rights of the Crimean Tatar people, including the right to self-determination and the restoration of national statehood.

Resolute opposition to attempts to revise existing borders between states or the territorial disintegration or division of Crimea, as a violation of the national sovereignty of the Crimean Tatar people.

## In the Socioeconomic Sphere

The utilization of foreign economic links and political-legal means to enlist the Central Asian states' participation in the material-financial guarantee of the return and reestablishment of Crimean Tatars on their homeland. The activation of all-round measures to bring pressure on Russia, as the party that takes the primary responsibility for the genocide of Crimean Tatars, with the aim of its financing the process of return, rehabilitation, and compensation for damages brought on the Crimean Tatar people.

Bringing to the attention of other states and international organizations the problems of the Crimean Tatar people with the aim of receiving necessary financial and material assistance.

The realization of measures to attract foreign investment, helping contribute to a solution to the problem of repatriation and support for business activity in the Crimean Tatar environment, with the aim of rendering financial and material assistance to compatriots through tax privileges.

Legislative activity to secure the defense of the interests of the Crimean Tatar people in the process of privatization of state and municipal property, taking into account the right to such property of that part of the [Crimean Tatar] people who have not yet returned [to Crimea].

The initiation of the elaboration and realization of special programs, including legislative acts and normative materials directed at a just compensation for material and moral damages caused to Crimean Tatars.

The securing of the social defense of invalids, low-income groups, dependent families, and aged citizens.

The consideration by state organs of Ukrayina of proposals to change legislation on military service, designed to take all-round consideration of the specific features connected with the observance of the national, religious, and other habits and traditions of Crimean Tatars, and during the period of building homes and reestablishment [of Crimean Tatars in Crimea]—defer or completely exempt citizens of Crimean Tatar nationality from fixed-term military service.

Bringing to general attention the problems of ecological defense of the peninsula, preserving its historical landscape, including the adjoining basins of the Black and Azov Seas, the elaboration of correspondingly tough legislative acts.

*In the Sphere of Education, Culture, and Religion*

The revival of general education Crimean Tatar national schools, and a system of middle and higher textbooks designed for the preparation of national cadres.

The passing of a law on the conversion of the Crimean Tatar alphabet into the Latin graphic, and the realization of this law.

The elaboration of systems of measures to accelerate the preparation of national cadres for work in all spheres of social life.

The passing of measures for the reconstruction and development of the national-cultural infrastructure of Crimea: national theaters, music and dance assemblies, creative and craft studios, philharmonic collectives, museums, exhibitions, national youth clubs, and so forth. The passing of special laws on the restoration and protecton of historical, religious, and cultural monuments of the Crimean Tatar people.

The passing of measures to restore the traditional historical place names [*toponimiki*] of Crimea.

## Document 3

"Lilia Budzhurova, Woman with a Passion for Communication—a Brief Autobiography" (Simferopol', 6 July 1996, typescript). Translated by Edward A. Allworth.

The Crimean Tatar Lilia Budzhurova (shown in fig. 14.2) stands out in the culture and society of her people for numerous reasons. She first gained close attention in this book owing to the power and relevance of her poetry, two short specimens of which appear in chapter 1. Personally, she exemplifies the new generation born and educated mainly in Central Asia. And Budzhurova embodies that intermingling of culture and humanity inevitable in the closeness of ethnic contact among nationalities in both Central Asia and other regions of the former Soviet Union. Observers would agree, without doubt, that her talent as a communicator through literature and journalism as well as her service in the Mejlis of the Crimean Tatar Qurultay (parliament) stand as the most important of those achievements. She provides a glimpse of her many accomplishments in the following brief autobiographical sketch.

I was born on 1 November 1958 in the town of Angren, Tashkent *oblast*, Uzbekistan. My father—Rustem Murtazaev—a Crimean Tatar, had been deported at the age of twelve from the Crimean village of Demirji. My mother, Margarita Murtazaeva (née Ermolova), is Russian. I lived in Angren until I was twenty-five, finished school here, then the pedagogical institute, specializing in Russian philology. Here I began to work, first in the pedagogical institute in the department of Russian and foreign literature. Then I was head of the extension division of the Angren Economic Planning Technicum. In 1983, I married and moved to Tashkent.

In 1987, I began to write verses after the first massive demonstration of Crimean Tatars occurred in Moscow.[1] Gradually, my verses became very well known among my people. They circulated them in manuscript copies, then issued them as samizdat.[2] The first collection, *The Ticket Unbought* [*Nekuplennyi bilet*], published in the Baltics, came out in 1989, the second, *When We Return* [*Kogda my vernemsia*], within a year.

When I returned to Crimea in 1990, they already knew me as a poet. Evidently, it was also due to the fact that in 1989 I entered the Organization of the Crimean Tatar National Movement [Organizatsiia krymskotatarskogo natsional'nogo dvizheniia] that made Mustafa Jemiloglu propose that I work on the first independent newspaper about the problems of Crimean Tatars, *Avdet* [*Vozvrashchenie*]. From 1991 on, I have been the editor-in-chief of this newspaper.

In 1991, at the Second Qurultay of the Crimean Tatar people, I was elected to the highest representative body of Crimean Tatars, the Mejlis. In that same year, I tried my strength on television, and since that time I have had my own author's program, "Ana-Yurt" [Homeland] on Crimean television. On becoming a journalist, I moved away from poetry and now busy myself with political publicity. I work with the agencies of France-Presse, Intel-News, and Ekspress-Khronika and publish articles in the area-wide press of Ukrayina. Besides this, in 1995, on the establishment of the Crimean Union of Free Journalists (Krymskii Soiuz Svobodnykh Zhurnalistov), I was elected its president. In 1992, I became the first laureate of the Ismail Gasprinskii [Gaspirali] Prize.

They elected me deputy to the Crimean parliament [Qurultay] in 1994. In the summer of 1996, at the Third Qurultay, I was once again elected to

---

1. A photograph made during that demonstration appears on the dust jacket of the first edition of this volume.
2. Self-published, usually in typescript.

the Mejlis, where, as before, I am the sole woman, which really delights but also saddens me.

I owe everything in life to my father and my homeland. They gave and give me strength. They are my pride.

## Document 4

Nuri Abdulaev, "Biz-Qïrïmlïlarmïz" (We are Crimeans), *Dostluq*, no. 3 (18 January 1991): 4. Translated by Nermin Eren.

My personal opinion is that it is necessary for us to document the real name of our nation and from now on live with that name. It is time to abandon the imposed pseudonym *Tatar*. Furthermore, it is imperative to bring the issue of our nation's name to the attention of the Qurultay [the congress of the Crimean Tatar people] soon to be convened. Moreover, the issue should also be discussed in the conference of All-Crimean Tatar Scholars.

In the past we had our name as Crimeans [*Qïrïmlïlar/Krimtsy*]. It is important that we use and write our name as it was in the past. Also, we should make every effort to reflect that name in our passports as such....

In the newspapers *Dostluq* and *Lenin Bayraghï* (from now on *Yangi Dünya*) the Russian word *krimchane* is translated into our language as *Crimeans* [*Qïrïmlïlar*]. This is not correct because, among our Crimeans, *Qïrïmlïlar* is understood as the same as *Crimean Tatar*. Every nation in the world bears the name of its native land. My thinking is that the correct translation of the word *krimchane* into the Crimean Tatar language should be "People living in Crimea" [*Qïrïmda yashaghanlar*], "Peoples of Crimea" [*Qïrïmdaki khalqlar*], or "Inhabitants of Crimea" [*Qïrïmdaki eali*]. The word *Crimeans* [*Qïrïmlïlar*] should be spared for us, for Crimean Tatars.

## Document 5

The Useinov family, "Bitaraf Kalïp Olamadïq" (We couldn't remain impartial), *Dostluq*, no. 7 (15 February 1991): 4. Translated by Nermin Eren.

We became very excited after reading the article "We Are Crimeans" ["Biz Qïrïmlïlarmïz"]. It is very pleasing to see some of our own people attempting to correct and bring into use the real and historic name of our nation. The purpose of writing this letter is to invite our own people to participate in this important and necessary discussion. This matter, that is, the real name of our nation, should be resolved together. Also, we should inform the other brother nations living in our homeland about who we are and how our history occurred.

If we pay close attention to our history and go back about 150 or 200 years, we will see that our past generations had never considered themselves *Tatar*. They used the name of their own land, *Crimean* [*Qïrïmlï*]. The pseudonym [*laqab*] *Tatar* is a remnant to us from the Slavs [*Slavyanlar*]. They [the Slavs] had given pseudonyms to Russians, *katsap*; to Ukrayinans, *khokhol*; and for us, *Tatar*. But neither Russians nor Ukrayinans allow the pseudonyms to be used and written in their passports. Only we continue to be called with that pseudonym, *Crimean Tatar*. Recently, they made it "pretty" by abandoning *Crimean* and using only *Tatar*. If everything were just and humane, only *Crimean* [*Qïrïmlï*] should have remained.

## Document 6

Sh. Muradasïlova, "Biz-Qïrïmtatarlarmïz" (We are Crimean Tatars), *Dostluq*, no. 7 (15 February 1991): 4. Translated by Nermin Eren.

After I had read the article "We are Crimeans" ["Biz-Qïrïmlïlarmïz"] in *Dostluq*, I felt compelled to express my own opinion on this matter.

I think that we could not gain anything until all our people have returned to and settled in our homeland and the peninsula is proclaimed as the Crimean Tatar Autonomous Republic. Furthermore, to be mingled with the nonnative settlers of Crimea and become *Crimean* [*Krimchane*] cannot help the survival of our people. Our fathers and grandfathers called themselves *Crimean Tatars*. Now, how could we abandon the *Tatar* part of it? Today, *Crimean Tatar* is our nation's name. We have to keep in mind that, after our people were deported to Uzbekistan, the Crimean Tatar children born there were registered and referred to, not as *Uzbek Tatar*, but *Crimean Tatar*. Why, then, should I abandon the *Tatar* part of it? After all, who will I become? Crimean? Who is my nation? Representatives of different nationalities live in Crimea. They all consider themselves as Crimeans. If we mingle with them, do we not further lose our nationality?

# *Bibliography of Recent Publications in English about Crimea*

Compiled by Edward Allworth, with the generous advice of other contributors to this book. The following list of English-language titles represents published writings by the authors of the second edition of *The Tatars of Crimea* and includes, as well, some important recent books and articles relevant to this subject by other writers.

Aksyonov (Aksënov), Vassily. 1981. *The Island of Crimea: A Novel.* Translated from Russian by Michael Henry Heim. Ann Arbor, Mich.: Ardis. Reprint, New York: Random House, 1983; London: Hutchinson, 1985.
Alexeyeva, Ludmilla. 1978. "The Tenth Anniversary of a Chronicle of Current Events." *Chronicle of Human Rights*, no. 29:57–66.
———. 1979. "The Human Rights Movement in the USSR and the Moscow Helsinki Group." *Survey*, no. 4:71–85.
———. 1980. "A Commentary on the Questionnaire, 'The National Problem in the USSR.'" *Prolog*, no. 11:106–27.
———. 1982a. "The Movement for Social and Economic Rights in the Soviet Union." *Russia*, nos. 5/6:81–89.
———. 1982b. "The Status of Soviet Political Prisoners' Rights to Correspondence and Visits." *Chronicle of Human Rights*, no. 47:49–52.
———. 1983. "Quantitative and Qualitative Characteristics of Soviet Dissent." *Russia*, nos. 7/8:114–35.
———. 1985. *Soviet Dissent: Contemporary Movements for National, Religious and Human Rights.* Translated by Carol Pearce and John Glad. Middletown, Conn.: Wesleyan University Press.
———. 1986. *U.S. Radio Broadcasts to the Soviet Union.* New York: Helsinki Watch.
Allworth, Edward. 1971. "Crimean Tatar." In *Nationalities of the Soviet East: Publications and Writing Systems.* New York: Columbia University Press.
———. 1975. "Crimea and Crimean Tatar." In *Soviet Asia: Bibliographies: A Compilation of Social Science and Humanities Sources on the Iranian, Mongolian and Turkic Nationalities: With an Essay on the Soviet-Asian Controversy.* New York: Praeger.

———. 1984. "Tatar Literature." In *Encyclopedia of World Literature in the Twentieth Century*, vol. 4. New York: Frederick Ungar.

———. 1988a. "The Crimean Tatar Case." In Allworth (1988c).

———. 1988b. "Mass Exile, Ethnocide, Group Derogation—Anomaly or Norm in Soviet Nationality Politics?" In Allworth (1988c).

———. 1993. "The Precarious Existence of Small Nationalities in Russia and Georgia." *Central Asian Survey*, no. 1:5–12.

———, ed. 1988c. *Tatars of the Crimea: Their Struggle for Survival*. 1st ed. Central Asia Book Series. Durham, N.C.: Duke University Press.

Altan, Mübeyyin Batu. 1986a. "Mustafa Dzhemilev Deserves the Nobel Prize." *Crimean Review* 1, no. 1 (18 May): 30–31.

———. 1986b. "The Plight of the Crimean Tatar People." *Crimean Review* 1, no. 1 (18 May): 6–15.

———. 1988. "Structures: The Importance of Family—a Personal Memoir." In Allworth (1988c).

———. 1989. "Vladimir Pozner in Concord, Massachusetts." *Crimean Review* 4, no. 1 (18 June): 9–11.

———. 1990. "Ismail Bey Gaspirali (1851–1914)." *Crimean Review* 5, no. 1:6–7.

———. 1991. "Sefername and Togai Bei—a Brief Introduction to Two Seventeenth-Century Crimean Tatar Epic Poems." *Crimean Review* 6, nos. 1–2:28–32.

———. 1995a. "The Tragedy of Crimean Tatars Continues." *Beacon*, 18 May, 6.

———. 1995b. "Ukraine's Nationalities Problem—The Plight of the Crimean Tatar People." *Crimean Review* 7, no. 7:15–28.

Altan, Mübeyyin Batu, and Fikret Turan. 1996. *Crimea: A General Bibliographic Survey*. Cambridge, Mass.: Widener Library (Middle Eastern Section), Harvard University.

Baraheni, Reza, Pavel Litvinov, Ralph Schoenman, and Martin Sostre, eds. 1976. *In Defense of Mustafa Dzhemilev*. New York: Mustafa Dzhemilev Defense Committee.

Barkovets, Aliya, Zinaida Peregudova, and Lyubov Tyutyunnik, comps. 1993. *The Romanovs and the Crimea*. Moscow: Russia-Wide Nobility Descendants' Union, "Rurik" Publishers, and Publishing Firm "Kruk."

Barringer, Felicity. 1987. "Tatars Stage a Noisy Protest in Moscow." *New York Times*, 26 July, 3.

Bekirov, Nadir. *See* Doroszewska (1995b).

Bennigsen, Alexander. 1980. "Tatars." In *Harvard Encyclopedia of American Ethnic Groups*, ed. Stephan Thernstrom. Cambridge, Mass.: Harvard University Press.

Bezanis, Lowell. 1992. "Volga-Ural Tatars in Emigration." *Central Asian Survey* 11, no. 4:29–74.

———. 1994. "Soviet Muslim Emigres in the Republic of Turkey." *Central Asian Survey* 13, no. 1:59–180.

Burke, Justin, et al. 1996. *Crimean Tatars: Repatriation and Conflict Prevention.* New York: Open Society Institute, Forced Migration Projects.

Cemilev. *See* Jemilev.

Conquest, Robert. 1970. *The Nation Killers: The Soviet Deportation of Nationalities.* London: Macmillan.

———. 1991. *Stalin: Breaker of Nations.* London: Weidenfeld & Nicolson.

"Crimean Tatar Is Freed." 1986. *New York Times*, 21 December, 14.

Doroszewska, Urszula. 1992a. "Crimea: Whose Country?" *Uncaptive Minds* 5, no. 3, Serial no. 21:39–50.

———. 1992b. "Reclaiming a Homeland: An Interview with Mustafa Dzhemilev." *Uncaptive Minds* 5, no. 3 (21) (Fall): 51–62.

———. 1995a. "Sevastopol—City of Russian Glory." *Uncaptive Minds* 8, no. 2 (29) (Summer): 49–54.

———. 1995b. "We Prefer Ukraine: An Interview with Nadir Bekirov." *Uncaptive Minds* 8, no. 2 (29) (Summer): 55–61.

De Zwager, Nicolaas. 1996. *Crimea: A Programme for the Future in Ukraine.* Geneva: International Organization for Migration.

Drohobycky, Maria, ed. 1995. *Crimea: Dynamics, Challenges, Prospects.* Lanham, Md.: American Association for the Advancement of Science; Rowman and Littlefield.

Duke, David F. See Marples and Duke (1995).

Dzhemilev. *See* Jemilev.

Eren, Nermin. 1995. "The Eurasian Nationalities Collection in Non-Slavic Languages Held by the Slavic and Baltic Division of the New York Public Library." *Nationalities Papers* 23, no. 4 (December): 789–95.

Fisher, Alan W. 1967. "Shahin Giray, the Reformer Khan, and the Russian Annexation of the Crimea." *Jahrbücher für Geschichte Osteuropas*, n.s. 15, no. 4:375–94.

———. 1970. *The Russian Annexation of the Crimea, 1772–1783.* Cambridge: Cambridge University Press.

———. 1972a. "Muscovy and the Black Sea Slave Trade." *Canadian-American Slavic Studies* 6, no. 4:575–94.

———. 1972b. "Les rapports entre l'Empire ottoman et la Crimee: L'aspect financier." *Cahiers du monde russe et soviétique* 13, no. 4:368–81.

———. 1973. "Azov in the Sixteenth and Seventeenth Centuries." *Jahrbücher für Geschichte Osteuropas*, n.s., 21, no. 2:161–74.

———. 1977. "Crimean Separatism in the Ottoman Empire." In *Nationalism in a Non-National State: The Dissolution of the Ottoman Empire*, ed. William W. Haddad and William Ochsenwald. Columbus: Ohio State University Press.

———. 1978a. *The Crimean Tatars*. Stanford, Calif.: Hoover Institution Press. 2d printing, 1987.

———. 1978b. "Ottoman Sources for a Study of Kefe Vilayet: The *Maliyeden Müdevver Fond* in the Bashbakanlik Arshivi in Istanbul." *Cahiers du monde russe et soviétique* 19, nos. 1–2:191–205.

———. 1979. "The Crimean Tatars, the USSR, and Turkey." In *Soviet Asian Frontiers*, ed. William O. McCagg and Brian D. Silver. New York: Pergamon.

———. 1979–80. "The Ottoman Crimea in the Mid-Seventeenth Century: Some Problems and Preliminary Considerations." *Harvard Ukrainian Studies* 3–4: 215–26.

———. 1981. "The Ottoman Crimea in the Sixteenth Century." *Harvard Ukrainian Studies* 5:135–70.

———. 1987. "The Emigration of Russian Muslims after the Crimean War." *Jahrbücher für Geschichte Osteuropas* 37, no. 4:356–71.

———. 1988. "Ismail Gaspirali, Model Leader for Asia." In Allworth (1988c).

———. 1994. "Crimean Khanate." In *Oxford Encyclopaedia of Modern Islam*, vol. 1. Oxford: Oxford University Press.

Gaspirali, Ismail Bey. 1988. "Russian-Oriental Relations." Translated by Edward J. Lazzerini. In Allworth (1988c).

Grigorenko, Petr G. 1976. *The Grigorenko Papers: Writings by General P. G. Grigorenko and Documents on His Case*. Boulder, Colo.: Westview.

"Gromyko to Study Homeland for Resettled Crimean Tatars," 1987. *New York Times*, 24 July, A9.

Guboglo, Mikhail, and Svetlana Chervonnaia. 1995. "The Crimean Tatar Question and the Present Ethnopolitical Situation in Crimea." *Russian Politics and Law* 33, no. 6 (November–December): 31–60.

Gülüm, Riza. 1988. "Rituals: Artistic, Cultural, and Social Activities." In Allworth (1988c).

Inalcik, Halil. 1946–47. "The Origin of the Ottoman-Russian Rivalry and the Volga-Don Canal (1569)." *Ankara Üniversitesi Yıllığı*, no. 1:47–106.

Jemilev (Dzhemilev), Mustafa. See Doroszewska (1992b).

Jemilev, Reshat, comp. 1986. *Musa Mamut—Human Torch: List of Documents*. Publication no. 8. New York: Crimea Foundation.

Kamınskaıa, Dina. 1982. *Final Judgment: My Life as a Soviet Defense Attorney*. New York: Simon & Schuster.

Karpat, Kemal H. 1984–85. "Ottoman Urbanism: The Crimean Emigration to Dobruja and the Founding of Mejidiye, 1856–1878." *International Journal of Turkish Studies* 3, no. 1 (Winter): 1–25.

———. 1985. *Ottoman Population, 1830–1914: Demographic and Social Characteristics*. Madison, Wis.: University of Wisconsin Press.

Kirimal, Edige. 1958. "The Crimean Turks." In *Genocide in the USSR: Studies in Group Destruction*. New York: Institute for the Study of the USSR.

———. 1964. "Mass Deportations and Massacres in the Crimea." *Cultura Turcica*, no. 2 (1964): 253–65.

———. 1970. "The Crimean Tatars." *Studies on the Soviet Union*, n.s., no. 1 (1970): 70–97.

———. 1971. *The Crimean Tatars*. Munich: Institute for the Study of the USSR.

Kirimca, Seyit Ahmet. 1988. "Symbols: The National Anthem and Patriotic Songs by Three Poets." In Allworth (1988c).

Kirimli, Hakan. 1996. *National Movements and National Identity among the Crimean Tatars, 1905–1916*. Ottoman Empire and Its Heritage, vol. 7. Leiden: E. J. Brill.

Kuzio, Taras. 1994. *Russia-Crimea-Ukraine: Triangle of Conflict*. London: Research Institute for the Study of Conflict and Terrorism.

Kuzio, Taras, and Andrew Wilson. 1994. *Ukraine: Perestroika to Independence*. Basingstoke: Macmillan; New York: St. Martin's.

Lazzerini, Edward J. 1975a. "Gadidism at the Turn of the Twentieth Century: A View from Within." *Cahiers du monde russe et soviétique* 16, no. 2 (April–June): 245–77.

———. 1980. "Sayyid Jamal ad-Din al-Afghani from the Perspective of a Russian Muslim." In *Iran: Toward Modernity: Studies in Thought, Politics and Society*, ed. Elie Kedourie and S. Haim. London: Frank Case.

———. 1981. "Tatarovedenie and the 'New Historiography' in the USSR: Revising the Interpretation of the Tatar-Russian Relationship." *Slavic Review* 40, no. 4 (Winter): 625–35.

———. 1982–83. "Ethnicity and the Uses of History: The Case of the Volga Tatars and Jadidism." *Central Asian Survey* 1, nos. 2–3 (October–January): 61–69.

———. 1984. "From Bakhchisarai to Bukhara in 1893: Ismail Bey Gasprinskii's Journey to Central Asia." *Central Asian Survey* 4, no. 4 (1984): 77–88.

———. 1985. "Crimean Tatar: The Fate of a Severed Tongue." In *Socio-Linguistic*

*Perspectives on Soviet National Languages*, ed. Isabelle T. Kreindler. Amsterdam: Mouton deGruyter.

———. 1986. "The Revival of Islam in Pre-Revolutionary Russia; or, Why a Prosopography of the Tatar Ulema?" In *Passé turko-tatar, présent soviétique*, ed. Gilles Veinstein, Chantal Lemercier-Quelquejay, and S. Enders Wimbush. Louvain: Peeter.

———. 1988a. "The Crimea under Russia Rule: 1783 to the Great Reforms." In *Russian Colonial Expansion to 1917*, ed. Michael Rywkin. London: Mansell.

———. 1988b. "Ismail Bey Gasprinskii (Gaspirali), the Discourse of Modernism, and the Russians." In Allworth (1988c).

———. 1992a. "Beyond Renewal: The *Jadid* Response to Pressure for Change in the Modern Age." In *Muslims of Central Asia: Expressions of Identity and Change*, ed. Jo-Ann Gross. Durham, N.C.: Duke University Press.

———. 1992b. "The Debate over Instruction of Muslims in Post-1905 Russia: A Local Perspective." In *Secular and Religious Forces in Late Tsarist Russia*, ed. Charles Timberlake. Seattle: University of Washington Press.

———. 1992c. "Ismail Bey Gasprinskii's *Perevodchik/Tercuman*: A Clarion of Modernism." In *Central Asian Monuments*, ed. Hasan B. Paksoy. Istanbul: Isis.

———. 1993. *The Volga Tatars in Central Asia, 18th–20th Centuries: From Diaspora to Hegemony?* Washington, D.C.: National Council for Soviet and East European Research.

———. 1994. "Defining the Orient" A Nineteenth-Century Russo-Tatar Polemic over Identity and Cultural Representation." In *Muslim Communities Reemerge: Historical Perspectives on Nationality, Politics, and Opposition in the Former Soviet Union and Yugoslavia*, ed. Andreas Kappeler, Gerhard Simon, Georg Brunner, and Edward Allworth. Central Asia Book Series. Durham, N.C.: Duke University Press.

———. 1996. "Crimean Tatars." In *The Nationalities Question in the Post-Soviet States*, 2d ed., ed. Graham Smith. London: Longman.

Marples, David R., and David F. Duke. 1995. "Ukraine, Russia, and the Question of Crimea." *Nationalities Papers* 23, no. 2 (Summer): 261–90.

Nahaylo, Bohdan. See Sheehy and Nahaylo (1973).

Nekrich, Aleksandr M. 1978. *The Punished Peoples: The Deportation and Fate of Soviet Minorities at the End of the Second World War*. New York: W. W. Norton.

———. 1991. *"Punished Peoples" of the Soviet Union: The Continuing Legacy of Stalin's Deportations*. New York: Human Rights Watch.

Peregudova, Zinaida. See Barkovets, Peregudova, and Tyutyunnik (1993).

"Persecution of Crimean Tatars." *A Chronicle of Current Events*. London: Amnesty International Publications. No. 31 (1974): entire issue; nos. 40/41/42 (1979): no. 41: 165–73, no. 42: 247–50; nos. 43/44/45 (1979): no. 43: 52–54, no. 44: 169–79; no. 51 (1979): 114–28; no. 52 (1980): 79–96; no. 54 (1980): 86–88; no. 57 (1981): 53–55; nos. 59/60/61 (1982): no. 60: 50–51.

Pinson, Mark. 1972–73/74. "Russian Policy and the Emigration of the Crimean Tatars to the Ottoman Empire, 1854–1862." *Güney Dogu Avrupa Araştirmalari Dergisi*, no. 1:37–56; nos. 2–3:101–14.

Plyusch, Leonid. 1979. "The Crimean Tatars." In *History's Carnival*. New York: Harcourt Brace Jovanovich.

Potichnyi, Peter J. 1975. "The Struggle of the Crimean Tatars." *Canadian Slavonic Papers*, nos. 2–3:301–19. Reprinted in *Nationalism and Human Rights: Processes of Modernization in the USSR*, ed. Ihor Kamenetsky (Littleton, Colo.: Libraries Unlimited for the Association for the Study of the Nationalities [USSR and Eastern Europe], 1977).

Prytula, Volodymyr. 1995. "The Crimean Deadlock." *Uncaptive Minds* 8, no. 2 (29): 43–47.

Reddaway, Peter. 1969. "The Soviet Treatment of Dissenters and the Growth of a Civil Rights Movement." In *Rights and Wrongs: Some Essays on Human Rights*, ed. C. Hill. Harmondsworth: Penguin.

———. 1976. "The Development of Dissent in the USSR." In *The Soviet Empire: Expansion and Détente*, ed. William E. Griffith. Lexington, Mass.: Lexington.

———. 1984. *Soviet Policies on Dissent and Emigration: The Radical Change of Course since 1979*. Occasional Paper no. 192. Washington, D.C.: Kennan Institute for Advanced Russian Studies.

———. 1988. "The Crimean Tatar Drive for Repatriation: Some Comparisons with Other Movements of Dissent in the USSR." In Allworth (1988c).

———. 1993a. "Research on Soviet Decline." *Post-Soviet Affairs* 9, no. 2 (April–June): 176–81.

———. 1993b. "Sovietology and Dissent: New Sources of Protest." *RFE/RL Research Report* 1, no. 5 (January): 12–16.

———, chair. 1993c. "Two Years after the Collapse of the USSR: A Panel of Specialists." *Post-Soviet Affairs* 9, no. 4 (October/December): 281–313.

———, ed. 1972. *Uncensored Russia: The Human Rights Movement in the Soviet Union*. London: Cape.

Rupert, James. 1996. "Coming Home to Poverty: Tatars' Return Roils Crimea's Politics." *Washington Post*, 5 January.

Sasse, Gwendolyn. "The Crimean Issue." *Journal of Communist Studies and Transitional Politics* 12, no. 1 (1996): 83–116.

Sckolnick, Lewis B. 1994. *Crimean Tatars and Volga Germans*. Civil Rights Reporter Series. Leverett, Mass.: Rector.

Seytmuratova, Ayshe. 1980a. "People Who Refuse to Die." *Impact International*, 11–24 July, 5–7.

———. 1980b. [Testimony.] In *Basket III: Implementation of the Helsinki Accords; Hearings before the Commission on Security and Cooperation in Europe; Ninety-sixth Congress, Second Session on Implementation of the Helsinki Accords*, vol. 13, *Soviet Treatment of Ethnic Groups, April 29, 1980*. Washington, D.C.: U.S. Government Printing Office.

———. 1981. "The Plight of the Crimean Tatars." *Rabitat al-Alam al-Islami*, no. 4 (February): 24–27.

———. 1984. "Deportation of the Crimean Tatar Nation on May 18, 1944." *Religion in Communist Dominated Areas*, nos. 4–6:82–84, 94.

———. 1986. *Mustafa Dzhemilev and the Crimean Tatars: Story of a Man and His People: Facts, Documents, How to Help*. New York: Center for Democracy.

———. 1988. "The Elders of the New National Movement: Recollections." In Allworth (1988c).

Sheehy, Ann, and Bohdan Nahaylo. 1973. *The Crimean Tatars and Volga Germans: Soviet Treatment of Two National Minorities*. Report no. 6. London: Minority Rights Group. New, rev. ed., 1973; 3d ed., 1980.

Solzhenitsyn, Aleksandr. I. 1979. *The Gulag Archipelago, 1918–1956: An Experiment in Literary Investigation*. Translated by Harry Willetts. New York: Harper and Row.

Stearns, MacDonald. 1978. *Crimean Gothic: Analysis and Etymology of the Corpus*. Saratoga, Calif.: Anma Libri.

Stewart, Susan. 1994. "The Tatar Dimension." *RFE/RFL Research Report* 3, no. 19 (13 May): 22–26.

Turan, Fikret. *See* Altan and Turan (1996).

Turkay, Osman. 1974. "The Tragedy of the Crimean Tatars." *Index on Censorship*, no. 1:67–68.

Tyutyunnik, Lyubov. *See* Barkovets, Peregudova, and Tyutyunnik (1993).

Vardys, V. Stanley. 1971. "The Case of the Crimean Tatars." *Russian Review*, no. 2:100–109.

Wilson, Andrew. 1993. "Crimea's Political Cauldron." *RFE/RL Research Report* 2, no. 45 (12 November): 1–8.

———. 1994a. *The Crimean Tatars: A Situation Report on the Crimean Tatars*. London: International Alert.
———. 1994b. "The Elections in Crimea." *RFE/RL Research Report* 3, no. 25 (24 June): 7–19.
———. 1995. "Parliamentary and Presidential Elections in Ukraine: The Issue of Crimea." In *Crimea: Dynamics, Challenges, Prospects*, ed. Maria Drohobycky.
———. 1996. *Ukrainian Nationalism in the 1990s: A Minority Faith*. Cambridge: Cambridge University Press.
———. *See also* Kuzio and Wilson (1994).

## *Notes on the Authors*

*Ludmilla Alexeyeva*, born in Kezlev (Eupatoria), Crimea, studied at the University of Moscow, graduating in 1950, and pursued graduate work in the Institute of Economics of the Academy of Sciences, also in Moscow. Thereafter, she worked as an editor in scientific publishing houses in the same city, 1958–77. A founding member of the Moscow Helsinki Group, since emigration from the Soviet Union in 1977 she has served as a consultant to the Helsinki Watch Group, New York. She also serves on the board of the Open Society Institute, Forced Migration Projects, New York. Having spent fifteen years as an emigrant in the United States, she returned to Moscow as a consultant to the AFL-CIO's Free Trade Union Institute after the fall of the Soviet regime.

*Edward A. Allworth* holds a Ph.D. in Slavic and Turkic languages and cultures from Columbia University (1959). Since 1994, he has been Emeritus Professor at Columbia University. He is a member of the Executive Committee, The Harriman Institute, Columbia University; chief editor of the Central Asia Book Series, Duke University Press; a member of the editorial board of the *Central Asia Monitor*; and advisory editor of the *Nationalities Papers* journal. He served as Visiting Fellow in the Post-Soviet States in Transition Programme, Sidney Sussex College, University of Cambridge, England, for the 1995 autumn term. He is an in-house advisor to the Baltic and Slavic Division and Eurasian collections at the New York Public Library.

*Mübeyyin Batu Altan*, born in Külchora, Crimean ASSR, emigrated to the West in the spring of 1944 and to the United States in 1962. He holds an M.A. in political science from the University of Bridgeport (1972) and is currently a research associate and Ph.D. candidate at the Institute of Oriental Studies, Kyiv, Ukrayina. He also works in the Massachusetts Rehabilitation Commission, Commonwealth of Massachusetts. He is the cofounder and vice president of the Crimea Foundation and the editor and publisher of the *Crimean Review.*

*Nermin Eren*, born in Ruse, Bulgaria, to a Crimean Tatar family, immigrated to Turkiye in 1972. He holds an M.A. in history from the Social Science Institute, Marmara University (1988); an M.Phil. in Central Asian cultural history from Columbia University (1993); and is a candidate for the Ph.D. in cultural history at Columbia University. He has also worked as a research assistant at the Turkic Institute, Marmara University, taught spoken Turkish at Columbia University (fall semester, 1996), and served as bibliographic assistant at the Columbia University

Libraries and the New York Public Library (1992–96). Since 1996, he has been national executive director of the Federation of Turkish-American Associations, Inc.

*Alan W. Fisher* holds a Ph.D. in Russian and Ottoman history and language from Columbia University (1967). He is currently a professor in the Department of History at Michigan State University; director of the Center for Integrative Studies in the Arts and Humanities, Michigan State University; secretary-treasurer of the Institute of Turkish Studies, Washington, D.C.; and vice-president of the American Research Institute in Turkiye.

*Riza Gülüm*, born in Kalimtay, Crimea, was educated in the Crimean Tatar high school Aqyar (Sevastopol), the mechanics' school, Dnepropetrovsk, and the cadets' school, Odessa, from which he graduated in 1940. He emigrated from the Soviet Union during World War II, residing in Europe and Turkiye before coming to the United States. He has served as vice president of the American Association of Crimean Turks. He has led many music and dance groups.

*Seyit Ahmet Kirimca* was born in Jungelager Camp, Kassel, West Germany, of Crimean Tatar parents who emigrated from Crimea in March 1944 to Europe and Turkiye before coming to the United States in late 1963. He was educated in Mamure Koy, with secondary education through the lycée level in Eskishehir, Turkiye. He holds the B.S. degree in geology from Brooklyn College (1974) and now works in transportation. He is the organizer and cofounder of the Ismail Gaspirali Fund, Columbia University.

*Edward J. Lazzerini* holds a Ph.D. in history, from the University of Washington, Seattle (1973). He is a professor of history at the University of New Orleans; director of the Asian Studies Program, University of New Orleans; a member of the editorial advisory boards of *Central Asian Survey* and *Nationalities Papers*; the editor of the *Modern Encyclopedia of Russian, Soviet, and Eurasian History*; and president of the Association for the Advancement of Central Asian Research. He has traveled extensively to Crimea since 1991, conducting research in archives and libraries.

*Peter Reddaway* holds an M.A. in Russian area studies from Cambridge University (1966) and did graduate work in Soviet politics at Harvard University, Moscow State University, and the London School of Economics (1962–65). He is now a professor of political science and international affairs at the Institute for European, Russian, and Eurasian Studies, George Washington University. He was directing secretary of the Kennan Institute for Advanced Russian Studies, Washington, D.C., from 1986 to 1989 and served on the editorial board of *Religion in Communist Lands*. He has made frequent research trips to the Soviet Union and to Russia.

*Ayshe Seytmuratova*, born in Aji Elin (Derzhavin), Crimean ASSR, was educated in Uzbekistan, graduating from Russian-language middle school in 1957 and from the University of Samarkand in 1963 in history. She did graduate study in the

Institute of History, Uzbekistan SSR Academy of Sciences. She received three years' imprisonment in camps for political prisoners in the Mordvin ASSR. She emigrated from the Soviet Union in 1978 and came to the United States in early 1979. She serves as a consultant to the Center for Democracy, New York. Since the breakup of the Soviet Union, she has actively engaged in humanitarian assistance in Crimea, especially aid to elderly Crimean Tatars through the charitable organization "Merhamet (Mercy)," which she heads.

*Andrew Wilson* holds a Ph.D. from the London School of Economics and Political Science (1993), writing on modern Ukrayinan nationalism. He is a senior research fellow at Sidney Sussex College, University of Cambridge, and lecturer in Ukrayinan Studies at the School of Slavonic and East European Studies (SSEES), London. He has made several research trips to Crimea, including one sponsored by the organization International Alert in September–October 1993 and one in October 1997 to investigate the political and social conditions of Crimean Tatars.

# Index

This index thoroughly covers the twelve studies making up this book and selectively refers to materials provided in the chapters devoted exclusively to documents. In subentries, the initials CT stand for Crimean Tatar, CTs for Crimean Tatars.

Abdüljemil: father of Mustafa Jemiloglu, vii

Abkhazians: consider CTs good neighbors, 273

Akchokrakli, Osman: CT educator and folklorist, 30, 85, 88

Aksyonov, Vassily: Russian dissident author, 5

"Alim the Crimean Brave" (play), 87

Andropov, Yurii V.: meets with CT petitioners, 164

Bagrov, N. (Mykola, in Ukrayinan): moderate chairman of Crimea Council, 295; signs 1993 decree renaming CTs, 14

Bakhshish, Ilyas: composer, 89; manager of Qaytarma Ensemble, 89, 91–92; musical director of Crimean Tatar State Drama Theater, 92; Uzbekistan national opera superviser, 92

Bakkal family: dancer Hüseyin, 92–93; students of, 93–95; Tajikistan actress and choreographer Remziye, 93–94

Bektore, Emin: dance and music teacher, drama producer, 343; emigrant CT born in Romania, 343

Bektore, Shevki: author of memoir *Red Flows the Volga*, 343; second-generation emigrant teacher and poet, 71, 78–79, 340, 343

Cemeteries: Communist desecration of, 196; of CT Khans, 22; CT respect for, 22–23; of Qaraims, 22; in Turkiye, 22

Chobanzade, Bekir Sitki: CT educator, poet, and scholar, 71, 80–81

Chubarov, Refat: denies arming of CTs, 298; deputy head (1991–) of CT Mejlis (Executive Committee), 285; elected a vice-chairman under Supruniuk, 309; leader (1991–93) OKND, 285; rejects idea of CT independence, 292–93; sits on Crimean Council Presidium, 308

Colonialism: Gaspirali excuses Russians for, 57–62

CPC (Communist Party of Crimea—KPK), 297; banned in August 1991, 297

CPSU (Communist Party of the Soviet Union–SSSR), 99; nationality policies of, 180–81; Twenty-fourth Congress of, 212; Twenty-third Congress of, 183. *See also* Political parties and governmental structures

"Crimea for Crimeans" slogan, 9

Crimean Tatar authors and poets, 73; Cherkez Ali, 2; Yusuf Bolat, 89–90; Lilia Budzhurova, 3–4, 19, 357–59; Remzi Burnash, 18; Eskender Fazil, 2–3; folk *akeys* and *kedays*, 73; folk *manes* and *chins*, 85–86; Ümer Ipchi, dramatist, 86–87; literary intelligentsia destroyed by Communist Party, 174; Party officials refuse Crimean burial to poet Eshref Shemizade, 106. *See also* Bakhshish; Chobanzade; Ipchi: "I Pledge"

Crimean Tatars: appeal to CPSU, 99; considered cunning by Russian missionaries, 52; 18 May 1944 deportation to Central Asia of, 12; nonviolence of, 186, 220–23, 312; poetic expression of, 2–5; restoring confidence of, 254; staunch character of, 1, 22, 192, 217, 224, 234; violence against, 186–87, 258–59, 272, 310–11. *See also* Protest methods of CTs

Crimean Tatar State Drama Theater (CTSDT), 87–88

Crimea's districts, geography, towns, and topography: Aqmesjit (Simferopol'), 8; Aqyar (Sevastopol), 9; Bakhchesaray, 8, 111; Chirchik, assaults on CTs witnessed in, 165, 239–40; Chukurja village flooded, 13; Itil (Volga) river, 6; Kefe, 80; Kerch, 5; Salgir River forms Simferopol' Reservoir, 13

CTSDT. *See* Crimean Tatar State Drama Theater

Education: administrators deny admission to CT activist, 160, 162–63, 248; Akchora Seminary near Jankoy, 75; CT graduates reject appointments, 199–200; CT history denied to exiles, 100, 157; Dar ul-Malumat girls' school, 76; Gaspirali's own training, 131; Russia considered defamed by European scholars, 113; Rustiye Medrese of Aqmesjit, 75; Rustiye Medrese of Qarasuvbazar, 80; secondary and primary schools teach only Russian, 199; of women, 39, 140; Zinjirli Medrese near Bakhchesaray, 75, 151

Elections, 299–307; CTs lose local single-member voting, 303; Russia bloc wins majority of Crimean council seats, 304

The Emigration (see chap. 15): actively supports CT rebuilding, 324, 343–46; controversy over group name among, 335–37; CTs concentrated in four foreign countries, 325; helps preserve CT culture, 347; important leaders of, 340–43, 347; largest group of CTs located in Turkiye, 328; small numbers in Bulgaria, 331; twenty-four CT organizations in Turkiye, 330

Emir Zade, Hayri: brave man, 96; dancer, 92, 95–97

"The Enemy" (*Düshman;* drama), 88

Erejepova, Sabriye: actress and singer, 90–91

Ethnic-group and ethnic identity: rejection of, 7. *See also* Identity

Exile(s): actress dies in, 90; Bekabad, Uzbekistan, zone of, 20, 177–78; in Chirchik, Uzbekistan, 185; CTs forced into, 154–56; in German refugee camps, 102; half of CTs remain in Central Asia, 156–57, 323; Slavs resist premature CT return from, 227; in Transcaucasus, Turkiye, and Ukrayina, 102

*Funereal Information Document No. 69:* CTs appeal to Uzbekistan Writers' Union, 185–87; denounced as slander, 187

Gaspirali (Gasprinskii), Ismail Bey (chaps. 2–3): advocates CT-Russian rapprochement, 55–57, 120–21; buried beside *medrese,* 151; conversations in Istanbul of, 125–26; death of, 30, 151; educational reforms of, 41–43, 135–36; emphasizes religious, not ethnic unity, 23; his name, 67n; lifestyle of, 149; Soviet scholars ignore, 32; vital statistics for, 129–31; works by, 132–33

Genocide: CTs charge Soviet regime with, 190–192, 197

*Gesture of Respect* (*Temenna;* poetry collection), 2–3

Giray dynasty of Crimea. Islam Giray Khan II, 85; Khan Giray's fateful decision, 211; Khansaray Palace of the Crimean Khans, 74; loses independence to Russians, 4; Mengli Giray Khan founds Zinjirli Medrese, 75; Mengli Giray Khan's tomb, 151; *Shahin Giray* (drama), 88

*The Girl Arzi (Arzï qïz;* musical), 89, 91–92

Gorchakova, Princess Elena S.: 1881 memoirs by, 257

Grigorenko, General Petr, 103; advocates using legalism, 231; CTs hear speech of, 215–16; Mustafa Jemiloglu's letter to, 211; son of, 219

Homeland (*vatan/rodina*): CT definition of, 274; ideas of, 269, 271, 274; incomplete, 265–67; qualifications of a, 263–65; Russian definitions of, 261–63; symbol of group identity for the emigration, 338; verses about, 3–5, 274–75, 323, 338

Homeless, 266–67

Hook, Sidney: about leadership, vii

Ibrahimov, Veli: institutes affirmative action for CTs, 291; president of Crimean ASSR, 96; pro-Communist CT leader, 10; Soviet authorities execute, 96

Identity: art and culture focus on, 84; CT citizenship in Ukrayina, 295; CTs lack group recognition, 184; European antagonism to CTs' Islamic identity, 110–14; flag and songs symbolize Crimea for the emigration, 338–39; symbols of, 81–82. *See also* Name(s), naming, and namesakes

Il'minskii, Nikolai Ivanovich: opposed Gaspirali's Muslim reforms, 38, 41, 52; orthodox Christian missionary, 51

Ipchi, Ümer: theater and drama school director, 87–88. *See also* Crimean Tatar authors and poets

"I Pledge" national anthem: banned by czarist regime, 73; translation and text of, 74–76; written by Numan Chelebi Jihan, 72

*The Island Crimea* (novel), 5

Jemiloglu, Mustafa (chap. 10): broad outlook of, 219; convicted of defaming Soviet nationality policies, 198; harassed and imprisoned by Soviet authorities, 192–98, 206, 217; heart and soul of CT nationality, 104–5; infancy of, vii, 206; leadership of, 29, 214–15; 1970 trial transcript of, 237–45; vital statistics for, 237–38; young adulthood of, viii, 210–11

Jemiloglu, Safinar: provides photos for this book, xiii, 21, 100; vital statistics of, 107; wife of Mustafa, 107–8

Jihan, Numan Chelebi: creates CT national anthem, 72; Crimean government's president, 9, 71, 75–77; killing of, 9

*Journeys over Poland* (*Polonya üzerine seferleri;* travels), 85

KGB (USSR Committee for State Security): accused by Mustafa Jemiloglu, 213–14; jails CT dissidents, 163–64, 166, 192–96; repeatedly imprisons CT protesters, 170–71

Khrushchev, Nikita S.: denounced mass deportations, 202, 281

Kïrïmal, Edige Mustafa: emigrant activist, scholar, and editor, 342

Kïrïmer, Jafer Seydahmet: emigrant author, editor, and political leader, 340–41.

Kravchuk, Leonid: CTs appeal to, 294; elected president of Ukrayina Re-

Kravchuk, Leonid (*cont.*)
public, 293; opposes Yurii Meshkov's Republic Movement of Crimea, 295; rebuffs CT overtures, 295; supports Mykola Bagrov as Crimea Council chairman, 295

Kuchma, Leonid: abolishes 1992 Crimea constitution and presidency, 308; successful candidate for Ukrayinan presidency (1994), 305; unsuccessfully opposed in elections by CTs, 305

Language and group identity: All-Turkic, 7; CT language untaught, 15, 17; ethnically neutral, 7; Gaspirali's common language for all Turkic people, 37–38, 137–41; mother tongue, 18–19; Ottoman Turkish, 7; phonetic method of teaching, 139; Russian used by many CTs, 17–18

Makhfure: mother of Mustafa Jemiloglu, vii

Mamut, Musa: self-immolation of, in protest, 167–69

*Memoirs about Crimea (Vospominaniia o Krymie)*, 257

Meshkov, Yurii: anti-CT candidate for presidency, 302; defeats Mykola Bagrov, 302; heads Russia bloc in Crimea, 301–2; his bloc wins majority of seats, 304

Meskhetians: CTs cooperate with, 231; suffer prolonged exile, 226

Migrations: CTs leave home after Russian conquest, 326, 327. *See also* Emigration

Mubarek and Baharistan *raions* of Uzbekistan: offered to CTs for settlement, 199–200

Muslim writers (not CTs), 142

"My Mother Tongue" (poems), 18–19, 80–81

"My Tatarness" (popular CT song), 71, 77–80, 82

Name(s), naming, and namesakes: Aq Mechet/Chernomorsk, 12; *Chersonesus Taurica* (Tauric Chersonese), 5; controversies among CTs in Crimea over, 359–60; Crimea/Krym/Qïrïm/Qrïm, 4–7; CTs or Tatars, 8; good name, 273–74; omission of CT designation, 104; Qarasuvbazar/Belogorskii, 12; Slavic and Tatar place names, 16 (table 1.1); Soviet renaming, 12–15; Tauris/Tavrida, 9

National sovereignty declaration by CTs, 288–89, 352–54

Osmanov, Aidar: *Yïldïz* journal editor, 2

Otar, Ibrahim and Ismail: second-generation emigrant authors and cultural leaders

Passport system: blocks CT residence in Crimea, 178

Political parties and governmental structures: Autonomous Crimean Socialist Soviet Republic, 8, 10; Communist Party of the Soviet Union (CPSU), 99, 180–81, 183, 212; Crimean Autonomous Soviet Socialist Republic (CASSR), 10; Crimean government, 8; Crimean People's Republic, 8; CT quotas in Crimean parliament of Ukrayina, 299–305; czarist state, 7; Eighth Union-Wide Congress of Soviets, 11; Golden Horde, 6; Karelo-Finnish SSR, 12; Mejlis (CT Executive Committee), 285, 286–87 (figs. 14.1 and 14.2), 289, 311; Milli Firqa (National Party), 9, 296, 298; Mongolians and Mongols, 6, 111–13; Musispolkom (Muslim Executive Committee), 9; National Movement of Crimean Tatars (NDKT), 283–84; Organization of the Crimean Tatar National Movement (OKND), 259–60, 284–85; Ottoman Empire, 7; Russian Socialist Federative Soviet Republic (RSFSR), 10; Second Crimean Tatar Delegate Congress, October 1917, 9; Socialist Soviet Republic of Tavrida, 9; Supreme Council of Crimea, 14; Supreme Council of the Soviet Union, 11. *See also* CPC; CPSU; Giray dynasty; Qurultay

Population of Crimea (tables 1.1 and 14.1): heterogeneity among, 268; indigenous category of enumerated, 255–56; Slavic proportion in, 268; 1926 and 1939 figures for CTs, 12, 291; 1926 and 1939 Tajik figures compared, 12; 1926 and 1939 Turkmen figures compared, 12; 1939 census for Crimea, 11; 1979–94 growth of CTs in, 282; 1980s distribution of CTs in Crimea, 101; 1993 distribution of CTs in, xvi; 1995 estimates for, 256

Press and publishing: bilingual CT-Russian newspaper *Qïrïm,* 18; Gaspirali's *Terjüman* (Interpreter), 30–34; Gaspirali's tracts, 35; *Lenin bayraghi* in Central Asia, 81, 347

*The Prostitute* (*Fahishe;* drama), 87

Protest methods of CTs: letters and petitions, 226–28; main later tactics, 230–31; public demonstrations, 232 (fig. 11.1)

Qaraims: alloted no representation, 300; indigenous to Crimea, 290; some abandon Crimea, 325

Qaytarma Ensemble for CT dance and song, 20, 88–90

Qipchaq Turkic horsemen, 6, 10

Qrymchaqs: alloted no representation, 300; indigenous to Crimea, 290; well reputed in Crimea, 273

Qur'ân: little known by Russia's Muslims, 114; most Muslims follow the, 123; viewed by Christians as pernicious, 114

Qurultay/Kurultay (CT constituent assembly): appeals to UN, 312; brings defining moment in CT politics, 286; First (1917), 8, 9, 72, 285; Second (1991), 4, 17, 255, 259, 263, 273, 286–88; Third (1996), 15, 260; more radical mood of Third Qurultay, 311

*Red Flows the Volga* (memoirs), 78

Religion and religious community: conservative CTs reject reform of, 53; CT mosque destroyed, 20–21; Islam/Muslim/Muslims, 7–8; strength of, 23

Russian generals: Whites and Bolsheviks in Crimea, 9

Seytmuratova, Ayshe: account of leaders of new CT national movement, 155–79; Uzbekistan accuses her of improper behavior, 248

Sherfedinov, Yahya: collaborates on musical *Arzï qïz,* 91; composer-musicologist collects CT folksongs, 19–20

Slavic vigilantes and robbers: repeatedly destroy CT housing, 20; vandalize CT cemeteries, 22

Sovereignty: CT declaration of, 352–54

Soysal, Abdullah Zihni: emigrant scholar and leader, 341–42

Special settlements, 155–56, 224n1

Stalin, Joseph (Iosif): sets rules for republic status, 11–12

Tashkent trial: charges ten CTs with defaming USSR, 187, 192

Territoriality discussed, 252–53

"To Mothers of the World" (poem), 2–3

Ukrayina Republic: CTs support independence of, 293; disappoints hopes of CTs, 295; establishes a pro-CT ministry for nationalities and migration (1993), 309–10; grants aid to CTs, 310; indifference to CT demands attacked, 311; inherits Crimea from USSR, 291–93

Ulkusal, Mustejip: emigrant teacher, cultural leader, editor, 341

Useinov, Ramazan: painter's works exhibited, 19

"We Returned Today" (poem), 4

"What Is the Homeland's Scent?" (poem), 3–4

*The Whirlwind* (*Boran;* poetry collection), 80

Women: Gaspirali's enlightened attitudes toward, 39; underrepresented in CT Mejlis, 359

Yurter, Fikret: emigrant activist in United States, 105–8; preserves and publishes CT cultural materials, 347

*Library of Congress Cataloging-in-Publication Data*

The Tatars of Crimea : return to the homeland / Edward Allworth, editor. — 2nd ed., rev. and expanded.

p. cm. — (Central Asia book series)

Includes bibliographical references and index.

ISBN 0-8223-1985-3 (cloth : alk. paper). — ISBN 0-8223-1994-2 (paper : alk. paper)

1. Crimean Tatars—Civil rights. 2. Crimean Tatars—Ethnic identity. 3. Human rights—Ukrayina. I. Allworth, Edward. II. Series.

DK508.9K78T37   1998

323.1'194388047'0904—dc21      97-19110